J. Howe Adams

History of the Life of D. Hayes Agnew

J. Howe Adams

History of the Life of D. Hayes Agnew

ISBN/EAN: 9783743399785

Manufactured in Europe, USA, Canada, Australia, Japa

Cover: Foto ©ninafisch / pixelio.de

Manufactured and distributed by brebook publishing software (www.brebook.com)

J. Howe Adams

History of the Life of D. Hayes Agnew

HISTORY OF THE LIFE

OF

D. HAYES AGNEW,

M.D., LL.D.

BY

J. HOWE ADAMS, M.D.

PHILADELPHIA AND LONDON:

THE F. A. DAVIS COMPANY, PUBLISHERS,

1892.

Philadelphia, Pa., U. S. A.
The Medical Bulletin Printing House,
1916 Cherry Street.

PREFACE.

Dr. Agnew lived his life without thought of a biographer; he took no care to preserve the data of his life-work; in consequence, after his death, but little available material could be found among his papers. Through the efforts of Mrs. Agnew, however, and from the memory and material in the hands of his friends, the work has been at length done. It was the intention of the writer to give the original sources from which data were obtained throughout the book, but these references have been so many and varied that it was soon found that it would constitute a source of annoyance to the reader; consequently, in the Appendix all credits are given.

It has been a great aid, as well as pleasure, to see the eagerness and love displayed by every one in giving information in regard to Dr. Agnew's life. It seemed to be a pleasant task, on the part of all, to do what they could for their beloved friend and colleague; at the expense of considerable toil, trouble, and time, they have fully performed this labor of love. Without such assistance the biography would have been sadly incomplete.

In writing this book the style and treatment have been modeled, as far as possible, upon Dr. Agnew's own idea of propriety and methods of thought. A biographer, in preparing the life of his hero, loves to dwell chiefly on those efforts and achievements which have attracted public admiration,—on those master-strokes in the life of his subject which have raised him above the level of his fellow-men,—leaving out those lesser

(iii)

characteristics which not only serve to consolidate the character and lead to success, but which, from their multiform points in which they come in contact with common humanity, confer a personal interest in the life. The glory of the Alps does not consist merely in the mighty mountain-peaks which send their spires to heaven, clothed with sunshine and cloud; the foot-hills clustering at the mountain-base, the rippling streams, and pleasant meadows catch equally the eye of the pleasure-seeking tourist and increase the beauties above by contrast.

And so with Dr. Agnew: it was not alone those achievements which bore the stamp of originality, which heralded his name on the wings of the wind and made it a tower of strength which we have endeavored to depict; but there were other charms of social and personal life which have made his memory fragrant in the minds of his friends. In endeavoring thus to show his life and its effect upon the American world, these lesser points have been included as far as possible.

If any better conception, however shadowy and undecided, of the life, character, and accomplishments of this grandest figure in American medicine, can be gained from reading this biography, the writer will feel that the labor of love was not done in vain.

December 20, 1892.

CONTENTS.

CHAPTER I.

PAGE

LINEAGE OF THE AGNEW FAMILY, ... 1

CHAPTER II.

THE EARLY LIFE OF DR. AGNEW, ... 36

CHAPTER III.

THE STORY OF DR. AGNEW'S BUSINESS VENTURE, ... 60

CHAPTER IV.

DR. AGNEW'S CONNECTION WITH THE PHILADELPHIA SCHOOL OF
ANATOMY, ... 76

CHAPTER V.

DR. AGNEW'S EARLY LIFE IN PHILADELPHIA, ... 106

CHAPTER VI.

DR. AGNEW'S LIFE FROM 1860 TO 1870, ... 128

CHAPTER VII.

DR. AGNEW AS PROFESSOR OF SURGERY, ... 154

CHAPTER VIII.

DR. AGNEW'S ORIGINAL WORK IN SURGERY, ... 173

CHAPTER IX.

DR. AGNEW AS A WRITER, ... 193

CHAPTER X.

THE GARFIELD CASE, ... 220

CHAPTER XI.

DR. AGNEW'S HOME-LIFE, ... 250

(v)

CHAPTER XII.

PAGE

Dr. Agnew's Later Life, ... 265

CHAPTER XIII.

The Jubilee of Dr. Agnew, ... 298

CHAPTER XIV.

Dr. Agnew's Retirement from the University of Pennsylvania, 318

CHAPTER XV.

Dr. Agnew's Final Sickness, Death, and Funeral, . . . 339

CHAPTER XVI.

Estimate of Dr. Agnew's Position in Surgery, ... 353

Appendix, ... 365

LIST OF ILLUSTRATIONS.

Uhle Portrait of Dr. Agnew, ... Frontispiece

The Agnew Coat of Arms, . . Facing page 18

The Charcoal-House of the Pleasant Garden Iron-
Works, ... " " 68

The Philadelphia School of Anatomy, . . . " " 78

Dr. Agnew in 1858, ... " " 108

Dr. Agnew in 1867, ... " " 132

Fac-simile of Title-Page of Japanese Edition of
Dr. Agnew's "Surgery," . . . " " 162

Dr. Agnew in 1876, ... " " 178

Dr. Agnew in 1879, ... " " 204

Dr. Agnew in 1882, ... " " 230

Dr. Agnew in 1884, ... " " 272

Dr. Agnew in 1887, ... " " 290

Dr. Agnew in Clinique, ... " " 332

Dr. Agnew in 1890, ... " " 348

(vii)

LIST OF ILLUSTRATIONS

CHAPTER I.

THE earliest record of the Agnew family, which can be definitely and connectedly followed down to the present time, comes from Agneaux, a quaint little village in northern France, from which the family derives its name. This form of origin of surname is not unusual, for the most ancient and most honorable names found at present in Great Britain and Ireland are derived from the names of places in Normandy or in neighboring parts of France. In fact, there is no village in Normandy which has not given its name to some family in England. Genealogists have decided that this is the most common form of the derivation of English and Scottish surnames, exceeding those derived from occupations, mental characteristics, Christian names, and sobriquets.

It has further been conceded, that it was the universal custom for the place to give the name to the family, not the family to the place. This is the reverse of the process in America. In this country the family has invariably given the name to the place. The little town of Agnew in Lancaster County, Nebraska, named in honor of Dr. Agnew, is a typical example of this method. It shows the space of time which has elapsed, and the changes in living and civilization, between the Agneaux of the old world and the Agnew of the newer continent.

The name Agneaux is Norman-French for "lamb," being derived, of course, originally, from the Latin term *agnus*, a word of the same signification. The variety of ways in which the name has been spelled is numerous, Agneau, Agneaux, Agneux, Aigneux, Aigneaux, Aignel; the Latinized forms are Agnelli, Agnella, Agnellus; the modernized forms are Agneu, Agnieu, and Agnew. The word "agneau" in French still bears its original signification of "lamb."

The Normans, or Norsemen, as is well known, were not of French origin, but were bold, adventurous explorers from the north of Europe, who fell in great swarms upon the neighboring sea-board countries, seizing lands for their own use, and carrying death and destruction to the original inhabitants.

Agneaux, this little Norman town, which has been dead to the world for many centuries, holds, then, the honor of being the originating place of the ancient and honorable family of Agnew. Here was moulded into permanent form, this clannish family, which all the vicissitudes of rude and stormy times could not tear asunder. This place is still a village of less than 500 inhabitants. It stands solitary and unprogressive, far from the nearest railroad station, although it seems unfair to compare such a quaint old place with such a modern creation as the railroad. It is not large or important enough to be found in the French gazetteers, and even a diligent search of maps in Paris fails to reveal its location. This quaint spot is large enough, however, to be governed, according to French customs, by a mayor. It is located in the Département de la Manche, near the city of Saint-Lo. The Department of Manche is on the northwestern coast of France, jutting into the English Channel; it derives its name from the French term for the English Channel, "La Manche." Its bold, unprotected position is just such an one open to the invasion of such hardy seamen as the Norsemen.

There still exists in Agneaux an ancient chateau, belonging to the Marquis de Ste. Marie d'Agneaux, which was quite capable of resisting a siege. Around the memory of this ancient castle many of the romantic legends of Normandy have been woven. At the time when the Huguenots were driven from France, during the reigns of Henri III and Henri IV, this castle formed one of the headquarters for the Protestants. The scion of this ancient family espoused this religion, and threw all his resources to the defense of its adherents.

The names of Agneaux and Aigneaux are not uncommon

in this region, although there has been a general exodus from
this country in the past eight hundred years.

The explanation of this exodus of the Agneaux from Normandy is seen in studying the history of the family. Family
tradition reports that at the time of the Norman conquest of
England by William the Conqueror, in the eleventh century, the
chief body of the family came with him, settling in England and
Scotland. This was an age of rough manners and brutal conquest, and it required the banding together of large bodies of
well-built, courageous men to survive. Some of the family,
filled with this restless spirit of conquest which was the feature
of the age, did not linger in Great Britain, but followed "Strong
Bow," Richard de Clare, Earl of Strigul, to Ireland, rendering
efficient aid to him in the conquest of this island, in the twelfth
century.

A further element which assisted in driving the Agneaux
who remained in France after the Norman conquest from their
native spot is explained in an exhaustive work entitled " Protestant Exiles from France in the Reign of Louis XIV, or the
Huguenots and their Descendants in Great Britain and Ireland,"
by the Rev. David C. A. Agnew. This work, which includes a
complete list of all the families which comprised this religious
body joining in the exodus, shows that many of the Agneaux
who were left behind at the time of the Norman conquest
became Huguenots at the time of the Reformation.

The Agneaux were moderately numerous in France from
the ninth to the sixteenth centuries. As early as the tenth
century, knights of this name swelled the ranks of French
chivalry and acquired landed estates in several French prov-
inces; their heraldic achievements are to be found recorded in
the rolls of the ancient nobility of Normandy, Burgundy, and
Provençe. The first member of the family whose name is definitely known, Agneaux de l'Isle, lived in the neighborhood of
Caen, in the arondissement of Bayeux. He was Lord of l'Isle
and Auval, his heraldic bearing being Three Holy Lambs, on

an azure shield. He was also entitled to carry "two bars vert on a golden shield surrounded by an orle of martlets" as Lord of Auval. This latter achievement, carried first as an addition, was soon afterward adopted, in place of the original bearing of the family, by his descendants,—these gentlemen probably considering the Holy Lamb as too peaceful an emblem for such restless adventurers.

From Agneaux de l'Isle sprang various families, all of which prospered,—four of which held seignorial fiefs in Normandy, a fifth in Burgundy, and a sixth branch in Provençe.

Sir Philip d'Agneaux, the heir of line of the senior branch, was created a banneret, for military services, in 1228; his father and uncle were already knights. Sir John d'Agneaux was one of the companions of de Harcourt, Admiral of France, in a voyage which he undertook in 1295; while in the Book of Achievements, drawn up by command of Charles V of France, in 1368, a Sir Fulke and a Sir William d'Agneaux are both honorably mentioned. An offshoot of the same stem, Agneaux, Lord of Alencourt, adopted as his arms "three crescent gules, upon a shield of gold." Both these crescents and the martlets are special indications of good service done against the infidels, or of long voyages of discovery and adventure.

The line of the Alencourts ended in an heiress; she gave her name, however, to her descendants, and this branch of the family is styled Ste. Marie d'Agneaux. These Agneaux are traced for many generations in the "Armorial de France." Jean Jacques Renè de Ste. Marie d'Agneaux, of this branch of the family, was famous during the reign of Louis XV.

History reports that a number of the members of the family who remained in Normandy after the Norman conquest gained distinction in other ways. Robert and Antoine Agneaux, or, as the name was then written, Aigneaux, born in Normandy in the sixteenth century, translated "Virgil" into French in 1582. This work became popular, and stands even to-day as one of the great landmarks among the translations of the Middle Ages.

The chief interest centres, however, in that branch of the Agnew family which settled in Scotland. It was in County Wigtown, in southwest Scotland, which juts with bold outline into the North Channel and the Irish Sea, that the principal branch of this bold, adventurous family finally settled. Here, in the wild and unsettled times of the early part of the history of Scotland, they held their own, and became prominent in that country at a time when great physical development was as necessary for existence as shrewdness and intelligence. The records of the time show that as early as the year 1330 they became the holders of the office of Hereditary Sheriff of County Wigtown. "The Sheriff of Wigtown" was the title of their office; yet in royal proclamations and even in acts of Parliament, and always in familiar intercourse, this official was addressed as "Sheriff of Galloway," the name of Galloway being applied to the counties of Wigtown and Kirkcudbright.

This office formed the very backbone of the feudal system; it was held in the Agnew family, despite all the various changes through the Middle Ages, for more than four hundred years, until the abolishment of hereditary jurisdictions in Scotland, in 1747. The abolition of this office—the removal of the last trace of the government of the Middle Ages—was the final blow struck at the feudal system. As a compensation to the Agnew family for the loss of this hereditary office, they were paid by the English government the sum of £4000.

The duties of an hereditary sheriff in Scotland were far more important than are commonly associated in these later days with the office of sheriff. Next to the king, the sheriff of that day was the most powerful individual in the land. On the performance of his duties rested the foundations of society; he was law, lawyer, judge, jury, and executioner of penalties. He owned allegiance and submission only to the king. This officer, unchecked by nearly all restraints, was not as oppressive and tyrannical as might be inferred from his powers. In medieval times those at the fountain-head of authority were the least inclined to be unjust and arbitrary. It was the resident owners of the soil who were the source of greatest oppression to the people.

The essence of feudalism was, that superior and vassal were alike bound together by ties of reciprocal good-will. "Gentleman's law," even to this day, is regarded respectfully by the peasants of Scotland. This absolute power of the sheriff can be estimated, when it is realized that even an earl in those days had not the power of shrievalty within his own earldom. In ancient times an appeal lay from the judgment of the earl, as proprietor, to the court of the sheriff.

It is at Lochnaw, Stranraer, Scotland, that the Agnew family holds its castle; the present incumbent of the title being the twenty-first in descent from the first Agnew who settled there.

Although some of the Agneaux family came over to England during the reign of William the Conqueror, nothing definite of their doings is known. The first Agneaux of whom any authentic record exists in Great Britain is that Agneaux de l'Isle who took part in the conquest of Ulster, in the reign of Henry II of England, in 1171. For his services in this conquest, he was allotted the Lordship of Larne, a beautiful spot on the northeastern coast of Ireland, with a view which was terminated only by the distant Scottish coast. In commemoration of the expedition in which they had gained their new possessions, "the sinister hand of Ulster" was introduced into their shield. Their name was also given to the highest mountain in the Antrim range, which still retains its appellation "Agnew's Hill."

Here this family of bold adventurers remained for more than one hundred years, and the descendants of the Lord of Larne in the fifth generation were in quiet possession of the land he had acquired. At the commencement of the fourteenth century the Lord of Larne, in common with his neighbors, was impatient of the English yoke. The English monarchs were looked upon rather as feudal superiors than as kings; indeed, they hardly assumed the latter title at this period. The Ulster lords wished to assert their entire independence, and have a king of their own. Hearing of the doughty deeds of Edward Bruce, brother of King Robert Bruce, across the channel, they offered to acknowledge him as their sovereign if he would undertake to bring them armed assistance and put himself at their head.

The restless Edward was delighted with a proposal so congenial to his tastes; and, organizing what forces he could in Galloway, he landed, with six thousand men, at Olderfleet Castle, the property of the Agnews,—the ruins of which may still be seen,—on the Lough of Larne, in 1315. Here the Lord of Larne and his retainers received him with great joy, and all the lords of Ulster, hearing of his arrival, flocked to his standard. In 1316 Bruce was crowned King of Ireland.

At this time the good King Robert Bruce lived at Lochnaw, in the castle which had been erected a century before. This was his own garrison, and there was no other fortress as suitable in respect to position, for the old castle was considered impregnable, commanding fine views of the Firth of Clyde and the opposite Irish coast, Agnew's Hill being a prominent feature in the background. Robert followed his brother Edward to Ireland, and together they advanced as far as Dublin. Two years later Edward Bruce was killed in battle, the English again came into supremacy, and the remnant of the Scottish army retreated to Scotland.

The Lord of Larne had been so seriously compromised with the English authorities, by this connection with the Bruces, that we are not surprised to learn that his son and heir appeared at the Scottish court after the death of Robert Bruce, when the Earl of Moray, his old commanding officer, was chosen Regent during the minority of King David II. As a reward for his past services, and to hold his allegiance in the future, the young Lord of Larne was installed in the keeping of the office of Constable of Lochnaw.

The young constable showing bravery and spirit,—qualities

necessary for an officer holding the king's commission among the wild Scots of Galloway,—was soon afterward appointed Sheriff of Wigtown The sheriffship is described as an hereditary gift, but the successions were not preserved at this time; for the Earl Douglas, in a later generation, forcibly denuded the Agnews of their office for some years. Hence the appointment of the first three sheriffs is regarded as personal; the office of Hereditary Sheriff of Wigtown being given again to the Agnews in a new charter, in 1452. It was only this latter commission which was recognized by the English government.

This is the historical story of the first settlement of the Agnews in Scotland; but the traditionary account, which is fully believed by the oldest inhabitants, points to a much bolder course, by which the Lord of Larne obtained a footing here.

According to this tradition among the peasantry of Wigtown, a member of the Agnew family once found himself in Galloway, and here he determined to stay; and, courting adventure in the true Norman spirit, he cast his eyes about him for a well-housed foe. The king's Castle of Lochnaw, according to our informants, had been captured by one M'Clellan, a chief of the native race; and here, strongly posted in the fortress, he set the royal authority at defiance. The castle was quite to young Agnew's taste, and he immediately besieged it, with the full approbation of the king.

M'Clellan was well armed and provisioned, and Agnew, with a small band of followers, could make no impression; hence, storming the castle was out of the question, and he was compelled to resort to strategy. It must be understood that the castle stood on an island, and, with the exception of a narrow rock at either end, the ground was entirely covered with the buildings of this fortress.

Agnew withdrew the besieging party from sight, and it was settled that his right-hand man should be hanged on a tree, the rope being so arranged that the victim could himself prevent strangulation. The hanging scene was duly enacted, and the executioners retired. The plot succeeded to their hearts' content. M'Clellan had watched their strange doings, and no sooner saw them off than, manning a boat, he rowed to the shore to see what had been done. No sooner had he landed than out rushed the besiegers from an ambush. M'Clellan's retreat to the island was instantly cut off; but he and his band fought their way out of the inclosure. Agnew followed him, and, when they reached the site of the Brig O'Doon, he succeeded in dispatching the old chieftain. Now, in the moment of triumph, he remembered, for the first time, his poor, half-hung lieutenant. When he arrived again on the shores of the white Loch of Lochnaw, there the poor decoy hung, stiff and cold.

On the death of the Bruces a civil war broke out, and in 1347 David II was taken prisoner by the English, and the Sheriff of Wigtown would have been destroyed had not Sir William Douglas come to his relief. A story of ravage and confiscation follows this event,—for a century the country was untilled, the woods were wasted, and the forester's art was utterly neglected.

The Douglases had always been friendly to the Agnews, but in 1390, Black Douglas, a natural son of the famous Earl Douglas, rose into power. He determined to reduce all the Scottish barons to a state of vassalage. The Constable of Lochnaw could offer no serious resistance to the forces of the earl, who besieged the Castle of Lochnaw. Eventually the Agnews were driven from Scotland, and sorrowfully the Laird of Lochnaw, the great-grandson of the first proprietor, sailed, with his family and retainers, across the channel to the Bay of Larne. In the words of Sir George Mackenzie, a chronicler of the period, " the Castell of Lochnaw was blowen up." This act of Black Douglas was extremely bold, for the castle was still the property of the king.

The ex-Constable of Lochnaw found Ireland little to his liking, and repaired shortly to the Scottish court at Perth, where he received from the aged monarch, Robert III, much commiseration, but no assistance. He became a member of the royal household, and stood in high favor. While at court the young Agnew had the good fortune to attract the favorable notice of Princess Margaret, who was married to Archibald, son of Black Douglas. Although not inclined to love the name of Douglas, yet he soon had cause to be grateful for her good offices. On the death of her husband, she received from her brother, King James I, the lordship of Galloway, and she took up her residence with feudal pomp at the old Castle of Threave. Here she was accompanied by her young *protégé*, Andrew Agnew.

Through her efforts Andrew Agnew was restored to the possessions of his fathers, in 1426, on his marriage to Princess Mary, the niece of his liege lady.

The old castle had been destroyed by Black Douglas, and the constable set bravely to work to build a better home for himself and his gentle bride. On the south shore of the Loch of Lochnaw he built a castle, a greater part of which stands to the present day, which, as has been said, is still owned by the Agnews, his lineal descendants.

In a "History of the Hereditary Sheriffs of Galloway," by Sir Andrew Agnew, Bart., M.P., there is a fine picture of Scottish life from the year 1170 to 1747. Sir Andrew Agnew has compiled this book from the archives of the Agnew family, including sasines, infeftments, summonses, discharges, letters of horning, inhibitions, informations, bonds, precepts of clareconstat, marriage contracts, reliefs, wills, tacks, commissions, rentals, acts of Parliament, processes and all sorts of papers connected with the proceedings of the Sheriff Courts; memoranda, charters under the Great Seal, and charters from bishops, abbots, and commendators. In this way the actual picture of Scottish life throughout this period has been depicted; the customs, the dresses, the value of money, the price of the necessaries of life, the food eaten, table manners, the rentals paid and received, and all the minutiæ of Scottish life have been drawn, making the book an invaluable treasure-house for the antiquarian or the novelist, especially as the greater part of this matter has never been published in any other form.

Patrick Agnew, the fourth hereditary sheriff, may be taken as a fair type of a Scottish hereditary official in 1500. As to law, he troubled himself little with studying the statutes. Custom was law to him, and he was not scrupulous in enforcing his supposed rights, in defiance of any acts of Parliament to the contrary. If an injury was to be redressed or a friend to be assisted, he sprang into his saddle and dealt out justice with his own good sword, caring little for the technicalities; if attacked, he was ready to defend himself; if his cattle were carried off, he was quite capable of returning the compliment with interest. Such assertions of the dignity of his office he, doubtless, considered necessary to sustain the traditionary status of a Galloway sheriff.

Through Margaret Kennedy, the wife of Sir Patrick Agnew, the eighth hereditary sheriff, the Agnews have a double royal descent,—on one side from King James II of Scotland, and on the other from King Henry VII of England.

Sir Andrew Agnew, the twelfth and last hereditary sheriff, was a famous soldier, but not a practical agriculturist. On the death of his father, when the paternal estates fell into his possession, he determined to acquaint himself with the routine of farming operations. One of his attempts at such superintendence is the subject of a favorite Galloway story, which is still extant:—

"Sir Andrew, though a grand soldier, was nae farmer ava'; he kent naething aboot it. A' the castle farm-wark in his days, an' lang before and after, was done by baillie wark. There was baillie pleuching, baillie harrowing, baillie shearing, baillie corn-leading,—aye, an' peat-leading, too! The tenants were a' warned in their turn to do as they were bun' in their tacks.

"Sir Andrew was new come hame; they had been a' warned in, and were shearing ower in the Beef-Park, an', as was aye the case when a wheen o' farmers met, they had great strivings wha wad be first oot at the lan's end. Horrid bad wark they made it, and whiles left as muckle as they took.

"Just as the sheriff came oot to see, they were kemping [1] a' they could, and the grieve, afeared the sheriff wad be angry, began and trod doon the lang stubbles wi' his feet, and made a show o' gathering as muckle o' the left corn as he could.

"'What's that ye're doing there?' says Sir Andrew, sharply.

"'Oh, please your honour,' answers the grieve, terribly frightened; 'oh, I'm just tramping doon a lot o' the o'erplus. There's plenty to tak' and plenty to leave here, please your honour. It's just to keep the grun' warm, your honour, for I expect a right guid awal crap here next year'; and so he ran on, scarce knowing what he said."

Greatly astonished was the grieve to find that his ridiculous invention was taken in good faith; but if he felt little compunction at thus shamefully imposing upon his master, his deceit drew upon him a retribution as sharp as it was unexpected; for the sheriff, greatly pleased with the theory of keeping the ground warm, "keepit him there a' the morning, aye treading doon the stubble, and whiles he wad begin and tread doon the corn himsel'." So the unjust steward cut a very sorry figure in the eyes of his own men. "Ye see," as is a usual remark after some similar stories, "although Sir Andrew was a bra' warrior, he didna ken the lea-side o' a rick!"

This Sir Andrew Agnew, on account of his daring military exploits and quaint humor, has become a famous figure in Scotch history. In his defense of Blair Castle from the attack of the rebels, in the spring of 1745, Sir Andrew was the hero of a number of characteristic incidents, which have been described by Sir Walter Scott in his "History of Scotland." The

---

[1] Kemping is an expression commonly applied to reapers trying to see who will cut most quickly their share of corn in the harvest-field. While the term strictly signifies rivalry, it implies undue haste, and that the work is hurriedly and badly done.

fame of Sir Andrew was already considerable, and the treatment which the rebels experienced at his hands went far to increase this reputation.

The rebels besieged this castle for a fortnight, during which time the sheriff showed himself too good a soldier to abandon his post,—although his men were in a state of semi-starvation,—and he was too old an one to be provoked into a sally. He knew that each day he could detain so large a force of rebels before Blair Castle would be of the greatest advantage to the king; and here he determined to stay as long as a single mouthful of biscuit remained in store.

Time, however, hung very heavily the while on the hands of the younger officers, who, in default of all other sources of diversion, at last bethought themselves of a joke at the expense of their commander. As a part of the plot, they purloined a portion of the great man's wardrobe,—taking a full suit of the brigadier's uniform,—with which, with the assistance of some straw, they soon produced an excellent imitation of his figure. Then they placed the stuffed sheriff at a window of the tower, with a spy-glass in his hand, in the attitude of reconnoitering the rebels.

"This apparition," says Sir Walter Scott, "did not escape the hawks' eyes of the Highlanders, who commenced to pour their fire upon the turret-window, without producing any adequate result. The best deer-stalkers of Athole and Badenoch persevered, nevertheless, and wasted their ammunition in vain upon this impassible commander. At length, Sir Andrew himself became anxious to know what could possibly induce so constant a fire upon that particular point; and ascending the turret himself, there he saw his other identity standing under fire,—as stiff, as fearless, as imperturbable as himself. The sheriff was scandalized at the irreverent deception, and, discovering the author of the plot, he delivered sentence upon the culprit to this effect:—

"'Let the loon that set it up just go up himsel' and tak' it doon again.' A great effect had been produced, however, upon the rebels, and the clansmen, already predisposed to regard the sheriff with superstitious awe, had found their surmises as to his invulnerability so thoroughly confirmed that henceforth they became hopeless of success."

A few days later, the sheriff was relieved from his unenviable position by the appearance of the king's Black Horse.

A camp-story, in which Sir Andrew did not come out victor, has been preserved of these days, to understand which it is necessary to bear in mind that, in the Lowlands of Scotland, a "Lammermuir lion" is a proverbial expression for a sheep.

After the affair at Ostend, in which Sir Andrew Agnew distinguished himself, when the English were at war with the French, the officers of the garrison were talking over the incidents of the siege at the dinner-table, and, becoming very noisy as they fought their battles over again, some of the younger ones became very eloquent on their own prowess, until the Commandant, Sir Andrew Agnew, becoming tired, thought it time to give them a hint. Behind his chair stood a faithful servant, a Lammermoor man, almost as great a character as his master, who had followed Sir Andrew closely in many a field. "John," said the sheriff, slyly, "I think I looked as bold a man yesterday as any in the brigade; what do you say, my man?" "Aye, Sir Andrew," answered the batman, with a twinkle in his eye, "you looked for all the world *just like a lion!*" An uproarious burst of merriment greeted this response, in which the sheriff heartily joined, supposing it was due to his own wit at the expense of his officers. The tables, however, were soon turned; for, as he good-humoredly continued, "And wherever did *you* see a lion, you scoundrel?" a jolly young subaltern interposed, "Oh, sir! there's plenty of lions in John's country; surely you know John's slain many a *Lammermuir lion!*"

The General James Agnew who was killed at the Battle of Germantown, Philadelphia, was a nephew of this sheriff.

In 1775 he was made Aide-de-camp to the king, with the rank of Colonel, being made Brigadier-General the following year. The description given of his death in Holmes' "Annals of America" and in the "Pictorial History of England" is incorrect. The correct account is given on another page of this biography.

This sheriff's sayings and doings have been the subject of innumerable traditions; "to give one of *Sir Andrew Agnew's broad hints*" has been a proverbial expression in Scotland for the last hundred years, the force of which is exemplified by a story from a book of Scotch humor, published toward the close of the last century:—

"Sir Andrew Agnew, of Lochnaw, a well-known Scotch baronet, was famous for giving what he called 'broad hints.' Having been long pestered by an impertinent intruder, it was one day remarked to the baronet that he was fortunate in having freed himself of the bore, and he was asked how he had contrived it. 'Ah!' he replied, 'I was obliged to give the loon a *broad hint*.' 'A broad hint!' said the friend; 'why, I thought he was one of those who would never take any hint!' 'By my faith,' rejoined Sir Andrew, 'but he was forced to take it; for, as the chiel wouldna gang oot at the door, I just threw him oot at the window.'"

He had been bred in the true old British prejudice against the French, and, although he had served often upon French soil, he hated the language, and disdained to learn a word of it. Once, when on a visit to his daughter, Lady Bruce, being at church, the minister, in his discourse, objected to the authorized translation of the text upon which he was preaching, and gave an amended version, in enforcing the superiority of which he proceeded to say: "The words in the original Hebrew are these: *Comment vous portez vous.*" The sheriff's wrath was raised to boiling-pitch; not only had an insult been offered to his understanding, but his peculiar antipathy had been aroused. He started from his seat, and it was with difficulty that he was persuaded by his daughter to sit still. No sooner, however, was the service over, than his righteous indignation was brought out before all the congregation. "The scoundrel!" he said; "and yet, I could have forgiven him had he not used the only French I ever knew."

Following the rebellion in Scotland in 1746, the British government, alarmed by its extent, were naturally anxious to increase the influence of the Crown in Scotland; the great barrier to the accomplishment of this purpose was the hereditable jurisdictions held by the barons and chieftains.

As these hereditary rights had been expressly reserved at the time of the union of England and Scotland, it was feared that their abolition would breed fresh dissatisfaction; but after a fierce battle over the subject in Parliament, a bill was passed abolishing hereditable jurisdictions and making arrangements for compensation to their owners.

It was found that in only sixteen cases the claims of hereditary sheriffs could be proved, viz., those of the shires of Argyle, Bute, Caithness, Clackmannan, Cromarty, Dumfries, Dumbarton, Elgin, Fife, Kinross, Kirkcudbright, Nairn, Orkney and Zetland, Peebles, Selkirk, and Wigtown.

In only four families had the sheriffships of their respective counties been continuous since 1567. These were:—

The Earls and Dukes of Argyle, . .	Tarbert and Argyle.
The Earls of Rothes, ...	Fife.
The Murrays of Philiphaugh, . . .	Selkirk.
The Agnews of Lochnaw, . . .	Wigtown.

Of these, the Duke of Argyle's commission was dated February 26, 1473; the Earl of Rothes', June 1, 1529; the Murray's is unknown; while the Agnew's was dated 1452, making it the oldest in Scotland, although, as has been shown, the Agnews held the office for over a century before that date. The Sheriff of Wigtown claimed less proportionally than any of the other office-holders, and received £4771 6s., being nearly six times as much as all of the rest collectively, showing that his office was considered of the greatest importance.

Thus ended the days of hereditable jurisdictions in Scotland. No rational person can now doubt that the change was a wise one, although this conviction grew only gradually upon the people.

This Scottish branch, which had long held the title of Knight, were given a baronetage on July 28, 1629, by Charles I. The circumstances under which the Agnew family received its baronetage forms an interesting page in English history. This title was not regarded by the Agnew family at the time as conferring any special dignity to their position, and they preferred the title of "Sheriff" to that of "Sir." Different members of the family had been knighted many times by different sovereigns, but they had not used their titles. It was not until later years that this title grew into greater prominence.

The title of baronet is of comparatively recent origin, having been revived by King James I, who constituted it an hereditary dignity. The term "baronet" was originally given to a class of bannarets, who were hereditary barons of Parliament. The existing baronetage of England dates from 1611, in which year James I established it by letters patent under the Great Seal; in 1619 he further extended the order to Ireland, and in 1624 adopted steps to create a Scottish branch, which intention was carried out, in 1625, by his son Charles I.

Every person who sought the dignity of a baronet was compelled to give proof that he was a gentleman of blood,—*i.e.*, descended on his father's side from a grandfather who bore arms, possessed of a good reputation, and had an annual revenue of not less than £1000.

These baronets, in turn for the honor granted them by their government, were expected to help in return in maintaining armies in different localities. Thus, the baronets of Ulster assisted the government in its management of affairs in Ireland; the baronets of Nova Scotia, among whom were the Agnews, rendered great aid in colonizing that recently-explored region. These latter baronets were granted special honors by Charles I,

being permitted to wear around the neck "an orange taunie
silk ribbon, whereon shall be pendent in a scutcheon argent, a
saltier azure, thereon an inescutcheon of the armes of Scotland,
with an imperial crown above the scutcheon, and encircled with
this motto :—

"*Fax mentis honestæ gloriæ.*"

The Hereditary Sheriffs of Galloway from 1452 to 1629
were as follow : Andrew, Andrew, Quentin, Patrick, Andrew,
Patrick (who was the first of his race to be buried as a Protestant, in 1590), Andrew, and Patrick Agnew.

It was this last Sir Patrick Agnew, Knt., who was created
a Baronet of Nova Scotia on July 28, 1629, by Charles I.   He
married Margaret, daughter of Sir Thomas Kennedy, and died
in 1661. His son, Sir Andrew Agnew, M.P. for Wigtownshire,
was appointed, on the suppression of hereditable jurisdictions,
by Cromwell, in 1656, Sheriff of all Galloway, and a member of
the Commission for governing the Kingdom of Scotland.   At
the restoration of Charles II, he was re-instated in his hereditary sheriffalty, in 1661.   Sir Andrew married Lady Anne
Stewart, daughter of Alexander, Earl of Galloway, and died
in 1671. His son and heir, also named Sir Andrew Agnew, on
refusing the test oath of 1682, was ejected, by the Privy Council
of Scotland, from his office, but was re-instated at the restoration, in 1689, by the Convention of Estates, of which he was a
member.   He married Jane, daughter of Sir Thomas Hay,
Baronet of Park, and died in 1701. His son, the fourth
baronet, Sir James Agnew, married Lady Mary Montgomerie,
daughter of Alexander, Earl of Eglinton.   He is particularly
famous in history for being the father of twenty-one children.

The fifth baronet, Sir Andrew Agnew, was the distinguished military officer of whom we have already read, being
a Lieutenant-General in the English army.   During his life-
time, hereditary jurisdictions were abolished finally in Scotland.   He had married his cousin, Eleanor, the only daughter
of Thomas Agnew, Esq., and was also remarkable in being

THE AGNEW COAT OF ARMS.

the father of eighteen children. He died in 1771, at the advanced age of 84 years, being succeeded by his fifth but eldest surviving son. Sir Stair Agnew, his son, sixth baronet, married Mary, daughter of Thomas Baillie, Esq. On account of the death of his eldest son, Andrew, who had married Martha De Courcy, eldest daughter of John, twenty-sixth Lord of Kinsale, he was succeeded by his grandson, Andrew, a posthumous child. The seventh baronet, Sir Andrew Agnew, married Madeline, daughter of the late Sir David Carnegie, and died in 1849. He was succeeded by Sir Andrew Agnew, who married Lady Louisa Noel, daughter of Charles, Earl of Gainsborough. The life of this baronet forms a remarkable coincidence with the head of the American branch of the Agnew family, for he was born in 1818, the same year as Dr. D. Hayes Agnew, and died March 25, 1892, three days after Dr. Agnew's death.

The present incumbent of the title, Sir Andrew Noel Agnew, was born in 1850. He married Gertrude, daughter of the Hon. Gowran Charles Vernon.

The coat of arms of the Agnew family is as follows :—

Arms, argent, a chevron between two cinquefoils in chief, gules, and a saltier couped in base, azure.

Crest, an eagle issuant and regardant, proper.

Supporters, two heraldic tigers, proper, collared and chained, or.

Motto, " Consilio, non impetu,"—by persuasion, rather than by force.

Seat, Lochnaw Castle, Stranraer, Wigtownshire.

Anciently the coat of arms was azure, three lambs passant, argent, with the motto " Agnus Miles."

Of those members of the Agnew family who migrated to America from the North of Ireland the greater number came originally from Scotland, becoming members of that brave, hardy, persevering, and Godly race, the Scotch-Irish. The earls of Tyrone and Tyrconnel, in the Province of Ulster, having conspired against the government, in the reign of James I, fled from the kingdom to escape punishment. Some of their accomplices were arrested, condemned, and executed, but the two earls were attainted by the process of outlawry, upon which their vast estates, containing about five hundred thousand acres of land, were escheated to the crown. King James resolved, if possible, to improve a country which was covered by forests, desolated by war, infested by robbers, or inhabited by ignorant natives. For this purpose he divided the escheated lands into small tracts, and these he gave to colonists, who were to settle them within four years with a certain number of subtenants.

According to his command, in 1610, the preference was given, in distributing the lands, to the inhabitants of the west of Scotland, as they were Protestants from his own country and were industrious people. The passage by water being very short, they could with greater ease settle the land according to their contracts. The establishment of prelacy in Scotland in the year 1637 and afterward in the year 1661, among people who had adopted the simpler form of Presbyterian worship, became additional cause of the numerous emigrations from that kingdom to the North of Ireland.

The superior knowledge, industry, and temperance of the Scotch in a short time enabled them to supplant the natives among whom they lived, and six of the northern counties, by the end of the seventeenth century, were inhabited chiefly by the descendants of Scottish families or the remnants of Cromwell's army. Their faithful services and uniform attachment to government had placed them in the ranks of good and faithful subjects, and their unshaken loyalty had entitled them to confidence and public favor; but they were treated like aliens and strangers by Charles II and James II, with marks of distrust for their civil capacity, and depressed in their religious observances by the spirit of intolerance, because they were not of the established Church of Ireland. Men who were thus degraded and vexed by burdens and slights emigrated in thousands to Pennsylvania, where they knew the principles of civil and religious liberty had their full operation.

Among this rare people stood prominently the Agnews. This class of people, who had reclaimed the desolated lands of Ulster, who had built towns and established manufactories, were Presbyterians; and neither the tyranny of Charles II nor James II, the dragoons of Claverhouse nor the intimidations of the Papacy, could compel them to surrender their independence or give up their religion. These were the people who had made famous the glens and moors of Scotland and Ireland, and who, rather than yield their convictions of faith and duty, suffered the sharpest persecutions, coming eventually to this side of the Atlantic Ocean to find homes more congenial to their taste. Men of strong intellect, independent thinkers, intolerant of oppression, gentle in peace, but terrible in war, they have left their impress upon all the institutions of the country of their adoption.

The bold position of County Wigtown, and the fact that the family were engaged in the colonization of one of the largest and most important of the American colonies, also naturally attracted the attention of the members of the family to America. In consequence, in the early part of the history of this country the Agnews became prominent. In the early part of the eighteenth century, three brothers of this family came to the then British colonies. One brother settled in New Jersey, another in Pennsylvania, and the third in South Carolina. The name of the brother who settled in South Carolina was Samuel. His descendants are still in existence in the South, a number of the family living in Mississippi, forming the branch of the "Southern Agnews." During the Revolution, the members of this branch of the family were Tories, and suffered, in consequence, many losses and privations. All traces have been lost of the brother who settled in New Jersey, even to his name; probably this branch of the family has become extinct.

It is with the third brother, who settled in Pennsylvania,— James Agnew,—that interest centres for the readers of this biography, for he was the great-grandfather of David Hayes Agnew.

Settlements were made on Octorara Creek by the Scotch and Irish colonists about 1717, and later throughout other portions of Lancaster and Bucks Counties. About 1737, many of the Agnew family settled in the northwestern part of York (now Adams) County, on Tom's and Marsh Creeks.

In the quaint, old, deserted burying-ground at Gettysburg, which is now completely overshadowed by that greater grave-yard which marks the high-water mark of rebellion, lie a number of the earlier members of the Agnew family in this country. In this quaint old burying-ground on Black's turn-pike, a mile and a half out of the village of Gettysburg, there are a number of grave-stones sacred to the memory of many of the Agnew family. On one stone there is a rude carving of weights and measures, with the further inscription : "The Weights and Measures of Scotland." On another is the coat of arms of the Agnews of Lochnaw.

Dr. Agnew took a pathetic interest in this deserted little spot, where so many of his family were laid to rest, and always, when he went to Gettysburg, spent a portion of his time in the place, taking tracings of the various stones.

There are few families which exhibit, to such a marked degree, the same physical, moral, and mental characteristics. The members of the Agnew family have always been re-markable for their great height and splendid physical devel-opment. It is, undoubtedly, this great physical activity which has held them so together as a family through all the tumultu-ous and disturbing periods which succeeded the Norman Con-quest in England, and the same rude separating influences of the similar period of European invasion in America. No finer example exists of this trait of height and physique than in the father and uncles of Dr. Agnew. His father, Dr. Robert Agnew, was the shortest of seven brothers, his height being six feet two inches. His tallest brother towered to the height of six feet seven inches. Another marked characteristic of the Agnew family was their extraordinary mental activity, and their keen perception of the duties and requirements of their life-work. No family exists which shows, on a whole, a higher degree of these traits. In whatever branch of life-work they are found, they stand pre-eminent.

Undoubtedly, however, the most remarkable characteristic possessed by the family has been their great prominence in religious matters. They have been always active in all the observances of religion, both in church-work and in their daily life. The three original heads of the Agnew family in this country were all elders of the same church,—the Seceder, or Associate Presbyterian.

It is a curious problem for students of genealogy to note that the Agneaux who remained in Normandy, wholly separated from their brethren, became Protestants, as well as did the Scotch Agnews. In fact, their Protestantism was more remarkable because of the adverse tendency of their surroundings.

Probably there exists no fuller or more comprehensive biographical record of any American family than that of the Agnew lineage. Imbued with a clannish love of race, they have kept religiously the history of their family. The various American branches, like the English, have been prolific of offspring; and yet, in the various phases and separations to which American families are subjected, which render any lineage of an American family so difficult to complete, no traces of the different ramifications have been lost. In regard to the American Agnew family, much of the credit for preserving these records and placing them together is due to the late Smith Agnew, of Pittsburgh, who devoted forty years of his life in traveling and collecting, in a permanent shape, the biographical outline of his family. These records he arranged in chronological order; in this shape they are invaluable to the American Agnew family.

James Agnew, the founder of this branch of the family, was born in October, 1711. He was married twice; by his first wife he had two children. It is, however, with his second wife, Rebecca Scott, that we are interested, for from her Dr. Agnew was descended. They were married in the year 1737, and, following out the traditions of the Agnew family, had nine children, — Samuel, Martha, James, David, Margaret, Rebecca, Sarah, Abraham, and Anne. Of these children, many became very well known in the early settlement of Pennsylvania. It is, however, the fourth child by his second wife that is of importance to this biography.

The name of this son was David Agnew, and he was born July 17, 1743. On attaining his maturity he was married, in Franklin County, Pennsylvania, April 2, 1772, to Mary Erwin. This couple are of historic interest, for they were the grandparents of Dr. Agnew. They had twelve children, which was a moderate-sized family for an Agnew. The record of the births of these children is so interesting that we venture to copy this portion of the family record in its entirety. It will be noticed that a child was born nearly every two years :—

Ann,					born January 9, 1773.
James,					born January 18, 1775.
John,					born April, 14, 1777.
David,					born May 20, 1779.
Rebecca,					born April 5, 1781.
Mary,					born June 29, 1783.
Robert,					born April 21, 1785.
Samuel,					born August 22, 1787.
Martha,					born December 2, 1789.
Smith,					born January 14, 1792.
James (2d),					born January 20, 1794.
Gibson,					born August 3, 1796.

David Agnew did not live to be an old man, dying soon after the birth of his last child, on the 17th of January, 1797, at the age of 53 years. After four years of widowhood, Mary Agnew, his relict, married the Rev. Alexander Dobbin, who was then a widower with seven children. This made a combined family of eighteen children. They lived happily together until her death, in 1824.

Robert Agnew, the seventh child of David and Mary Agnew, who was born April 21, 1785, became later the father of David Hayes Agnew, the subject of this biography. He was married, August 1, 1815, at 30 years of age, by Rev. Ebenezer Dickey, to Agnes Henderson, who was, at that time, a handsome widow with two children. Their only child was born three years later, November, 24, 1818, and named David Hayes Agnew.

Mrs. Agnew's maiden name was Agnes Noble. Her first husband was the Rev. Ebenezer Henderson, a Presbyterian minister, by whom she had two children,—James N. and Mary A. Henderson. The Rev. Ebenezer Henderson was one of the pioneer Presbyterian preachers of America. His father, the Rev. Matthew Henderson, had been sent to this country by the Associate Synod of Edinburgh, being the fourth minister of that church, in order of time, entering upon this work in America. The Rev. Ebenezer Henderson's first charge was in Pittsburgh, which was, at that time, in a very wild and uncivilized condition; it being necessary to make the trip over the Allegheny Mountains on horseback. Mrs. Henderson, on one of these trips, carried her infant son upon a pillow on the saddle before her.

Mrs. Agnew frequently described the church services of those early times, which, in the absence of a church building, were often held in the open air, even in mid-winter with the ground covered with snow. A call was given to Mr. Henderson to succeed Mr. Marshall as the pastor of the First Associate, now the First United Presbyterian Church in Philadelphia. The Presbytery placed it in his hands with the stipulation that before entering on his pastoral work he should visit the scattered flocks of their adherents in the South. This duty he fulfilled, but on his return he was attacked by a violent fever brought on by exposure to the elements, swimming rivers, etc. He died at Staunton, Va., before he reached home. Intelligence did not then fly with the speed of lightning, and, while the congregation eagerly awaited the arrival of their pastor-elect, they received the news of his death.

Robert Agnew, the father of the subject of this biography, was born in Adams County, Pennsylvania. He received his general education at Dickinson College, and studied medicine under that great teacher who elevated obstetrics into the dignity of a distinct branch of medical study,—Dr. Thomas Chalkey James, of Philadelphia. After the completion of his course in medicine, he became a surgeon in the U. S. Navy. On his first trip, which was to Canton, China, the vessel in which he sailed, left the port of Philadelphia, intending to round Cape Horn and cross the Pacific Ocean. This plan, fortunately for posterity, was frustrated by an accident. The vessel was wrecked, off the coast of North Carolina, in a storm, and Dr. Agnew, narrowly escaping death by drowning, reached shore in an exhausted condition. The vessel being totally destroyed, there was nothing left to do but to return to Philadelphia. Upon his return Dr. Agnew decided to give up his original intention, of becoming a naval surgeon, and remain on shore. Thus, providentially prevented from leaving his native land, he settled in Lancaster County, Pennsylvania, at Nobleville, a town which is now called Christiana. Here he became extensively known and respected, both as a physician and a man. He acquired a large practice after a comparatively short residence in this section of the country, and many of the older generation still remember him as having been their family physician. Scores of children in Lancaster and Chester Counties were named in his honor.

So influential did his opinions become that he was elected, against his wishes, to represent Lancaster County in the State Legislature for two successive terms. Dr. Agnew met and married his wife while living at Nobleville, and his only son was born in the quaint Noble homestead, near Nobleville. After twenty-five years of active practice as a country physician, Dr. Robert Agnew determined to be relieved of his laborious duties, on account of ill-health; but he was so popular and his services were so in demand that he found the only way to accomplish this was to leave his old home. Consequently, he removed to Baltimore County, Maryland, in 1840, where he purchased a handsome country-seat, "Blenheim." Even this change of residence did not prevent his being sought out by his former patients, or by those who had heard of his reputation as a practising physician. In consequence, with the compliance which was so noticeable in his son, he visited the sick and gave counsel for many years afterward, until shortly before his death; so that it can be truly said that he was engaged in the performance of the trying duties of a country physician for nearly half a century.

The description which exists of Dr. Robert Agnew's personal appearance shows whence his son derived much of his physical and mental composition. He was a very handsome man; his countenance expressed the mildness and modesty of his character, while his height gave him great dignity and impressiveness. Yet, while modest, retiring, and gentle in his disposition, he possessed great determination of character; and when he felt he was in the right, he was firm and inflexible. He was a close observer of men and things, and was a keen student on many questions. He read and studied much, not only in the department of medicine, but also in the domain of general science and literature. He was very methodical in all that he did, and showed great thoroughness and accuracy. In fact, it is stated, by all who knew him, that he showed, in his characteristics, the qualities which so distinguished at a later period his more celebrated son.

Dr. Robert Agnew was also prominent in the Presbyterian Church, carrying out the traditions of his family. In 1828 he was ordained a ruling elder of the congregation of the Presbyterian Church at Octorara, and until his removal to Maryland his relation with Session was sympathetic and cordial. He died of pneumonia, at his residence, "Blenheim," Baltimore County, Maryland, October 10, 1858, at the age of 73 years.

Mrs. Agnes Agnew, the mother of Dr. D. Hayes Agnew,

was born in Lancaster County, Pennsylvania, January 30, 1781, this making her four years older than her second husband. On her side of the house the associations with the Presbyterian Church had been as intimate and cordial as on the Agnew side. Her father, James Noble, had been an elder in the Associate Church at Octorara, while her grandfather, William Noble, had been one of the founders of this famous old church, which, with the neighboring congregation of Oxford, formed the original seat of Associate Presbyterianism in America. As has been said, Mrs. Agnew was wife first of a minister and then of a physician. She was well fitted to occupy these two prominent positions in American society, for she was a woman of the most extraordinary force of character, possessing a powerful mind and an indomitable energy. From her descent and her associations she was deeply religious in nature, which tendency increased as she grew older. As a young woman, possessing a magnificent physique and tireless energy, she had lived a life of greatest hardship as the wife of a frontier minister. The hardships of such a life, which would always fall harder on the wife and mother of the family, did not affect her health and spirits in the least, although her husband, the Rev. Ebenezer Henderson, succumbed to them early in his career.

As the wife of the active country practitioner, Mrs. Agnew brought into use the energies and faculties which, by long training, were suited pre-eminently for such work. Always serene, contented, and cheerful, perfectly guileless, and ingenuous in character, she reached her old age with a mind unusually clear and full of the knowledge of Divine truth. Undoubtedly, to her training and influence her distinguished son owed many of his characteristic traits. She walked daily with God, and ripened for glory until she reached her ninety-first year, dying, February 25, 1871, of a paralytic stroke. Although she was 37 years of age when her famous son was born, she lived to see him reach a foremost position in his professional work.

To the last she was employed in the reading of her favorite

books. Her study of the Bible occupied the principal portion of her time, but she was also devoted to the standard religious treatises of her youth: "Boston's Fourfold State," "Owen on Forgiveness and on the Spirit," "Edwards' History of Redemption," "Baxter's Saints' Rest," and "Henry's Commentaries." To her son, when he was summoned to her dying bed, she said, "You have come to see the broken frame of your old mother, but in my feebleness I have still great cause for thankfulness,—God has kept my mind untouched." And, as if to assure him of the fact, she commenced to repeat her favorite chapter, beginning "Let not your heart be troubled."

Her eldest son, James N. Henderson, born in 1803, was, consequently, fifteen years older than his half-brother. He was not married until late in life, dying in 1887, at the family seat near Baltimore, aged 84 years. Mary A. Henderson, her only daughter, was born in 1805. She married Davies Wallace and raised a large family. She is still living, her home being in Lancaster County. Between this sister and Dr. Agnew there always existed the greatest love and sympathy.

A number of Dr. Agnew's relatives became so prominent in the history of Pennsylvania that they demand brief biographies in any history of the Agnew family. David Agnew, Dr. Agnew's grandfather, was quite as ready to resist oppression as his ancestors had been, and, when hostilities commenced in the colonies against the British rule, he espoused the colonial cause. Dr. Agnew's great-uncle, James Agnew, was a colonel in the Continental army, and was wounded in one of the battles in New Jersey. In that struggle many members of the family bore honorable and patriotic parts, although they knew that in the English army were many relatives and friends. Among these was General James Agnew, who fell at the Battle of Germantown, a commanding officer in the English army. The following account of his death at the Battle of Germantown, Philadelphia, while a member of the staff of General Howe, is found in Watson's "Annals of Philadelphia":—

"At the time of the battle, General Howe came as far as the market-square and staid there, giving his commands. General Agnew rode on at the head of his men, and when he got as far as the wall of the Mennonite Church he was shot by Hans P. Boyer, who lay in ambush and took deliberate aim at the star on his breast. He fell from his horse, and was carried to Mr. Wistar's house, where he died in the front parlor. General Agnew was a very civil and gentlemanly man. The man who killed him was not an enlisted soldier. . . . General Agnew and Colonel Bird, of the British army, are both buried in the lower burying-ground, side by side. General Agnew showed great kindness to those with whom he came in contact."

The house in which General Agnew died was one of the celebrated places of the city fifty years ago. It was photographed on account of this incident, and many of the older collections of the famous houses of Philadelphia contain a copy of this quaint, old, typical Germantown home, which still stands on Germantown Road.

Dr. Agnew's uncle, Samuel Agnew, was killed during the War of 1812, at the Battle of Chippewa. A cousin, Dr. Samuel Agnew, was a surgeon in the army during that period.

Among the best-known members of the family was Colonel James Agnew, a cousin of Dr. Agnew, who was born in Adams County, Pa., July 21, 1769. His parents were of the Reformed Presbyterian (Covenanter) branch of the Church; but at the time of the union of that body with the Associate (Seceders) Church, forming the Associate Reform Church of North America, they joined in the Union. The following incident, related of his mother, Mary Ramsey, shows the unsettled condition of the country: She was attending school, living for the purpose at the house of a brother, Colonel Ramsey, in Franklin County. One day she felt a special aversion to going to school, which became so strong that she yielded to it and remained at home. That day a band of hostile Indians came upon the school-house, murdering and scalping the teacher and all the small children, and carrying the larger boys and girls into captivity. Had she gone to school that day, she would either have been killed or taken captive.

At an early age young James Agnew went to live with his maternal uncle, Colonel Ramsey, who owned an estate on West Conococheague, near Mercersburg. At the time of his advent, emigration to Western Pennsylvania had been inaugurated, and a considerable trade was carried on between the settlers west of the Alleghenies and the older settlements of Cumberland Valley. This trade was carried on by means of pack-horses, and the route corresponded nearly with the present turnpike. By the assistance of his uncle, young Agnew established a trading-post in the "Great Cove"; the nearest store to the east was kept by a Mr. Buchanan, whose son, James Buchanan, afterward became President of the United States. At this station, where McConnelsburg now stands, James Agnew built up a very prosperous business, so that he subsequently became one of the wealthiest men in Pennsylvania. He was for many years a ruling elder in the church, and his home was known as "the ministers' hotel." This arose from the cordial hospitality with which clergymen of all denominations were received and entertained; this hospitality being practised for weeks and months at a time. He was killed by falling down stairs, in 1855, in the eighty-seventh year of his age.

An incident which illustrates his character for brave and firm adherence to principle and law is as follows: In those days, before canals and railroads, the Conestoga wagon was the only means of conveying freight from Philadelphia to Pittsburgh. These sometimes formed a long caravan on the road that passed through McConnelsburg.

Very few teamsters gave themselves and their horses the benefit of the Sabbath's rest; the noise of the wagons and horses, and the boisterous voices and oaths of the drivers, became a nuisance to the people along the route. It was known that Colonel Agnew was one of the persons opposed to this, and it aroused opposition among a portion of the community; they conspired to annoy him by nominating him for the office of constable. He was elected, and accepted at once his duties. He now determined to enforce the law, which he did with the greatest zeal and firmness, as it was illegal for the teamsters to do this transportation on Sunday. One Monday morning, attempting to arrest a large and powerful teamster, who had violated the law the day before, he was resisted. Colonel Agnew was a large, finely-built man, over six feet in height, and very strong; the teamster was also stalwart and violent, and withstood so fiercely that the colonel was not equal to the task. Dr. George Junkin, who was his guest at the time, rushed to the help of the officer; by his aid the giant wagoner was overpowered and carried before the magistrate.

Colonel Agnew was an early and consistent friend of the temperance reformation. He determined to banish all liquors from his own store; his partner, to whom one-third of the profits was given, objected, as it was a very profitable portion of the business. Colonel Agnew, however, directed his partner to make a calculation of the usual amount of income from this source. This was done, and one-third of the amount was ordered to be added to the partner's receipts, and all wines and liquors were banished from the place.

Dr. Samuel Agnew, brother of James, was a physician, being born, August 10, 1777, near Gettysburg. After his graduation at Dickinson College, in 1798, he studied medicine. During the War of 1812 he served as Surgeon in the Army, but settled afterward in Harrisburg, Pennsylvania. He became so well known that the late Professor Samuel Jackson, of the University of Pennsylvania, remarked, on one occasion, that "if he had an only son dangerously sick, there was no physician between Philadelphia and New Orleans whose services he would rather have than those of Dr. Samuel Agnew." His eldest son was the Rev. John Holmes Agnew; his second son, Judge James C. Agnew. He was a ruling elder in the first Presbyterian Church in Harrisburg for fifteen years, and a corporate member of the American Board of Commissioners for Foreign Missions for a long time.

Rev. John Holmes Agnew, son of Dr. Samuel Agnew, and cousin of Dr. D. Hayes Agnew, was born in Gettysburg in 1804. He became a minister, but soon relinquished pastoral work and was elected Professor of Languages in Washington College in 1831. He subsequently became professor in a similar position in Newark College, Delaware, from which he withdrew because the funds for the institution were raised by lottery. He was also editor of *The Knickerbocker*, *The Eclectic Magazine*, and the *Biblical Repertory*, a quarterly in the interest of the then new-school branch of the Presbyterian Church. He was also author of a valuable work on the Sabbath, and he assisted in the translation of Winer's "Grammar of the New Testament." He died in 1865.

Samuel Agnew was born, November 18, 1814, in McConnelsburg, Fulton County, Pennsylvania. He was the youngest of eight children of Colonel James Agnew. He was a student for some time at Washington College; subsequently he removed to Philadelphia, where he entered into business. After remaining several years in business, he retired from mercantile pursuits and engaged in the book-publishing business at Sixth and Chestnut, bringing out the series of Goodrich's (Peter Parley's) School Histories. He withdrew from this business about 1855 and devoted his leisure time to the formation of a library for the Presbyterian Historical Society, which he originated in 1852, and of which he was, until the time of his death, Treasurer and Librarian. In addition, Mr. Agnew made special collections of books on this subject; for example, his collection of works on the subject of Baptism numbered 7000 volumes. He was married, December 10, 1840, to Susan, daughter of Robert and Susan Coxe Erwin, and left one child, Dr. Erwin Agnew. He died in Philadelphia, March 6, 1880.

His son, Dr. Erwin Agnew, was born February 22, 1842, graduating in medicine, at the University of Pennsylvania, in

1864. He gave up the practice of medicine early in his career, and devoted himself to the care of his estate. Although a man of most vigorous constitution and methodical habits, and coming of a long-lived race, yet his life of great usefulness was cut short by his sudden death, September 4, 1891.

The Hon. Daniel Agnew, ex-Chief Justice of the Supreme Court of Pennsylvania, is also a member of the Agnew family, his ancestors coming from the County of Antrim, in the north of Ireland, in 1764. Although no definite relationship can be traced between Dr. Agnew and him, yet the resemblance between his father and uncles and Dr. Agnew's family was so striking that there would be no hesitation on the part of a stranger to proclaim them near relatives. He was born, January 5, 1809, in Trenton, New Jersey, and was brought west, in 1813, to Beaver, Pennsylvania, where he resides at present. Judge Agnew has always borne a prominent part in the history of Pennsylvania, and his clear expoundings of constitutional law and legal points have been received with the greatest confidence and respect

His father, James Agnew, A.M., M.D., graduated at the University of Pennsylvania, in the Medical Department, in 1800. His graduation thesis was on the subject of " Perspiration," and, as was the custom at that period, it was printed in pamphlet form, bound with others in a handsome volume, and presented to the different libraries of the time.

Another member of the family, a cousin of Dr. Agnew, was Dr. Cornelius R. Agnew, of New York, who was born in that city in 1830, and graduated at Columbia College in 1848, and afterward at the College of Physicians and Surgeons. He became a distinguished oculist, and died in the midst of his usefulness, April 18, 1888.

Rev. Benjamin L. Agnew, son of Smith Agnew, and a cousin of Dr. Agnew, born October 2, 1833, is a prominent minister in the Presbyterian Church, having at present a charge in Philadelphia.

The history of the Agnew family is given in its barest outlines, in order to show from whence the family sprung. Dr. Agnew had an honest appreciation of family; he did not value a man more or less on account of his ancestry,—not for a single moment,—but he was fond, from his earliest childhood, of hearing the chronicles of olden times, in which his family bore prominent parts, and of studying and comparing the lives of its different members. His mind was stored with the tales and anecdotes of years ago, and his love for his family was one of his most marked characteristics.

An honest regard for an honorable ancestry is allowable in the most democratic of countries.

CHAPTER II.

THE EARLY LIFE OF DR. AGNEW.

DR. AGNEW received his name of David in honor of his grandfather, David Agnew. The name of David has always been a favorite one in the Agnew family, and his parents, in giving him this appellation, simply followed out one of the customs of the family in having a David among their children. He received the name of Hayes for his uncle by marriage,— Robert Hayes, of Gettysburg; this gentleman had married Rebecca Agnew, fifth child of David and Mary Agnew.

Dr. Agnew was a "born doctor"; he never remembered a time when he did not desire to be a physician. His father's profession possessed for him, from his earliest childhood, the keenest and most irresistible fascination. From the time that he was first able to play, he would ride a cane for a horse, and, clad in one of his father's vests, which reached nearly to his heels, he would stuff his pockets with bottles and powders, and pretend to visit his patients. At these times, if any one called at the house requiring his father's services, he would tell them that he had sent the young doctor out to see a patient, but that the old doctor—meaning himself—was at home.

The stories which are told of the early life of Dr. Agnew show that he possessed a keen sense of humor and a remarkable intelligence, even as a very little child. When scarcely able to walk and talk he would take his Grandmother Noble by the hand and walk through the garden with her. When he grew weary he would say, "Now let us sit down and talk over old times." He loved to hear her tell of Revolutionary days,— the trials, anecdotes, and incidents of that great struggle for independence. He knew no enjoyment equal to this, and his memory was early stored with many of the daring adventures and thrilling stories of Revolutionary history.

(36)

He was never very fond of going to school, possibly because he lived in what might be called the "Birchen Age" of American education. This was the time when a teacher was regarded as incompetent unless he made liberal use of the old-fashioned birch-rod. Unfortunately, young Agnew had a very cross teacher, who was most proficient in the use of this very necessary instrument of education, and he did not escape an occasional punishment at the hands of this pedagogue. At one time, after being corrected in this manner, young David felt very sick. His half-brother, James Henderson, who was considerably older than himself, happened to be near the school, when he heard a sad, small voice cry, "Jimmy, I've got the ague." The little boy had slipped out of school, and, seeing his brother in the distance, had followed him. As soon as "Davy"—as he was then called—reached his mother, the ague quickly disappeared, and David was himself again. This little incident was repeated a number of times, until the conviction was forced upon the family that it was a childish expedient to get away from his terrible teacher.

When about four years of age his mother took him to a camp-meeting, which was considered, in those days, a necessary adjunct to religious training. Young David possessed a very vivid imagination, and, unfortunately, one of the preachers happened to be telling the congregation about the Devil—a favorite subject at that time—just after the arrival of his young auditor. Becoming very warm in his efforts, the minister pointed his finger and cried out, dramatically: "There he is! Don't you see him?" Young David at this moment chanced to espy a lizard, and called out in return, at the top of his small voice, "Yes, I see him, and I'll catch him, too." He caught the lizard, and held it up in triumph. It is needless to say that his mother took him into custody as quickly as possible, but the effect upon the congregation is still remembered by those now living who were present.

When he was three years of age he was being prepared for

bed one night, when suddenly he disappeared and could not be found. After a time, his sister, Mary Henderson, who was thirteen years older than he, was entertaining a gentleman in the parlor, when she chanced to hear a small voice. This small voice exclaimed "Here me is," and out stepped young David, proudly, from under the table in the corner, clad only in Nature's covering, to the great confusion of the young people present.

There are some children who, from their earliest childhood, seem to realize fully the duties and responsibilities of life. Such a child was young David Agnew; he gave his attention from the outset to his religious duties, and his mother stated subsequently that she could never remember the time when she did not feel that her son was a Christian.

In those days Sabbath-schools were few, and it was the universal custom for the minister to catechise children publicly before the church service. This was an ordeal that helped to make unhappy the existence of the younger members of the congregation. In these trials, however, young David always knew his lesson perfectly, although frequently his study of his Bible and catechism would be put off until the very last thing Saturday night; but his memory was, from the earliest period, most retentive, and it was never any trouble for him to learn quickly and thoroughly.

His determination and kindness of thought were exhibited from his earliest childhood. At one time he was sick,—so sick that his family thought he could not live; and, in consequence, his mother was so much distressed by the thought that she left the sick-room for a moment. At once he missed his mother, and said that they should call her back and tell her not to feel worried about him, for he did not intend to die.

A pretty story is told of his first meeting with his future wife. While he was still a small boy, a gentleman stopped to see his father on business, bringing with him a pretty, dark-haired little girl. The boy fell in love with her at once, and made the childish remark at the time, at which every one laughed, that he had made up his mind that he would marry her when he grew up. Although he did not meet the lady who was to be his wife for many years afterward, to know her well, strangely enough, the little ideal of his boyhood days was the one love of his life—the woman to whom he owed so much of his success—the woman who became to him, in after years, a real helpmeet.

Young Agnew was growing up in the most favorable surroundings for his future career. He was born in a doctor's home; he faced that life from infancy. It was his childish sport to play the doctor, and he grew naturally into the doctor. His father and mother were thoughtful and honorable folk, devoted members of the old Presbyterian Church, lovers of their Bibles, students of Confession and Catechism, who gave many proofs of the faith of their ancestors and the strong, uplifting convictions of their own devout souls. Their boy was well trained, and his life-record is their monument.

Through these early years he was perfecting the elements of his vigorous constitution, which stood him in later years in such good stead. The boy's life in the country then was even more out-door and wild than it is now, for game was then more plentiful in the woods and the country itself less under the control of civilization. In all the boyish sports and games young Agnew early took the lead by his vigor and intelligence. His habits and customs were being instilled into him by his parents and companions too firmly to be changed to the day of his death by the enervating influences of city life. Fortunate in his parents, he was no less fortunate in the location of his early home.

After his experience at the country school, young David was sent to begin his classical education at the Moscow Academy, which was a flourishing Chester County institution of that period, in charge of the Rev. Francis Latta.

The incidents by which this academy received its curious name are interesting. At the close of the War of 1812 with

Great Britain, there developed in Pennsylvania a mania for laying out towns. Among others engaged in this project was the owner of a tavern called "The General Wayne," on the Philadelphia and Lancaster Turnpike, who sold his property, with fifty acres, for the exorbitant sum of $16,000 to speculators, who laid out thereon a town, to which they gave the name of Moscow, from the city of Moscow in Russia, which had just been consumed by fire started by Russian torches to prevent its occupation by Napoleon Bonaparte. These speculators disposed of the property by lottery, the public-house being the highest prize. The streets were called by Russian names, and the lots were disposed of in this way at high prices.

The town flourished only on paper, and the project failed. "Cossack Street" became again the common Lancaster Pike, and the others, with their Russian names, returned to the bosom of the farm from which they had sprung. It was on this property that, in 1826, the "Moscow Academy" was built by Mr. Latta.

Here he received the foundations of a good classical education, and from here he was sent to Jefferson College at Cannonsburgh, Pa. This institution was at that time the stronghold of Presbyterianism in the western part of the State, and as such, naturally, attracted the attention of Dr. Agnew's parents, when it became necessary to complete the education of their son. This college was an outgrowth of the Cannonsburgh Academy of the early part of the present century. It had been named for Thomas Jefferson, in the hope that it would receive aid from him similar to that given by Washington to the college named in his honor. Dr. Agnew was a student here in the winter of 1833–34, during the *régime* of Rev. Matthew Brown, who had been elected Principal in 1822, holding the position for twenty-three years. A further circumstance which probably influenced his family in the selection of this institution for the education of their son was the fact that Rev. James Ramsey, a connection of the family, had been a trustee of the college from 1805 to 1824.

Dr. Agnew did not stay to graduate at this institution, as he had intended, but left to enter Newark College, which had just then been established at Newark, Delaware, by the Legislature of that State. He was attracted to this institution because his cousin, Rev. John Holmes Agnew, had been elected Professor of Languages there. Newark College had been established by the Legislature of Delaware to afford higher educational facilities for the residents of that State; on May 8, 1834, it was opened officially; the inauguration addresses being delivered by Professors Nathan Munroe and John Holmes Agnew. The college opened with sixty-three students on the roll, but all were so young that only one was entered in the college course. In 1843 the name of this institution was changed to Delaware College. It was closed from 1859 to 1870, on account of difficulties in its management, but was re-opened and is now in a flourishing condition.

Dr. Agnew was one of the earliest students at Newark College, entering in the session of 1834–35. He leaves a record of his experience here, then a boy of 16, as follows: "We were a lively set of boys, and guilty of many foolish pranks, but, on the whole, not worse than the young men in similar institutions at the present time. The refectory was infamous,—poor food, and badly served."

While he was at Newark College, Dr. Agnew was active in college life; with eleven colleagues he founded the Atheneum Literary Society, and was one of its most earnest supporters. Professor Holmes Agnew left Newark College because it was supported in part by the proceeds of a lottery,—a means of sustenance of which he could not approve; in consequence, there was no further inducement for his student-cousin to remain. Therefore, Dr. Agnew did not stay to graduate in this institution.

He had been looking forward eagerly for years to the time when his father would feel that he was old enough to study medicine. He now felt that he had reached an age when he could enter upon the study of that profession, the performance of whose duties had been the dream of his boyhood.   Therefore, after studying for a time at home, under his father's directions, he entered the Medical Department of the University of Pennsylvania in 1836, being one of the youngest members of the class.

His selection of the University of Pennsylvania as his school for study was a natural one.   At that time this oldest American medical school stood easily at the head of medical instruction in America.   Philadelphia was then the undisputed centre of medical instruction, and students were attracted, as they are to-day, from all over the Union, and, in many instances, from far beyond the seas.

His advent at the University of Pennsylvania chanced to be at a very fortunate period, for between the years 1834 and 1840 the Medical Department rose with a bound, as it were, from a state of stagnation and torpor to one of vivid and productive activity, in which the student who felt ambition stirring within him was amply furnished with incentives to vigorous effort, with a better provision for future usefulness.   With the reorganization of the Medical Department, in 1835, the chair of the Practice of Medicine had been separated from that of the Institutes of Medicine, and Dr. Samuel Jackson was raised to this chair; while Dr. Chapman retained strictly the teaching of Practice.   Dr. George B. Wood was elected to the vacant chair of Materia Medica and Pharmacy.   At the same time, ill health obliging the Professor of Obstetrics, Dr. Dewees, to resign the chair he had so brilliantly illustrated, it was filled by Dr. Hugh L. Hodge, whose thorough, systematic, and impressive lectures inspired and guided his pupils for twenty-eight years.

These changes were most fortunate; they supplied fresh stimulus to the teaching force and strengthened the weak spots in the curriculum.

In consequence of these alterations, the Faculty at this time consisted of the following professors :—

Faculty of Medicine at the University of Pennsylvania, 1838.

NATHANIEL CHAPMAN, M.D., Professor of the Practice of Physic.

ROBERT HARE, M.D., Professor of Chemistry.

WILLIAM GIBSON, M.D., Professor of Surgery.

WILLIAM E. HORNER, M.D., Professor of Anatomy.

SAMUEL JACKSON, M.D., Professor of the Institutes.

GEORGE B. WOOD, M.D., Professor of Materia Medica and Pharmacy.

HUGH L. HODGE, M.D., Professor of Obstetrics and the Diseases of Women and Children.

WILLIAM E. HORNER, M.D., Dean of the Faculty.

From 1835 until the year 1847 no change took place in the Faculty, when Dr. Hare resigned the Professorship of Chemistry, having been in possession of the chair twenty-seven years. As a lecturer, Dr. Hare had been remarkable for the skill of his experiments, which were uniformly successful, impressing the minds of the students with their grandeur. His most remarkable discovery was the contrivance of the oxyhydrogen blow-pipe.

The elevation of Dr. Samuel Jackson to the Professorship of the Institutes of Medicine was a fortunate circumstance for the University. Beyond comparison the most brilliant and speculative lecturer in the Faculty of that period, he had the very rare power of swaying his audiences with his words and tones, using this power to take lofty views of Medicine as a science and an art.

Dr. Nathaniel Chapman, as a lecturer, was self-possessed, deliberate, and emphatic. Whenever warmed with his subject, his animation became oratorical. Often the theme of dry matter would be enlivened by some stroke of wit, happy pun, anecdote, or quotation. He was fresh with stores of facts and cases drawn from his own large experience and observation. His bearing was dignified, his manners easy, and his gestures graceful. He had a thorough command over the attention of his class, with whom he always possessed unbounded popularity. His voice had a peculiar intonation, depending upon some defect in the conformation of the palate, which rendered the articulation of some words an effort. When one became accustomed, however, to the tone, his enunciation was remarkable for its distinctness.[1]

Dr. William Gibson, as a teacher, was clear and emphatic; his voice was distinct and melodious, his language was well-chosen, and his style of enunciation was attractive. His demonstrations of surgical anatomy were readily comprehended by the student; some of them could not be surpassed in any respect. For the purposes of demonstration, Dr. Gibson had prepared himself, and procured by purchase, an ample collection of morbid structures, of diseased and fractured bones, models and casts, as well as pictures of large size, illustrative of diseases, or of the anatomical parts of the body involved in operations. To these were added the approved mechanical appliances of that day. In teaching in this manner, he set the example that has been followed extensively by other surgeons ever since. As an operator he was undoubtedly dexterous.

Professor Horner was not fluent or copious in language, nor had he any pretensions to elocution. His plan of teaching, to a certain extent, was novel. He composed a text-book which was a complete but concise treatise on anatomy. It was written in strict reference to the course of study in the University of Pennsylvania, and was kept in as concise a style as possible, so that there should be no unnecessary loss of time in reading it. In the lecture-room he confined himself chiefly to the demonstrations of the text of his work by discussions, preparations, drawings, and models. As to the value of this method there may be different opinions, but it made good anatomists. The students of the time frequently declared that, plain, simple, and unadorned as were the lectures of Dr. Horner, they learned

---

[1] Dr. Chapman's readiness in repartee may be illustrated by the following, in connection with the election of a colleague. When Dr. Dorsey was chosen to succeed Dr. Wistar, he was much gratified and elated at the prospect presented him of distinction in the chair of Anatomy. Expressing himself enthusiastically with reference to his hope of acquiring reputation in that branch, Dr. Chapman remarked that this had been already accomplished, as a muscle had been named after him,—the latissimus dorsi.

anatomy better from him than from any other teacher. The Anatomical Museum of the University, which had been founded by Dr. Wistar, was greatly enlarged by the anatomical skill and untiring application of Dr. Horner.

Professor Wood's connection with the University forms one of its brightest glories. His election to the chair of Materia Medica and Pharmacy had been productive of new interest in that branch in consequence of its being made more demonstrative.

This constituted the faculty which gave Dr. Agnew his first medical instruction. He was always particularly fond of describing their traits and characteristics, and the last speech he ever made, less than a month before his death, was devoted to this congenial theme. Dr. Agnew believed firmly what another student of the period has pleasantly said: "It is my pleasure to imagine that they have not been excelled to the present day." This is the universal, loyal consensus of belief of all the students of the thirties.

In order to see the extent of medical instruction of that day, with its advantages and limitations, a short *résumé* of the curriculum is necessary. The instruction in the medical schools at this period can be seen from the roster, which included the fundamental branches of Medical Science, Materia Medica and Pharmacy, Surgery, Practice of Medicine, Chemistry, Anatomy, Midwifery, and Institutes of Medicine. The very insignificant proportion of practical work formerly required of the student, and the preponderance of it at the present time, is the most noticeable change in medical instruction.

It is the spirit of the age to deride the past and underrate its advantages. There is no doubt but that there is too low an estimate placed on the extent and thoroughness of the medical teaching in the thirties. The minuter points of medical science are forgotten by the physician soon after his graduation, and only the practical knowledge which he needs remains. This does not vary so much from the knowledge of fifty years ago as would appear at first sight.

Fifty years ago personal practical work was not required of the students; they derived nearly all they learned from didactic lectures and " clinical conferences," so called. Only a few enjoyed the good fortune of receiving the personal bedside teaching of gentlemen who had themselves been trained in the Paris hospitals. Through these younger men a wider knowledge of practical medicine and surgery became disseminated. A similar revolution gradually took place in other cities, until, at the present day, the American graduate in medicine enters upon his professional life with a far completer panoply than was dreamed of by the reformers of half a century ago.

Still, the young men of the period were as studious as those of any other decade, and many of them were anxious to pursue a longer course than was demanded by the medical schools,— attendance on two courses of lectures being all that was required. In the course of 1832–33 there were forty-seven students who were in attendance beyond the second course and twenty-six who held the degree of M.D. In 1833–34 there were forty-three of the former class and thirty-one of the latter class. In 1834–35 there were forty-seven on a longer course and twenty-six doctors of medicine. After this time the catalogues did not report such students. It is known that many of those who were the most successful in their professional life attended three courses of lectures by their own choice.

It was not in didactic lectures only that improvement took place. From the commencement of medical teaching in Philadelphia bedside instruction had indeed been given at the Pennsylvania Hospital and at the Almshouse, but the credit of introducing medical patients before students in a lecture-room is ascribed to Dr. Benjamin H. Coates,[1] physician to the Pennsylvania Hospital, in 1834, although these cliniques were but little less than informal didactic expositions of the diseases which the patients who were exhibited happened to present. It was not

---

[1] Dr. Tralll Green states that, when he was a student at the University, in 1834, cliniques at the Pennsylvania Hospital had been held for some time prior to this date.

until the return of Drs. Gerhard and Pennock from Europe, and the election of the former to the Pennsylvania Hospital as attending physician, and of both gentlemen as attending physicians to the Philadelphia Hospital, that clinical medicine began to be taught in a systematic and fruitful manner.

With surgical cliniques the case was somewhat different, since they conveyed, for the most part, instruction through the eye rather than through the understanding, and, therefore, they have always attracted students by their spectacular qualities. During the period 1833 to 1840, the two great hospitals were served by surgeons who were most eminent. At the Almshouse Hospital, the staff included Drs. William Gibson, Joseph Pancoast, William E. Horner, and Richard Harlan; at the Pennsylvania Hospital, Drs. Thomas T. Hewson, John Rhea Barton, Thomas Harris, Jacob Randolph, and George W. Norris.

It would be difficult to find, anywhere, a corps of surgeons more skillful, judicious, and successful than these. Horner was distinguished by his precision, Gibson by his clearness, Pancoast by his vast experience, Hewson by his learning, Harris by his prudence and knowledge of principles, Norris by his wise conservatism and clinical investigations, and Barton by his ambidextrous skill, which he, as it were, bequeathed to one of his successors,—Agnew.

In these surgical operations, before the introduction of anesthesia, pain was not in all cases a depressing influence; for example, a boy was cut for stone, in the Pennsylvania Hospital, by lateral section; he promised that he would lie perfectly still if he were allowed to smoke a cigar during the operation. He bore the cutting with impassive tranquility.

The infusion of new life and vigor into the Medical Faculty of the University of Pennsylvania was not followed by an immediate and permanent increase in the size of the classes. Probably, in the present instance, the critics were too far away and too ill-informed to learn of the improvement in the medical instruction here. The greater number of students were drawn from the Southern States; in 1833–34, out of a total number of four hundred and thirty-two, no less than two hundred and thirty came from States south and west of Delaware. Yet, under the new *régime* begun in 1835, there was a steady increase in numbers until the Civil War, in 1861–62.

At about this date, 1836, student life became more sedate, owing probably to the changes made in the Faculty, which tended to inspire the young men with more serious ideas of the nature and purpose of their studies. This reformation occurred almost simultaneously with a similar improvement, which took place in London, and which had been attributed in that instance to the genial but biting satire of the "Medical Student," in *Punch*.

During the period 1830 to 1840 the medical department occupied what was then its new hall on Ninth Street above Chestnut. A large proportion of the first-course students wore a decidedly bucolic aspect in manners and apparel. Very many of the classes of those days came from the Old Dominion; they brought with them, along with the wealth they lavishly dispensed, a freedom, not to say a license of bearing, which caused not only themselves, but the whole medical class they were supposed to typify, to be called "'Ginny Students" by the vulgar. They were specially looked at askance by the colored people, among whom a superstition prevailed that these gay young doctors "burked" negroes for the anatomical rooms.

In those days it was no uncommon occurrence for medical students to engage in brawls in theatres and other public places, and to pass more or less of the night in the lock-up, unless liberated by the intervention of some professor. Indeed, going bail for disorderly students was regarded as an incident of the professorial functions. This custom was a natural result of the closer personal relations existing between the professors and students than have prevailed of later years. Almost every professor had a large class of private and office students, being so large in some instances as to become cumbrous. This fact led, on the one hand, to the establishment of the Medical Institute by Professor Chapman, in which he associated with himself several of his colleagues in the Faculty, together with one or two physicians who were not connected with the University, and, on the other hand, to the organization of several more or less private quiz classes. The first of these was established by the late Dr. Thomas Dent Mütter, afterward Professor of Surgery in the Jefferson Medical College, and by Dr. Paul Beck Goddard, so distinguished as an anatomist. The classes for private instruction were numerous.

A great feature of medical instruction at this time was the summer courses of lectures with private instruction. In some instances, it was absolutely necessary for the students to take some of these courses; for example, Dr. Chapman's lectures on Practice at the University was not completed there, and his lectures in the Medical Institute filled out the course. His lectures on the diseases of the nervous system he delivered during the summer months.

It was the practice of the students of this period to form quiz clubs, consisting of six or seven members, each member representing a professor. The duty of the member was to listen diligently to the instruction of the lecturer or professor he represented and record notes. The club met in the evening, and each member in turn quizzed the others. Every week or every two weeks, the members changed the subjects; for example, the man who had quizzed on chemistry exchanged with the man who had quizzed on materia medica; so that each member of the club, in turn, quizzed on all the branches during the lecture course. These quiz clubs were possibly more effectual than the modern method of employing quiz masters, for each member had a motive in taking notes on his subject, in the hope that he might have the pleasure of " stumping " some of his colleagues at the club meetings. In this way a spirit of rivalry and competition was begotten, which spurred the students on to acquire fuller and more accurate medical knowledge.

4

It was the custom of two of the professors to entertain the graduating class at their houses on Commencement eve, when the provision was less ascetic than is usual in these abstemious days. The consequences were not always edifying from a decorous point of view, but the soberest among them may, perhaps, be pardoned for indulging a little in the greatest saturnalia of their lives. They had, but a short time before, passed through the ordeal of the "Green Box," which was once a literal closet where the candidate for the degree was given over to his tormentors.

The "Green Box," or "Green Room," which is still even employed as the term for an examination in medical subjects, arose from the practice of the professors at one period—1810 to 1821—examining the candidates for the degree of medicine behind a screen. This was a modification of the method which had been in operation before 1810, when the professors examined first the student privately, and then publicly before the trustees to exhibit his fitness for the honor of the doctorate.

The number graduating with Dr. Agnew at the Medical Commencement, April 6, 1838, was 144; at the Commencement of the college department on July 12th 12 more were added to this list, making a total of 156. In the "General Catalogue of the Medical Department of the University of Pennsylvania, with an Historical Sketch of the Medical Department, published by the Direction of the Medical Faculty of the University of Pennsylvania, third edition, 1845," the number of matriculates is given as 380 and the graduates as 157. This slight mistake in the number of graduates is due to the duplication of the name of one of the students.

The Commencement was held at Musical Fund Hall, on Locust Street, between Eighth and Ninth Streets. It occurred during a period of a few years, in which the University term was prolonged to six months, being afterward reduced again to a period of five months. Among his class-mates and fellow-graduates were John Forsyth Meigs; Joseph K. Barnes, late

Surgeon-General U. S. Army; Philip Lansdale, Surgeon U. S. Navy; James L. Tyson, now living at Penllyn, Montgomery County, Pennsylvania, formerly Professor of Materia Medica in the Philadelphia Medical College; Azariah B. Newell, at one time Governor of New Jersey; John D. Griscom, formerly a well-known practitioner in, Philadelphia, who was subsequently a neighbor of Dr. Agnew at Haverford; Henry E. Muhlenburg, of Reading; and Joseph Hopkinson, Jr., who was in charge of the Mower Hospital during the Civil War.

A search through the "National Directory of Physicians for the United States" discloses the fact that in 1890 there were at least twelve members of the class of 1838 still living. Subsequent inquiries, made during the summer of 1892, revealed the fact that, out of this number, probably only four members remained, the other eight dying in the last two years. The living members (1892) as far as are known are Drs. James L. Tyson, Penllyn, Pennsylvania; S. G. Fauntleroy, Dragonsville, Virginia; James L. Motley, Sharp's Wharf, Virginia; and Philip Lansdale, retired Medical Director in the U. S. Navy, Philadelphia.

The following description of Dr. Agnew at this period is given by a former class-mate:—

"I knew D. Hayes Agnew in 1838, when I graduated at the University of Pennsylvania, but my relations with him were not intimate. He was a quiet gentleman, as I remember him, but indefatigable in his close attendance in the lecture-room. It was the custom of some of the professors, in that day, to catechise the two first rows of students on the subjects of the preceding lectures,—particularly by Horner on Anatomy, Wood on Materia Medica, and Hodge on Obstetrics, as well as occasionally Gibson on Surgery,—so that the questions and answers could be heard throughout the rotunda. Being one of these, and familiar with most of the others who underwent this somewhat trying ordeal, I remember that Agnew's well-marked presence was seldom absent at these times, especially if anatomy or surgery were the themes. More than half a century has elapsed since the time referred to; but I find that my memory, although occasionally a little treacherous, is more tenacious of distant events than of those of more recent origin.

"The subject of slavery in the South was at that period rife in the minds of all, and many collisions, engendered by discussions on the prolific theme, gave rise to divers canings and fisticuffs among the malcontents; so much so that Professor Gibson one day made the remark that 'the very devil seemed to have broken out among the students.' In none of these dissensions, however, did Mr. Agnew in any way participate, but quietly pursued his studies, undeterred by the conflicting elements around him.

"Not far from the University, which was, at the time I refer to, on Ninth Street, north of Chestnut, there was, in a back street, near by, a certain house whose rooms were appropriated for anatomical dissections by some specialists in that department, which I had desired to possess, with a view of pursuing and perfecting my studies in that branch; but to my chagrin, at the time, I learned they had already come into the possession of Mr. Agnew, and I have little doubt that here he laid the first foundation of his great skill in surgical operations, which was destined to place his name high on the rolls of fame in Surgery, unsurpassed as he was in this or any country in the world."

As shown in this account, there was a custom among the students at this period of engaging such rooms for anatomical work. They were not connected in any way with the School of Anatomy, which was then in active operation, under the care of Dr. Joseph Pancoast, although on the same street.

Agnew's determination to study anatomy more fully even than was required by the curriculum throws an interesting light on his ambition. His love for this laborious and too frequently neglected branch of medicine was not acquired; it was instinctive. As he expressed it himself, in speaking of the dissecting-room of the School of Anatomy: "Those dingy old rooms had more attractions for me than the frescoed and fretted walls of a palace, and those anatomical odors were sweeter far than those of Araby the blest."

Dr. Agnew registered himself for graduation as David H. Agnew, the title of his graduating thesis being "Medical Science, and the Responsibility of Medical Character." Up to this time, and until after his marriage, he signed himself in this manner, making the change to D. Hayes Agnew at the solicitation of his wife, who disliked greatly the name of David.

During the fire in the Medical Department at the University, May 30, 1888, the Stillé Library, a valuable collection of medical books, in the third story of the Medical Hall, was damaged by water to such an extent that, at the recent re-arrangement of the books in the University Library, those that had been rendered illegible were destroyed. Unfortunately, all the theses for the year 1838 were among this number to be destroyed; consequently, all trace is gone forever of Dr. Agnew's graduating essay. Curiously enough, the essays for the years prior to 1838 are in a good state of preservation, as are also those after the year 1839, the years missing being 1838 and 1839. Fate seems to have decreed that one of the few essays which would be of interest at present should be lost.

It is to be doubted, however, whether the entire loss of these graduating theses would be a serious blow to medical literature. They were composed under unfortunate circumstances, at a time when the medical students were worn out and depressed by a hard winter's course; their composition was regarded as an irksome and unpleasant task; but little time could be given for original investigation, consequently they were copied largely from the text-books, and they were shirked as much as possible. In consequence, many of them are decidedly schoolboyish in composition and in the treatment of their subjects. On the other hand, the necessity for reading one hundred and fifty of these essays annually was an equally unpleasant task for the Faculty. The removal of this requisite for graduation within the past fifteen years was a wise act on the part of the authorities of the Medical Department.

Although Dr. Agnew's graduating thesis has been destroyed, yet it is possible to see its drift from its title; he always held strict ideas upon the special responsibilities of a physician, and, undoubtedly, in this first essay, wrote on a subject which was an especial favorite with him during his whole life.

After graduating at the University of Pennsylvania, in 1838, Dr. Agnew returned to Nobleville in order to assist his father in his very extensive practice. He remained with his father in this capacity for two years, until the latter's removal to Maryland, in 1840. The elder Agnew was a terrible sufferer from asthma, and his removal was made not merely to get rid of the exactions of a laborious country practice, but also in the hope of finding a climate more suited to his constitution. After his removal to Maryland, he suffered but little from his asthmatic attacks. The younger Agnew lived, at this time, in the old Noble homestead, where his parents had lived before him for many years.

His mother's family had long dwelt in this location. The village had been called for a long time Nobleville, in honor of the family. It was south of the Philadelphia and Columbia Railroad, subsequently the Pennsylvania Railroad, which had just been built to connect Philadelphia with the canals farther west. Its title was changed to Christiana, in 1847, in honor of Christiana Noble, wife of William Noble, Dr. Agnew's uncle.

While living here he formed the acquaintance of the lady who was to play, subsequently, an important part in his career, Margaret Creighton Irwin, daughter of Samuel Irwin, of Pleasant Garden Iron-Works. Their parents had been friends for a long time, Dr. Robert Agnew having been their family physician for many years. On his removal south, in 1840, the younger Dr. Agnew was called in to attend some members of the Irwin family who had been injured in an accident. The relations between Dr. Agnew and the Irwin family continued to grow more intimate, until, finally, the strong attachment between Miss Irwin and himself culminated in their marriage at the old homestead, at Pleasant Garden, Chester County, Pennsylvania, the wedding ceremony being performed by Rev. Wm. Easton, on November 21, 1841, three days before the doctor's twenty-third birthday.

Mrs. Agnew's family were so solicitous for the young couple to live at home with them that they spent the winter of 1841–42 at Pleasant Garden, Dr. Agnew continuing his practice at this point. In the spring, however, they determined to return to his original office, in the old homestead at Nobleville. They remained here until Dr. Agnew decided to give up practice, a year later.

Samuel Irwin, Mrs. Agnew's father, died March 17, 1842, leaving his large business to his children.

The selection of his future companion and helpmate was one of the most fortunate circumstances of his life. It is hard to say how much of Dr. Agnew's success was due to his wife, but certainly a large portion of it was the result of her energy, intelligence, and determination; for she supplied the tireless, ever-active impetus which kept him from being satisfied with his first efforts. He learned at this time a young doctor's life of incessant and ill-paid toil in that finest of first fields for medical activity, —a diversified country practice,—where a man of medicine is saved for all time from cramping one-sidedness, and where, of necessity, he endures hardness and makes firm backbone. They were days of wearing toil, of sturdy effort, and steady struggle. He has told, in his own calm, crisp, cheery sentences, of those first years of professional life,—"hard riding, hard reading, hard working, and small fees." Here it was he gained first his own resistless eye of instantaneous insight from which nothing seemed to be hidden, that marvelous judgment for the subtle secrets of the human body, those nimble fingers apt for any delicate operation, and those unrivaled hands of co-equal power.

Dr. Agnew was, at that time, a famous sportsman; he loved

to take his gun and go in search of game, which was then very plentiful in the woods of Lancaster and Chester Counties. In such expeditions he became a leader from his earliest youth, and his fame as a hunter still lingers as a legend in those regions. There were one or two incidents of this wild out-door life that he could never forget, especially as, in one of these occurrences, he nearly lost his life. In Lancaster County, in those years, fox-hunts were a great source of amusement and recreation. Dr. Agnew took the foremost place in these hunts, riding a famous jumper called "Tom." This was not so much an individual as a generic equine appellation, for the steed was of a breed called "Toms," found only in Baltimore County, Maryland. History says, no doubt with truth, that a British officer, during the Revolutionary war, left a magnificent stallion in Baltimore County, which was the sire of the "Tom" breed of horses, famous for more than a century in Maryland. They are closely built, muscular, great jumpers, with wonderful en-durance, intelligence, and spirits. Most of them are of a bay color, with black manes and tails, and arched necks. All these peculiarities, in a remarkable degree, were possessed by Dr. Agnew's fox-hunter,—an animal that was long famous, even in Lancaster County, for its speed and abilities as a jumper.

It was a frosty morning in the fall when Dr. Agnew and several other gentlemen followed a pack of fox-hounds to the fields in a particularly beautiful portion of fair old " Lancaster "; the dogs soon striking the trail of the fox, dashed off in full cry. After them rode the hunters, with rapidly increasing speed, over corn-fields and across ditches, jumping such fences as came in their way, filled with the delight of the ride in the crisp air and the excitement of the chase. The fox led toward a range of hills, and, while the others kept on directly after the hounds, Dr. Agnew took a " short cut " across country, intending to head off reynard as he turned back on his tracks, as he was almost sure to do.

" Tom " bore his master gallantly across a decidedly rough

country, leaping ditches as if the task were sport and sailing over low fences and hedges as birds sail over a line of trees. The cries of the hounds grew fainter in the distance as they kept straight on upon the trail of the fox, and the other hunters had long passed out of sight; but, knowing well "the lay of the land," Dr. Agnew pressed on until he saw an exceedingly high fence before him, and pulled on the bridle to check "Tom" until he could lower the rails for a passage. The horse's blood was up; he, too, felt all the excitement of the chase, and, taking the bit in his teeth, he rushed on. His rider, seeing how near the fence was, whipped the steed and let him go as he would. The horse, when a few feet from the fence, made a long jump, rising in the air like a lark from her nest; but his hoofs struck the top rail and down he fell on the opposite side, throwing his rider off with a stirrup entangled about one foot.

Dr. Agnew was thrown partially in front of the horse, and he knew that if the animal stirred he would be dragged. He knew, too, in a moment, that "Tom" might roll forward— the animal was on its knees—and crush him to death; but the blooded animal did not stir. Although the horse was on his knees, with his hind legs half crushed under him, he lay like a block of stone, looking at his master. Slowly, painfully, the bruised physician disentangled the stirrup, and, rising to his feet, found that no bones were broken. Not until then did "Tom" rise. The physician gratefully reflected, as he rode slowly homeward, pretty well shaken up, upon the intelligence displayed by the horse, which saved his master from injury, probably from death.

Some years later Dr. Agnew became fond of duck-shooting. For a number of years he went regularly to Chesapeake Bay to indulge in this fascinating sport. About eighteen miles below Havre-de-Grace there is an island famous among duck-shooters, where Dr. Agnew had many remarkable experiences, so far as exciting sport was concerned. On one occasion the doctor's boatman told him, as the sun began to decline, that he would have a wonderful experience, if he did not mind standing in water up to his knees for about half an hour.

Twenty minutes later, just as the sun dipped beyond the western horizon, and it was "neither day nor night," Dr. Agnew and his boatman, standing in water near the edge of the bay, and concealed in the tussocks, held their guns in readiness. Pretty soon a cloud appeared,—a cloud of black ducks coming to roost. As they passed overhead, the guns re-echoed and scores of the water-fowl fell dead. The sportsmen hardly had time to reload before another flock came. Many more were bagged. Then the ducks were seen on all sides. They came in flocks of hundreds each, to roost in the tussocks as the twilight deepened, and in the aggregate they numbered thousands. The hunters killed ducks by the score until it became dark, which was about twenty minutes after the arrival of the first bunch of water-fowl. There are not now many such duck-roosts in the world.

Dr. Agnew was never a happier or more attractive companion than when off for a day with dog and gun. During his connection with the School of Anatomy this formed his only recreation, and in after years he often spoke of these happy days with the greatest pleasure. At that time he was a superb shot and a stranger to fatigue. His steadiness of hand, quick, decisive judgment, and sharp eye were as useful to him as the successful sportsman as they were in the successful surgeon.

As Dr. Agnew grew older, he gave up entirely all his expeditions as a sportsman, although he still retained a love and appreciation for the pleasure of the chase; but his time was too fully occupied for him to indulge in this favorite pastime of his earlier manhood.

Dr. Agnew was one of the best judges of horse-flesh that it is possible to become. All his life he had a fondness and admiration for that noble animal, and he could take in at a glance all its good qualities and defects. If he approved of the selection of an animal, its purchaser could rest satisfied that it was all that had been claimed for it.

Dr. Agnew had now been in practice for nearly five years, during which time he had been busily engaged in work. He was happily married, and had apparently settled down to his life-work as a country physician; but just at this time, through the instrumentality of his marriage, he gave up his profession for a time, and unconsciously mapped out for himself a totally different career, even, from the new work which he had undertaken. As he said himself, in his speech at his own jubilee banquet: "Any man who has lived long in this world, and has taken a thoughtful retrospect of his life, must be forced to confess that the influences and forces which have conspired to mold his character and to shape his destiny are most mysterious indeed. Plans constructed with infinite care have miscarried; fondly-cherished hopes have suddenly been crushed with a shock; glowing anticipations just about to become realizations are dissipated in a moment into thin, viewless air, like earth-mists before the morning sun."

The details of this change in the life of Dr. Agnew, which gave him eventually a career undreamed of at this time, are given in the next chapter.

CHAPTER III.

THE story has been told that Dr. Agnew, discouraged by his prospects in medicine and feeling himself unfitted for its practice, determined to give up his professional life and go into business. This incident has often been cited as an illustration to encourage the medical graduate of to-day who sees in the future no opening for himself; its application is obvious. This story is partly true, and partly false. Dr. Agnew did not give up the practice of medicine because he felt that he was unfitted for it, or because he felt that there was no future in it for him, but because he thought he saw a much greater opening in another direction. There came an opportunity to him of immediate advancement, in his early professional life, which he did not dare ignore, although it is true that his consent to it was most reluctantly given; for his love for medical work, as he has said himself, was inborn, wrought into the very fibre of his mental organization.

His father-in-law, Samuel Irwin, was a well-known and prosperous iron-founder of the early part of the century. He had furnaces on Bush River, near Baltimore; at Pleasant Garden and at Washington Forges, near Bellefonte, in this State. The firm in Baltimore was Irwin & Patterson,—the Patterson being the brother-in-law of Jerome Bonaparte; the firm name in Pleasant Garden was simply Samuel Irwin; in Bellefonte it was Irwin & Houston. He had, in addition, a number of large stores, to supply the necessaries of life to his workmen at these different points. As he grew older, the care of these industries devolved more and more upon his sons, until at his death they assumed control of his large business. Then it was that Dr. Agnew was invited to enter the firm, to represent the interests of his wife.

(60)

His progress in practice in the country had been fairly successful. He had been cordially received by the people, on account of the pleasant memories which had been left by his father, who had been a practising physician in this locality for many years; but, of course, practice in the country, as well as elsewhere, is, at the outset, not particularly lucrative to a young man. It requires years to establish the confidence and to acquire that acquaintanceship which lays the foundation of a physician's success. His principal competitor was Dr. Nathaniel Sample, who at that time had reached an honorable old age, having earned a reputation which made him the leading practitioner of the region,—skillful, capable, and honest.

Consequently, this admission into the partnership of a large manufacturing concern was a flattering opportunity to the young country practitioner; although, knowing his own nature so thoroughly, his consent was given reluctantly. Therefore, in 1843 Dr. Agnew relinquished all idea of continuing his medical work, and joined his brothers-in-law in the management of the iron-works at Pleasant Garden, Chester County, Pennsylvania.

At this time that great revolution in business methods— the logical sequence of the introduction of new agencies in the mercantile world—was just beginning. The electric telegraph, the railroad, the extended use of steam as a power, and the invention of improved machinery were all making new conditions in the industrial world. New competitors were springing up everywhere in every business; competition was becoming closer and keener; those industries which were disadvantageously placed in any way, in the new order of things, were being pushed slowly but inevitably to the wall.

It was the mill-race against the steam-engine, the Conestoga wagon against the freight-car. No such revolution had been known before in the business world; consequently, its forces and powers were not quickly grasped or utilized by all the business men of the period. Because their fathers or grandfathers had made money in the old way, many clung to their old locations, old machinery, old methods of business, old means of transportation.   It was this spirit which drove the great whaling firms of New Bedford, bringing their oil from far-distant, perilous, and uncertain sources, to attempt to compete with the great oil-wells of Pennsylvania, spouting their thousands of gallons daily.   The result was typical of the conflict everywhere. The great fortunes of the whalers[1] melted away like mist before the summer sun, in the fierce but unequal competition with the penniless but clear-headed men who saw the real outlook of the future, and who were straining every nerve to get money to buy oil-lands.   This struggle went on in every business; the simple rules of political economy were being fought against in vain.

The wrecks of this terrific storm still strew the country, forming its only ruins.   How often, in a drive through the shaded roads, alongside many of the tumultuous streams of central New York or Pennsylvania, can be found the romantically-deserted mill or moss-covered factory which once echoed to the ceaseless hum of industry!   These romantic spots, now so suggestive of legend or story, were made by the practical demands of commonplace, commonsense business.   It is stern reality, curiously enough, that makes the romance of this world.

Among other industries, there occurred no greater revolution than in the iron business.   Formerly, the iron was found in small quantities in isolated spots and hauled by wagon many miles to the foundry or the rolling-mill, where it was smelted by specially prepared charcoal or by coal brought from a distance. The manner in which the work was done, as compared with the tremendous modern methods, was mere child's play.   Often great works were built which depended on the iron found in the peat of swamps along the coast-line.   "The ruined village of Allaire," near Spring Lake Beach, New Jersey, with its rows of empty houses opening on grass-grown streets, and its gaunt, huge foundry buildings, with their gaping windows, forming as

[1] In justice, it must be stated that some of the whaling firms saw the temporary nature of their business long before its destruction.

true a deserted village as ever was painted by Goldsmith, is a typical example of this kind.

In order to see the position of the Pleasant Garden Iron-Works in the business world of the period, and the various agencies which were at work, it is necessary to present a brief outline of the history of iron-making, and the various sudden revolutions which have occurred in its history. As far as can be determined, the first iron-works in Pennsylvania were established in 1718, by Thomas Rutter, near the present city of Pottstown.

Of course, the works of the eighteenth century were of the most primitive character; such a works, in those days, being called a "bloomary," or Pool forge. The forge, at that time, occupied a far more prominent position than it does at present, being the great means by which pig-iron was converted into marketable articles. This work, which is now done by the rolling-mill, was hammered out by hand on the forge, the product being called "bloom," deriving its name from the fact that when hammered into shape on the anvil, it was the flower of the metal, gaining its name from the German term "blume," a flower. This product was made from cast- or pig- iron, or even directly from the ore. Until 1838, all iron-furnaces in the United States, with the exception of a few coke-furnaces, used charcoal as fuel. All furnaces, at this time, were blown by water-power, and the blast was always cold.

In 1838 anthracite or stone coal first came into use as fuel for iron-works. Its introduction into the manufacture of iron gave a great impetus to the industry everywhere, and it was followed by the establishment of many other furnaces in other parts of the country. Raw bituminous coal was used as fuel for the same purpose in 1843. The first Lake Superior iron-ore used in a blast-furnace, curiously enough, was brought by David and John P. Agnew to their furnaces at Sharpsville, Pennsylvania, in 1853.

At this time, outside communication and the means of transportation being limited and equally good to all, and the demand coming from no great distance, the importance of being accessible to the market was not appreciated. In those days there were no railroads or canals in existence, and every one was obliged to cart his merchandise by wagon. In consequence, these forges were placed in locations which, nowadays, seem out of the way.

One of the favorite situations at this time, for an iron-works, was in the range of hills running down from the Alleghenies to the sea, extending through the pleasant, fertile farm-lands of Chester County, on the border of Mason's and Dixon's Line. These ranges of high hills afforded two great advantages: in the first place, charcoal, which was then the great means for smelting iron, was one of the most expensive factors in the iron industry; consequently, the location of the iron-works in the midst of a densely wooded region afforded access to a large and practically inexhaustible supply of fuel. In the second place, the waters of the rapid streams which were found among these hills afforded the great source of power. The arrangement of the land by nature was such that dams could be built and fine water-supplies obtained at a very moderate outlay of money.

As time wore by, the disadvantages of such a location as that chosen by Samuel Irwin for the site of his iron-works, on the Big Elk Creek, became more apparent. The Reading Railroad was finished in 1838; the great Pennsylvania Canal, with its Portage and Columbia Auxiliary Railroad, was opened for traffic in 1834; and by 1840 communication had been opened with the Great Lakes at Cleveland, by means of the Beaver River and the Ohio Canal. In 1840 the State of Pennsylvania had 974 miles of canals and 953 miles of railroads; thus, it can be seen that the means of transportation were being rapidly extended.

Forges, at this time, were beginning to stop the manufacture of bar-iron, leaving its production to the rolling-mills, forced by the many improvements in the various processes which were made continually in the manufacture of iron; in 1836 furnace gases were first utilized for increasing the heat of the fuel; in 1838 the hot blast came into use.

The business life of the iron-manufacturer, at this period, was particularly hard and precarious. His business was open to such disadvantages and losses that it early dawned upon the government that protection must be given to this branch of industry; in consequence, in 1836, corporations for the mining and working of iron were favored by legislative act. This was necessary on account of the panic which was approaching, and because of the strong alien influence at work, exerted by the English iron-workers, who were at that time in a more prosperous position than their American competitors. It has been stated, on good authority, that scarcely an American firm engaged in the iron industry made money between the years 1840 and 1850, and countless numbers of firms were forced to succumb.

The iron industry of Pennsylvania has always been one of the most important and typical features of this commonwealth. The iron-workers of Pennsylvania were most influential in the settlement of the State. Except for the thinning out of the forests to obtain the charcoal for their furnaces, there would not have been a sufficient number of acres cleared to have allowed the farmer to do his work satisfactorily, for the farmer did not have sufficient inducement to do this work for himself. In consequence, agriculture would have lagged. The forgemen and furnacemen, in the history of Pennsylvania, were never far behind the pioneer with his rifle. If it were not for the existence of forges, furnaces, and rolling-mills, also, there would not have been so much inducement for the improvement of the means of transportation. History shows that canals were first used for this branch of industry. Again, the necessity for a larger quantity and a better quality of fuel led the way to the introduction and utilization of anthracite coal. The history of the coal industry goes hand in hand with that of iron.

The panic of 1837, which was followed by a period of intense financial depression throughout the country, was felt most severely in the iron industries. It handicapped the iron-workers, who were already at a disadvantage in competition with Great Britain. The amount of pig-iron produced fell, in one year, to 233,000 tons, from 390,000 tons of the year before. It was only by the imposition of a high protective tariff, by the organization of corporations, with large amounts of capital to draw upon, and by many favors of legislative action, that the iron business was nursed until it grew to its present colossal proportions.

The Pleasant Garden Iron-Works was a most perfect example of the old-fashioned method of producing iron. In 1811 Ellis Passmore built a forge on the Big Elk Creek, five miles southeast of Oxford, and two and one-half miles southwest of New London, in Chester County. He also erected, in this beautiful valley, a handsome colonial residence, two and one-half stories high, built of stone, and a typical example of this pretty style of architecture. Shortly after this time he sold the works to his brother-in-law, Samuel Irwin. Mr. Irwin conducted these works most successfully, and at his death, in 1842, the business had grown until there was a large collection of buildings here, in which the work was carried on, or in which the workmen lived.

When Dr. Agnew was admitted to the firm, some of these disadvantages were already felt. Realizing that they must keep up with the advances and improvements in the iron industry, they added a rolling-mill, at the expense of many thousand dollars, in 1845. Their location had been excellently selected. It is conceded to-day to be one of the best water-rights in the State. The dam supplied a water-power dependent on a lake extending backward for a mile and a half; but by this time the works were far from railroad, river, and canal; its ore had to be hauled from a distance; its fuel was old-fashioned and second-rate; its power uncertain and weak, compared to the newer sources of power.

The transformation occurred almost in the twinkling of an eye, from the time when the old-fashioned iron-works in the densely grown woods on the babbling streams of Pennsylvania made its owners' fortunes, to the period when an iron-works required, for its successful continuance, three vital factors,—the cheapest fuel, the most extensive connections by rail and canal, and the best ore. The change took place with such lightning rapidity that it startles even the observer of to-day studying its phenomena.

It was just at this time that Dr. Agnew was admitted to partnership, and the firm name became Irwin & Agnew. Had he gone into the industry ten years before he would have been successful in it, and America would have lost her greatest surgeon. How inscrutable are the ways of Providence!

The iron used at Pleasant Garden was not mined here, but was hauled by eight-horse teams from Port Deposit, Elkton, Perryville, and other points at a considerable distance, necessitating, of course, a considerable expense in the manufacture of its products. The iron-foundry was in a most unfavorable natural position to compete with the newer mines in better locations being worked everywhere. These influences had not been felt in the original growth of the concern.

To the credit of Dr. Agnew's business sagacity it must be said that the circumstances of the business made it such that it had to struggle at this point, without the possibility of seeking a newer and more favorable location. Many different interests were involved, and no concerted action to remove was feasible.

The firm of Irwin & Agnew made a long and determined struggle against unequal forces. In this they were somewhat handicapped by the fact that the resources of the firm had been lost to a considerable extent in various ways. After the maintenance of the firm for three years after the admission of Dr. Agnew, they were eventually obliged to succumb, and consequently to assign. During this time Dr. Agnew worked with the greatest zeal and intelligence to maintain the sinking fortunes of the estate. He made a desperate attempt to stem the current which was sweeping them along; his attention and absorption in business was unrelenting day and night, but the firm was too heavily handicapped; it was doomed to failure.

It is difficult now to trace the site of the forges and the rolling-mill, for the buildings themselves have long since fallen to the ground. With the aid of a guide, however, it is possible to see where the different buildings stood, although now only masses of crumbling stone mark the locations. The dam which supplied the water-power gave way about ten years ago; in strength and size it had been the wonder of the neighborhood.

Only portions of the walls of one building remain. At the edge of the road, half-hidden by the dense foliage of the surrounding trees, stands a solitary stone wall, as solidly built as the corner of a prison. It is probably twenty feet high, and forms one of the corners of the old charcoal house, inclosing, probably, one-half of the building. In the deep vault, still shadowed and hidden by this wall, was stored the fuel, from time to time as it was needed, for the forges.

Scattered over the ground can still be found large quantities of iron-slag, which, at the time of the running of the iron-works, had been discarded as worthless, being full of fragments of charcoal. At that time there was no method to separate the charcoal from the iron; in consequence, tons of this material had to be discarded. Recently, a method was devised which separated the charcoal from the iron, and tons of this worthless iron-slag have been removed from the place; while it lasted, it was quite in demand, for it contained plenty of good iron.

Curiously enough, the revolutions of time and the requirements of later days render it possible that this old, deserted site, which marks the wreck of a large fortune, will probably be again the scene of industry. The Big Elk is a valuable stream in the manufacture of paper, for paper-mills require water of a certain degree of purity with which to wash their paper. In

THE CHARCOAL-HOUSE OF THE PLEASANT GARDEN IRON-WORKS.

consequence, there has sprung up on this stream a number of paper-mills; the paper which is used in the Philadelphia *Public Ledger* and the *Philadelphia Record* is made on this stream, not ten miles away.

Since the projection of a new railroad—the Lancaster Southern—through this region, a branch from the Baltimore and Ohio, locating a station within a mile of this place, there has been good prospects of establishing another paper-mill here; so that probably industry will again be seen at this deserted spot, which, unless ruined by the changing improvements of time, as its predecessor was, should be eminently prosperous.

Dr. Agnew felt keenly the failure of his firm, and, endowed with the same sensitive feeling of honor in business as Sir Walter Scott, determined to make up to his creditors, at the earliest opportunity, all that had been lost. Through his ability to do successful work elsewhere, in another line, he was able to pay back to the creditors every cent of indebtedness against the firm.

This is the simple story of Dr. Agnew's venture into mercantile pursuits. It has been distorted in many particulars, as have many other facts in connection with his life.

Although it was regarded as unfortunate at the time that the firm should have failed, it was the most fortunate thing that it did occur, not only for the medical world and the general public, but also for Dr. Agnew himself; for he was undoubtedly intended by nature to do the work which he met subsequently in his professional career.

During these years of hard, unceasing toil it became the custom for Dr. and Mrs. Agnew to make an annual pilgrimage by carriage down into Maryland to spend a few days with his parents. In these expeditions they were joined by his half-sister and her husband, Mr. and Mrs. Davies Wallace, and their daughter, afterward Mrs. Mary A. Falls. It took two days to reach the home of the elder Dr. Agnew, in Baltimore County, but in pleasant weather it was a beautiful drive.

The second evening found them all at their journey's end, tired and hungry, but the elder Mrs. Agnew was always ready with her cheerful welcome and a steaming supper for their comfort. After supper they talked over the events which had transpired since their last union until it was time to retire; then the family Bible was brought out and the Psalm-books. All joined voice; if not always in chord, at least it was done heartily. Then "Good-night" and "God bless you" were said. In the morning the party gave themselves to their enjoyments. Frequently the younger Dr. Agnew would bring out his violin, on which he was a skillful performer, and discourse sweet music for their pleasure.

Those were busy days for all. Dinners and suppers through the region were given for them; all the amusements of the Maryland country life were brought into requisition,—fox-hunting, gunning, and riding for the men; dinners and visiting for the women.

Just before the party returned home, every one who had shown them attention was invited to the house to a bountiful dinner, after which the party of children, now in middle age, returned to their Pennsylvania homes, just over Mason's and Dixon's Line.

Feeling that he had lost a number of valuable years in which he might have been gaining practice, Dr. Agnew returned again to medicine with redoubled energy and power. Consequently, he settled in Cochranville, which was then a flourishing, growing village in the central part of Chester County, a few miles south of Parkesburg. He remained here for seven months, and his success was most re-assuring, although he had in the small town a very popular competitor,—a Dr. Windall.

On his return to medicine he determined to make the practice of surgery his life-work. He had long been decided to become a surgeon; in order to do this, he saw that it was necessary to study anatomy. In consequence, he put into action a long-cherished plan which, unconsciously, changed his whole future life, and gave him another wholly different career from any of which he had yet dreamed.

He began to dissect and study bodies sent to him from Philadelphia; but it was not long before this anatomical work threw him into bad repute with the people of the district in which he lived; the country gossips began to criticise the young doctor's methods of investigation, and he became much disliked in the country for the work which was bringing his future colleague, Leidy, fame in the city.

This dislike for his work among the country people was increased by several unfortunate incidents. He was in the habit of employing a farmer to remove the bones of his subjects to a neighboring pond, after he had dissected the soft parts. This pond was well stocked with eels, which completed the work of cleaning the bones for him,—a process all anatomists know to be extremely slow and troublesome when done by the dissector. The bones being cleaned, he was thus enabled to study them carefully.

At this time, unfortunately, there happened to be a fisherman in this region, who supplied the entire country with the best quality of fish; his eels, especially, were famed for their size and fatness. There was a flavor and a snap about the eels which this particular fisherman supplied that put despair into the heart of every other fisherman in the county. In consequence, this fisherman's reputation grew,—his eels were in greater demand,—until, finally, he was hardly able to supply his many customers with this toothsome viand. The farmer who assisted Dr. Agnew in his anatomical pursuits was among the customers of this prosperous fisherman. Working in his field one day, while the fisherman was passing, the farmer became curious to know where such magnificent eels could be found. "Well," replied the fisherman, "if you will promise to keep it a secret where I get my eels, I will tell you; I get them from a pond down here, on your own farm." "What!" cried the farmer, "you don't mean to tell me that you get them from my pond?" It proved too true for the farmer, before whose unhappy vision floated the

memory of many a hearty meal on these eels.   When this story
became known, it did not increase the popularity of the young
anatomist to any great extent.   The neighbors began to inves-
tigate this mysterious pond, and, among other relics, fished
up a skull with what they supposed to be a bullet-hole through
it.   Some of the country people—possibly some of those who
had partaken too bountifully of the eels,—suggested that it
was some one who had been shot by this too enterprising
scientist.   Fortunately for all concerned, Dr. Agnew was able
to demonstrate to the community that this mysterious hole was
made by a trephine, and was done for practice, and not a bullet-
hole at all.

All these incidents, instead of discouraging Dr. Agnew,
only intensified his desire to get into a wider field, where he
could pursue his labors unmolested by too curious neighbors.
Naturally, too, his practice was seriously injured.   He relates
that after the occurrence of these incidents, while driving along
the country roads, it was no uncommon thing for the people of
the district to ignore utterly his existence.   He determined not
to give up his study of anatomy, although it rendered his
future most precarious.   He had a wife to support and no one
to aid him, yet he did not turn back.   Having at last fixed on
his course of action, he determined that nothing should deter
him from reaching the goal of his ambition.

He looked toward Philadelphia,—the seat of his Alma
Mater,—and he decided to make arrangements to go there to
carry out his plans.

In consequence, in the spring of 1848 Dr. Agnew came to
Philadelphia.[1]   Realizing the fact that a physician's prospects
are dependent somewhat on his location, he determined not to
select his future residence too hastily; in consequence, he lived
temporarily with his brother-in-law, William Irwin, on Filbert
Street, west of Sixteenth, at that time a very pretty part of the

---

[1] In all previous accounts of Dr. Agnew's life the time of his coming to Philadelphia
has been stated as 1852, or later.

city, until he could find a suitable residence. The summer, however, came on before he reached a decision, and at this time Dr.
Nathaniel Sample invited him to return to the country, to take
charge, temporarily, of the practice of his son, who had been
sick for some time. Accordingly, Dr. Agnew went to Soudersburg, ten miles from Lancaster, and spent the summer of 1848
in the country. He soon found out that the younger Dr. Sample
had been sick so long that his practice had been scattered, and
his services were but little in demand. He determined, however, to take the vacation which the opportunity afforded.

A few years ago, meeting one of the citizens of Soudersburg, Dr. Agnew said: "I located at Soudersburg when a young
man; I stayed there long enough to know all the roads in that
district; but I found that the people around there wanted a
better doctor than I was likely to prove, so I moved."

While here during this summer there occurred an accident,
the effect of which he carried to his grave, causing the slight
limp in his gait which acute observers could always see. He
was driving with Mrs. Agnew one afternoon, to visit some one at
a distance, when his horse took fright at a flock of sheep and
ran away. In turning a sharp corner in the road the carriage
was flung violently around, and Dr. Agnew was thrown to the
ground. Mrs. Agnew was carried for some distance beyond,
until, creeping over the edge of the carriage, she dropped out at
the back, falling upon her head, inflicting a severe scalp wound.
She did not lose consciousness, however, and, regaining her feet,
she returned to seek her husband. It was nearly a mile beyond
where she had been thrown, but she soon found him, stretched
out white and limp on the porch of a neighboring house. She
quickly secured a vehicle and removed him to her mother's
home, where he spent nine weeks in bed. His hip had been
very severely injured, and he suffered more or less inconvenience
from it until the day of his death. As soon as he was well
enough to return to the city, they came again to Philadelphia.
In the meantime, being unable to select his own location, and

not wishing to delay any longer, he left the decision to his brother-in-law. This gentleman selected a house on Tenth Street, above Race, to which Dr. Agnew came when he had sufficiently recovered. The location did not meet with the approval of Dr. and Mrs. Agnew at all, and they determined, at once, to select one that would be more congenial. Accordingly, they took a house, temporarily, on Sixteenth Street, below Arch, where they stayed until they selected a permanent home, which was at the corner of Eleventh and Hunter Streets,—16 North Eleventh Street. At this time this selection was a very central and excellent location. It was in the best part of the city, close to the best class of practice, besides being within easy reach of the School of Anatomy, in which he spent later so many hours a day.

He had not been forgotten by many old friends in the city, and he determined to start to work as quickly as possible. Deprived of his fortune by his failure, he wished to find something which would at once make him a comfortable living and furnish him the means of future advancement. He saw at once the advantages of such an institution as the Philadelphia School of Anatomy, which was then rapidly dwindling into nonentity. It was just such a chance for which he was looking; it afforded him a means of support and also a means for education, fulfilling a two-fold mission.

It is hard now, in the lapse of years, at a time when Dr. Agnew has become the hero in surgery to the American world and his memory an inspiration to his profession, to realize the boldness of his course which forced him eventually to Philadelphia. When he began to dissect in the country, he knew that his course might imperil his future there, but, once determined on it, nothing could thwart him. His position was not one to which such independence was suited. By the failure of the iron-works all his means of sustenance had been given to his creditors; everything had been swept away. This was the only region in which he was well known, by the memories of his parents, by his own life-long friends and associates, and by his wife's relatives and friends. He knew every one, and by education and temper-. ament he was suited to these people. In estranging them, he was estranging relatives and friends, and at the same time he was destroying his only means of support without increasing, apparently, his opportunities elsewhere.

When Dr. and Mrs. Agnew came to Philadelphia they had burned their bridges behind them, and the future was a vast blank uncertainty. Dr. Agnew did not come as the successful surgeon to fill the professorship at a well-known medical school; nor did he come with the prowess of the discovery of some new and wonderful advance in gynecology, by which a hitherto intractable disease was conquered; but he came with youth, health and strength, and a determination to carry out his line of action.

CHAPTER IV.

DR. AGNEW'S CONNECTION WITH THE PHILADELPHIA SCHOOL OF ANATOMY.

ONE of the principal factors in the success attained by Dr. Agnew was undoubtedly the Philadelphia School of Anatomy. The advantages which the training of such a school imparts, with the consequent reputation which is sure to follow the successful administration of its affairs, can scarcely be overestimated. Philadelphia, in many respects wonderfully similar in its methods of life to London, was like it in the possession of this unique school; the English prototype being the Great Windmill Street School, of London. This school, founded in 1770 by William Hunter, which boasted such names as the Hunters, Hewson, Cruikshank, Baillie, Wilson, Brodie, Bell, Shaw, and others, came to an end in 1833, after an existence of sixty-three years,—a period which has been exceeded by its American companion.

The Philadelphia School of Anatomy, established as an independent school, without the dignity or privileges of a chartered institution, without the prestige of the collection of well-known names as a faculty, without the privilege of granting diplomas or degrees, has outlasted many larger and more pretentious institutions. This school must not be considered as in any sense a "quiz class," although it performed some of the duties of a quiz. It was an independent school, doing original work in demonstrations, teaching, and dissections. It has always been remarkable for the character of men it has attracted as teachers. In nearly every instance of change in its long and varied existence, it has depended, for its popularity and usefulness, more or less upon the ability and reputation of one man.

The undertaking of such a school meant the greatest risks to a medical teacher, but it also included the greatest prospects

(76)

of success. Failure meant financial loss as well as the acknowl-
edgment of defeat, undoubtedly closing further avenues of advance in the line of medical teaching: Success, on the other
hand, meant the gathering of a large class of enterprizing and
enthusiastic students,—the most congenial happiness in the
world to a real teacher. It meant, also, considerable financial
return ; but, far more, it opened quickly and thoroughly future
prospects. It attracted attention from all quarters. The school
stood as a stepping-stone to professorships in the regular medical
colleges. This is shown by the fact that nearly every teacher
who left the School of Anatomy was called to some important
professorial position. It also meant the rapid distribution of
pupils throughout the country, with the consequent growth of
consultation practice. In short, the Philadelphia School of
Anatomy could be an element for great good, or for great evil,
in the hands of its teachers.

The successful prosecution of a school of the style of the
Philadelphia School of Anatomy was dependent upon a number
of factors. It required the immediate presence of several large
medical schools from which it could draw its students. In addition to this, it implied a lack of strength in the dissecting
courses of these regular chartered institutions, for it showed that
the attractions of the school were greater than the attractions of
the colleges. At the height of its prosperity it was the custom
for the medical schools in Philadelphia to charge each student
for each branch in which he received instruction, and hence
many students preferred to receive their anatomical education
at this school ; students being permitted by the authorities of
the various colleges to do their dissecting wherever they desired.
This gave the opportunity for opening such a school. Subsequently, this privilege was withdrawn ; but even after the withdrawal of this privilege the school held its usual attendance.

With the removal of the Medical Department of the University to West Philadelphia, with the strengthening of the
Jefferson Medical College and the Dental Colleges, however,

such a school must necessarily deteriorate. It is no criticism on the later teachers of anatomy in this school to say that the importance of this institution, as an independent educational factor in Philadelphia medical circles, has become less. The conditions of medical teaching are so different at the present time, that this is a natural sequence.

The demonstrations of anatomy and the dissecting which were done in this school were intended to be eminently practical in their nature. While it was the intention of the lecturers to present anatomy in as scientific and thorough a manner as possible, at the same time the subject was taught for use to practising physicians. The work done by Dr. Leidy at the University of Pennsylvania, and that done by Dr. Agnew at this school, stand out as typical examples of the two great methods of teaching anatomy. Dr. Leidy dissected as the eminent scientist, whose vast knowledge of comparative anatomy and its allied branches was constantly drawn on for record and comparison. On the other hand, Dr. Agnew dissected as the practical surgeon, whose intention it was to use his knowledge of anatomy, and teach others to use theirs, for operating. With that clearness which marked his entire life-work, he saw, when he knowingly incurred a second defeat in the country, that anatomy is the mother of successful surgery, and he became the the great anatomist in order to become the great surgeon. He went so far in this belief as to state that he believed a surgeon could not become pre-eminent unless he had spent a number of years in the actual demonstration of practical anatomy.

This school, which stands unique in medical history in this country, was opened in March, 1820, as the private anatomical school of Dr. Jason Valentine O'Brien Lawrance, under the title of the "Philadelphia Anatomical Rooms." It started at the location at which it stood for fifty-five years, at the upper end of Chant Street, which was then called College Avenue. The building in which the school was carried on stood on the north side of the street. At various times the building adjoin-

THE PHILADELPHIA SCHOOL OF ANATOMY.

ing to the westward was utilized in addition. It remained in this location until 1875, when the government took the ground on which the easternmost building stood as a portion of the site for the new post-office.

The location of the School of Anatomy, as selected by Dr. Lawrance, was an excellent one. It was within a stone's throw of the University of Pennsylvania, and it happened also to be close to the Jefferson Medical College, which was started at a later date. When the government seized the eastern building, as a portion of the site for the new post-office, it left the other building untouched. It stands to-day, a solitary and deserted memorial of the former school. It is unchanged in appearance, and the old sign, which can be seen on the left-hand side of the illustration, still remains.

At the beginning of the present century, in Philadelphia, it was the custom of well-known physicians to have private dissecting-rooms for their office pupils, not depending entirely upon the anatomical rooms of the University of Pennsylvania. In 1818 Dr. Joseph Parrish opened a private dissecting-room in the rear of Christ Church, and in 1822 Dr. Thomas T. Hewson opened another over his stable on Library Street, next door to the present Custom House, removing it subsequently, in 1829, to Blackberry Alley, in the rear of his house on Walnut Street, above Ninth. Dr. George McClellan had another private dissecting-room on Sansom Street above Sixth, and a fourth existed on Eighth Street above Jayne, which was then called Lodge Alley.

All of these schools differed from the Philadelphia School of Anatomy, in that they were ephemeral in character, and were intended principally for the instruction of the office students of their proprietors; while Lawrance, on the other hand, opened his school for all who cared to come, and so established an institution which has educated thousands of students and scores of teachers for their life-work. Tradition says that Lawrance was an unusually brilliant teacher. He was born in New

Orleans in 1791, and graduated at the University of Pennsylvania in 1815. He returned to New Orleans, and began the practice of medicine there, but, thirsting for the advantages he had found in Philadelphia during his student life, he returned in 1818, and at once resumed his scientific labors. At that time the University of Pennsylvania, which was then the only medical school in Philadelphia, closed its doors from April until November.

To fill out this long vacation Lawrance gave a course on anatomy and surgery, which began in March, had a recess in August, and ended in November. He gave six lectures a week, and his personal qualities, as well as the ease and clearness of his style as a lecturer, made his school a decided success. In the fall of the same year he became assistant to Dr. Gibson, who was then Professor of Surgery in the University, and in 1822 he was also made assistant to Dr. Horner, then Adjunct Professor of Anatomy. He was also surgeon to the Philadelphia Hospital. He did not live long to conduct his school, for, while attending the poor in the Ridge Road district, during an epidemic of typhus fever in the summer of 1823, he was attacked by the disease and died, at the age of 32.

Dr. Lawrance was a diligent writer; he left behind him over three thousand pages of unpublished manuscript, much of it intended for use in a projected work on pathological anatomy, —a subject then very much neglected in America. After Dr. Lawrance's death the school passed into the hands of Dr. John D. Godman. Dr. Godman was also from the South, having been born in Annapolis in 1794. He studied medicine at the University of Maryland, and soon after his graduation, in 1821, he was appointed Professor of Anatomy in the Medical School of Ohio. He came to Philadelphia in 1822, retiring from practice in 1823, when he began to teach in the Anatomical School. The first winter he had a class of seventy students. As was the custom for many years afterward, he gave three courses a year, viz.: The autumn course, twice a week, from September to

November; the winter course, four times a week, from November to March; and the spring course, twice a day, with a view to graduation, from March 1st to April 1st, the remainder of the year being a vacation from teaching, but devoted to work. The fee was $10, the same as it was later, although but two annual courses were given subsequently, lasting from October to March and April to October, with a recess in July and August.

Dr. Godman's lectures were characterized by simplicity of language, directness of statement, and fertility of illustration. It was his invariable habit to dissect before the class while he lectured, no previous dissection, however incomplete, having been made,—a method which was only practical before the introduction of the use of chloride of zinc, which hardens the tissues too much for such rapid work. He frequently used bodies for dissection which were in quite advanced stages of putrefaction.

In 1824 he established in the school a reading-room supplied with text-books and journals, and, not long after, he intended to enlarge the sphere of the school by adding associate lecturers. Accordingly, he invited Dr. R. E. Griffiths, afterward of the University of Virginia, to lecture on practice and materia medica, and Dr. Isaac Hays on surgery and the eye, lecturing himself on anatomy and surgery. This programme was never carried out, however, for in 1826 the widely-spread fame of Dr. Godman had called attention to him so prominently that he was called to the Chair of Anatomy in Rutgers Medical College, then established in New York City. Unfortunately, his health broke down during his second course at this school, and, after vainly traveling in search of health, he settled in Germantown, where he died in 1830. He also was a voluminous writer. In 1825 he became one of the editors of the *Philadelphia Journal of the Medical and Physical Sciences*, which was enlarged in 1827, by the agreement that the profession in New York would support the journal if it dropped its local name, which it did, becoming the *American Journal of the Medical Sciences*.

When Dr. Godman went to Rutgers College, in 1826, he was succeeded by Dr. James Webster. Dr. Webster retained the school for four years, when, in 1830, he was called to the Chair of Anatomy in the Geneva Medical College. Although not so polished a man nor so industrious a worker as Godman, he was an excellent teacher and a good anatomist. He was thoroughly devoted to the interests of his class, and when there was greater difficulty than usual in getting subjects,—a chronic complaint in dissecting-rooms,—he sat up night after night to see that neither the University nor any private room should obtain them until he was supplied. After Dr. Webster left the school its doors remained closed for a year, making the only break in its history until 1875.

In 1831 Dr. Joseph Pancoast reopened the rooms, three years after his graduation from the University of Pennsylvania, and in the seven years which he spent in lecturing and working here he laid the foundation of his subsequent career as anatomist and surgeon. He gave the usual three annual courses which Godman had established, but no other lectures were given in the building during his administration. In 1838, following the usual custom of the teachers in this school, he went to Jefferson Medical College as Professor of Anatomy, in which position he won world-wide fame. After Dr. Pancoast was elected to Jefferson Medical College he was succeeded by Dr. Justus Dunott, who lectured in the school alone for about three years.

Until 1839 the "Philadelphia Anatomical Rooms" consisted solely of the east building, the adjacent structure containing a carpenter-shop and warehouse; but in 1839 the two buildings contained rival schools, for Dr. James McClintock then rented and fitted up the western building as a lecture-room. Dr. McClintock had started a dissecting-room the year before at the southeast corner of Eighth and Walnut Streets, and called it the "Philadelphia School of Anatomy"; this was the first time this title had been used by any school. His neighbors complained so vigorously to him, on account of the odor coming from his rooms, that Dr. McClintock moved to Chant Street, next door to the older school. Here he gathered a very large class by his brilliant demonstrations, remaining here until 1841, when he was elected Professor of Anatomy in the Vermont Academy of Medicine, afterward called the Castleton Medical College. He was succeeded by Dr. Jonathan M. Allen, who had been a former office pupil and subsequently his assistant. Dr. Allen joined forces with Dr. Dunott, after Dr. McClintock's removal from the city, and they occupied both buildings, taking the new title of the "Philadelphia School of Anatomy."

It has been claimed, by good authority, that Dr. McClintock founded the Philadelphia School of Anatomy. This statement is a mistake. He founded a school which he called the "Philadelphia School of Anatomy," and which was subsequently merged into the older school, giving it its new title; but by the Philadelphia School of Anatomy is meant, undoubtedly, the original school which was established in Chant Street in 1820 by Dr. Lawrance, and which stood on that site for fifty-five years. The title, "Philadelphia Anatomical Rooms," clung for many years as an explanatory sub-title. Shortly after this Dr. Allen was left in sole charge of the school.

In 1842 Dr. William R. Grant, who had been Demonstrator of Anatomy at Jefferson Medical College, held the western building for a year, when, becoming Professor of Anatomy and Physiology in the Pennsylvania Medical College, he relinquished it to Dr. McClintock, who returned to Philadelphia and occupied the western building again, from 1843 to 1847.

In 1844 Dr. McClintock enlarged his school, having lectures on practice by Dr. James X. McCloskey, and on materia medica by Dr. Jackson Van Stavern. Dr. McClintock in 1847 secured the charter of the Philadelphia Medical College, and left the School of Anatomy. From 1847 to 1852 Dr. Allen assumed control again of both buildings. At this latter date he also left the school forever, being elected Professor of Anatomy at the Pennsylvania Medical College. One incident is remarkable to note which occurred during his administration: a woman dissected in the school as a medical student, probably, for the first time,—the date being 1843 or 1844. During the early part of this decade the school received its most famous scholar of anatomy, Dr. Joseph Leidy. He was a pupil here for some time during the *régime* of Dr. McClintock.

Dr. Allen was succeeded by Dr. Agnew in ·1852, who held the responsibility of the school for ten years. When he entered the school, as he has stated in one of his addresses, "that single front bench afforded ample accommodations for my audience." This was strictly true, for the records of the school show that there were but nine students when he began lecturing there. For many long years he toiled patiently and unceasingly, spending from twelve to eighteen hours a day in the dissection of that marvelous human structure which he learned to know so well. His industry during these years may be judged by the fact that, in addition to his dissections and practical work, he lectured five evenings a week from September 1st to March 1st, and three times a week from April 1st to August 1st. The school naturally prospered, until he was obliged to enlarge its capacity, throwing the small room on the third story into the lecture-room, to accommodate the throngs of students who gathered to see and hear his lucid demonstrations. In 1854 Dr. Agnew altered the second story of the eastern building, and started the Philadelphia School of Operative Surgery, in which his classes were also large. While teaching here he published his "Dissector's Manual," his lecture on the "Career of Baron Larrey," a valued and prolonged series of papers in the *Medical and Surgical Reporter*, on the "Relations of Anatomy to Surgery and Medicine," and prepared a work on the "Fasciæ of the Human Body," which, however, he never published.

As the school grew in size and importance, Dr. Agnew found it necessary to add demonstrators of anatomy to assist him in his work. Drs. R. J. Barclay and J. R. Sanderson were his demonstrators from 1857 to 1859. Later, they were Drs. R.

J. Levis, William Flynn, J. K. Kane, and Morris J. Asch; in 1860 they were five in number, Drs. R. J. Levis, William Flynn, D. R. Richardson, J. T. Darby, and Robert Bolling. Later, Drs. James E. Garretson, John W. Lodge, and S. W. Gross[1] were added to this number.

The duties of a demonstrator of anatomy, during Dr. Agnew's administration of the school, consisted in being present each evening, in the dissecting-room, to aid the students in their dissections, and to demonstrate the different regions of the body. The only remuneration which they received was the advantage of constantly reviewing their knowledge of anatomy, and the opportunity of practising ligations and studying accurately the parts involved in hernia, tracheotomy, etc., together with the privilege of attending all the lectures delivered by Dr. Agnew free of charge.

During each winter course Dr. Agnew met his students one hundred and thirty evenings to discuss the high theme of God's master-piece of handiwork. He began the teaching of anatomy by a study of the constituent elements of the body, which was followed by a study of the subject of osteology and syndesmology, in which, as Dr. Agnew humorously stated, his "students' thoughts often embodied the language of the prophet: 'And, lo, they were very dry.'" Next came a study of the apparatus of locomotion, which included the muscular system; then the organs performing the functions of digestion; then the organs of circulation and respiration, and, finally, the organs of special sense.

The School of Operative Surgery was totally distinct from the School of Anatomy. On usually two, and sometimes three, evenings a week, this special class for operative surgery met. On these evenings, lectures were given to explain the surgical

---

[1] By a typographical error, Dr. Agnew was made to state in an address that Dr. S. D. Gross was his demonstrator; the incorrectness of this statement is manifest, for Dr. S. D. Gross, besides being a much older man than Dr. Agnew, was Professor of Surgery at the Jefferson Medical College at this time.

anatomy of the different regions, illustrated with drawings, skeletons, wet and dry preparations, etc.; for example, first would be studied the surgical anatomy of the femoral artery; next, the various points at which it could be ligated, with the advantages and disadvantages of each, and the description of the actual steps of each operation. Then each class of five went to its own table with its own assistant demonstrator, and, if the operation was on the common femoral artery, the superficial femoral in Scarpa's triangle and in Hunter's canal were then divided amongst the class, according to a "table of operations." When three operations could be done on each side of each artery, there were more than enough to go round; when a single operation could be done, such as in tracheotomy, or two, as in ligation of the subclavian artery, they were apportioned equitably among the different members of the class. The length of the course in operative surgery was about sixteen sessions, of two hours each; but the course was always continued until all the operations feasible on a cadaver had been done. Some classes worked more rapidly than others. The number of students ran from six to eight or ten classes, of five each.

The students came from the University of Pennsylvania, Jefferson and Pennsylvania Medical Colleges, and the Dental Colleges, to attend this course of instruction on general, special, and surgical anatomy; so that Dr. Agnew's students were by no means confined to one school.

There are many hundreds of graduates of Jefferson Medical College who justly and proudly claim that they were students of Dr. Agnew.

So crowded did the lecture-room become, under Dr. Agnew's administration, that it was necessary to arrive in good time in order to get a satisfactory seat. As these lectures were given in the evening, so as not to interfere with the courses of instruction at the medical colleges, many were the cases of dyspepsia among the students, who hurried through their evening meal on this account. The classes increased each year until they averaged in size about two hundred and seventy students. The school was limited to this number only by the size and capacity of its buildings; if the accommodations had been larger, the classes would have been much larger.

Dr. Agnew inspired his students with an interest in the difficult and dry subject which he taught; so that many who entered the old Chant Street school became zealous and earnest workers, and in after years did honor to their grand old master by becoming themselves distinguished anatomists and surgeons.

Dr. Agnew lectured every evening except Saturday and Sunday, making five lectures a week for six months, averaging one hundred and thirty lectures in each winter course; in the spring and summer course he delivered lectures three times a week for four months. As there are but three hundred and thirteen working days in the year, it will be seen that Dr. Agnew, in delivering one hundred and eighty lectures, lectured, on an average, oftener than once every other day for the entire year. Of course, these lectures were in addition to his dissections and practical work. As Dr. Agnew was connected with the school for over ten years, he delivered over eighteen hundred lectures; the lectures in the eleventh year not being counted to offset the few appointments which he did not keep.

The lecture-room of the School of Anatomy was built in imitation of the ordinary lecture-room of a medical college. It had tier above tier of benches, rising so abruptly above each other that the seventh or highest row was fully twenty feet above the arena. It may be interesting to those who have sat for hours upon the ordinary clinique-room bench, which seems always to be made of boards particularly unyielding in their texture, to know that these benches were covered with cushions. This unparalleled luxury was the only portion of the " royal road to learning " reached by the embryo anatomists of Chant Street. In the arena was a revolving table on which the cadaver to be demonstrated could be placed. Over this was a series of lights, so arranged as to throw their illumination over the lecturer and the subject. Hanging in mid-air, by a wire from the ceiling, was a skeleton, which could be lowered when needed. On a shelf back of the lecturer stood a number of statues, representing, classically, the human form. One was a representation of Hercules, another of Mercury, a third of Venus, and a fourth "The Discus Thrower." This room was surprisingly similar in appearance to the well-known quiz-room of the Medical Institute, now at 3451 Woodland Avenue, Philadelphia.

The dissecting-room was above, in a long, low apartment in the third story. This room is the only trace left of the old school, being situated in the western building, which still stands. Careful search shows that the rest of the building has been completely altered.

A curious character which is found in every medical school is the janitor of the dissecting-room. He always has an air of better days; he is extremely stoical and cynical in his work; and he always commands respect among the students on account of the many stories of his wonderful ability as a hard drinker. That the janitor of this date was of this kind is shown in a resolution passed by the class in 1857. At a stated meeting of the class, held during the winter of 1857–58, it was resolved "That in justice to the merits of our faithful janitor, John Campbell, we are compelled to say that, as the *genius* of the anatomical rooms, he must be known to be appreciated."

During the winter of 1854–55 Dr. Agnew became seriously ill, as the result of a wound received while making an autopsy on a woman who had died of peritonitis. He was ill for some time, and during that period Dr. William Goodell took charge of the school, supervising the dissections made by the students.

Through Dr. Agnew's administration of affairs at the School of Anatomy, the subject of the supply of material was always a difficult one. It was necessary for him to be constantly on the outlook to obtain bodies for his students' use, but he obtained them in a perfectly legitimate way; for example, during the terrible epidemic of Asiatic cholera in Philadelphia, in 1854, there were so many deaths daily, at the Philadelphia Hospital, that deep pits were dug in the neighboring fields, into which the bodies were rudely thrown. At that time, in order to render these bodies suitable for use, Dr. Agnew would descend into these pits, and, with the sun beating fiercely upon his head, he would inject a sufficient number of bodies for his purpose.

Obtaining proper material for dissection is a source of difficulty, in the management of a dissecting-room, which is rarely brought to the attention of the public. This question, which has now been settled legally,—a regular supply, through proper channels, being portioned to the different medical schools of the country, from the proper officials,—has been, in times gone by, a very burning consideration. From the days when Vesalius was compelled to spoil the gallows of its victims, hiding the bodies even in his own bed; when Sir Astley Cooper barely escaped mobbing for the same offense; and Dr. Shippen was assaulted in Philadelphia, in 1765, by a mob, for the same reason, it can be seen that this forms another unpleasant phase of the already hard lot of the demonstrator of anatomy.

The increase of the demand for bodies which came with the advance of medicine, with the lack of supply which existed until within recent years, resulted in the production, especially in England, of a class of people known as "Resurrectionists." These body-snatchers became so expert at their work that they could rob a grave in very short order. The demand became so great, and the price so much higher, that finally the victims were even selected from among the living, and were murdered, in order that they might be sold to the dissecting-rooms. The infamous crimes of William Burke, in Edinburgh, are among the most interesting in criminal annals. This man killed a number of persons, in order to sell their bodies to the local dissecting-rooms. Similar instances occurred elsewhere, until the authorities, aroused to the necessity of regulating this question, passed the "Anatomy Acts." In England, the Warburton Anatomy Bill, enacted in 1832, gave all unclaimed bodies, under certain regulations, to the various schools. This was followed by the passage of similar acts in this country.[1]

The great mass of ignorant people are so slow in acquiring their knowledge, being generally about a hundred years behind the times, that it is a common belief, among many of this strata of society, that the authorities of certain hospitals murder their patients in order that they may be dissected by medical students. The Philadelphia Hospital has a great reputation for this thing among the negroes of the city; they believe firmly that when they go to this hospital they need never expect to come back alive. In consequence, it is only as a last resort that they apply for admission to this institution.

This ignorant belief, curiously enough, is heightened by some of the conditions of admission in the hospital rules. This hospital is the only regular hospital in the city which will take any large number of chronic cases. Consequently, when a negro falls sick with pneumonia, he can go to the Pennsylvania Hospital, where, as a rule, he recovers; but, if he contracts consumption, he applies in vain at every other hospital, until he is at death's door, when he is forced into the Philadelphia Hospital, from which his non-appearance alive is only confirmation, to all of his friends, of·their belief. To show that these are not idle statements, it is only necessary to state that on August 26, 1892, a negro minister, named Moulton, was hanged in Camden, New Jersey, for the murder of an aged colored woman, who was boarding with him. In accordance with this commonly-accepted belief of killing persons for use on the dissecting-table, he had offered her body, before her murder, to a medical student at the University of Pennsylvania. When asked by the student how he could supply a living per-

[1] The history of this outgrowth of medical work, which is intensely interesting, can be found in the London Lancet; the Life of Sir Astley Cooper; the Life of Robert Knox, the Anatomist; The London Medical Times and Gazette, etc. Dickens also, in his novel of Our Mutual Friend, presents a sketch of the life of a resurrectionist.

son for this purpose, he replied, nonchalantly, that he would "put her out of the way." The circumstances of the case were reported to the police, but they believed the whole affair to be a joke, and so took no action in the matter until the unfortunate old woman lost her life.

The School of Anatomy continued to prosper for nearly eight years, until the mutterings of the Civil War were first heard, when the old school was the scene of one of the earliest breaks in our national life. For a few short months its career was crippled, and it lost its principal source of revenue,—its Southern students. A very large proportion of the medical students of that day, as well as of this, who were attracted to Philadelphia, came from the South and Southwest. In the winter of 1859–60, so much excitement was created in Philadelphia by John Brown's invasion of Virginia, and so much sympathy was shown for him and his adherents, that the spirit and enthusiasm of the Southern students were thoroughly aroused, and they determined to leave Philadelphia and seek more congenial localities for study. A telegram from Governor Wise, of Virginia, requesting them to leave Philadelphia, precipitated this action. In consequence, by the middle of February, 1860, most of the Southern students left Philadelphia in a body, to go to the medical schools in Baltimore and Richmond. This occurred before the people of the North were fully aroused to the fact that a struggle was approaching. It was feared, at this time, that the school would suffer severely from this defection of the larger portion of its students; but many new students from the South, despite the uncertain condition of the country, came in the fall of 1860. When, however, war was actually declared, the school lost all its Southern patronage.

Dr. Agnew's records of his students, at this time, show only an occasional pupil from neighboring Southern States. Fortunately, however, the school was not injured at all, financially, for, of course, the fees of the term during which the defection took place were already paid, and, as compensation for the loss of these students, the demands of the war sent, in their places, students preparing for field service; so that the classes continued about the same in number.

The receipts from the School of Anatomy, when it was in successful operation, were sufficient to repay a physician moderately for his work. The uniform fee for each course was $10 from the starting of the school to the present day. There were two courses through the year; so that the receipts from the school, with several hundreds of students, were considerable. The extent to which the school could attain in its financial returns is shown in the case of Dr. McClintock when he had the school, from 1838 to 1840. His receipts from his winter classes for 1838 to 1839 were $190. His receipts from his spring course were $40; so that he made from his lecturing, for the year, $230. The next year, the winter of 1839–40, his receipts were $1155 for his winter course and $50 for his spring course.

As the years rolled by and the school came into Dr. Agnew's hands, the receipts were increased many-fold. It is an easy calculation to see what his income was; but any estimate would be too low, from the fact that he gave two courses in the year, the summer session attracting from twenty-five to fifty students at the same fees as paid for the winter work. In addition, the fees from the School of Operative Surgery, founded by Dr. Agnew, also greatly increased his income. As has been said, his classes in this school varied from thirty to fifty in each course, which was comparatively short. At the same time, this was far below the pecuniary returns for successful work in other professions or occupations.

Dr. Agnew paid $600 for this school, which, considering the fact that he had but nine students and but a small number of specimens for demonstration, was a considerable sum. He sold the school to Dr. Garretson for the same amount,—a characteristic stroke of business,—although his students had increased from nine to two hundred and sixty-seven, making, probably, the largest private class, under an individual, independent medical teacher, in the history of the world.

In 1862 Dr. Agnew relinquished the anatomical department of the school to Dr. James E. Garretson, who had been his demonstrator for several years. Dr. Agnew retained the course in operative surgery for a year longer, until he was made Demonstrator of Anatomy and Lecturer on Clinical Surgery at the University of Pennsylvania. He was succeeded in the Department of Operative Surgery, from 1864 to 1867, by Dr. J. M. Boisnot. After two years of successful teaching Dr. Garretson withdrew from the anatomical department, on his election to the Chair of Surgery in the Philadelphia Dental College. In accordance with the influence of the school, Dr. Garretson was not idle with his pen, for he has since published his large work on "Oral Surgery" and a number of charming philosophical and metaphysical reflections, under the pen-name of "John Darby."

In the summer of 1865 Dr. James P. Andrews assumed the duties of Lecturer on Anatomy, but, his health failing, he was succeeded, in the fall, by Dr. R. S. Sutton. After teaching for a year, Dr. Sutton was succeeded by Dr. W. W. Keen, who conducted the school successfully until 1875.

From 1866 to 1870 Dr. Keen occupied only the western building, Dr. D. D. Richardson having the lower story of the other for his quiz class, and Dr. H. Lenox Hodge, from 1866 to 1870, the upper story for his courses on operative surgery; but, in order to accommodate his increasing class, Dr. Keen was obliged, in 1870, to obtain the use of that building, and, later still, enlarged the lecture-room by placing a gallery over his head. While connected with the school, Dr. Keen published many articles, besides gathering the materials for more extended subsequent publications.

In 1873 the University of Pennsylvania had been removed to West Philadelphia. Previously the school had drawn its pupils from both the University and Jefferson Medical College.

It was clear to Dr. Keen that he must become an appendage to one school or the other, for, if he attempted to build at a point between the two schools, he would not receive sufficient support to make his venture a success. Moreover, at the same time, the government took the ground on which the principal building stood as a portion of the site for the new post-office, and so prevented the possibility of the school remaining where it was. Dr. Keen went so far as to purchase two properties on Sansom Street above Sixteenth as a site for a new school, but, after consultation with friends, he decided not to build. Therefore, on March 1, 1875, Dr. Keen delivered the final lecture in the old Chant Street building. This lecture was appropriately devoted to a carefully-verified history of the old school and its honored teachers.

Dr. Keen's death-song proved to be, however, only a lullaby. The vitality of the old name was greater than had been expected, for Dr. J. M. Boisnot, one of the old teachers of the school, opened another institution under this name at 1022–24 Hunter Street, a short distance from the old location, the year after the closing of the school by Dr. Keen. As the school was not continued in its original location and the good-will and fixtures not purchased, as had been the custom through all the various vicissitudes of its existence, it is a matter of dispute as to what degree of relationship should be conceded as existing. On the other hand, it can be claimed by the later teachers that, as the site of the old school was gone, its scholars and teaching-material scattered, there were no fixtures and good-will to be purchased. Moreover, the new school was started by a former teacher in the original school.

Undoubtedly, however, this was the most serious break in the history of the school. Dr. Boisnot associated with him, in the latter part of his career, Dr. J. M. Barton, who lectured on operative surgery. Dr. John B. Roberts obtained possession of the school in 1878, Dr. Barton continuing his lectures. The new school grew, until it retained a number of lecturers: Dr.

H. Augustus Wilson, on orthopedic surgery; Henry Leffman, on chemistry; J. T. Eskridge, on physical diagnosis; Wm. H. Parish, on obstetrics and gynecology; C. W. Dulles, on venereal diseases; E. H. Bell, on obstetrics and gynecology; and C. E. Sajous, on the throat and nose.

It was from this nucleus that the Philadelphia Polyclinic and College for Graduates in Medicine started, in 1882–83, at Thirteenth and Locust Streets. After the withdrawal of the staff of lecturers for this purpose, the school again contracted to its original work of teaching anatomy, while its brilliant off-spring started on its broader career. The inroads of business finally drove the school from Hunter Street to Cuthbert Street above Eleventh in 1883, when Dr. L. W. Steinbach became owner of the school. It wandered from here to the northwest corner of Tenth and Arch Streets in 1883. In 1884 the school passed into the hands of Dr. Henry C. Boenning, who holds it at the present time (1892). In 1887 the school again moved, this time to the building of the Third National Bank, at Broad and Market Streets, opposite the Pennsylvania Railroad Depot.

It is still in a flourishing location, being now situated in the building of the Medico-Chirurgical College, on Cherry Street below Eighteenth, where it exists in connection with that school and the Philadelphia Dental College; it is, however, still an independent school, paying its own way, and holding the privilege of accepting or rejecting the students who present themselves. It draws its pupils still from the Medico-Chirurgical College, the Philadelphia Dental College, the University of Pennsylvania, Jefferson, the Women's Medical College, and those art students from the Academy of Fine Arts who wish to study human anatomy.

While the Philadelphia School of Anatomy was in no sense a "quiz class," remaining always an independent factor in medical teaching, yet at the same time it gathered in its train, naturally, the elements which subsequently developed into quiz work. The quiz is a coaching class in which the knowledge of the medical student is reviewed, systematized, and stamped upon his mind. It is generally the ivy clinging to the oak,—the ground covered being regulated by the lectures of the professor who is in charge of the subject in the medical school. A large part of the brilliant reputation of the School of Anatomy is due to the men who used its accommodations for this work.

The first one, as far as can be determined, who established a quiz, thereby enlarging the facilities of his office students, was Dr. Nathaniel Chapman. In 1817 he associated with himself Dr. Horner, on anatomy, and they occupied a room over his stable—a rather favorite place, it would seem, for anatomists—. in the rear of his house, on the south side of Walnut Street, the second door below Eighth. In 1819-20 Dr. Dewees joined them, and, soon after, Drs. Hodge, Bell, Jackson, J. K. Mitchell, and, for some time, Dr. T. P. Harris. This afterward became the "Medical Institute," obtained a charter, and erected a building in Locust Street above Eleventh, afterward occupied, from 1846 to 1848, by the "Franklin Medical College." This quiz organization is still in existence at the University of Pennsylvania.

In 1818 Dr. Joseph Parrish began a similar association with Dr. George B. Wood, and afterward also Drs. Richard Harlan and Shoemaker. From this, in 1830, arose the "Philadelphia Association for Medical Instruction," consisting of Drs. Parrish, Wood, Samuel George Morton, John Rhea Barton, and Franklin Bache, who were joined at various times by Jacob Randolph, W. W. Gerhard, Joseph Pancoast, and William Rush. For six years the association continued its labors; but then, as some grew in years and practice, and others were absorbed by the colleges, it was dissolved. The "School of Medicine" was a third similar organization formed about the same time, in which were Drs. William Gibson, Jacob Randolph, B. H. Coates, Rene La Roche, John Hopkinson, and Charles D. Meigs. Nearly all of these became professors in the University of Pennsylvania or the Jefferson Medical College.

In 1842, while Dr. Jonathan M. Allen was at the head of the Philadelphia School of Anatomy, the second "Philadelphia Association for Medical Instruction," generally known as the "Summer Association," was formed for the purpose of giving lectures during the long recess in the colleges from March to November. It consisted, originally, of Drs. John F. Meigs, on obstetrics; Joshua M. Wallace, on surgery; Robert Bridges, on chemistry; Francis Gurney Smith, on physiology; and Jonathan M. Allen, on anatomy. The lectures were given in the eastern building till about 1847, when they changed to the western one, and in 1854 to Butler's Avenue, in the rear of the Jefferson Medical College. Here they continued till 1860, when they disbanded.

In 1845 Dr. J. F. Meigs began to lecture at the School of Anatomy on diseases of children, Dr. D. H. Tucker on obstetrics, and in 1850, on his removal to the Richmond Medical College as Professor of Obstetrics, he was followed by Dr. William V. Keating. At Dr. J. M. Wallace's death the surgical lecture-ship was filled by the appointment of Dr. J. H. B. McClellan in 1851, Dr. Addinell Hewson in 1853, and Dr. John H. Brinton in 1860. Dr. Bridges, although elected to the College of Pharmacy, retained his lectureship on chemistry from 1842 to 1860, —the only constituent member of the association who remained to its close. In anatomy, when Dr. Allen became Professor of Anatomy in the Pennsylvania College, in 1852, Dr. Ellerslie Wallace, then also Demonstrator of Anatomy, and later Professor of Obstetrics at Jefferson, became his successor.

Dr. Francis Gurney Smith continued to lecture on physiology till 1852, when he was elected to the professorship of physiology in the Pennsylvania College, and was succeeded by Dr. S. Weir Mitchell until 1860. The first lecturer on practice was Dr. Alfred Stillé, who joined the association in 1844 and resigned in 1850 on account of ill health. In 1854 he became Professor of Practice in Pennsylvania College, and later filled the same chair in the University. He was succeeded by Dr. John F.

Meigs from 1850 to 1854, and he again, in 1855, by Dr. Moreton Stillé, the brother of Alfred Stillé, and already widely known as the joint author of "Wharton and Stillé's Medical Jurisprudence." A career of great prominence was then suddenly cut short by a sad accident. A decomposing subject left in the lecture-room from Friday until Monday, in July, so poisoned the air that Stillé and several of the class were made faint and sick. Stillé still lectured as long as he could, but finally was compelled to yield, went home, and, after a brief illness, died from blood-poisoning. The next year the place was filled by Dr. J. M. Da Costa, subsequently Professor of Practice at Jefferson Medical College. Dr. Francis West lectured on materia medica from 1844 till the last year, when Dr. James Parrish succeeded him. On diseases of children Dr. John F. Meigs was the only lecturer from 1840 to 1850, and on medical jurisprudence Dr. Edward Hartshorne from 1847 to 1849.

Dr. Da Costa also gave private courses on physical diagnosis from 1854 to 1863. Such was his reputation at this time, especially a year before their close, that he was compelled to refuse many anxious applicants, lest the classes should become unwieldy for his methods of personal instruction.

The front room on the lower floor, and afterward that in the second story, was occupied by Dr. S. Weir Mitchell as his physiological laboratory. Besides his lectures on physiology in the association, from 1853 to 1860, he gave, in 1856, the first purely experimental course on physiology in the city, and also made in these rooms nearly all of his extremely important physiological experiments and discoveries, working with dogs, cats, and copperhead, moccasin, and rattle snakes. Many are the amusing stories that could be told of this somewhat perilous work with snakes; of the rude and insecure boxes in which they were received, sometimes a section from the hollow trunk of a tree battened at each end with scanty nails; of the suddenly-discovered escape of a snake or two on more than one occasion,—a dis-

covery none the less disquieting from the fact that no antidote had
as yet been found among the scientific harvest; or of the janitor
who, one night, when locking up, being slightly mystified by
sundry potations, and treading on a headless snake, that rattled
vigorously and struck him with its stump, ran to a brick-pile
near by, and, filling his arms with the bricks, let fly at random
into the dark room,—he had more than St. Patrick's aversion to
snakes,—and bottles, crucibles, costly thermometers, and two
weeks of carefully prepared results were in the morrow's woeful
count of cost.   Many were the assistants who came, and, not
liking the work, quietly disappeared; one of them, however,
rather hurriedly, for he sat down all unconscious upon a lighted
cigar, and, leaning rudely against the snake-box, started them to
rattling just as the cigar burned through, when, leaping up in
affright, he ran away, crying "I'm bitten! I'm bitten!" and
was seen no more.

It can now be easily understood how not so much even as
a chip had ever been stolen with such objects in the building,
both dead and alive, although the door often went unlocked and
the cellar was almost always accessible.   Even a former office-boy
of Dr. Keen, of African extraction, could never be induced to
put foot inside the building, alleging that he had "heerd of
their layin' for colored boys afore now!"

It is interesting to note that the only thing reported to have
been stolen during the *régime* of Dr. Agnew was a valuable
paper which he had intrusted to an assistant, and which the
latter had stuffed in the pocket of his overcoat, leaving it in the
museum as he stepped into the lecture-hall of the school.   On
returning from his lecture, the demonstrator found that some-
body had stolen the coat.   He was naturally much more concerned over the loss of the paper than over the article of clothing, and spent a restless night thinking of his loss.   Curiously
enough, however, the thief had the interest of the school sufficiently at heart to return the abstracted paper by the next
morning's mail.

No more brilliant corps of teachers, perhaps, has ever been gathered in this city than this old "Summer Association." Tucker became Professor of Obstetrics first in Franklin College, and then in Richmond; Keating went to the Jefferson; Bridges to the Franklin College and the College of Pharmacy; Allen, as Professor of Anatomy, to the Pennsylvania College; Ellerslie Wallace, first as Demonstrator of Anatomy, and then Professor of Obstetrics, to the Jefferson; Francis Gurney Smith to the Chair of Physiology in the Pennsylvania College, and then in the University of Pennsylvania; Alfred Stillé to that of Practice in Pennsylvania College, and then to the University; Da Costa to the Chair of Practice in the Jefferson; Mitchell here formed that habit of exact scientific observation and sagacious deduction which has given him a reputation on two continents, while Meigs, McClellan, Hewson, Brinton, Darrach, and Hartshorne have all become well-known hospital teachers and practitioners.

As writers, during this period, few men have been busier. Among the medical books and papers which were the direct results of their labors here, the following may be mentioned: Dr. Tucker wrote his " Principles and Practice of Midwifery." Dr. Alfred Stillé published a part of his lectures under the title of "Elements of General Pathology," while the lectures on "Practice," most carefully and "elaborately written out, have formed the foundation of all those upon the same subject which he has since delivered." He also published his "Medical Institutions of the United States" and his "Report on Medical Literature," and with Dr. Meigs translated Andral's "Pathological Hæmatology." Dr. John F. Meigs published his lectures on the " Diseases of Children," the well-thumbed book of multitudes of practitioners, now grown to be a most portly volume. Dr. F. G. Smith translated Barth & Roget's "Manual of Auscultation and Percussion," and edited Carpenter's various physiological works, "Kirkes' Paget's Physiology," and "Churchill on Obstetrics." Dr. Keating edited "Ramsbotham's Obstetrics" and "Churchill on Children." Dr. Bridges edited "Fowne's

Chemistry " and " Graham's Chemistry." Dr. Hewson edited " Mackenzie on the Eye " and " Wilde on the Ear," and all of them wrote numerous papers, reviews, etc., and practised medicine into the bargain ! Truly, they were busy men.

In 1855, during Dr. Agnew's administration, another association was started, which, like the one just named, was called after an older one, already noticed, the " Pennsylvania Academy of Medicine." It consisted of Drs. W. W. Gerhard, Henry H. Smith, D. Hayes Agnew, Bernard Henry, R. A. F. Penrose, and Mr. Edward Parrish, the son of Dr. Joseph Parrish, who lectured on practical pharmacy; the next year they were joined also by Dr. Edward Shippen. For two years they continued as an association of lecturers; then Drs. Gerhard, Agnew, Penrose and Mr. Parrish went on as a quiz association for a year, when they disbanded. Dr. Agnew went on with his usual courses in the School of Anatomy, and Dr. Penrose continued to lecture here on obstetrics until called to the University, in 1863. They were equally fortunate in promotion with the members of the other association, for four of the seven went to the University as professors,—Gerhard on clinical medicine, Henry H. Smith and Agnew as professors of surgery, and Penrose of obstetrics.

Besides these distinct associations for lecturing, numerous other independent experimenters have availed themselves of the facilities afforded by the School of Anatomy for their work.

In 1849 Dr. Brown-Séquard gave his first lecture in America in this school, to Dr. Francis Gurney Smith's class in physiology, in the " Summer Association." It was on the physiology of the nervous system; and during the lecture, with that extraordinary manual dexterity for which he is noted, he cut the anterior and posterior roots of the spinal nerves in some frogs, and demonstrated the cross-sensibility of the spinal marrow by sections of its lateral halves in the guinea-pig. This was followed by a course to the physicians of the city. His next course was given in the Franklin Institute. About this time, also, Dr. John Hastings, of the navy, gave some lectures on yellow fever,—apropos of the then existing epidemic,— based on his personal observations during the Mexican War. In 1859 Dr. Samuel W. Gross, while one of Dr. Agnew's demonstrators, gave courses on operative surgery and surgical anatomy, and again in 1866–67. In 1860, and for some time afterward, Dr. John W. Lodge gave courses in experimental physiology in the summer, and on urinary pathology in the winter. In obstetrics, Dr. J. M. Corse also lectured here. In 1864 to 1867 Dr. J. M. Boisnot, and also, in 1865 to 1867, Dr. J. Bernard Brinton, each gave courses in operative surgery.

When Dr. Keen had charge of the school, Dr. Isaac Ott experimented on cocaine and other poisons, and Dr. H. C. Wood on the physiological action of the alkaloids of veratrum viride. Besides these, the following regular courses of lectures have been given here: On obstetrics, Drs. F. H. Getchell and W. F. Jenks; on the microscope, Dr. James Tyson; Dr. Hodge gave independent courses on operative surgery from 1868 to 1870 in the eastern building; Drs. J. Ewing Mears and O. H. Allis on bandaging and fractures; Drs. John S. Parry, O. P. Rex, Stanley Smith, and Hamilton Osgood, on physical diagnosis; on venereal diseases, Dr. William G. Porter; on ophthalmology, Drs. George C. Harlan, George Strawbridge, and W. W. McClure; and on laryngoscopy, Dr. J. Solis Cohen. For a number of years, also, the Naval Examining Board examined all their candidates for admission and promotion here. In 1837 Dr. E. G. Davis quizzed on all the branches himself, as also, at first, was Dr. D. D. Richardson's habit. Dr. Richardson's quiz lasted from 1860 to 1871, and in the last few years he was assisted by Drs. Boisnot, Cohen, and Witmer. From 1866 to 1868 Dr. Keen quizzed with Drs. Duer, Dunglison, and Maury; in 1868–69 with Drs. Warder, McArthur, Leaman, and Mears; and from 1869 to 1872 with Drs. Hutchins, Allis, Rex, Getchell, Leffman, and Loughlin. In 1874–75 Drs. Wilson, West, Greene, and Osgood gave quiz courses. From 1869 to

1871, also, the eastern building was occupied by the quizzes of Drs. Willard, Curtin, Cheston, Jenks, Wilson, and Githens.

Such, in brief, is the history of this venerable school, and of the many teachers associated with it. Over one hundred teachers won their spurs in its lecture-rooms, formed here their habits of thought, style of lecturing, methods of scientific research, and gained their early fame as writers and teachers, so that thirty-two have become professors in sixteen medical colleges, here and elsewhere, and seventy hospital and clinical physicians, surgeons, obstetricians, etc., of distinction. Thirty-two books have been written or edited, and many pamphlets and papers of value have been published by its various teachers.

Its assistant demonstrators are too numerous even for mention. The students of this old school can never be traced, but this much is known, that, spread all over the world, doing faithfully their daily work in relieving the suffering, soothing the dying, helping the poor, assuaging the pestilence that walketh in darkness, improving the public health, advancing the domain of pure and applied science, teaching earnestly its results to thousands of eager students who, in turn, will swell their noble ranks, promoting in general the moral and material welfare of mankind, some in lofty, some in lowly station, they will confess that here they first developed their scientific tastes and aspirations; here they were taught to look beyond the lower to the highest and noblest aims of their profession; here they first caught the inspiration that has made them what they are, and here they learned to love this old school and its faithful teachers.

So great had grown the reputation of Dr. Agnew in later years, and his connection with the School of Anatomy was so quoted in all accounts of his life, that the public at large and the younger members of the medical profession are inclined to suppose that he was its originator, and that he constituted its only glory. On the contrary, this brief history shows the close connection between the old school and a large proportion of the medical profession of Philadelphia. The majority of the names mentioned in this brief *résumé* are famous ones in Philadelphia to-day.   Dr. Agnew practically built a new school here, but it was made on the ruins of an older structure.   He did found, however, the School of Operative Surgery, which put into practical use the knowledge gained in the School of Anatomy.

So great was the concentration of mind of Dr. Agnew in his earlier years upon his work that those who were his assistants for many years, and intimately associated with him in his daily work at the School of Anatomy, were unable to refer subsequently to any special conversation held during those years which was not related in some way with anatomy or surgery.   To Dr. Garretson, who was his demonstrator for several years, Dr. Agnew, at this period, possessed the most unspeculative mind on the subject of religion of any man he had ever met.   Distinctions often propounded by Dr. Garretson regarding human hypostoses of body, ego, and soul, as the dissectors worked together over a cadaver, failed always to elicit from the elder any other response than that he was sure of the body and was willing to leave ego to philosophy and soul to church,—a most characteristic reply.

In the later years of his connection with the School of Anatomy, Dr. Agnew did not feel, however, the necessity for that terrible expenditure of force and energy which had so characterized his earlier work.   His practice was growing; he was being called more and more into consultation; his hospital opportunities were increasing; consequently, he devolved the manual work more and more upon his demonstrators.

Undoubtedly, much of the grace, ease, and sureness with which Dr. Agnew operated was due to his perfect knowledge of anatomy which he learned in this school.   He never had to stop to think out the answers to questions in regional anatomy. He reached his conclusions as quickly and as naturally as if he were reading an open book, which justified the statement that he seemed to see the positions and relations of the internal organs of the body as well as if their coverings were made of glass.

He acquired also a most beautiful and attractive style of lecturing, which drew students because of its naturalness. He learned, as has been truthfully said, to present Nature's truths in Nature's simplicity, without the deadly paralysis of unnecessary words. He learned to go at once to the gist of the matter, and, having seized upon the central point of demonstration, he grouped all the secondary features in beautiful sequence about it. His demonstrations of the surgical anatomy of hernia or the regional anatomy of the perineum will always be remembered by those who were fortunate enough to have been his students, as most clear, concise, and yet comprehensive.

Dr. Agnew, when he relinquished this school, had been connected longer with it than any other of its proprietors, his whole term of service, including his connection with the School of Operative Surgery, being eleven years. Although he had grown famous here, and had been by far its most successful teacher, yet he was only the second to leave it not receiving a professorship. His progress forward had been of the slowest nature. He would not push himself, and, consequently, his advance was not rapid, but it was natural. Other men were pushing rapidly by him, younger and less well known; but Dr. Agnew's progress was satisfactory to himself. He was receiving as much as he felt he deserved; and his reputation was not a hot-house plant, ready to wither at the first chilly touch, but a sturdy out-door growth, which the colds and snows of winter could not affect.

Dr. Agnew's final separation from the School of Anatomy occurred in December, 1863, on his appointment as Demonstrator of Anatomy at the University of Pennsylvania.

CHAPTER V.

DR. AGNEW's coming to Philadelphia was not an unusual thing for a country physician to do; for probably one-half, at the lowest estimation, of the successful city practitioners of to-day were country boys. This can be seen by taking a list of the prominent physicians of Philadelphia, New York, and Boston, and ascertaining their birth-places.

To the credit of the Philadelphia physicians of that day, it must be said that Dr. Agnew was received with considerable cordiality. He was known, already, to a large part of the profession in the city; among the residents of the town he had some relatives and many friends. He was not treated with the coldness and neglect experienced by Dr. Sims in New York, although he had no such reputation to sustain him at this time as had that gentleman. On the other hand, he did not come to Philadelphia like Dr. Gross, with the appointment to a prominent position in an important medical school.

He had his name to make and his fortune to acquire. His experience as a surgeon had been, as yet, limited. He had done a number of major .surgical operations, performing some of them as early as 1840; but he had fallen behind many of his classmates in this work, on account of giving up his professional duties for over three years.

Possibly, it was the quiet, unobtrusive, but determined, manner in which he began his new career that caused him to be well treated and warmly welcomed by his fellow-practitioners in Philadelphia. In his early years, as well as later, his career was never aggressive; he forced no one from his place or practice; while his hard and conscientious work won for him hosts of friends and confidence in his abilities.

As years rolled by, his position became easier and pleas-
(106)

anter; his practice grew; his consultation work steadily increased, and slowly, but surely, he was forging to the front. By
1860 he was acknowledged to be one of the foremost of Philadelphia surgeons.

Undoubtedly, one reason why his reputation was so firmly
established was because of its natural growth. It rested on a
foundation of the broadest and firmest description. He did not
buy his way into a professorship; nor did the influence of his
friends or family put him there. Dr. Agnew's progress corresponded to his own ideas and beliefs. He has frequently stated
that "promotion, to be permanent and successful, must be of
slow growth."

He did not attempt to attract the attention of the public to
himself by any eccentricity of conduct, speech, or dress. He did
not utilize the newspapers to force his learning and attainments
upon the reading world. He instinctively avoided such reputation, and always felt a gentle contempt for "newspaper doctors."
He realized the hollow mockery of the false position of those
physicians whose true qualities are known to the rank and file
of their profession, but who win, now and then, from the public
a false estimate which sets them on dangerous levels of apparent
competence.

During the decade that Dr. Agnew taught at the School
of Anatomy, he was not wholly absorbed by that work, exhaust-
ing and exhaustive as it was; on the contrary, he was quite
active in other branches of medical endeavor.

In all the fields of activity in which he worked, Dr.
Agnew's connection with hospital duties forms a large part of
the history of his life.

The greater portion of the most valuable surgical work
performed by Dr. Agnew was done in the surgical wards of the
various hospitals with which he was connected from time to
time. He was connected as surgeon, first, with the Philadelphia Hospital, from 1854 to 1865; with the Wills' Eye Hospital,
from 1864 to 1868; with the Pennsylvania Hospital, from 1865

to 1871, and from 1877 to 1884. He was surgeon to the Orthopedic Hospital from its inception, in 1868, until 1871, when his increasing duties compelled his resignation, although he remained consulting surgeon until his death. His service at the University Hospital dates from its erection, 1873–74, until his death. In addition, during the Civil War he had a most extensive and valuable hospital experience.

At the majority of these hospitals the attending physician acts in a dual capacity,—as a practitioner in charge of patients, and as a teacher demonstrating the various phases of disease and their treatment to the students. It is customary to have Wednesday and Saturday morning cliniques, at which the different physicians on the staff are given opportunities to perform this latter duty. It forms a great training-school for those gentlemen who are anxious to review and classify their own knowledge and learn to impart it to others.

The variety of operations which he performed during this long period of service and the number of patients under his care were countless, many thousands of cases being under his charge during these many years of faithful work.

The first hospital in point of time with which Dr. Agnew was connected was the official hospital of the City of Philadelphia, called the " Philadelphia Hospital," and popularly known as " Blockley," from the district in which it was erected. He was elected to this hospital in 1854, two years after assuming control of the School of Anatomy. This hospital, one of the largest in the world, with its four thousand beds, is peculiarly rich in all clinical material. Its fame has spread all over the continent. As such, it is a fortunate berth for the ambitious and enterprising physician or surgeon.

As referred to humorously by Dr. Agnew in his speech at his jubilee banquet, the Philadelphia Hospital had closed its doors to students of medicine in 1845. In the lecture on the "Medical History of the Philadelphia Almshouse," delivered at the opening of the clinical lectures, October 15, 1862, by Dr.

Dr. Agnew in 1858.

Agnew, and published by request of the Board of Guardians, the following amusing account of the incident which caused the abolishment of clinical instruction at the Philadelphia Hospital for nine years is given :—

"The 30th of June, 1845, is somewhat remarkable in consequence of the culmination of the trouble which had been developing for some time. The Resident Physicians were boarded at the table of the steward, where, as I understand, in consequence of the want of due formality in the destruction of an unfortunate cockroach, which had rashly taken a cut across the table, instead of going around it, these gentlemen became indignant and demanded of the Managers to be transferred to the table of the matron. Their refusal to comply with this request determined a unanimous resignation, leaving the hospital unprovided with any medical assistance. The evening of that day Drs. Horner and Clymer attended and prescribed for the sick. Here was the *causus belli*, and the Managers promptly passed a resolution of dismissal.

"With the hope of adjusting these difficulties a joint meeting was called for July 2d, at which Drs. Jackson, Horner, Clymer, Gillingham, and Pancoast attended, representing as a committee the Medical Board. Dr. Jackson, who seems to have been the advocate in the case, spoke in behalf of the committee, urging the Managers to allow the Residents to remain, at least until their places could be properly supplied, and declining to pass any censure, or interfere in any way in the matter of personal conflict between the Residents and Guardians, as foreign altogether to their legitimate jurisdiction.

"The Guardians, however, were inexorable, and refused to recede from their dismissal, thus forever closing the door of compromise. The seceders, after retiring, availed themselves of the columns of the *Ledger* newspaper, in which there appeared a card betraying, to say the least of it, a good deal of youthful indiscretion.

"On the same day of this meeting Mr. Flanagan offered the following resolution :—

" ' *Resolved*, That the Hospital Committee be requested to inquire into the expediency of reorganizing the Medical Department of the house, and report to this Board.'

"On the 21st of July that report was made, which, after going over the ground of the trouble, recommended the abolishment of the Medical Board and the substitution of a chief resident and assistant resident physician, and two consulting physicians and surgeons. On September 15th the report was taken up and passed, modified as follows: 'After the first of October, 1845, there shall be one chief resident physician, at a salary of $1800 per annum; one consulting surgeon, one consulting physician, one accoucheur, each at a salary of $100 a year.'

"What great results proceed from small and unlikely causes! Who would have thought that the official existence of a medical board composed of the best and ablest men in their various departments on the continent would be suspended on the life of a contemptible cockroach!

"In this manner the doors of the Philadelphia Hospital, as a school of instruction, were sealed for nine years."

On the 1st of May, 1854, the Philadelphia County Medical Society addressed a communication to the Board of Guardians of this hospital, asking that its doors be re-opened for medical instruction. This document, although forcibly expressed, produced no change in the views of that body. In August of the same year Dr. John J. Reese, Registrar of the Medical Faculty of Pennsylvania Medical College, communicated with the Board of Guardians on the same subject, and guaranteed, if its wards were opened to public instruction, the sale of fifty tickets from that school alone.

These appeals had some weight with the Guardians, but, in Dr. Agnew's opinion, it was to Drs. Henry H. Smith, R. A. F. Penrose, and James L. Ludlow that the profession in Philadelphia and the country at large were indebted for the re-establishment of the clinical school within the walls of this institution. Dr. Agnew modestly made no mention of his own efforts in this direction, for he felt that he was comparatively a stranger in the city, and that he had no influence whatsoever; but other reports gave him equal claim with these three in the success of this opening.

Consequently, on the 6th of September, 1854, the rules for the government of the cliniques were reported, and arrangements were made for the election of two additional surgeons and physicians. On this day the Guardians elected Drs. J. L. Ludlow and Robert Coleman as physicians, and Drs. Henry H. Smith and D. Hayes Agnew as surgeons. On the 30th of October the staff was increased by the appointment of Dr. R. A. F. Penrose as obstetrician. Tickets of admission were fixed at $10, including transportation to the hospital two days in the week—Wednesday and Saturday—for four months. The Westchester Railroad, which passed through the grounds of the institution, was just being completed, and an arrangement was made with the superintendent to run cars from Broad and Market Streets to some point opposite the building, on the days of the clinical lectures. The second week in October, 1854, an immense train left Broad Street, filled to overflowing with medical students, to witness the inauguration of this important event.

Dr. Agnew has stated that he believed this train to have been the first to have passed over the long trestle-work supporting the road across the meadows of this property. There were at least 700 persons present in the old amphitheatre when the first clinique was held by the new staff. The affairs of the Philadelphia Hospital, never particularly tranquil at any time, were rudely disturbed when, in 1856, clinical instruction was again abolished. In the summer of 1857, the visiting members of the entire medical organization resigned, several of the resident physicians withdrew, and again the institution ceased to administer to the wants of the medical students of Philadelphia.

In 1858 it was proposed to re-establish the course of clinical lectures, and, on the 22d of November, 1858, the Guardians again revived the courses of medical instruction, and elected Drs. Joseph Carson, J. B. Biddle, J. Aitken Meigs, and Samuel Dickson, lecturers on clinical medicine; Drs. John Neill, W. S. Halsey, Richard J. Levis, and D. Hayes Agnew on clinical surgery; and Drs. R. A. F. Penrose and E. McClellan on obstetrics and diseases of women and children. Dr. Dickson's health did not allow him any increase of his labors; so he resigned, and in his place Dr. J. M. Da Costa was elected.

On the 4th of July, 1859, the old Board of Guardians, which for many years had been elected by popular vote, was abolished, and a new board, consisting of twelve members appointed by the Courts and Councils, came into power. This organization, consisting of the most respectable and intelligent gentlemen in the community, entered upon the work of reform, after a careful survey of the field. As a result of their investigations, they placed the hospital department under the charge of twelve members, consisting of physicians, surgeons, and obstetricians, who were to visit the institution four times a week. The election of these officers took place on the 8th of August, 1859, at which Drs. James L. Ludlow, William F. Mayburry, Charles P. Tutt, and Robert Lucket were elected to constitute the medical staff; Drs. S. W. Gross, Richard J. Levis, Robert Kenderdine, and D. Hayes Agnew, the surgical staff; and Drs. R. A. F. Penrose, John Wiltbank, William D. Stroud, and Louis Harlow, the obstetrical staff. On the 24th of September, 1860, the wards of the hospital were again thrown open, this time for free clinical instruction.

The cliniques at the Philadelphia Hospital were held originally in the Insane Department; they were afterward held, commencing in the winter of 1860–61, in a new building built for the purpose. This clinique-room, which was described at the time as elegant and commodious, was anything but convenient and pleasant to either the operator or the students. The accommodations were most cramped and the ventilation was so wretched that, at times, it was almost impossible to stay in the room on account of the closeness of the air. This serious defect has recently been remedied by the erection of a new clinique-building within the present year.

It is interesting to note, in the records of the reports to the Board of Guardians, that during these years Drs. Agnew and Kenderdine were the only surgeons who made complete reports of their surgical work. In 1865 Dr. Agnew resigned his position as physician and teacher in this school, Drs. Gross and Kenderdine going off at the same time.

Dr. Agnew established the Pathological Museum in this hospital and was its first Curator. He retained this position, after giving up his surgical post, until 1867. On January 1, 1867, he presented a report on the flourishing condition of this museum, while under his care, to the Board of Guardians. This was the last of several letters on this subject addressed by him to this Board. He was succeeded in this position by Dr. William Pepper. During the fifties this hospital was the only one with which Dr. Agnew was connected. He received no other hospital appointment until the outbreak of the Civil War.

As a writer, Dr. Agnew was not prolific. Excepting his treatise on surgery, he wrote but very little. Nearly all of his published articles were written in pursuance of some purpose, such as an address before a society, or to give utterance to his views on some subject important at the moment. The first book published by Dr. Agnew was prepared to aid his students in their study of anatomy. "Agnew's Anatomy," as it is popularly called, or, with its full title, "Practical Anatomy: A New Arrangement of the London Dissector, with Numerous Modifications and Additions," was first issued by J. B. Lippincott & Co., in August, 1856. Possibly, with the memory of Professor Horner's method of teaching anatomy in his mind, Dr. Agnew prepared this concise volume " with an eye single to the faithful economy of the student's time," believing that a dissector suited to the wants of American students should be much more condensed than those in general use.

Dr. Agnew modestly called the work "a new arrange ment of the 'London Dissector,'" when, in reality, he changed completely this famous volume. The treatment of the subject was entirely altered and the system of nomenclature changed. This work was not intended to teach the student anatomy, but it was to be taken to the dissecting-table, where it was to be consulted by the student. It was an anatomical libretto. It showed him how to learn anatomy from the cadaver; as such it is a most excellent work, still used occasionally by students.

This modest little volume compares favorably with the more elaborate publications on the same subject at the present day. The first edition was quite rapidly exhausted, compelling Dr. Agnew to publish a second revised edition in 1867, in which he still compressed the matter into as small a compass as possible.

His first article published in a medical journal appeared in the *Medical and Surgical Reporter*, October 15, 1858, in which he made report of a case of facial neuralgia successfully treated by excision of the inferior maxillary nerve.

It was the custom of the medical journals of that day to report more fully than is done at present the clinical lectures of the various professors, many of the reports of Dr. Agnew's service at the Philadelphia Hospital and at the University of Pennsylvania, where he frequently substituted for Dr. H. H. Smith, then Professor of Surgery, being published. The class of cases operated on at this time by Dr. Agnew were most varied,— hernia, lachrymal fistula, cataract, removal of cancer, etc.,— while he included such special subjects as the treatment of skin, throat, nose diseases, etc.

In the issue of the *Medical and Surgical Reporter* for April, 1859, Dr. Agnew gave his first communication on the subject of "Regional Anatomy in its Relations to Medicine and Surgery." It was Dr. Agnew's dream that anatomy should be more closely and practically united with the work of the practising physician; and in this series of articles which he commenced this year, he hoped to show that the subject of anatomy was so important to the ordinary practitioner that a good anatomical education would increase his powers of diagnosis and treatment, not merely in surgical but also in medical diseases.

In the next few volumes of the *Medical and Surgical Reporter* he continued these papers; so thoroughly did he go into this subject that, although he frequently published these articles as often as every week for two years, yet, at the end of this time, although he began with the head, he had not finished this division of his topic. The illustrations which he used to illuminate his thoughts were grouped in his clear, inimitable manner. In 1862–63 the increase of his duties incident to the Civil War broke off his communications on this question, and it was not until 1864 that he was again enabled to publish two papers on this subject; but here, again, his duties increased, and he was never able to complete the series. This is a distinct loss to medicine, for it was his intention to republish the series in book form. It was his desire, after he retired permanently from the University, to return to this favorite topic. He had in course of preparation, at the time of his death, an article on this subject, for which space had been reserved in the *University Medical Magazine.*

The following remarks in relation to this series of articles were published in the *North American Medical Reporter*, a New York journal of the period :—

"The series of illustrated papers, of seven of which we have imperfectly indicated the contents, will, if completed, form the best body of practical anatomy extant. These papers wonderfully approach actual work, most perfectly bringing back to the mind the dimmed impressions of actual dissection; while of the 'bearings and practice' there are single paragraphs to be found, so far as we know, in no printed book in the world, making them worth, to any practitioner, more than the amount of the year's subscription to the journal containing these practically invaluable communications. Collected in a volume, they form, as far as they go, a fair set-off in the English language to Hyrtl's 'Handbuch' in the German."

The only other publications from Dr. Agnew's pen during the fifties were the series of annual valedictory lectures to his classes, published at their request; a pamphlet on "Theatrical Amusements, with Some Remarks on the Rev. Henry W. Bellows' Address before the Dramatic Fund Society," in 1857; and an obituary notice on the late Frederick S. Geiger, M.D., in the *Medical and Surgical Reporter*, May 14, 1859.

Dr. Agnew's valedictory address to the anatomical class of the Philadelphia School of Anatomy, on February 19, 1856, affords an opportunity to estimate intelligently his knowledge, his beliefs, and his style at this period, and at the same time it expresses his views on the duties and privileges of a physician:—

" GENTLEMEN:

"This evening we bring our instructions in the lecture-room to a close. In all things I recognize a superintending *Providence*, by which I have been enabled, amid many and varied engagements, some indeed the saddest of my life, to stand here in my place at each appointed hour to communicate the great lessons of a branch which constitutes the substructure of medicine. In taking a retrospect of the last few months, there are many points on which it is pleasant to linger, and among these I assure you there are none which kindle more kindly associations, and which I rejoice to have this public opportunity to acknowledge, than the unexceptionable decorum, courteous attention, and untiring industry of the very large class who have honored me by their presence.

"In closing our winter course of instruction, I cannot allow the present opportunity to pass away without dropping a few observations such as the time, the place, and the occasion suggest. Disclaiming all intention to indulge in heartless compliment, I should do great injustice to you, and violence to my own feelings, did I refrain to acknowledge in the kindest manner the uniform courtesy, good feeling, and attention which have characterized your demeanor toward one who, in an honest conscience, has labored to instruct you in a branch which lies at the foundation of a medical education.

"For very many years the department of Anatomy has been taught within these humble walls by many masters of our Art. Some have gone to their reward, others remain as living and successful expounders of their branch, whilst those who have drawn wisdom from their teachings are found occupying every position, and planted over every portion of our great and happy country. But a very few years ago I entered this room as a teacher, and that single front seat furnished ample accommodations for my audience. Every succeeding year has added largely to its numbers, and it now constitutes the largest private class in this country; one which, for intelligence, application, and all the requisites for gentlemanly bearing,—I say it in no spirit of boasting,—has not its superior in the world.

"There is something of more than ordinary interest and solemnity in the rupture of an intercourse which has grown and strengthened by those affinities and sympathies naturally springing up from the prosecution of subjects of common investigation and interest. A few more days and most of you will have turned your backs upon the scenes which have become familiar as haunts of study.

"I can picture to my mind the various feelings which agitate your bosoms. Some filled with the enthusiasm of the Doctorate long for the opportunity, like some valiant knight, to test the temper of their armor in the tournament of medical conflict. Others long for the renewal of that holy and friendly interchange of feelings which clusters around the sacred circle of home. There is a charm and power about this familiar word which exerts a most mysterious influence over the human mind.

"Who has not read and wept over that beautiful and touching description of Xenophon, where the hacked and scarred Greeks, after enduring untold hardships, and scathed by the fortunes of war, in their homeward return first caught a glimpse of the broad waters which washed the shores of their native

land, and rushed into its friendly bosom with the impetuous joy
of the pilgrim enthusiast who, coming from the ends of the earth,
descries in the distance the banks of his sacred Jordan! The
inspiration of this most praiseworthy sentiment cements the
heart to forms and principles; it is perpetuating in all its tendencies; it constitutes the 'bulwark of civil liberty, and under
its power a people become terrible in war and influential in
peace. It is the paradoxical embodiment of *strength in division*
—*harmony in disagreement*. The idea is happily expressed by
Goldsmith, in his 'Traveller':—

> "'The shuddering tenant of the frigid zone
> Boldly proclaims that happiest spot his home;
> Extols the treasures of his stormy seas,
> And his long nights of revelry and ease.
> The naked negro, panting at the Line,
> Boasts of his golden sands and palmy wine.
> *   *   *   *   *
> Such is the patriot's boast where'er we roam,
> His first best country ever is at home.'

"You have, gentlemen, adopted the profession of medicine
as the pursuit of your life, and I doubt not it is your desire to
make the resources of that profession tributary to your name,
your wealth, and the happiness of your race.

"I am aware it is customary to exalt the disinterestedness
of medicine, so as to exclude all considerations of self; to libel
name as vanity, and *gold* as contemptible dross; but I have no
objection to that selfishness which would rather provide for one's
own house than be esteemed a heathen man.[1] And even were
it true either in principle or fact, the public are not prone to
sin very grievously against your dignity or conscientious delicacy. If, however, you enter upon the duties of your calling
entertaining such puerile fancies, your mind will soon become
disabused. And why not? Are we not made of the same stuff
as other men? We cannot live as a plant, upon the air; nor can
we subsist upon the benisons of grateful convalescents.

[1] I Timothy, 5th chapter, 8th verse.

"May we not exclaim with the Jew in the 'Merchant of Venice'—Hath not a Doctor eyes? Hath not he hands, organs and dimensions, affections, passions, as others have? If you prick us, do we not bleed? If you tickle us, do we not laugh, feed with the same food, and hurt with the same weapons? It so happens that the Great Creator most generally connects our duties with our interests; so that, the more ardently we prosecute our partialities, the more do we contribute to the general good of the human family.

"In medicine, as in every other occupation, the first step is the most important. For its successful prosecution, qualifications of no ordinary character are required; and to have a full comprehension of these is a very essential step toward success. You all aspire to distinction in life. It is a noble sentiment, and yet there is none so commonly doomed to disappointment. Who can tell how many professional hopes have vanished like dew before the morning sun? How many brilliant anticipations disappointed, and noble plans miscarried? Why is this the case? Certainly not from a defect of talent.

"Not one of the liberal professions comprise so large a share of talent as our own. It brings into its ranks, in point of education and manly endowments, every qualification essential to the accomplishment of any reasonable result. For the explanation we must look, therefore, not to the want of talent, but its misapplication, and a little investigation will reveal the true cause. Let us examine some of these for a short time.

"Many are prone to consider that, as soon as they are released from their collegiate minority, labor is at an end and their education completed. They carry with them the views of instructors, adopting these as axioms in science and undeviating rules for their future practice. It is all well to regard with the highest consideration these teachings. The idea that they are not worthy of your confidence and application is not for a moment entertained; but it is that servility of conduct, that forfeiture of independent thought, which is to be deplored and condemned; for it is the sure precursor of a routinist, who is ever content to follow, never aspires to lead. It should be the first great duty of one just initiated into the brotherhood of medicine to test the truth and validity of the basis upon which his education has been erected. Our science courts investigation—nay, challenges examination. It is not to be supposed that the multitude of opinions gathered into the literature of medicine would fail to create doubts upon some points. These are questions for your own solution, and the exercise of a doubt involves no sin. Indeed, there can be no progress without it. It has ever, and will ever, be the great pioneer in all reforms.

"In fact, conformity of sentiment cannot be expected. Men, from their very organization, examine subjects from different points and in different modes, and the various accumulations of facts which are thus garnered into the great depository of the science become the property of some future medical philosopher, who fashions out of them some general law, whose every part beams with the harmony and light of proportion and truth. Universal conformity in any department, even were it possible, would be fatal to progress. 'What a fool have I been,' exclaimed Charles V, when, to relieve the tedium of his kingly exile, he amused himself in attempting to regulate a few watches to a common time. 'What a fool have I been in endeavoring to compel living men to think alike, when I cannot make two dumb watches keep time together!'

"It should be remembered that, in espousing the profession, you incur solemn moral obligations which may not be lightly shaken off. It is no trivial consideration to assume the management of the health and lives of a community. You have seen enough in your anatomical pursuits to teach you that to comprehend the workings of so complex and curiously-constructed a system as that of man is a task of no mean magnitude, and to fathom the laws by which its mysterious processes are conducted requires all the concentration of mind, acuteness of observation, and philosophical disposition of facts you can command. The expounder of your art can hope to do no more than to inculcate principles which are universal and general in their character. The applications of these to special conditions must depend for success upon the logical correctness of conclusions formed by rigid analysis.

"*Inordinate expectation* from the resources of the profession is another source of difficulty. The public are exacting in their demands and expect you to accomplish very many unreasonable results. Voltaire's definition of a Physician expresses the idea: 'An unfortunate gentleman who is expected to perform a miracle every day in reconciling health with intemperance.'

"The student enters upon duty as though he had little else to do than to level with a stroke every enemy of human life. Failing to accomplish all his sanguine confidence would desire, he loses faith in its potency for good and pursues it as a trade rather than a science. A moment's consideration will correct all such unreasonable impressions. The system is a kind of federal compact, an assemblage of numerous distinct independencies. There are laws belonging to the individual organs, and so are there laws regulative of the combined operations of its parts, and, as each individual part is considered sovereign, one does not entrench upon the other; and as the general laws grow out of the combined necessities of individual portions, their influence must be in a great measure conservative.

"Interruptions of these laws constitute disease; and when the quiet and normal exercise of the legitimate functions of an organ have been assailed by some enemy who secretly gains access to the citadel, see how promptly all the other portions resent the injury and combine to eject the intruder! See how the skin mantles with generous indignation and sweats with arduous toil! How the heart thumps like an imprisoned giant against the bars of his cell and lashes the crimson torrent along the shores of the systemic rivers, as if to wash out the very foot-prints of the invader! The lungs breathe a tempest. The glands, for the most part, shut up their bosom and refuse supplies; the eyes melt with pity and shed tears of sympathy. The little *absorbent* traders, who visit all the avenues of the body in search of wares, refuse to replenish at the great marts of commerce; all work is suspended until safety and peace is restored.

"What a lesson to a people, citizens of a country of different aggregated interests like our own! May the same principles of fraternity bind every member to the great centre of our national Union, and may its enemies, whether at home or abroad, meet with the same unterrified rebuke! Now, the tendency of deranged organic actions is generally sanitary, and, in a large proportion of cases, adequate to accomplish their own relief. It is only, therefore, when these processes are likely to fail that medicine legitimately interferes. The judgment and address of the Physician consist not in the *administration of remedies*, but in knowing *when to administer*; not only in employing weapons, but *when* to employ them. Habitual inattention to these considerations will defeat the best intentions of the profession, and, under the hue and cry of *an unsuccessful Doctor*, he too often beats an inglorious retreat into some of the innumerable sinks of quackery. Another prolific source of failure is the wide-spread idea that some *lucky chance or accidental good future* will elevate suddenly to position, as the breaker catches upon its bosom the bubble of surf and drops it high upon the sea-beach. How unlike our conduct in the common affairs of life! Would you linger at the risk of starvation upon some barren island of the sea in full view of land, with all the materials to construct a raft in profusion around, in the hope that, perchance, the friendly winds would bring some propitious sail?

"Look into the world of matter. Do the small particles which in the aggregate construct the glittering crystal take their definitive posts at hazard? Do the elements which the chemist brings into relation settle into place by accident, and form fortuitously the various compounds? Do those brilliant orbs which sparkle in the vault of heaven move through the highways of space, impelled by chance? There is no such thing. All are acting under laws emanating from the *throne*, as unalterable and fixed as the God who sits upon it, whose operations are seen as well in the mote which floats in the sunbeam as the mightiest planet which wheels in his orbit; as manifest in the tint of an insect's wing, the creature of a day, as in the rainbow arch which spans the sky.

"Others toil in search of *specific agents* wherewith to medicate. They are like those ancient philosophers who spent their lives in the fruitless attempt to discover that magic stone which was to turn all the baser metals into gold. Or those Castilian adventurers who, led by the Cavalier Ferdinand de Soto, wandered over our continent in quest of precious mines, or some potent spring, whose recuperative waters should stay the march of years and clothe the body with the bloom of perpetual youth. 'Leave that to the winds,' said the impetuous Alaric, in answer to his pilot whither should they turn their prow,—'Leave that to the winds; they will be sure to waft us to the desired coast.' There can be no greater mistake, gentlemen, than to suppose the instrumentalities which lead to success in other vocations of life will be suspended in favor of you. There must be a diligent and patient employment of means, if you expect desired ends; you must invoke causes if you hope for consequences. It was not fortune which filled the world with the name of Napoleon. All his great successes and master-strokes, as they were wont to be termed, were nothing more than the execution of plans rigidly constructed in the mind of the *First Consul*, both for ordinary and extraordinary circumstances.

"It was not chance which made a great constitutional lawyer of Daniel Webster. Nor was it chance which made a Physick or a Rush the ornaments of your own profession.

"Promotion is a plant of slow growth. The road which leads to distinction is rough and rugged, and many pilgrims grow faint

and sink by the way.   The grain does not ripen to the perfect
harvest by gentle gales and unbroken sunshine; it must have the
storms, the winds, and the frosts of heaven.   Navigators tell us,
and our own intrepid countryman and professional brother,
Kane, whom the world delights to honor, has verified its truth,
that around the pole flows a sea of open water; to reach it, however, the mariner must encounter icebergs and storms.   Just so
it is with the goal of scientific distinction.   It is an inviting spot
of rare and dazzling beauty, but to reach it there are many Mont
Blancs to scale.

"Still, let your peculiar difficulties be what they may, history
has placed on record examples for encouragement.   Is your time
distracted with onerous cares?   Be it so!   Cæsar wrote his
Commentaries and governed a kingdom.   Does poverty pinch
with its Shylock grip?   Poverty produced the immortal poet
Dante, the 'Iliad' of Homer, the 'Maxims' of Terrence; and the
owner of but four acres of land, by the unanimous acclamation
of the Senate, became the Dictator of Rome.   There is a power,
a moral sublimity in undismayed perseverance and virtue, which,
planting its shoulder resolutely against the wheel of life, and not
idly supplicating the aid of Jupiter, forces and compels the world
to respect and homage.

" The unfortunate author of 'Lacon' has said that many men
fail in life from the want, as they suppose, of those great occasions wherein they might have shown their trustworthiness.
But all such persons should remember that before we place wine
in a vessel we try its integrity with water; and it is attention to
what are frequently termed the trivial duties of a profession
which paves the way for higher advancements.   This landing
at a single bound from the cradle into mature manhood is one
of the remarkable characteristics of the age.   In the high-crown
hats, Shanghai coats, and air of *nonchalance*, we fail to recognize
any longer the boy.   Scarcely are many loosed from the leading-
strings of the schools, when they appear as the expositors and
oracles of science.   We would not assert that early genius

may not render important contributions to our branch.   Dante was an author at a very early age ; Schiller wrote an epic before he had attained his fifteenth year ; Tasso was a prodigy at five ; and Mozart astonished his friends at three years of age with wonderful executions which foreshadowed his future triumphs. Visconti knew his alphabet at eighteen months, and ere he had attained his fourth year read fluently the ancient classics. Years have rolled away, and their productions still stand as the models of our literature, gathering additional strength and brilliancy with age.   What think you will be the judgment of opinion two generations hence upon much of our early authorship?

"Time is the great adjudicator ; it will preserve and burnish the gold, and it will bury the dross.   When the immortal Kepler discovered the laws which harmonize the movements of the heavenly bodies, he is said to have exclaimed 'Whether my discoveries will be read by posterity or by my contemporaries is a matter that concerns them more than me.   I can wait a century for a reader, when God has waited some thousands of years for an observer like myself.'   We think many care little about the decisions of the future if they can secure the approval of the present.

"But I fear I have wearied your patience, and, though I would feign linger among you, I hasten to conclude.   Many of you are about to enter the lists and measure arms with the multiplied enemies of our race.   Take care—take care that your armor befits you.   The stripling shepherd of Israel in vain essayed to meet the giant of Gath in the cumbrous panoply of Saul ; and it will be better with you, as with him, to venture with the simple staff and sling of unpretense.

"There is everything in preparation.   I take it, no man living, who has carefully watched the drift of life, but will have marked certain periods when he might have embarked in business with every prospect of success.   These may be termed seasons of opportunity.   They pass along some time or other

by every man's door.   The great secret, gentlemen, is to be fully
equipped, and seize the moment when it comes.

> "'We must take the current when it serves,
>   Or lose our venture.'

"Wherever, in the will of Providence, your lot may be·
cast, you have my warmest wishes for your personal and professional happiness and success."

This address was written by Dr. Agnew in one evening;
it stands exactly as it was prepared, without corrections or
additions.

At this period a coincidence showing the unity of mind of
the Agnews upon religious subjects occurred :—

"A Manual on the Christian Sabbath," written by Rev.
John Holmes Agnew, D.D., was published by the Presbyterian
Board of Publication in Philadelphia, in 1852.   In this work,
this learned professor studied the institution, perpetual obligation, change of day, utility and duties of the Sabbath.   He
also waged warfare on all Sabbath-breakers in most valiant
style.   Curiously enough, in the Appendix are abstracts from
the report of a committee of the British House of Commons on
the observances of the Sabbath, of which another member of
the family, Sir Andrew Agnew, was chairman.   In this report
the cudgels are taken up in favor of the Scottish Sabbath, and,
among other things, the description given by Sir Walter Scott
of the Sunday of the Covenanters is disputed.

In the latter part of the fifties, Dr. Agnew was honored
by election to membership in the Board of Managers of the
House of Refuge, the appointment being made by the Judges
of the Courts of the City of Philadelphia.   He joined, also, in
these years, the Philadelphia County Medical Society and the
College of Physicians.

Keen eyes in the city were fixed upon him ; men of skill
and eminence were talking about him.   Signs of his strength
had aroused attention.   Smith and Jackson, then foremost in

their profession, had tested the stranger, and they found what, in after years, we have all come to know—that Agnew never failed when he was tried. So the doors began to open; the doctor and surgeon began to be known; the path grew easier; he drew longer breaths, and felt that the battle was now in his own hands, under that merciful Providence whom he had ever trusted, and now trusted more than ever; but those stern years never left his memory In speaking of these days, he has said, frequently, "The time a man needs God the most is when he feels that he deserves success and doesn't get it."

Work had not ceased with him, but it had changed its character; it was not now a struggle for sustenance, but unconsciously for supremacy.

CHAPTER VI.

DR. AGNEW'S LIFE FROM 1860 TO 1870.

LIKE other Americans, Dr. Agnew's quiet, tranquil life was rudely disturbed in 1860 by the commencement of the terrific struggle of the Southern States to separate themselves from the Union. The part borne by Dr. Agnew in this conflict was no small one. A surgeon's position in war-time is always most important; but for his skill and work the horrors of war, already terrible, would be increased a thousand-fold.

Dr. Agnew, in common with many other clear-headed men before the commencement of the war, such as Abraham Lincoln, while in favor of the abolition of slavery, was opposed to the methods by which the Abolitionists proposed to bring about the accomplishment of this purpose. He believed thoroughly in the extinction of slavery, and had studied the problem for many years.

It seemed to him that the removal of slaves to the country from which they had originally come, in a climate to which their constitutions adapted them, with the addition of all the agencies of civilization to which they had grown accustomed, was the proper solution of the vexed slavery question. He was well enough acquainted with the temper of the South to know that the Abolition movement in itself tended inevitably toward war, and, possibly, toward dissolution of the country. On this account, years before, he had become an active member of the American Colonization Society. He had hoped that, in the foundation of the Liberian Colony, the solution of this terrible question would be found; but as the country was swept along irresistibly to the terrible vortex of a civil war, the subject of slavery and the threatened dissolution of the government were forced upon his attention, in the most practical manner, before the outside world had felt the rigors of war,—when he

(128)

lost, in a night, the majority of his Southern students.   At this time this action, together with the request of a portion of his class to hurry the course of instruction, led him to speak on the all-absorbing question of the abolition of slavery.   The temperate tone in which he discussed this burning question shows that he had taken up its study with his characteristic calmness. He spoke as follows :—

"When I cast a glance over these seats, I discover many faces absent which had grown familiar from the regularity of their presence. This circumstance and also a request from a portion of the class constrain me to notice one of the most extraordinary incidents,—one without a precedent in the history of this country,—that of a large number of educated young men, prosecuting their professional studies, suddenly abandoning the institutions of one section for those of another.

"The question naturally presents itself,—What circumstances have caused this remarkable action?   Have the schools of Philadelphia, so long famous for their devotion to medical education, become degenerate plants of a noble vine?   Have those, their functionaries, who now stand forth as the expositors of our art, lost their power to charm,—their voices become mute, and their cunning departed?   Has the Philadelphia Hospital,—with a population of over three thousand souls,—the Pennsylvania Hospital, The Wills, and other eleomosynary institutions no sick, no halt, no blind upon which to demonstrate the practical power of medicine, and introduce the student into the beneficent functions of his profession?   Have the resources so necessary to sustain a body of zealous young men during the period of pupilage suddenly become dried up?   Has some modern development cleft the great body of medicine in twain, an opinion, separated by a vast, unbridged chasm, created independent and uncompromising parties?   Medicine once held her court in Edinburgh, then her empire moved to London, then to Paris, and now, perhaps, to Vienna; yet the science was one, and still so continues indissoluble, cemented unity,—the same in Maine as at the Pacific, in Oregon as at the Gulf of Mexico.

"Not one of these catastrophes has happened.   Then, to what shall we look for an explanation?   Whatever other circumstances may have conspired to bring about this event, it cannot be doubted but that the agitation of the long-vexed question of negro slavery was the exciting cause.   Long confined to the arena of politics, this subject has, from various influences, been rising in magnitude, until it has assumed an importance full of peril, and, like some mighty Maelstrom, it has drawn

9

into its revolving currents all occupations, trades, and professions. A subject, therefore, which has become so disturbing an element to the peace of the States; which has rent asunder large bodies of denominational Christians; which avows, with unblushing insolence, the most horrible doctrines, inciting to riot, rapine, and murder, and openly counselling and practicing resistance to the supreme authority of the land; and which even threatens the proscription of our very seats of learning on account of their geographical relation to a particular line, may well challenge our most earnest attention."

Continuing in this strain, Dr. Agnew made a stirring address, in which he reviewed the past history of the country, and urged the love of patriotism and forbearance upon his students. He believed that the dissolution of the country would be most calamitous. He believed that it would settle none of the questions at stake; that it would doom the slave population to the most rigorous and most hopeless servitude, and possibly to entire extermination. He believed that the line of separation, if drawn, would be crimson with the blood of border warfare. He felt that it would be better to have war, pestilence, and famine a thousand times together than that such a catastrophe should occur. In concluding this stirring address, he hoped that all his students would carry with them, to whatever spot they went, love and honor for their country and the memory of his admonitions.

He published, during the winter of 1860–61, his lecture on the "Career of Baron Larrey," the great surgeon of the Napoleonic wars, in order to present the life-work of one who stood pre-eminent among military surgeons,—"whose example may serve as a model for the ambition of my professional countrymen at a period when events portend a struggle of no ordinary magnitude."

When war was eventually declared, Dr. Agnew threw all the resources of his training into the service of the government. From the position of his school,—near the seat of war,—it attracted, naturally, hundreds of students who were anxious to complete their education to such a degree that they could serve as assistant surgeons in the army. The line of teaching which he had been following on anatomy and surgery was exactly suited to the requirements which they were expected to meet as army-surgeons. In consequence, countless surgeons went to the war prepared, through the teachings and demonstrations of Dr. Agnew, to aid their countrymen, to alleviate their sufferings, and to ward off disease and death.

On June 11, 1862, he entered into contract with the government for service as Acting Assistant Surgeon in the United States Army, on duty at Satterlee General Hospital, in West Philadelphia. On July 17, 1862, he was transferred to duty at the Hestonville General Hospital. On October 26, 1862, his contract terminated, he being appointed Surgeon of Volunteers, to date from October 6, 1862. He continued on duty at this hospital, as Surgeon-in-Charge, until April 7, 1863, when his resignation was accepted, as his professional services as lecturer on anatomy and operative surgery did not permit of his transfer to duty elsewhere. From December, 1862, to January, 1863, he was also a member of the Medical Examining Board for Volunteer Surgeons. On August 11, 1863, he again entered into contract for service as Acting Assistant Surgeon, being assigned again to duty at Satterlee General Hospital, in West Philadelphia. This contract was terminated October 7, 1863. On May 12, 1864, he entered into contract for service as Consulting Surgeon, on duty at the Mower General Hospital, Chestnut Hill, Philadelphia, where he remained on duty for nearly fourteen months,—until July 8, 1865,—when his contract was terminated.

As can be seen from this official report of Dr. Agnew's service during the Civil War, his first connection with a military hospital was with the Satterlee General Hospital; but he was transferred, after a month of service, to the Hestonville General Hospital, where he was Surgeon-in-Charge.

The United States Military Hospital at Hestonville was opened in July, 1862, with Dr. Agnew as Surgeon-in-Charge,

and with Dr. John W. Lodge as Assistant Surgeon and Executive Officer. The large room over the *dépôt* of the Race and
Vine Streets Passenger Railway Company was utilized for this
purpose, containing two hundred beds. The place was not well
adapted for hospital purposes at first, but later the room was
divided and the various offices attached. Under the direction
of the Surgeon-in-Charge it soon became one of the best in the
city. It was here that Dr. Agnew had his first experience with
military surgery and the management of gunshot wounds. He
bestowed the greatest care on all his cases; his interest in their
condition and welfare was absorbing. This was a new field for
American surgeons; it was their first experience with the injuries, accidents, and diseases incident to military operations in
the field, since the introduction of anesthesia and the improvement in modern war-implements. Dr. Agnew, among many
others, studied his cases with care and spent many hours each
day in the wards.

At this time Dr. Agnew's great kindness of heart and
simplicity of character showed themselves most strongly.
Among the wounded were many Confederate soldiers, far from
home, among a people something more than strangers, and
utterly penniless. To these he was especially tender, and aided
many materially from his own then limited means.

The Hestonville Hospital was closed in April, 1863, having
been open nearly a year, Dr. Agnew continuing in charge until
its close. Without previous experience Dr. Agnew managed the
hospital, from the beginning to the end, without complaint from
the government. Much of the routine of the government was
complicated at the beginning of the war, and many of the hospitals had much trouble in their settlements; but there never was
a question as to the disposition of the property intrusted to him.
The trouble was usually due to inexperience in the preparation
of papers; Dr. Agnew's papers were always correct.

It was not at Mower Hospital, as is generally supposed,
but at Hestonville, that Dr. Agnew had his first great opportunity

Dr. Agnew in 1867.

of studying gunshot injuries; here he had ample time and ample material. His studious life, his previous experience as a surgeon, and his natural aptitude fully equipped him to deal with every emergency.

On the closing of the Hestonville General Hospital, Dr. Agnew was too busily engaged at the School of Anatomy to be transferred elsewhere; but in the fall he returned to service, being assigned to duty at the Satterlee General Hospital, where he remained several months.

The Satterlee General Hospital was located at Forty-fourth and Pine Streets, in West Philadelphia. It had twenty-eight wards, with a capacity for 70 patients in each, making a total capacity of nearly 2000 patients. The erection of this hospital was due to the liberality of the merchants of Philadelphia. Dr. Isaac Hayes, the celebrated Arctic explorer, was the Superintendent.

After the Battle of Gettysburg Dr. Agnew went to the battle-field, and performed efficient service in the hospitals there. Among other patients, he had charge of the case of General Winfield S. Hancock, who was severely wounded during the battle. When General Hancock was candidate for the Presidency, twenty years later, it made a strange coincidence, for, as a result, Dr. Agnew had charge, in his life-time, of the cases of both candidates for President of the United States in 1880; both being under his care for the same kind of injury,—gunshot wound.

The most important commission held by Dr. Agnew during the war was at the Mower General Hospital, at Chestnut Hill, Philadelphia. His commission here was dated May 12, 1864. This was followed by the appointment of Dr. Thomas G. Morton to a similar position, June 25, 1864.

The Mower General Hospital, located by the government at Chestnut Hill, Philadelphia, was built in the form of a flattened ellipsoid, the length of its main corridor being one-half mile. An idea of its size and capacity can be gained from the fact that twenty-seven acres were inclosed within its walls, and the circumference of its grounds was just one mile. The ward buildings ran off from the main corridor like the spokes of a wheel. It had a capacity for 3600 people, 3100 of these being patients and 500 attendants and guards. Its position was most fortunate; it was located in a most healthful position, on an elevated plateau, four hundred feet above tide-water.

It was arranged that each consulting surgeon went out to the hospital on alternate days, Sunday being omitted except in cases of emergency, when they were sent for. There were forty-eight wards, in each of which was stationed an assistant surgeon. Twenty-four wards were assigned to Dr. Agnew and the same number to Dr. Morton. It was the custom of the surgeons to reach the hospital at 1 o'clock and remain all the afternoon, first going through each ward with the ward-surgeon, then examining all cases for operation. These were then conveyed to the very commodious operating-room.

Only the minor operations were performed by the resident surgeons. Emergency operations which could not wait for the consulting surgeons were performed by Dr. Moon, the first assistant under Dr. Hopkinson, the Superintendent.

Although the hospital had been built to accommodate only 3100 patients, yet it was frequently so crowded that over 5000 cases were at one time within its walls. The possibilities of the service can be estimated when it is seen that this number would make a good-sized town, each inhabitant representing an important injury, no two of which were exactly alike. Each case was a problem in itself, and the task of caring for them was a terrific undertaking.

The operations performed were frequently of the greatest magnitude, such as ligations of the principal vessels, as the common carotid, the femorals, etc.; amputations of all sorts, resections, trephinings; extractions of balls and missiles generally. It was no uncommon occurrence that a number of these major operations would be performed on the same afternoon.

The geographical relation of Philadelphia to the various points of conflict made it one of the most convenient points to which to send the wounded soldiers. In consequence, the Philadelphia surgeons of the period acquired reputation and experience which served to strengthen their position as being the most brilliant and successful operators in America.

When the war was ended, in 1865, Dr. Agnew's contract was terminated and he returned once more to the quieter routine of his regular professional work.

It was by this extensive experience during the war that Dr. Agnew acquired his reputation as the great authority in America on gunshot wounds, which led to his selection as consulting surgeon in the Garfield case.

The other members of the Agnew family were not idle during the period of the Civil War. Professor John Holmes Agnew published, in conjunction with J. S. Wright, a most elaborate article on the subject of the Federal Union, entitled "Citizenship Sovereignty." In this work, reply was made to the arguments brought forward that the government had no right, by the power of the Constitution, to prevent the Southern States from seceding, and that slavery was a divine institution. The amount of work expended on this little volume must have been tremendous. Professor Agnew supplied quotations from Biblical authorities, Grotius, Pufendorf, Vattel, Montesquieu, *The Federalist*, Madison's Debates, Curtis's "History of the Constitution," etc., in order to strengthen and verify the statements made. This work was published in 1863.

At the same time the Hon. Daniel Agnew, at that period President Judge of the Seventeenth Judicial District of Pennsylvania, delivered an address on "Our National Constitution: its Adaptation to a State of War or Insurrection." In this essay he presented clear views of the change wrought by war upon this frame-work of our national life, and the dormant energies it starts into activity. In this argument he proved that the Constitution was legally enabled to act in such an emergency as arose at the beginning of the late Civil War. In eloquent and patriotic terms, he proved logically and fully that the government had the right to levy war when the necessity arose.

During the Civil War Dr. Agnew finally severed his connection with the School of Anatomy, and received his first appointment at the University of Pennsylvania. For some time considerable hostility had been shown to the School of Anatomy by the two medical schools of Philadelphia on account of its tremendous size and reputation. They felt, naturally, that their position was being usurped. By this move the breach was happily sealed.

The earliest connection of Dr. Agnew with the University of Pennsylvania as a teacher was unofficial, dating back as far as 1858, when, at the solicitation of Dr. Henry H. Smith, then Professor of Surgery, Dr. Agnew substituted for him at his cliniques, in the course of regular clinical instruction. He continued this relation with Dr. Smith, frequently acting as his substitute in the instruction of the students, until December 21, 1863, when he received his first official appointment to the University, being made Demonstrator of Anatomy and Assistant Lecturer on Clinical Surgery. This latter title was not accorded him, however, in the catalogues of the period. He succeeded Dr. William Hunt as Demonstrator of Anatomy.

This was a fortunate move on the part of the University; for she obtained a lecturer who had proved himself the best and most successful teacher of the period, who would also tend to attract to her lecture-halls many of the students from other schools, who had been studying under Dr. Agnew's care at the School of Anatomy. This is a potent influence in medical instruction, which can be seen in any medical school; one man's reputation can have much to do in attracting medical students. Medical students are very much given to the worship of some ideal teacher or operator, and frequently go long distances simply to study under a certain professor. Being, as a class, much older than ordinary collegiate students, and more independent as to their movements, they are able to do this.

An example of this tendency is seen in the autobiography of that eminent surgeon, Dr. Samuel D. Gross. He stated, in this history of his life, that he left his preceptor in Easton to enter the Medical Department of the University of Pennsylvania, having in his pocket letters of introduction to several of the professors; but, visiting the clinique of Dr. George McClellan, who was then Professor of Surgery at the recently established Jefferson Medical College, he became so fascinated with the personality of this distinguished surgeon that he gave up at once all thought of going to the University.

The number of students who were attracted to the University by Dr. Agnew's reputation can never be estimated, of course; but, undoubtedly, Dr. Agnew added as much to her financial condition as he did to her moral and scientific side.

Dr. Agnew, on the other hand, obtained, in his demonstratorship and lecturership, a fair position in the University, but not one at all commensurate with his reputation and talents. He was not made a member of the Faculty, although his position, of course, was one which was directly in the line of promotion. The appointment to the position of Demonstrator of Anatomy at the University of Pennsylvania rests in the hands of the Professor of Anatomy; consequently, Dr. Agnew owed this position to the courtesy of Dr. Leidy. As Assistant Lecturer on Clinical Surgery, he was requested to assist the Professor of Surgery in the conduct of the surgical cliniques.

The composition of the medical faculty at this time was as follows :—

Emeritus Professors.

WILLIAM GIBSON, Professor of Surgery.
GEORGE B. WOOD, Professor of the Practice of Medicine.
SAMUEL JACKSON, Professor of the Institutes of Medicine.
HUGH L. HODGE, Professor of Obstetrics and Diseases of Women and Children.

Medical Faculty of the University of Pennsylvania in 1863.

JOSEPH CARSON, Professor of Materia Medica and Pharmacy.

R. E. ROGERS, Professor of Chemistry.

JOSEPH LEIDY, Professor of Anatomy.

HENRY H. SMITH, Professor of Surgery.

WILLIAM PEPPER, Professor of the Theory and Practice of Medicine.

FRANCIS GURNEY SMITH, Professor of the Institutes of Medicine.

RICHARD ALEXANDER F. PENROSE, Professor of Obstetrics and Diseases of Women and Children.

On the appointment of Dr. Agnew as Demonstrator of Anatomy there was the commencement of the extension of clinical teaching at the University again. Just as before his admission as a student in 1836 there had been an impetus given to clinical teaching, so again on his admission as teacher at the University a similar impetus was imparted. He gave, during the winter months, a course of lectures on "Regional Anatomy," and a course on "Operative Surgery" in the spring. In the years 1865 and 1866 he gave summer instruction for students at the University, the course consisting of a series of lectures on "Operative Surgery and Anatomy." These lectures ran through the spring and summer season, beginning in March.

For the next seven years Dr. Agnew served faithfully the University in the position of Demonstrator of Anatomy. As the years rolled by, he grew to be more valuable as an acquisition to the teaching corps of the University, and his general reputation advanced rapidly. He lectured in the evening, twice a week, from 7.30 to 8.30, spending the remainder of the evening in the dissecting-room; but he was there frequently also on other evenings. The duties of his position were the same as those which he had administered when in charge of the School of Anatomy. He experienced, through all this period, a great lack of supply of anatomical material; the Minutes of the Faculty meetings of this time contain several pleas from him, urging upon the Faculty the importance of their taking active measures to make arrangements by which the supply would be made more certain and more regular.

After seven years of hard service, finally, in 1870, Dr.

Agnew intimated his intention of resigning his position as Demonstrator of Anatomy in the Medical Department of the University. This intention on the part of Dr. Agnew was deemed of sufficient importance for the calling of a Faculty meeting. As a result of the conference at this meeting, at a stated meeting of the Board of Trustees held March 1, 1870, Dr. Agnew was nominated for the Chair of Clinical Surgery; at the stated meeting held April 5, 1870, Dr. Agnew was elected to this chair, the title being changed to that of " Professor of Clinical and Demonstrative Surgery," the term " demonstrative " being added in order that he might be empowered to carry out fuller instruction in demonstrative surgery. This chair had been unoccupied since it had been vacated by Professor Norris, in 1857.

At the request of the Faculty, the Trustees had revived this Chair of Clinical Surgery, which had formerly been held by the late Dr. George W. Norris, conferring it upon Dr. Agnew, who thus became a member of the Faculty of Medicine in the University of Pennsylvania at the age of 52, and after practising medicine for thirty-one years. The student who expects to be a professor a year or so after graduation can find here a good lesson in patience.

Dr. Agnew, in being made Professor of Clinical and Demonstrative Surgery, was put more upon an equality with his fellow-teachers. There is no reason why he should not have been given this position on his first connection with the University, excepting the fact that he was perfectly contented with the demonstratorship; his own ambition being satisfied, there was no one to suggest his further advancement to the professorship in the clinical chair. He was not forcing Dr. Smith, the Professor of Surgery, from his lawful position; on the contrary, he was aiding that chair and lightening its duties.

The history of clinical instruction at the University is so connected with the history of this chair that it is briefly quoted. In 1841 the system of dispensary cliniques was adopted by the University; the first that was instituted under its auspices was conducted by Drs. Gerhard and William P. Johnston, in the building of the Medical Institute, in Locust Street above Eleventh. It was there carried on until the commencement of the course of 1843, when it was transferred to the University building under the immediate supervision of the professors, with the assistance of these gentlemen. From that time to the present, this mode of practical instruction has constituted a part of the regular course of medical teaching conducted by the University.

In connection with the clinical service, two rooms within the building were appropriated for the accommodation of patients requiring operations who could not be immediately removed. By this arrangement, the same attention, nursing, and care was bestowed upon the subjects of capital operations as in a hospital.

With a view of completing the plan for clinical instruction so as to give it the greatest efficiency compatible with the progress of medical education, it was resolved in 1845, by the Faculty, that a surgeon connected with the Pennsylvania Hospital, and whose duties there were performed during the session of the University, be requested to officiate as clinical lecturer on surgery. This led to the creation of a Chair of Clinical Surgery in the University, by the Trustees, and the appointment by the Board, in 1847, of Dr. Jacob Randolph to perform the duties of this office in the hospital. In 1848 Dr. Randolph died, and Dr. George W. Norris, who had delivered the course of clinical lectures under the auspices of the University during Dr. Randolph's illness, was elected his successor in the professorship. Dr. Norris continued to perform his duties as Clinical Professor until 1857, when, upon being elected a Trustee of the University, he resigned.

Dr. Agnew was succeeded by Dr. H. Lenox Hodge as Demonstrator of Anatomy. There was still great growth in the clinical department, clinical lectures being delivered daily throughout the year.

In the following year Professor Henry H. Smith, not being in sympathy with the expansion of clinical teaching, resigned the Chair of Surgery, and Dr. Agnew was chosen his successor, the surgical teaching of the University being thus again united in a single person.   The chair which had been revived to serve as a medium for admission of Dr. Agnew to the Faculty was abolished.   On the establishment of the University Hospital, in 1873–74, Dr. Agnew was made Professor of Clinical Surgery, still retaining, however, his didactic chair, and the late Dr. John Neill was associated with him also as Professor of Clinical Surgery.   The University had now gone to West Philadelphia, and this fine new hospital at last afforded ample clinical material.   On the endowment of the Chair of Surgery by Mrs. Susan R. Barton, widow of Dr. Barton, in 1878, by the gift of $50,000, the title was changed to that of the "John Rhea Barton Professorship of Surgery,"—a title which it still bears.

Dr. Agnew and Dr. Smith had long been as Damon and Pythias to each other.   For many years they had been inseparable companions, always together whenever the opportunity offered.   They had always felt the greatest love, sympathy, and admiration for each other.

For many years they remained most intimate in their relations; as has been stated, as far back as 1858, Dr. Agnew had been in the habit of substituting for his friend, while he was Professor of Surgery; and still earlier, in 1854, they had been associated together in the work of re-opening the Philadelphia Hospital for clinical instruction.   When Dr. Smith was a candidate for the position of Professor of Surgery at the University of Pennsylvania, in 1855, Dr. Agnew was one of his most earnest workers and supporters.   It was, probably, somewhat through Dr. Smith's solicitation that Dr. Agnew came to the University.   Unfortunately, however, Dr. Agnew's reputation grew so great that it greatly overshadowed that of Dr. Smith. This was not the fault in any way of either.   It was simply the inevitable result when one skillful, famous physician comes unconsciously and slowly into competition with another. Dr. Agnew's progress had been very slow; he had not forced his way at all; but, coming as it did, simply the natural growth and demand of the times, it was resistless even to Dr. Agnew himself. Dr. Agnew never sought the position of Professor of Surgery in the slightest way; never by word or deed did he intimate that he wanted it. He would have been satisfied for them to have retained their old relationship. As he said in his farewell speech, at his last didactic lecture, " The post was one that I had never sought."

The opportunities for clinical instruction at the University Hospital opened the way for the appointment of a Staff of Demonstrators of Practical Surgery to assist Dr. Agnew. They were: Drs. Hunter, Willard, Muhlenburg, and Elliott Richardson. Later, the Surgical Dispensary's staff was increased, Dr. Charles T. Hunter being made Chief. His assistants were: Drs. Stryker, Muhlenburg, Ashbridge, Allison, Willard, Richardson, and Porter.

The second civil hospital with which Dr. Agnew was connected was the Wills Eye Hospital. He applied for this position in order to round out his surgical experience.

At a stated meeting of the Board of Managers of the Wills Hospital for Diseases of the Eye, held January 4, 1864, with the President, Dr. Paul, in the chair, the Board elected, as attending surgeons, Drs. A. D. Hall, T. G. Morton, Richard J. Levis, and D. Hayes Agnew. The management of the hospital was arranged in such a way that it required the annual election of its medical officers; therefore, on January 2, 1865, Dr. Agnew was re-elected. His third election occurred December 3, 1866. On September 7, 1868, Dr. Agnew's resignation was received and accepted, Dr. Harlan being unanimously elected to fill his position. On October 5, 1868, a complimentary Minute was adopted by the Board of Managers, in which they placed on record their high estimation of Dr. Agnew's professional services in connection with that institution. He was made Emeritus Surgeon to the hospital, remaining such until his death.

As there is a complete record kept at the Wills Hospital
of the major operations performed by the different surgeons, it
has been easy to complete Dr. Agnew's record of eye-work
during his term of service. In comparing it with the work of
the present day, it must be remembered that the accommodations
of the hospital have grown considerably since his connection with
the institution; for example, in the month of January, 1864,
there were only 38 new patients admitted to and 38 discharged
from the house, while the total number of new out-door patients
was 119. The number runs now four times as great for house
patients, while out-door patients number over 1000 monthly.
In addition, Dr. Agnew's terms of service were principally during
the summer months of these years, affording the smallest *clien-
tele;* yet he performed, during this short period of time, 69
operations for cataract, 15 iridectomies, 24 tenotomies, 5 divisions of the ciliary muscle, and 1 enucleation. This shows that
a very large percentage of his work was operative.

Undoubtedly, the most important position held by Dr.
Agnew, as far as concerned purely operative surgical work, was
his connection with the Surgical Staff of the Pennsylvania Hospital. This institution, from its location, from its size, and
the length of time it has been in operation, is easily the first
of the Philadelphia hospitals, and its staff of physicians has
always consisted of the leaders of the profession in Philadelphia.

Philadelphia, one of the largest manufacturing cities in
the United States, is the scene, daily, of countless accidents.
Her busy streets also teem with the ordinary dangers of city life,
and the extent and variety of her population afford material
for the study of diseases of every kind. It is opportunities of
this sort which constitute a centre for medical education. These
facilities have been recognized from the earliest days of medical
study in America. The Pennsylvania Hospital is typical of
Philadelphia; within its colonial walls the greatest variety of
acute diseases, accidents, and curious medical phases of Philadelphians have been found, from the days of Gabriel and Evan-

geline down to the present time. Its quaint buildings and pleasant grounds caused the poet Longfellow to end here the career of these two famed lovers, the hero and heroine of the greatest American poem ever written.

While a member of the Surgical Staff of this hospital, Dr. Agnew was given a practical opportunity to demonstrate the degree of fidelity which he held for his convictions. The circumstances of the occurrence are as follow: He was elected a member of the Staff of Attending Surgeons to the Pennsylvania Hospital on March 27, 1865, serving in this connection, acceptably, for six years. On May 29, 1871, a resolution was passed by the Board of Managers of the Pennsylvania Hospital, requesting the staff to give appropriate clinical instruction to the students of the Women's Medical College. This question had long been discussed by the management of the hospital, and the following are the details in connection with it :—

"On motion of Samuel Mason, the following resolution was offered at the meeting of the Board of Managers of the Pennsylvania Hospital :—

"The Contributors, at their annual meeting in fifth month, 1870, having directed that appropriate thorough clinical instruction be given to the students of the Women's Medical College, if practicable, at the Pennsylvania Hospital, and having, at the last annual meeting, given reiterated instructions to the same effect,

"*Resolved*, That it is hereby made the duty of the Medical and Surgical Staff to carry into effect the instructions given by the Contributors, as above mentioned, during their term of office.

"Yeas 6, and Nays 5. Those who voted in the affirmative were: John Farnum, William Biddle, Samuel Mason, Samuel Welsh, Benjamin H. Shoemaker, Mordecai L. Dawson. Those voting negatively were: Alexander J. Derbyshire, Jacob P. Jones, Alexander Biddle, Joseph B. Townsend, and Joseph C. Turnpenny."

This action having been taken by the Board, they received, at the same meeting, the following letter from Dr. D. Hayes Agnew :—

1011 CHESTNUT STREET.

MR. JACOB P. JONES.

DEAR FRIEND: Should a willingness to give surgical instruction to female students be required as a condition of election on Monday, I desire that you will do me the favor to withdraw my name, as I should regret to do anything which would embarrass the Board in carrying out the wishes of the Contributors.

Very truly your friend,

D. HAYES AGNEW.

Immediately upon receiving this communication, the following resolutions were passed by the Board of Managers:—

" WHEREAS, A communication has this day been received from Dr. D. Hayes Agnew declining to be considered a candidate for re-election if surgical instruction be given to female students, in accordance with the directions of the Contributors at the last annual meeting; and

" WHEREAS, The Board feel bound to carry out the instructions of the Contributors; therefore,

" *Resolved*, That in accepting the declination of Dr. Agnew the Board desires to express their deep sense of his eminent abilities as a surgeon, as well as the faithful manner in which he has discharged the arduous duties devolving upon him while connected with the institution.

" *Resolved*, That a copy of the above be furnished Dr. Agnew, signed by the President and Secretary on our behalf."

Dr. Agnew, consequently, was not a member of the Staff of the Pennsylvania Hospital for the next six years. During this period he devoted such time and energy as was not spent in practice on his work in connection with the University of Pennsylvania. On the 7th of May, 1877, however, he was re-elected to the Staff and served for over six years, resigning, eventually, April 17, 1884.

It was always understood by Dr. Agnew and his friends that his re-election to the Staff of the Pennsylvania Hospital meant also that female students would not be allowed to attend his lectures, as that was the ground upon which he had resigned six years before, and as he still retained the same views. It has been discovered, however, recently, that when he resumed duties at the hospital no stipulation in regard to the presence or absence of female students was put upon record in the Minutes of the Board of Managers, although a suggestion was made in the Board, at the time of re-election, that women should not be present at his lectures, or should be asked to withdraw if, in the judgment of the lecturer, an operation was to be performed which he considered unfit for their presence. Dr. Agnew resigned on the very day that the resolution was passed by the Board allowing female students to be present at the cliniques at the Pennsylvania Hospital, and he did not change his views in later years. Consequently, his connection with the Pennsylvania Hospital at this later period needs explanation. It is undoubtedly shown in the following letter of acceptance, which is copied from the Minutes of the meeting of the Board held May 28, 1877:—

1611 CHESTNUT STREET.

To the Board of Managers of the Pennsylvania Hospital.

GENTLEMEN: I am deeply touched by both the compliment and the confidence implied in the recent action of your Board in electing me, without solicitation on my part, and with singular unanimity, as one of the surgeons to the institution over whose interests you preside. Though pressed with many arduous and exacting duties, yet, under the circumstances, I do not feel at liberty to decline, and shall, therefore, enter upon the duties of the place with the determination to serve the hospital to the best of my ability.

With considerations of the highest respect, I am, respectfully, your obedient servant, 　　　　　　　　D. HAYES AGNEW.

From this letter it can be seen that Dr. Agnew was re-elected without solicitation for the position and without stipulation on his part, and that, consequently, he took it for granted that the Board intended to remove the obstacle which had caused his separation from the hospital some years before. He was a man to meet such an action half-way. He knew that the Board could not have been led to believe that he had changed his unalterable determination not to lecture to women students. He believed that they had come over to his views in the matter, and he wisely let further discussion drop. After

consideration of these circumstances, it can be seen that the
Board of Managers of the Pennsylvania Hospital, by re-electing
him, retreated from the position which they had assumed some
years before.

After his election there were, undoubtedly, a number of
female students who attended his lectures, but he interpreted
their presence to ignorance of his views on the subject; and,
moreover, he was entirely too courteous and kindly in his feelings toward every one to object to the presence of the women,
—if he found them in his clinique-room,—even if they over-
whelmed him.

In order to see whether Dr. Agnew's belief in regard to
cliniques in which male and female students were admitted was
wrong, it is necessary to know of what a clinique consists and who
the students are. From time immemorial it has been customary,
at the surgical cliniques, to display the cases of venereal diseases
which are present in the hospital, and study them carefully;
this forms a part of the regular instruction of a surgical clinique.
In order to study these cases thoroughly, it is necessary, of
course, to enter fully into the minutest details of the diseases,—
their causes, diagnosis, and their treatment, making, at the same
time, the necessary exposure of the patients. The utmost freedom of speech and actions is required. On the other hand, the
audience which is to view this exhibition is not composed of
physicians, but of young men and women who are studying
medicine.

The large majority of such students who attend clinical lectures at such an institution as the Pennsylvania Hospital are the new-comers at the medical schools. They have not
become fully accustomed yet to the sights and work to which
every practising physician has long been familiar. There can
be found among them many young men and women who are
not of mature age,—some of the students being frequently as
young as seventeen or eighteen years of age. Taking such a
mixed class as this, containing many boys and girls unaccus-

tomed to such work, and exposing to them the unpleasant sights
and facts of venereal diseases, is a task from which a modest-
minded physician would naturally shrink.

Dr. Agnew did not wish to deprive the female students of
an opportunity to study these diseases; simply he did not think
that the "mixed clinique" was the proper place for them to
acquire this knowledge. In this belief Dr. Agnew did not
stand at all alone. A great number among his friends and
colleagues have taken the same ground.

Dr. Agnew's belief in regard to female medical students is
a corollary of his ideas on the subject of women studying medicine. Dr. Agnew was not opposed to the higher education of
women. He believed that the ideal place for woman was at
home, as the head of the household, but he realized the fact
that such a position was not intended for all women. He held
the sex in great respect and consideration, and he did not belittle
their powers or capacity for work.

Dr. Agnew did not oppose the admission of women into
the medical profession. The field of medicine is so broad, and
there is so much room for minds of the most diverse dispo-
sitions and talents, that he realized that there were certain
branches of medicine to which they were peculiarly adapted,
such as the preparation and mounting of microscopical specimens, where their delicacy of touch and deftness of fingers
made them well adapted. He believed that their minds were
sufficiently powerful for them to grasp the amount of learning
and training necessary to pass successful examinations; but he
had a deep, insurmountable distrust in the ability to train the
special talents of woman into the attributes of the really successful *practising* physician. He did not believe that, either
naturally or by their centuries of inherited training, women
made good practitioners. In a similar way he did not believe
that men made good nurses, no matter how well trained; and,
if he could avoid it, he never employed a male nurse. In addition, he believed that the environments of society were arranged

in such a way, at present, that a woman could not practise medicine without being exposed to many hardening, unpleasant influences.

At the same time Dr. Agnew recognized the futility of opposing the admission of women into the practice of medicine. If the State would allow them to practise, and they cared to study and could obtain a sufficient number of patients to make the practice of the profession profitable, he knew enough of the world's ways to realize that his protest would be unavailing; so that, when any measure came up in which he felt that they would be successful, he did not attempt to defeat them; for example, at the time of the last agitation of the question of the admission of women to the Philadelphia County Medical Society he listened courteously to the statements of the then-existing status of the question as seen by the women physicians, and expressed his entire willingness to let the movement take its course, saying that he should make no objections to the admission of women, should the Society see fit so to vote. When it was proposed that the women of the medical profession in and around Philadelphia should give a reception to Dr. Hiram Corson, Dr. Agnew allowed his name to go on the joint committee of medical men and women without a moment's hesitation.

Dr. Agnew served at the Pennsylvania Hospital, after his second election, until April 17, 1884. It is a strange coincidence that he served as a surgeon at this hospital for a short time over six years; he was out of office six years, and on his return to service he remained on the staff again for six years.

Dr. Agnew's appointment at the Orthopedic Hospital came next in point of time.

Although in Europe, by the year 1867, there were a few hospitals devoted to the science of orthopraxy, yet in the United States there existed no such charter institution for the treatment of bodily deformities. There were, of course, operations performed for club-foot, etc., at all the cliniques of the large hospitals, but the after-treatment of adjusting proper apparatus, the constant manipulation and vigilance necessary to prevent recurrence after operation, could not always be fully carried out, due to the very limited accommodations existing in general hospitals for this purpose, and to the fact that few hospitals were able to defray such expense. Thus many cases of club-feet among poor children were operated upon with necessarily ill attention later. Often the apparatus was left off, and in some cases the contractions following the operations produced worse deformities than the original. Drs. Thomas G. Morton, H. Earnest Goodman, S. W. Gross, and D. Hayes Agnew, believing that such an institution had long been needed in Philadelphia, took up the movement for the accomplishment of this purpose. In consequence, these four gentlemen met, October 1, 1867, to advise as to the best means for a hospital for deformities in this large and constantly increasing city.

A charter had been prepared and a second meeting was held October 11, 1867, and Drs. Agnew, Morton, Goodman, and S. W. Gross consented to act as a board of surgeons, with Professors S. D. Gross and George W. Norris as consultants. At this meeting a committee was appointed to confer with those gentlemen who had consented to serve as managers of the hospital. On October 23, 1867, the attending surgeons, with Dr. S. D. Gross, met Edward Hopper, Dillwyn Parrish, and Joseph C. Turnpenny, when the following Minute was read and adopted:—

" WHEREAS, There exist in all large communities many persons suffering from bodily deformities, such as hunchback, hip disease, club-foot, knock-knees, wryneck, etc.; and

" WHEREAS, A large proportion of such persons of adult age seen in our streets have never received in early life the requisite treatment for such deformities; and

" WHEREAS, Such deformities require constant care and attention by operation and mechanical appliances for greater or less period of time; and

" WHEREAS, No institution now exists in this city or state specially devoted to the treatment of this unfortunate class, and believing that

many persons may be saved from growing up deformed and a burden to
society, by a scientific course of treatment in a well-organized Orthopædic Hospital, we, citizens of Philadelphia, trusting in the liberality
of the public for support, met in Parlor No. 9 of the La Pierre House,
on Wednesday, October 23, at 5 o'clock P.M., for the purpose of organizing an Orthopædic Hospital for the cure of such deformed persons as
hereinbefore mentioned."

Mr. Edward Hopper was appointed temporary chairman
and Dr. Goodman was appointed acting secretary of the Board.

The charter prepared by the medical gentlemen was revised,
and while waiting its approval, which took place by "An Act
of the Court of Appeals" in December, 1867, temporary quarters were opened at 15 South Ninth Street, over the surgical-
instrument establishment of Mr. D. W. Kolbe, who had been
active in the suggestion for its establishment. The hospital
was opened for the reception of patients on February 25, 1868.
Only out-patients were then treated, while funds were being
solicited for the establishment of a well-regulated and organized
hospital.

The first Board of Managers appointed under the charter
consisted of Edward Hopper (president), J. Gillingham Fell,
Charles Macalester, Samuel S. White, Judge William S. Pierce,
Dillwyn Parrish, Joseph C. Turnpenny (treasurer), Charles F.
Norton, James B. Nicholson, J. B. McCreary, Thomas G. Mor-
ton, and D. Hayes Agnew.[1]

Thus, Dr. Agnew was a member of the first Board of
Managers, and, at the same time, served as surgeon on the
Medical Staff. The other surgeons were Drs. Thomas G. Morton, H. Earnest Goodman, and S. W. Gross, with Drs. S. D.
Gross and George W. Norris as consultants. The hospital rapidly increased in size and usefulness, although at the beginning
of the second year only four beds existed. The mission of the
hospital was so well carried out that only $48 remained in the

---

[1] A group photograph of these gentlemen, together with those of Prof. S. D. Gross,
George W. Norris, M.D., and S. W. Gross, M.D., consulting and attending surgeons, and
D. W. Kolbe, now hangs in the Board-room of the new hospital.

treasury at this time. Each year showed an increase in the number of patients treated and operations performed. Drs. Morton and Goodman did the largest part of the operative work, while Dr. Agnew held the position of influence and help rather than that of active operator. On account of the increase of his other duties, Dr. Agnew resigned his position as attending surgeon in 1871, at which time he became a member of the Faculty of Medicine at the University. Since that time, Dr. Agnew held the position of consulting surgeon up to the time of his death.

In the fall of 1870 a department for nervous diseases was created, to which were elected physicians for this work. It was thought advisable to treat these two classes of disease in the same institution, because of the relation many of the deformities bore to nervous diseases, and as many cases of nervous disease exacted at some time the use of instruments to aid in locomotion.

In 1872 the hospital removed to its new quarters, where it still remains, at the northwest corner of Seventeenth and Summer Streets. The other consultants with Dr. Agnew, during this period of service, were Drs. Gross, Norris, Hunt, Morehouse, and Keen.

From the founding of the institution up to November 30, 1892, there have been 11,560 surgical cases and 11,850 nervous cases treated at the daily clinique, with 3235 cases that have received house care, making a grand total of 26,645 cases treated since its foundation.

Thus it was that he grew gradually from the Master of the Anatomical School to the clear-voiced professor, the clinical teacher with marvelous hands, and the trusted surgeon of enormous practice, known from sea to sea, from the lakes to the gulf, as the last great appeal in practical operative surgery.

The professor in his chair had become a marvel. The most eminent members of his profession gave public testimony to the marvelous clearness of his statements, the sound common sense of his teaching, the reliable data founded upon his own operations and observations; the large forecasts, wonderfully suggestive and helpful, which he threw out before benches of eagerly listening students, and the inspiration to faithful work which he continually breathed into those who hearkened to him.

He became the consultant of consultants. The best men of his noble craft felt in their souls that Agnew had won all that he knew, and, pouring out volumes of proof for what he stated, would lead them ever in safe paths.

During this period Dr. Agnew changed his residence. He remained on Eleventh Street for over sixteen years. As years rolled by, however, the centre of residences had moved westward. Dr. Agnew finally concluded that he should go with it. Accordingly, in 1866, he purchased the house, 1611 Chestnut Street, combining, curiously, the figures of his former home,—16 North 11th Street. He lived in this house for nearly twenty-one years,—until the fall of 1886. It was an excellently timed selection, for it placed him again in the centre of the best section of the city,—a most fortunate thing for a physician.

CHAPTER VII.

DR. AGNEW AS PROFESSOR OF SURGERY.

DR. AGNEW's appointment as Professor of Surgery at the University of Pennsylvania was made May 2, 1871, by the Trustees. He began now to carry fully into effect his ideas on the teaching of surgery. He was a firm believer in actual experience and observation as being the best means to impress students with the principles and practice of surgery. He increased the size and scope of the Surgical Dispensary and added a *corps* of Demonstrators of Surgery.

The University of Pennsylvania had decided at this period to change its location to some such position which, while adapted fully to its purpose, would be permanent. Consequently, steps were taken to settle in West Philadelphia, on the strip of land extending south from Thirty-fourth Street and Darby Road.

In the meantime the Medical Department left their quarters at Ninth and Chestnut Streets in the spring of 1873. The winter of 1873-74 was spent in the building, 252 South Ninth Street, formerly occupied by the Philadelphia University of Medicine and Surgery. They remained here until June, 1874.

The first course in the new quarters in West Philadelphia began October 12, 1874. The Hospital which had been erected was inaugurated by Governor Hartranft in 1874 and opened for patients. There was some trouble experienced at first to place the officers of the Medical Department and those of the Hospital on a satisfactory footing. This was finally accomplished by making the professors of medicine, surgery, and obstetrics *ex-officio* officers in the hospital and making the professors of clinical medicine, surgery, etc., members of the Faculty. This was done in March, 1875. On March 6, 1874, Dr. John Neill was appointed Associate Clinical Professor of Surgery by the Trustees.

(154)

Dr. Neill retained this position for several years, until his election to the position of Emeritus Professor. He was succeeded by Dr. John Ashhurst, Jr., who was elected, June 5, 1877, by the Trustees to the position of Professor of Clinical Surgery. Dr. Ashhurst retained this position until Dr. Agnew retired from active service, in 1889, when he was advanced to the John Rhea Barton Professorship of Surgery.

During this period of the reconstruction of the Medical Department, Dr. Agnew took an active part. He bore, to a large extent, the burden of the responsibilities of the financial questions arising from the increase of size and consequent expense. The Minutes of the Faculty meetings of this period, meagre as they are, are filled with references to Dr. Agnew's work on these questions.

The organization and successful formation of the Dental Department was entered into by Dr. Agnew with great interest. Some influential members of the Faculty strongly opposed such a venture; it is interesting to note that Dr. Agnew was a member of the various committees appointed to overcome these objections and remove this opposition. The successful establishment and operation of this department since 1877 show the soundness of this judgment of its suggesters and promoters.

The Faculty meetings were held the third Monday in each month, at the homes of different members. Frequently they were held at Dr. Agnew's residence, 1611 Chestnut Street.

By Dr. Agnew's suggestion, orthopedic and venereal dispensaries were established at a meeting of the Faculty, June 29, 1877. By these two cliniques, an immense amount of work has been done. The Spring course of lectures inaugurated in 1878 was strongly advocated by Dr. Agnew, and to him was left the selection of a number of its lecturers.

He asked during this time that some remuneration be given his demonstrators of surgery, four in number. In consequence, the sum of fifty dollars annually to each was voted as salary. Following out his ideas of actual experience in teaching, he inaugurated the system of teaching bandaging and fracture-dressing to first-course students.

During this period of Dr. Agnew's connection with the Faculty, there was a very wide difference of opinion between those who regarded the curriculum as the best possible, and those who, on the other hand, thought it, on principle, the worst possible, and only redeemed by the honesty of those who ignorantly employed it.

Dr. Agnew was never far from the front of the party of progress, and he did much, by the impression of his earnest convictions, to encourage some who felt their spirits fail in the apparent hopelessness of the conflict. Apart from this special question, it may be safely asserted that in the Medical Faculty there was no one whose judgment was held in higher esteem by all of his colleagues ; for it was always temperate, deliberate, and untainted by any expression of selfish interest.

The following estimate of Dr. Agnew's services in the Faculty of Medicine at this time is prepared by the Provost of the University :—

"Dr. Agnew's powerful personality made itself felt, in the work and development of the Medical School of the University of Pennsylvania, from the beginning of his connection with it down to the last days of his life. His great success as a teacher has been fully referred to elsewhere in this work. I remember well, in my student days, the admiration and devotion which we felt for him.

"When he was added to the Faculty of the Medical School it was felt by all that he would be the peer of the great men who have honored the chairs they held in that school. This expectation was more than realized. He grew and developed steadily year by year, both as a great teacher and practitioner of surgery. It is not for me to allude to the magnificent reputation he achieved at home and abroad, or to the great work that he did for the community at large, and for surgical science. I am more especially concerned with his personal relations with the Medical Faculty, and with his influence upon the progress and growth of the medical school.

" He was admirably faithful in his attendance at Faculty meetings, and showed there the same conscientious care in the discharge of every duty that marked him in all relations of life.

" The last fifteen years have witnessed a complete reorganization of the Medical School of the University. Large interests were concerned and there were honest differences of opinion as to the wisdom and safety of the progressive policy pursued. Dr. Agnew's attitude was unswerving. He believed in honest, thorough work in education just as he did in every other field of effort. Medical teaching, with him, was a sacred trust. Its duties never sat lightly upon him. He welcomed every substantial advance in the interests of the science and of the students, no matter at what increased cost of personal exertion. Just as we know his open and impartial mind made him among the first to welcome the great truths of modern antiseptic surgery, so he accepted with equal readiness and completeness, as soon as convinced of their soundness, the advanced views upon medical education.

" It was most fortunate that in Agnew, Leidy, and Stillé the Medical Faculty contained men whose names and characters were towers of strength during these years of struggle.

" Dr. Agnew's personal relations with the members of the Faculty were so affectionate; their confidence in his sincerity and disinterestedness and genuine sympathy was so great that his advocacy of any measure went far to secure its success. His influence in the councils of the Faculty was, therefore, powerful, conciliating, and elevating. No one who had not the privilege of frequent personal and official intercourse with him can fully appreciate the charm which his character and consistent conduct conferred upon such relation.

" In the actual work of the Medical School his services and achievements were fully as conspicuous. He was an ideal teacher of surgery. In the first place, he kept his appointments with his class with scrupulous fidelity. At a time when every minute of his day was of golden value and was greedily sought in all quarters, he would travel all night and subject himself to every fatigue and exposure, or would unhesitatingly sacrifice the most important and lucrative consultations rather than miss a lecture or keep a class waiting. The high purpose he had in teaching impressed every student. There was no display of himself, of his vast attainments, or of his marvelous skill. He said only so much as would best instruct the student, and he did only what was demanded by the best interest of the patients upon whom he operated before the class.

"He taught not only by what he said and did, but by what he refrained from saying or doing. I am sure that, during his long career as a teacher, not one word was uttered nor a single operation performed which was hasty or ill-advised. His students depended upon his teachings with that fullness of confidence which is the highest tribute to any teacher. This trust in him began in their earliest student days, and it continued in all their subsequent relations with him after they had entered upon the practice of their profession. He did, at least, as much as any other man to sustain and carry forward the fame and success of the Medical School of the University during all the years he was connected with it.

"He threw himself into the movement for the establishment of the University Hospital with characteristic energy and directness of purpose. It is, indeed, fitting that the splendid portrait of this great master in surgery should adorn the hall-entrance to this great hospital which owes so much to him.

"His best thought, his valuable time, his personal exertions were always at its disposal. In the advocacy of its claims before the State Legislature; in personal appeals to his numerous friends in behalf of its funds; in generous personal gifts to it which only heralded the munificent benefaction announced in his last testament, he displayed a love and solicitous anxiety for its welfare and growth which were of incalculable value.

" His name and memory will forever be inseparably associated with the Medical School and the Hospital of the University of Pennsylvania, and they will be cherished there as a glorious example to the Faculties and students of all coming times."

In 1861 Dr. Agnew had been given the honorary degree of A.M. by Princeton College, as a mark of appreciation for his work in advancing the position of surgical science. This college, ever friendly to him and his ambitions, conferred on him, in 1874, the honorary degree of LL.D.

In the summer of 1872 Dr. and Mrs. Agnew went abroad to remain a few months. The details of this trip are given in another chapter. They were accompanied by Dr. Agnew's assistant, Dr. Charles T. Hunter. Dr. Hunter was regarded by Dr. and Mrs. Agnew almost in the light of a son ; he stood easily at the head of the corps of assistants, and his death, in 1884, was a terrible shock and irreparable loss, for, not only did Dr. Agnew feel that he had lost a brilliant assistant and loving companion, who was bound to him by many ties, but he realized that Dr. Hunter's place could never be filled again so ably and satisfactorily.

During this time Dr. Agnew continued his occasional contributions to medical literature. In 1865 was published his essay on " Lacerations of the Female Perineum," in which he reported a new operation for the relief of this condition, devised by himself. On July 6, 1866, he began the series of papers in the *Medical and Surgical Reporter* on " Vesico-Vaginal Fistula," which was subsequently reprinted in pamphlet form in 1867. In 1882 he combined and rewrote these two essays and published them in book form, through the firm of Lindsay & Blakiston.

This book stands as a landmark in gynecology. In all good historical accounts of advance in this branch of surgery its force and advancing influence is noted. In such standard works as Mann's "System of Gynecology," the proper importance of this work has been recognized.

Dr. Agnew increased at this time his fame as a syphilographer; he became the authority in America on this division of medical work.

Dr. Agnew delivered the introductory lecture, October 10, 1870, to the incoming class at the Medical School. During the period 1869–71 reports of his clinical work were published in the *Medical and Surgical Reporter*, by Dr. De Forest Willard. Dr. Willard collected the data of many cliniques, and by re-arrangement was enabled to report one clinique on the various phases of one disease, operation, etc., making the cliniques more valuable than when published as delivered.

The number of papers on anatomy in its relations to surgery and medicine reached sixty by 1864, but, as has been stated before, at this date they stopped forever.

He delivered an address to the Philadelphia County Medical Society, January 5, 1875, when retiring from its presidency. He took as his subject, "The Results of a Series of Experimental Observations Connected with the Repair and Development of Bone-Tissue." This essay was afterward incorporated in his work on surgery. In this work he was assisted by Drs. Charles T. Hunter, Henry C. Chapman, and James Tyson.

In 1876 he was selected to deliver the "Address on Surgery" before the Pennsylvania State Medical Society. Later, when President of this body, he delivered an address on "Errors of Diagnosis."

During this period the great literary work of his life was begun, "The Principles and Practice of Surgery," which was issued in three volumes. The first volume of Dr. Agnew's "Surgery" was published in 1878, the second volume in 1881, and the third in 1883. The mere mechanical labor involved in writing this work was tremendous. There were over 1100 pages in the first and second volumes, and nearly 800 in the third, making a total of 3000 pages. As each page contains, on an average, 650 words, this makes a total of nearly 2,000,000 words for the entire work.

As Dr. Agnew wrote the entire book with his own pen, allowing that he could write ten words a minute, which was far faster than he worked, for he was constantly compelled to recall cases of his own, to consult other authorities, and do similar work, which makes the progress of such a work extremely slow, it would take 3333 hours of constant work to produce it. Allowing eight hours as a working day, this would keep him occupied steadily for 417 days. He was engaged many years upon the work, doing it at odd times, such as working late into the night and getting up early in the morning, working before his early breakfast. The tremendous resources of his vitality may be better estimated when it is realized that this work was done at the very time of life when he was busiest in practice, busiest at the University, and busiest in consultation work. The work on the second and third volumes came about the time of the Garfield case, which added to his already tremendous routine of work. The number of illustrations in the work are 2198, each one of them being selected for its appropriateness, and the majority of them being original to the work. In order to show the tremendous range of the subjects treated, it is interesting to note that the index of the three volumes occupy seventy-three pages.

The opportunities which gave Dr. Agnew the ability to write this work are unique in the history of surgery. It has truthfully been said that never again can such a work on the subject of surgery, with all its broad ramifications, be produced from one man's experience. Dr. Agnew began his surgical work before the introduction of anesthesia, and he was able to keep pace with the advancement of surgery in all directions. Such an opportunity did not exist before his time, and no surgeon now can keep in touch with the entire subject of surgery, for the field has grown too vast. In this ability to keep in touch with the entire field of surgical activity, Dr. Agnew stands in the same position to surgery that Dr. Leidy did to biology. No worker in either of these fields can ever hope to occupy their pre-eminent positions. "Agnew's Surgery" is the medical diary of his professional life for fifty-one years. In this work he has recorded his own views upon every surgical subject, giving the history of countless cases of his own, his experiences, and his conclusions upon every surgical procedure.

This makes the work invaluable to the surgeon, for it gives him an Agnew perpetually at his elbow. A busy practitioner opening its pages never fails to find clearly-drawn lines for diagnosis, useful directions for treatment, carefully-delineated deductions in regard to operation, and positive opinions as to the arguments for and against operations; for Dr. Agnew knew as well when not to operate as when to cut, a quality not possessed by all surgeons. While Dr. Agnew endeavored to express his own views independently on all subjects, as far as was consistent with the scope and limits of the work, he recorded the views of other writers, that different plans of treatment might be contrasted. A student finds in its pages, also, well-selected notes of medical history and the famous and curious surgical appliances of former days; but through the whole work runs the distinctive thread of Agnew's own personal experiences, from which his thoughtful and practical brain had gleaned so much. Although he never obtrudes himself into the work, yet his own individuality stands out most markedly. It is written in much the same manner as he lectured. He was instinctively a teacher; when he theorized, his thoughts at once carried him to some practical conclusion.

During the last few years of his life the spirit of extraordinary vitality which pervaded every department of medicine was most active in the domain of surgery. During these years Dr. Agnew was not an idle spectator, but he carefully watched all that occurred within the region of his special study, and, consequently, he felt that a revised edition of his book should be published, in which he could embody whatever new things, by observation and experience, appeared to him worthy of professional confidence. Early committed to the parasitic theory

of disease, and adopting methods of practice in harmony with its acceptance, every year but served to strengthen his faith in the value of the germicidal agents of aseptic and antiseptic surgery.   He realized that the medical statistician must begin anew to collect and formulate surgical data, in order to arrive at conclusions which would be trustworthy at present.   Consequently, in 1889 he revised his work and the second edition was published.   He was surprised, when he came to the actual work of revision, how little he had to change in his words written before the introduction of antiseptic surgery.

After his death the publishers of the work, The J. B. Lippincott Co., feeling that there was a necessity again for its revision, suggested that the work be done.   As the ownership of the work was left to the trustees of the University, they discussed this matter, but at the wishes of Mrs. Agnew, who felt that this monument to his life-work should stand as he had erected it, they decided, permanently, that it should go down to posterity as it had been written by Dr. Agnew, being the most complete and exhaustive description of one man's surgical experiences in the history of the world.

In 1888 Dr. Agnew's " Surgery " was translated into Japanese, and published in Tokio, Japan.   The fac-simile of the title-page of this work in Japanese is given on the opposite page ; according to Japanese customs, it is at the back of the book.   The translation of this page begins at the upper right-hand corner and reads downward, the Japanese words saying : " The American edition by Dr. D. Hayes Agnew.   Translator, the Japanese Doctor, Masahito Toyabe."   The larger marks in the central column are the title of the book,—" New Treatise on the Principles and Practice of Surgery."   The figure at the bottom of the page is a word used to signify the first volume of a set of two or three volumes, meaning, literally, " top," as Japanese books are piled one on top of another, instead of being placed side by side.   The left-hand column says : " The original was published in 1886, the translation was made in

1888 "; or, in the Japanese method of writing dates, in the twenty-first year of the reign of the Mikado.

On the second page of the book is a large stamp in red, which corresponds to the American copyright, being the sanction of the government for its publication.

The book begins with an old Japanese motto about the value of scraping bones, eliminating poisons, removing obstructions, and washing uncleanness. Then the translator gives his estimate of the value of the book and the necessity for its study by Japanese students. Professor Gross's " Surgery " and this edition are the two great standards on that branch in Japanese medicine. The price of the book in Japanese is $6, which represents in American money about the value of $4.50. This is not cheaper in comparison, for probably not more than one-tenth of the work has been translated.

Theories change, new doctrines become old, and most medical books, even the most successful, have a life-time which rarely exceeds in duration that of their authors; but it is safe to say that surgical writers in future ages will still turn to " Agnew's Surgery " as a rich store-house of clinical facts and personal observations, just as they do now to the writings of Paré and Chelius, and as pathologists do to the works of Morgagni or Rokitanski.

As a surgeon, Dr. Agnew was fearless, yet conservative; not shrinking from any operation, however hazardous, but never eager to operate, and always glad if he could see a way to cure the patient by bloodless methods. His honesty and candor in this matter of advising operations may be seen by his recorded judgment as to the so-called radical cure of hernia. It is well known that in his earlier days Dr. Agnew had himself devised an operation for this purpose,—one of the most ingenious of the many ingenious procedures suggested for the cure of this incurable affection,—and that this operation he had performed in a number of cases with excellent immediate results; had he been a surgeon less judicious in conservativeness, less severe in his conscientiousness, or more sanguine in his prognostic habits, he would, no doubt, have continued to resort to it to his own manifest pecuniary advantage, if not to his patients' permanent benefit; but experience convinced him that its ultimate results did not justify its dangers, and he not only abandoned it, but publicly declared that he made it no exception in professing his profound distrust of all operations of this character.

In no phase of his career did Dr. Agnew appear in a better or more favorable light than in his position as a consultant. As a consulting physician, undoubtedly, he stood as a model. He happily accomplished the ofttimes difficult task of being perfectly loyal to the doctor, while being also loyal to the interests of the patient,—for the consulting physician occupies a most delicate and perilous position for all concerned. This position is rarely realized by any one but the physician who has been tried in such a capacity.

Dr. Agnew's manner was perfection. While he examined the case thoroughly, quietly, and exhaustively himself, he showed at all times a proper deference for the feelings and opinions of the physician who called him in. He never attempted, at any time, to place the attending physician in any unfortunate or uncertain light. If he felt that an error of diagnosis or treatment had been made, he suggested a change to the attending physician in such an adroit and pleasant way that the physician himself frequently felt that it was his own suggestion.

Dr. Agnew's appearance was always such as to command respect. Nearly every one who saw him, and did not know him, asked, instinctively, "Who is that man?" He had the faculty of impressing every one at once with his ability and conscientiousness. Colonel Rockwell, the intimate friend and faithful nurse of President Garfield, said, "When I saw Dr. Agnew at the President's bedside, I felt instinctively that the President was in the hands of a man of power and ability; Dr. Agnew's personal appearance was just such as I imagined the ideal surgeon should be."

Dr. Agnew in his lectures used no notes; at least, never more than a scrap of paper with the heads of the various topics on which he intended to speak for the day. He lectured as a didactic professor three times a week,—on Tuesday, Thursday, and Friday. On Wednesday at 12 o'clock he held his surgical clinique at the University Hospital, where he displayed and diagnosed cases and operated. By long training he was able to lecture on the case and operate at the same time,—a difficult achievement to learn, for it requires the following of two distinct lines of thought.

As an operator, Dr. Agnew was skillful, rapid, and success-ful. His superiority as a surgeon could be seen in his operating, even by the merest tyro, unfamiliar with surgical work. Here he showed to what an extent a naturally adept and skillful operator can be developed by a long training and experience. He worked with the utmost rapidity, confidence, and grace at all times, and yet always without the semblance of haste. He never gave one the impression that he was hurrying, although he showed that he was keenly alert to everything; when he was in the midst of an operation he would not tolerate the slightest in-attention, stupidity, or awkwardness on the part of his assistants. It was only at such times that he was imperative and brusque in his manner; he felt that the safety of the patient demanded that everything be sacrificed for his or her case. When he picked up his knife, he had a line of action mapped out; with-out a flourish or a sweep, his knife sank with unerring quickness to the exact depth he intended, and as quickly was withdrawn. There was no undecided dissections, consultations, wonderings, and considerations in this work.

His tall and erect figure was always the first object which caught the eye of the incomer into these cliniques. It is im-possible to express his wonderful tranquility of mind and confi-dence while operating. It made the most difficult feats in sur-gery a pleasant task to witness, for he never imparted any sense of uneasiness to spectators or friends.

At all times he was thoroughly collected in his manner, in the midst of the most startling accidents or incidents. Under the most dangerous conditions he never lost his head, but quickly and quietly adopted the best method of action; for example, one writer states that he well remembers the sudden rupture of an axillary vein during the reduction of a dislocation of old standing at the shoulder-joint. The patient instantly collapsed, becoming lifeless in appearance. A quiet but quick movement of the hand on the part of Dr. Agnew placed his thumb upon the subclavian artery. The danger of death from an appalling hemorrhage was averted, and the patient's life was saved.

Again, in an operation for cancer of the breast, in which, through neglect, the disease had far advanced, the glands in the axilla being deeply involved, all at once there was terrific hemorrhage; Dr. Agnew quietly said, "I guess we had better clamp this," applying, as he spoke, a clamp over the seat of hemorrhage. Then he resumed the operation composedly; when it was finished, he said, "Let us see what caused this bleeding." It proved to be due to a rupture in the axillary vein, owing to invasion of the cancerous process into its vicinity. He applied a ligature to the vein and dressed the wound, not in the least disconcerted by the appearance of a startling accident which would have unnerved completely many surgeons. Such instances in his career could be quoted in great numbers.

The surgeon's dexterity, unfortunately, is like the work of an actor; for, while it delights and impresses the spectators, it is impossible to represent it adequately to posterity. Dr. Agnew's skillfulness was shown as much in little operations and in small matters as in greater ones; for example, the way in which he plunged a trocar and canula into a hydrocele, to draw off the fluid contained in it, would frequently create enthusiasm among his students. As this little operation is done without the use of anesthetics, it can be made quite painful if done unskillfully, but when it is well done it is only the first shock which is unpleasant. The lightning-like rapidity with which Dr. Agnew would perform this operation, and finish it before the patient was fairly conscious of what had happened,—although it is the custom of such a patient to watch the surgeon's hands most anxiously,—was most pleasant to witness.

His recognition of surgical conditions was remarkable, and the accuracy of his diagnosis was seldom questioned. He was the recognized counsel of last resort,—the chief-justice of the medical supreme court,—and, whatever difficulty of diagnosis arose, a decision by the "old gentleman," as he was affectionately called, was always decisive. Often in examining cases some physician would say, "*I think*" so and so. Dr. Agnew would invariably say, "*It is*" so and so. This was not from any egotism on his part or self-assertiveness, but simply the result of his training; his logical mind, stored with the knowledge of so many years' gathering, could grasp at once a case and pronounce upon it so quickly that frequently it seemed almost impossible that he could have given it proper consideration.

An incident which occurred in the course of the Garfield case typifies exactly his quickness of decision and action. The physicians in consultation upon the case were deciding where the lines of incision should be made to liberate the pus. Some said one place, some said another. Dr. Agnew was the only one silent. He stood, knife in hand, waiting their decisions, for he was to do the operating. The *coterie* of physicians turned to him and asked his opinion. Dr. Agnew said: "This is where I believe the incision should be made." As he said the words he made the incision.

There was one result of Dr. Agnew's long experience,—no matter how strange a case appeared, or how rare a thing was seen in medicine, he was able always, from his long list of cases, to compare it intelligently and comprehensively with similar cases of his own. This made him a most fortunate companion in the study of any rare, obscure, or interesting case.

He was an example of punctuality; when one had an engagement to meet him, it was always wiser to be ten minutes in advance of the appointment than two minutes late; yet he was never in a hurry. In driving with him through many years, no one ever heard him use a more vigorous expression to his driver than "we must push on."

Dr. Agnew, as has been said, was, in the true sense of the term, "ambidextrous,"—not, as is often the case with those who claim this quality, dividing a limited modicum of skill between two hands instead of concentrating it in one, so that they might with more justice be called "ambisinistrous," but he really used his left hand as if it were his right, taking the knife in either hand indifferently, and often himself unconscious which he was employing. In his early youth he had injured his right hand in such a way as to render it useless for all practical purposes, and this loss of the use of the right hand continued so long that he was confirmed thoroughly in the practical use of the left hand. Upon the restoration of his right hand to its proper condition its dexterity came back coupled with the equally free use of his left hand. The facility with which he used either hand should serve as a lesson to parents to instruct children in the free use of both hands. The crippling of the left hand is a relic of the Middle Ages, when the right hand held the sword and the left the shield, and, as a natural sequence, the right hand was the hand of good faith, while the left was the reverse. This is crystallized in the two words *dexterity* and *sinister*.

If there were a shade of preference shown by Dr. Agnew in the use of his hands, it was for his left. Possibly this was in order to preserve the balance of utility. He carried his watch on the right side of his waistcoat, this being the pocket which his left hand would naturally seek with his arm half-flexed. A person who gives preference to the right hand instinctively places it in the corresponding pocket on the opposite side. It has been claimed that this is not a fair test that Dr. Agnew preferred his left hand instinctively. It does not imply at all, however, that he used his left hand when ascertaining the time of day, for watches are made for right-handed people. In his use of the scissors, which is a movement very difficult to acquire, he was indifferent as to which hand he used; although, in the majority of cases, he preferred to use the left hand because his right hand might happen to be occupied at the time.

It is generally considered an excellent test, in a case of acquired ambidexterity, for determining which hand is given the preference, to observe which hand is used most frequently in writing. Writing with the left hand is an unnatural procedure, as the thumb and fingers that hold the pen hide the letters that have already been written, while with the right hand the writing trails away from the already written word, leaving the full line visible. Dr. Agnew almost invariably used his left hand in writing, and, strangely enough, wrote with the back of his pen.

Reade, in "The Coming Man," mentions the wonderful accuracy of the action of the left-hand fingers in the case of a violinist, whose whole skill depends not so much upon drawing the bow backward and forward with the right hand as it does upon that wonderful readiness of touch that enables him, automatically, to select the string and to place his finger, with such marvelous accuracy, upon the spot which will develop the delicacy and the gradations of tone that are required to make music what it is when developed by the touch of a virtuoso.

This point, raised by Reade, was seen in the case of Dr. Agnew, for in his younger days he developed great skill in the use of the violin, which he played in the ordinary manner with the bow in his right hand.

This fondness of Dr. Agnew for the use of his left hand was seen by the artist, Mr. Eakens, when he was painting Dr. Agnew's picture for the University. This painting represents Dr. Agnew at the completion of an operation, and Mr. Eakens, who had been attending his cliniques for several months to get his characteristic attitudes and methods of operating, recognized at once this peculiarity.

This slight preference of Dr. Agnew for his left hand does not, of course, detract in the least from his ambidexterity. He could do equally good work with either hand.

In all kinds of surgical work Dr. Agnew was equally happy. He was just as capable of the extremely delicate work of extracting a cataract as he was in the expenditure of force necessary for refracturing a bone. Skillful in all operations, he was especially so in procedures which required great delicacy of touch, such as the removal of thin-walled cysts, in which his long habit of anatomical dissection came particularly into play.

The following estimate of Dr. Agnew's services as a surgeon was written by a colleague and friend of thirty-five years' standing, and his successor in the professorial chair:—

"During the last twenty years of his life it is probable that Dr. Agnew saw more patients in his office and in consultation than have ever been seen by any other Philadelphia surgeon. When it is remembered that he was at the same time constantly engaged in teaching, lecturing regularly during the winter months four or five times every week, it will be seen that he could have accomplished this amount of work only by carefully allotting his time and by being blessed with an unusual degree of physical endurance, enabling him to disregard fatigue by which another man would have been completely exhausted. Indeed, it was for years Dr. Agnew's habit to take a train, after a full day's work, in order to see a distant patient in consultation, making his visit late at night or in the very early morning, returning in time to be at his office as usual the next day and to fulfill his lecture engagements at the University of Pennsylvania.

"Possibly the best way to form an estimate of the position which Dr. Agnew occupied in his profession is to consider what would have been the state of affairs had his personality not existed; who can say what American surgery would have been during the last twenty years without his participation? Whether advising as consulting surgeon at the bedside of a wounded and dying President, imparting the principles of his art to large classes of attentive and eager students from all parts of our broad country, or giving the benefit of his great skill to the humblest clinique, his share in the surgical history of his time was such a large one that it is hard to imagine what that surgical history would have been without it.

"Our fair city has had ere now, in her professional rank, great operators, such as Barton and Pancoast; great writers and teachers, such as Gibson and Gross; and great consultants, such as Physick and Norris, who, by their strong personalities, established the tradition of surgical practice in their day and generation; but as consultant, teacher, and operator combined, the name of Agnew will long be spoken of as that of the height and glory of Philadelphia surgeons."

CHAPTER VIII.

DR. AGNEW'S ORIGINAL WORK IN SURGERY.

IT has been stated that, while Dr. Agnew was a wonderful operator, clear teacher, and thorough diagnostician, he had no originality; that he devised no new instruments or operations, and that his name was not associated with any great original investigation in new surgical fields.

There is no more necessity of a surgeon inventing new instruments or new operations or pursuing original investigations to become a great surgeon than there is in a great lawyer devising new legal procedures, or, to compare it with an occupation which approaches surgery on its manual side, for a carpenter to devise new tools or new methods of carpentry.

It is the faithful, intelligent way in which he uses the knowledge of his day in the regular routine of his life which constitutes the really valuable work in a surgeon. It is the fidelity with which the daily grinding application to work is undertaken—on which it is impossible to dilate—that forms the real basis of comparison of surgeons. It was here that Dr. Agnew stood pre-eminent; yet in a biography of his career this work can only be suggested. There is no way to show its extent without wearying the reader. The description of the invention of some trifling instrument or operation takes more room than any description of many years' work of this character in a surgeon's life.

There is more or less of a delusion in the claim of any originality in surgical work, for it is a gradual growth, to which every observer adds his quota. A surgeon may develop great pettiness of mind and spirit in devising methods or instruments just a little different from those in use already and claiming them as inventions of his own.

Dr. Agnew disdained such work; although he had that

(173)

adaptability of making anything suit his purpose. For example : After showing complicated or expensive instruments for certain purposes, at his lectures, he would invariably say : " But, gentlemen, you do not need these things," and he would proceed to improvise, out of simpler, cheaper instruments, the necessary articles.

On the other hand, it is the purpose of this chapter to show to some extent the variety of instruments and operations devised by Dr. Agnew, and some reports of the original investigations which he made. It must not be understood that this list comprises the entire number of operations or instruments which Dr. Agnew devised ; it is simply a sample of this work on his part. All those who are interested in this feature of his work sufficiently to pursue it further are referred to his treatise on surgery. The description of his own work in his "Surgery" is not complete. His well-known modesty impelled him instinctively to place himself in the background, and he does not claim, by any means, all that is his due.

Again, Dr. Agnew never blindly followed directions in any operation nor in the manufacture of instruments. Dr. Agnew probably never did two operations exactly alike; he modified every operation in each case to its own wants and needs. He always seemed to possess a great reserve fund of commonsense which fitted into the case before him exactly. He treated each case simply on its own demands, not on the lines laid down in text-books.

Among the instruments devised by Dr. Agnew was his well-known anterior angular splint with the posterior angular trough. Dr. Agnew devised this simple instrument for supracondyloid and condyloid fractures at the elbow- joint,—difficult conditions to treat properly.

To prevent bleeding in case of wounds of the chest from rupture of the intercostal vessels, Dr. Agnew devised a needle, strong, sharply-curved, with a blunt point, having in it an eye for the thread. This formed a very efficient instrument for putting a ligature around the rib and vessel. He also invented another ingenious instrument for compressing the wounded intercostal vessels. This instrument consisted of two branches,—a permanent one, having a little mortice on its concave surface, into the middle of which is fitted a short piece of sea-tangle; the other branch of the instrument is movable, and can be run up and down on the shanks by turning a handle. The object of the little piece of sea-tangle set into the groove on the inner branch of the instrument is, that by its swelling it may compress the vessel which lies below the common level of the rib in the costal groove.

Dr. Agnew also devised an artery-forceps, the blades of which are long and slender and armed each with a tooth, which can be made fast by a button-slide.

For the treatment of extra-capsular fractures of the humerus, Dr. Agnew devised an internal angular splint, and a cap for the shoulder and arm. By using his method the axillary wedge-shaped pad of Sir Astley Cooper is discarded.

Dr. Agnew also contrived a rectal chemise for use in dilatation of the internal and external sphincters, in operating for hemorrhoids. This rectal chemise is to be used when the surface removed is too extensive to be stopped from bleeding by the ordinary methods. This instrument, like others devised by Dr. Agnew, was extremely simple, consisting simply of the largest-sized gum catheter, through the openings at the end of which is passed a stout silk thread. Then three square pieces of ordinary mosquito-netting are taken and placed one on top of the other; at the centre of these squares or pieces an opening is made and the catheter passed through, and the two are fastened together by threads.

Dr. Agnew invented, for use in fracture of the patella or knee-cap, a simple, ingenious, and efficient splint, which takes the place of more elaborate instruments. It is the most common splint for this condition in use at present.

For the removal of the curious deformity of webbed fingers,

Dr. Agnew originated an operation which removes satisfactorily and permanently this condition. The trouble in this deformity has been to prevent its recurrence; by ingeniously dissecting flaps and stitching them together Dr. Agnew obviated this difficulty entirely.

Dr. Agnew devised a retractor for holding aside the sac of the peritoneum during operation upon the iliac arteries. This instrument was a great convenience in ligation of the external iliac artery. Dr. Agnew also devised a spiral wire probe for use when the sinuses passing down to diseased bone were tortuous; from its flexibility such a probe could follow the winding track.

Dr. Agnew also invented a thoracic trocar and canula for use in the operation of thoracentesis. This instrument consisted of a trocar and canula with a stop-cock and a gum bag or bottle, having a nozzle at one extremity fitted to the end of the canula and at the other a stop-cock by which it can be conveniently emptied and filled. By use of this instrument the fluid can be drawn out by suction, requiring no air-pump. In the absence of the rubber bag a bullock's or hog's bladder may be employed as a substitute. In this Dr. Agnew shows his adaptation of the ordinary implements and instruments found in the average country household to surgical use.

Dr. Agnew originated an operation for the treatment of salivary fistula. This annoying, disfiguring, and obstinate disease resisted all operations until Dr. Agnew devised an operation which was simplicity itself. It consisted in depositing a thread between the duct and the outside of the cheek with its two ends brought out at the corner of the mouth. As the threads cut their way out by ulceration the duct is detached from the external opening in the cheek.

Dr. Agnew also devised an operation for the radical cure of hernia, which he subsequently discarded.

Dr. Agnew also modified the method of reduction by manipulation of dislocations of the arm at the shoulder-joint. Dr. Agnew devised an apparatus for hip-joint disease which he advises for use under certain circumstances. When, on account of parental obstinacy, the surgeon is sometimes compelled to compromise by adopting a splint instead of following other treatment, such as rest in bed, Dr. Agnew advised the use of this splint.

Dr. Agnew also modified a number of amputations; for example, he modified the flap method (or the musculo-tegumentary method), in which, by an ingenious cutting of the flap, he was enabled to make the skin and muscles of the same length, avoiding the deformity which results from the retraction of the skin, which exists to a much greater degree than that of the muscles.

Dr. Agnew also devised a method for reducing paraphimosis, by which the methods in common practice were rendered unnecessary. It is a much more rational plan. Dr. Agnew also devised a blood-catheter, which serves the purpose very well.

Dr. Agnew also devised a stone-forceps for use in lithotomy in children. Dr. Agnew also contrived a pair of long, rat-toothed forceps for use in the operation of vesico-vaginal fistula. In gynecology Dr. Agnew also devised a mackerel-bill écraseur for use in dividing uterine polypi. Dr. Agnew also devised whalebone bougies of certain shapes and sizes.

In regard to the statement that Dr. Agnew possessed no specially original thoughts in surgery, because his name is not associated with many wonderful advances, this was due partly to the fact that Dr. Agnew held human life too dear to experiment on it, as must be done in all original work, and partly to the fact that he was so busily engaged that he did not have time for the research for which he was so eminently fitted. At the same time, no small amount of original investigation was done by him.

In strictly surgical and pathological work stand his experiments made to establish the fact of the transformation of the coagulum, clot, or thrombus into an organized structure, and

its unification with the walls of the vessel,—in other words, to
determine the method by which nature arrests hemorrhage. In
order to study this process satisfactorily he had a number of
· ligations made of the arteries of dogs, by Dr. William H.
Mastin, at the University Hospital. The animals were killed
at different periods and carefully injected, after which he had an
opportunity of studying each specimen as it was prepared by
Dr. E. O. Shakespeare.

Dr. Agnew's practical conclusions are quoted from the work
on surgery, vol. i, page 216, as follows:—

" When a ligature is placed about an artery and firmly tied,
the vessel is constricted and puckered up at the point of application. The effect of such constriction is to divide the middle
and internal coats, which become both incurved and retracted,
the external or fibrous coat remaining unsevered. The blood
thus arrested begins to coagulate first at the seat of ligation,
where it occupies the entire circumference of the canal of the
vessel. To this coagulum or thrombus are added successive
layers or laminæ, and as the column rises it becomes conical in
form, reaching up to the first collateral branch, and either not
touching the walls of the vessel or resting only against one of
its sides. The direction of these successive additions or laminæ
in the thrombus is transverse or slightly oblique.

" If a portion of this internal thrombus be examined at any
time after its coagulation, with a sufficient power, it will be seen
to consist of a vast crowd of red corpuscles, with here and there,
indiscriminately scattered, a few white ones, and all supported
in the fibrinous frame-work of the clot.

" Pressing the investigation further, let a section of the
artery and its clot be made twenty-four hours after ligature, and
a wonderful change will be noticed in the numerical relation of
the two kinds of corpuscles. Even in this short period of time
the red, which had predominated so greatly, have begun to disappear, and the white corpuscles are now seen thickly scattered

Dr. Agnew in 1876.

over the field.   If successive sections of this clot be made from
the base towards the summit, it will be seen that the white corpuscles diminish in numbers from below upwards; that is, they
are most numerous in the oldest part of the clot.   The secure
manner in which the clot or thrombus is first mechanically connected with the enclosing walls of the vessel is here worthy of
observation.   This connection is threefold: first, by being
crowded into the corrugations made by the puckering of the
vessel at the point of ligature; second, by moulding its surface
into the plications of the tunica intima, or internal coat; and
last, by the peculiar behavior of this coat, which, after being
severed by the ligature, splits into filaments or threads, which
float into the midst of the coagulating blood, and, like guys,
serve to moor the clot securely into place.   The questions
which, at this stage of the process, demand explanation, are
very difficult of solution.   We are not yet in a position to
answer them with any certainty, and any attempt in that direction brings us at once into the domain of conjecture.   These
questions are: Where do these crowds of white corpuscles
come from? and, What is the destiny of the red globules?

"With reference to the first, the origin of the white bodies,
several explanations may be advanced.   They may originate by
proliferation from the few which naturally belong to the thrombus, as no limit can be fixed to the rapidity of cell multiplication under certain stimulation; they may be emigrants wandering
into the clot from the vasa vasorum, according to the views of
Recklinghausen and Bubnoff; they may be derived from the
stable cells of the tunica intima, which accords with the opinions
of Romberg and Thiersch; and last, and least probable, they
may be but a retrograde metamorphosis of the red corpuscles,
on the supposition that the red are developed from the white
corpuscles.   I cannot, however, help believing that these cells
are derived from three sources: first, from the proliferating
white corpuscles of the clot; second, from the fixed corpuscles
of the endothelium; and last, from the emigrants from the vasa

vasorum. It is quite as probable that the endothelial cells should participate in the work of repair; in other words, change from a passive to an active state, as that those of connective tissue should do so under the disturbing influence of inflammation. Those experiments which show the presence of cells in new formations bearing granules of cinnabar previously injected into the blood would seem to establish a claim for emigration.

"This last view is not in accord with that of Billroth, who denies to the stable cells of the intima any participation in the work whatever, attributing multiplication of white corpuscles to the leucocytes of the clot and to wanderers from the neighboring vessel, coinciding in this respect with the statements of Recklinghausen and Bubnoff. As to the red corpuscles, they very soon become decolorized by the separation of crystals of hæmatoidin, and, it is supposed by some, form an intercellular substance by uniting with the fibrin of the thrombus. If the thrombus be examined on the fifth day, another notable change will be seen. Many of the cells have become spindle-shaped, one step in the direction of forming connective tissue; others have sent out prolongations, which, joining with similar processes from contiguous cells, form together a net-work with very distinct nuclei at the points of contact or communication. In this system of inosculating processes we have the provision for the vascularization of the thrombus. These processes become blood-channels, and, although as yet containing no blood, they are, like the irrigating canals which are cut in various directions through some arid waste, designed to receive the streams which are to give life and fruitage.

"While these changes are in operation within the thrombus the walls of the vessel are by no means passive. An active inflammatory transudation is going on, infiltrating its tunics and extending even into the loose cellular tissue of the adventitious coats. It is this which rives asunder the fibres, lamellæ, and fasciculi of the arterial tunics, and admits of their being interpenetrated by cell organisms or leucocytes, which wander out of the nutrient vessel, and which, like those of the clot within, assume the spindle forms, which are the promise of the future connective tissue. In the course of eight days the work foreshadowed in the thrombus of five days is well advanced. Many of the blood-channels are completed and others are in process of completion, the processes of the latter connecting with the nuclei on the walls of the former; the spindle form of the cells, both of the clot and walls, is more pronounced, and near to the intima they have reached the stage of immature connective tissue. The clot is beginning to shrink from loss of moisture in the intercellular substance, the whole becoming more compact.

"In all these changes or stages of transformation it would appear that the constructive force develops out of the materials of the original clot an organized tissue,—that is to say, the white cells of the thrombus retain their vitality and undergo multiplication, passing on to the spindle form; that the fibrin which determines the coagulation is not substituted by something else, but transformed into intercellular material, the fibrillation of which, with the spindle cells, constitutes true connective tissue; and, finally, that from other cells a system of inosculating canals is constructed, thus forming a vascularized structure. Thus far we have traced the leading changes in the clot toward organization.

"We have seen the infiltration of the tunics of the vessel with cell forms similar to those in the coagulum, and their intermingling at the tunica intima, obliterating in some degree their distinction from the latter. It still remains to establish a very important vital connection between the two, and that is the connection or inosculation of blood-vessels. The thrombus is in possession of a system of capillaries, but they contain no blood; and the next step is to form such a union with the vessel of the artery as will establish not only a unity of blood-channels, but also a oneness of circulation. To accomplish this it would appear, from certain preparations recently made by Dr. Shakespeare illustrative of this point, and which I had the opportunity of examining, that in this inosculation between the

vessels of the thrombus and those of the walls the former take
the initiative, penetrating the tunica intima, first, near to the
point where the artery has sustained the greatest injury by the
action of the ligature."

Dr. Agnew also performed a number of experiments to determine the process by which callus is converted into true bone.
It is a fair sample of the style of investigation he pursued:—

" The development of the organizable material of the callus
into true bone will be best illustrated by introducing, at this
point, the results of a number of experiments which I made
upon the bones of chickens, dogs, and guinea-pigs. For this
purpose numerous fractures were produced, and dissections, followed by microscopic examinations, made at various periods from
an hour and a half after the injury until the twenty-fifth day.

" These fractures were all simple. It has been stated that
after such an injury the blood finds its way into the medullary
canal between the fragments, adheres to the edges of the periosteum when torn, and permeates the muscular and the connective tissue next to the bone. This describes most accurately
the appearance presented in the first dissection I made one hour
and three-quarters after the injury. A second dissection was
made three days later. After removing the skin and fascia, the
seat of damage was recognized by a swelling over the break, of
a peculiar, spindle-shaped form. Even the tendons were curiously spread out into a ribbon-like expansion, and quite adherent
to the parts underneath. On the fifth day this enlargement is
probably at its height, and at this time a specimen was divided
longitudinally, for the purpose of study. The periosteum was
separated for over half an inch above and below the seat of
fracture. At the latter point the separation was greatest, becoming less above and below; hence the spindle form of the
enlargement. To the unaided vision the same material which
lay beneath the membrane was also external to it, so that the

periosteum was in reality embedded in or incorporated with it. It was also seen between the ends of the bone when not displaced, or between the contiguous surfaces when overlapping, and, finally, for some distance up and down the medullary canal. This preliminary formation was a light-colored, consistent substance, interspersed with dark-red spots, and gave to the fracture a considerable degree of fixation.

" This specimen was placed, for microscopic preparation, in charge of Dr. Rhoads, who furnished me with an opportunity to study each section, in order that the appearances might be more vividly impressed upon my mind. The material in contact with the fracture was found to consist of blood-corpuscles in various stages of disintegration, some adhering in rolls and preserving, in some degree, their form, some isolated, others collapsed, with irregular or stellated margins, homogeneous lymph, and great numbers of the so-called germinal corpuscles, or, in the light of more recent discovery, leucocytes. These components were irregularly intermixed, and here and there stained with what seemed to be the coloring matter of broken-down blood-corpuscles. The leucocytes varied much in form ; some were round, others oval. They varied also in size, as though under the active process of change.

" In the compact portion of the bone a noticeable contrast existed between the Haversian canals near the fractured ends and those more remote. The size of the former was much greater, and they presented at numerous points little recesses or loculi leading off from their sides. The blood-vessels could be distinctly seen, but they were pushed off from the sides of their bony canals, the intermediate space being occupied by crowds of cells in all respects like those exterior to the bone, and which came, no doubt, from the Haversian vessels. Now, as the Haversian canals open into the medullary space, and also upon the broken surfaces of the bone, the conclusion was inevitable that many of the cell-bodies seen in the medullary canal came from these sources, as well as from the vessels of the medullary membrane. In this rapid enlargement of the hard bony canals traversed by the blood-vessels we have an example of one of those singular changes which attend inflammation, and which it is difficult to explain. That it is due to absorption from the pressure exerted by the exudation is exceedingly improbable, as such pressure would destroy the contained vessels rather than affect the bony walls with which they are surrounded.

"In studying the inflammatory process in other tissues, an analogous phenomenon may be witnessed. In cartilage, for example, the normal corpuscles which lie embedded in the intermediate substance have their places occupied by a multitude of leucocytes, more changeable and active than those which they have replaced, and whose insatiate demand for pabulum compels them to prey upon the matrix, the consumption of which gives the structure an open, reticulated, or honeycombed appearance. It is quite probable, therefore, that the organic constituents of bone may be attacked by the migrated cells of its vessels, and, thus separated from the bone-salts, give rise to the enlarged canals and their irregularities. The phenomena presented in this first specimen appear, then, to have been those of an inflammatory character, in which all parts of the bone at and contiguous to the fracture were engaged. The periosteum incorporated with the reconstructive material in seven or eight days entirely disappeared as such, undergoing those changes which inflammation produces in ordinary connective tissue, while a new membrane was produced external to the spindle-shaped mass of new matter and continuous with the old periosteum at the limits of the separation.

"A second specimen, nine days old, was subjected to a similar examination. In this fracture the periosteum had not been entirely broken, and consequently there was no displacement of the fragments. It was divided longitudinally. The periosteum was not torn from the bone, but was separated by the exudation for about one inch above and below, in the same fusiform or spindle-like manner as in the specimen first studied, only to a greater degree. The reconstructive material lay between the bone and the periosteum, external to the latter, between the ends of the fracture in small amount, and within the medullary canal. This does not accord with Mr. Stanley's statement, who alleges that when thus apposed, and without disturbance, no provisional callus is supplied by nature, but that immediate union takes place,—an opinion in which, I believe, Mr. Paget concurs. The stage of organization was not alike in all portions of the new material. The development was evidently advancing from without inwards. The greater part of this new formation consisted of round, oval, and elongated masses of germinal matter, surrounded by a faintly granular and fibrillated intercellular or formed material.

"These cells were grouped irregularly, or arranged in an orderly manner in concentric ranks, corresponding to the canals seen a little later and foreshadowing the laminæ of the Haversian systems. The cells which lay between the ends of the bone and in the medullary canal were more numerous and less distinctly altered from the globular form, and were greatly in excess of the intercellular or formed material; this latter was still mingled with a little broken-down blood. In the angles between the periosteum and the bone, and in an oval space near the centre of the external or ensheathing matter, the transformation into soft bone had taken place by the deposit of bone-salts. In these situations the Haversian canals were large and numerous, running, some diagonally, others perpendicularly, between the periosteum and the old bone. Simultaneous with the calcareous conversion of the intercellular material were the formation of the canaliculi and the shaping of the previously-arranged cells into distinct lacunæ.

"In the spindle-shaped envelope or ferrule we have the ensheathing callus of Dupuytren, or what he termed 'provisional callus,' while the portion occupying the canal answers to the pin. These, according to this distinguished surgeon, were only temporary in their duration,—splints, in other words, to maintain a degree of connection until a secondary deposit took place between the ends of the bone, after which the former were removed, being no longer of use.

"Other specimens were examined on the thirteenth and seventeenth days. These exhibited a more advanced stage of ossification, though in some places many cells were seen which were not cartilage cells. Between the broken ends the intercellular substance had increased, and some progress had been made in its conversion into bone, permitting much less movement at the break. At other portions of the callus canaliculi were forming in the intercellular material, and which evidently commenced on that part of the callus most remote from the lacunæ. The entire mass of new bone was a trifle more open and spongy in its texture and of a slight rosy tint. Anxious to determine the vascularity of the reconstructing substance, on the fifth day after making a fracture of the wing of a chicken a delicate pipe was inserted into the brachial artery, through which I injected some ultramarine suspended in glycerin. A section was made of the bone and submitted to Dr. Rhoads for examination. Although the injection was not so satisfactorily done as I could have wished, yet the coloring matter had filled numerous vessels throughout the callus. These vessels in the external callus ran for the most part perpendicularly down, the callus ossifying around them.

"Two additional specimens, one twenty-one and the other twenty-three days old, were carefully studied. The appearances presented were entirely in harmony with the previous specimens. The entire reconstructing material had been converted into bone, so that scarcely a trace of cartilage could be seen. The amount of exterior callus had diminished and become more compact, and that between the ends of the bone, though much less perfectly transformed into osseous tissue by the deposit of the bone-salts in the intercellular substance than other portions, had nevertheless made material progress.

"Mœscher and Votsch state that ossification in birds is

always in cartilage ; Wagner states virtually the same in the case of rabbits, and in all the cases which furnished the subjects of the present experiments the same fact was observed.   It is asserted that in man the repair or ossification may take place either in cartilage or in fibrous or fibro-cartilaginous tissue.

"This statement needs confirmation.   At the time I was engaged in these experiments a patient was admitted into the Pennsylvania Hospital who had broken his femur in the lower third in the act of pulling off his boot.   Six weeks later the man died, and I had the opportunity of examining the bone.   Though the fractured limb had been kept perfectly quiet, the appearance presented was identical with that of the bones which I had under experiment.   There was the same spindle-shaped swelling on the exterior of the bone, extending for two inches above and below the fracture, and most of which had been converted into bone, while in that portion between the ends, and where the process was less advanced, lay cartilage-cells in a vitreous-like matrix, but not a trace of connective or fibrous tissue.

"Of course, it would be unsafe to speak dogmatically from a single example, but it is sufficient to excite a doubt as to union save through cartilage tissue.   It is certainly true that the amount of peripheral callus is greatly influenced both by the relation of the fragments to each other and by the degree of disturbance to which they are subjected, becoming exuberant when there is overlapping, and especially so when the ends are not sufficiently immobilized; but I think that any one who will study the fracture specimens in our museums will be convinced that in all long bones, whatever may be the age of the specimen, there is manifest evidence of an ensheathing callus, increasing somewhat the volume of the bone at the seat of injury.   The conclusions which I think are rendered probable by these and other observations are the following :—

"*First.* That there is no evidence founded on structure that the process of healing in the fractures of man may not be studied by experiments on the lower animals, or that the repair in the latter materially differs from that in the former.

"*Second.* That the reparative act is the result of inflammatory process.

"*Third.* That the reparative material is furnished by the vessels of the periosteum, endosteum, and bone, and, to some extent, by those of the adjacent soft parts.

"*Fourth.* That the uniting material is deposited external to the bone, constituting an ensheathing callus; also in the medullary canal when there is no displacement, and between the ends of the bones; that the conversion of this preliminary substance into bone proceeds from the surface towards the centre, so that the exterior is hard long before the interior, which will account for the movement discoverable in specimens apparently solidly united together.

"*Fifth.* That the union of bone is through cartilage, and even through cells which have not reached the typical form of cartilage, and in this respect does not materially differ from the process observed in the primary development of bone.

"*Sixth.* That the presence of the ensheathing and medullary callus, thought to be exceptional in man, should be considered the rule.

"*Seventh.* That the terms temporary and provisional callus, as used by Dupuytren in contradistinction to the definitive, must be accepted with considerable limitation, the one not differing in any particular of composition from the other; that the delay in the production and bony transformation of the intermediate or definitive callus, as compared with the exterior and interior portions, is due only to the comparatively small vascularity of the compact part of the bone.

"*Eighth.* That the complete absorption of the ensheathing callus never occurs, and that the re-absorption of the medullary callus is not a work of nature set in operation because the union at the ends of the bone has become complete, but is simply a repetition of the order followed in the development of the long bones, entirely independent of the fracture,—a work which contributes both to their lightness and to their mechanical strength.

"The time involved in the whole work of restoration varies, no doubt, in different persons, and is affected by various circumstances, such as the health of the patient, the quiet of the parts, and the accuracy of the adjustment. The process in its entirety may be described as follows:—

" First, there is a period of rest,—one in which there is no visible attempt made to repair the damage. All seems quiet. Everything within the area of injury remains in chaotic confusion ; and as an architect, before he begins the work of reconstruction, quietly surveys the mass of ruins of some noble building which has gone down under a sudden catastrophe, so the genetic forces of the parts seem to brood silently, for a time, over the scene of disorder before any note of preparation is sounded. This is of short duration, not generally extending beyond thirty-six hours. Following this comes a reactionary period, in which the ordinary phenomena of inflammation are present. There is an increased determination of blood to the part, accompanied by a transudation. This is sometimes very considerable, giving rise to much swelling and an exalted sensibility of the parts, and may continue for three or four days; so that the first five or six days are consumed in passing over the stages of local shock and inflammatory disturbance. It cannot be said that during this time any true reconstructive work has been inaugurated.

"In this respect the repair of fractures in lower animals, as chickens, rabbits, etc., differs from that in man. In the former the process of union is well established in seven or eight days. The acute symptoms having subsided, another period of three or four days elapses, during which a part of the inflammatory products and a portion of the extravasated blood and other *débris* consequent upon the injury are removed, and the tenderness and swelling, as well as the irritability of the surrounding muscles, become diminished. The vascularity, however, of the bone, periosteum, and endosteum does not diminish, but rather increases. From the eighth to the tenth day the real work of repair begins, that in which the true fibrogenous matter, swarming with cellular elements, assumes the appearance of order.

" The differentiation of this constructive material into cartilage or fibro-cartilage and intercellular substance, and the subsequent deposition of the bone-salts, ultimately permeating the mass and imparting solidity to the bone, are the work of four or five weeks.

" Now, while we have divided this process into stages, allotting to each an approximate number of days or of weeks, it must not be supposed that these gradations are sharply defined, and that one cannot begin until the other is ended; on the contrary, they may blend or co-exist, and can only be regarded as approximately true; but they are, nevertheless, convenient for purposes of description.

" In children, union will often occur with great rapidity; and I have even known an adult with a fracture of the femur to rise from his bed and walk at the expiration of four weeks; indeed, I am convinced that the healing of fractures takes place at an earlier period than is generally believed.

" Such is the ordinary mode of repair. It is alleged by some that where the apposition is very perfect, as where the fragments rest end to end or edge to edge, or where there is an incomplete separation of the fibres of the bone, immediate union may take place, just as it is alleged to occur under favorable circumstances in the soft parts. I have never seen any specimen which would induce me to adopt such a conclusion.

" In compound fractures the existence of an external wound and the suppuration which ensues modify the plan of restoration. The work is greatly delayed, and the union is effected through a larger amount of granulation than in simple fractures, which, after its transformation into fibro-cartilaginous tissues, becomes incorporated with the lime deposits. In other words, the difference between the healing of simple and that of compound fractures is much like that between the healing of subcutaneous and that of open wounds.

"In compound comminuted fractures the healing is still longer delayed.   Detached portions of the bone die from losing their connection with the periosteum and the medullary tissue, and from the influence of the inflammatory products.   The work of reparation is delayed until the sequestra are got rid of, after which granulations spring up abundantly from the medullary and periosteal tissues and undergo ossification.   The time required for the separation of such necrosed portions may be so great that the restorative powers entirely fail, and no union will take place; or, if united, the connection is established in a large sheath of irregular callus, without any cohesion of the ends of the fragments to each other.   It is in such fractures that we often find the hard and the soft parts extensively glued together by inflammatory lymph.   Where there is loss of bone, in most cases there will be shortening, particularly in the adult; although, as shown by M. Ollier, the preservation of the periosteum will often provide, to some extent, against this, by supplying the material for partially bridging the gap.

"When a cartilage is broken, the perichondrium behaves like the periosteum, furnishing the material for a bond of union, which consists not of cartilage, but of bone, and which envelops the parts like a firm ring, but often not filling the intermediate space, or that between the ends of the fragments. An epiphysis, when detached from its diaphysis, although the original conjunction was one of cartilage, will afterwards unite by bone; and as the bones grow in length by a deposit in the cartilage which exists between the ends of the shaft and the epiphyses, it has been stated that in such fractures the bone ceases to grow in the longitudinal direction.   I have reason to doubt the correctness of this statement, believing that, although no increase in length may take place at the injured part, the failure is compensated for by increased activity in the nutrition of the intermediate cartilage at the other extremity.   Fractures which extend through the articular incrusting cartilage seem to have no power to unite. There are other fractures which do not unite by callus. They are such as are subjected to the influence of the synovial fluid, or whose vascular supply is insufficient. Among these are fractures of the neck of the femur within the capsular ligament, of the head of the humerus, of the olecranon process of the ulna, and of the acromion process of the scapula. Fractures of the patella generally come under the same category."

CHAPTER IX.

DR. AGNEW AS A WRITER.

As has been said, Dr. Agnew was not a prolific writer; his articles were numerous, but not in comparison to the lists of many of his colleagues and the length of his life; they were always in response to some well-defined demand.

The following is the list of the books and articles published by Dr. Agnew. The majority of these are reports of his clinical lectures written not by himself, but by medical reporters :—

*The List of the Books, Articles, and Addresses Published by
Dr. Agnew.*

1856. Practical Anatomy; a New Arrangement of the London Dissector. 2d edition, 1867.
Valedictory Address, Philadelphia School of Anatomy.
1857. Valedictory Address, Philadelphia School of Anatomy.
Theatrical Amusements.
1858. Valedictory Address, Philadelphia School of Anatomy.
1859. Introductory Address, Philadelphia School of Anatomy.
Valedictory Address, Philadelphia School of Anatomy.
Obituary Notice on Frederick S. Geiger, M.D.
1859–64. Sixty articles: "Anatomy in its Relations to Medicine and Surgery." *Medical and Surgical Reporter.*
1859–71. Clinical Reports. *Medical and Surgical Reporter.*
1860. Valedictory Address, Philadelphia School of Anatomy.
Introductory Address, "Classification of the Animal Kingdom."
1861. Address, "Baron Larrey."
1862. History of the Philadelphia Almshouse Hospital. Reprinted in Philadelphia Hospital Reports, 1890, vol. i, p. 1.
1865. Lacerations of the Female Perineum.
1867. Vesico-Vaginal Fistula.
1870. Introductory Lecture, University of Pennsylvania.
1875. President's Address, Philadelphia County Medical Society.
1876. "Address on Surgery," Pennsylvania State Medical Society.
1877. "Hydrocele." G. P. Putnam & Sons.

13

(193)

1878. "Attitude and Expression in the Diagnosis of Surgical Diseases." *New York Medical Record*, vol. xiv, pp. 424–26.

"Errors of Diagnosis." President's Address, Pennsylvania State Medical Society.

Principles and Practice of Surgery, vol. i, 2d edition, 1889.

1879. "Popliteal Aneurism." *Hospital Gazette*, vol. vi, p. 387.

Biographical sketch of Dr. John Rhea Barton. Delivered at the Academy of Music, at the annual Commencement of the Medical Department.

"Pistol-Shot Wound of the Hand." *Hospital Gazette*, vol. vi, p. 369.

"Nævus." *Cincinnati Lancet-Clinic*, n. s., vol. iii, p. 434.

1880. "Anchylosis of the Elbow-Joint Following Dislocation, in a Medico-Legal Aspect." *Boston Medical and Surgical Journal*, vol. ciii, p. 33.

1881. "General Principles of Surgical Diagnosis." International Encyclopædia of Surgery, vol. i, p. 337.

"Treatment of Vesical Catarrh by Establishing Urinary Fistulæ." *Philadelphia Medical Times*, vol. xi, p. 300.

"Traumatic Tetanus." *Medical and Surgical Reporter*, Philadelphia, vol. xliv, p. 654.

' Popliteal Aneurism; Cure by Ligation." *Medical and Surgical Reporter*, Philadelphia, vol. xlv, p. 151–2.

"Clinical Remarks on Lithotomy in Children and its Complications." *New York Medical Record*, vol. xx, p. 681.

Principles and Practice of Surgery, vol. ii.

1882. Lacerations of the Female Perineum and Vesico-Vaginal Fistula.

"Abstract of a Clinical Lecture on the Recognition of the Early Stages of Pott's Disease." *Medical News*, vol. xl, p. 4.

"Clinical Lecture on Stone in the Bladder." *Virginia Medical Monthly*, Richmond, vol. ix, p. 12.

"A Case of Chronic Cystitis." *Medical Record*, vol. xxii, p. 92.

"Ununited Fracture of the Neck of the Femur." *Medical and Surgical Reporter*, Philadelphia, vol. xlvii, p. 65.

"Abscess of the Pharynx." *Medical and Surgical Reporter*, Philadelphia, vol. xlvii, p. 65.

"Vesical Calculus; Removal by Lateral Lithotomy." *Philadelphia Medical Times*, vol. xiii, p. 539.

1883. "Traumatic Urinary Fistula; External Perineal Urethrotomy." *Philadelphia Medical Times*, vol. xiii, p. 721.

"Necrosis of the Tibia." *Philadelphia Medical Times*, vol. xiii, p. 791.

1883. "Osteotomy upon the Left Superior Maxilla for the Removal of Post-nasal Fibrous Polypus." *Medical News*, vol. xliii, p. 141.

Principles and Practice of Surgery, vol. iii.

1885. "Note on the Use of Salvia Officinalis in Catarrhal Rhinitis." *Therapeutic Gazette*, 3, s. 1, p. 17.

Memoir of Elias R. Beadle, D.D.

Valedictory Address, Commencement of Medical Department.

1886. "Painful Muscular Spasm Treated by Excision of Portion of the Nerve-Trunk." *Medical Times*, vol. xvi, p. 279.

"Memoir of John Light Atlee." *Transactions of the College of Physicians.*

1887. "Nephrorrhaphy and Nephrectomy." *Medical News*, vol. l, p. 116.

"Excision of the Larynx and Pharynx." *Medical News*, vol. l. p. 401.

"Medico-Legal Aspect of Cranial and Heart Wounds." *Transactions of the American Surgical Association;* also, *Medical News*, vol. l, p. 561.

"Nephro-lithotomy." *Medical News*, vol. l, p. 682.

"A Death During and a Death Before the Administration of Ether." *Medical News*, vol. li, p. 589.

1888. "Nephro-lithotomy." *Medical News*, vol. lii, p. 115.

"The Relation of Social Life to Surgical Disease." *Transactions of the American Surgical Association; Medical News*, Philadelphia, vol. liii, p. 316.

"Laparotomy with Excision of a Portion of the Ileum." *Medical and Surgical Reporter*, vol. lix, p. 321.

"Practical Observations on Senile Hypertrophy of the Prostate Gland." *University Medical Magazine*, vol. i, p. 1.

1889. "Tracheotomy." *University Medical Magazine*, vol i, p. 519.

"The Choice of Operations for Vesical Calculus." *University Medical Magazine*, vol. ii, p. 1.

"The Radical Treatment of Hernia." *University Medical Magazine*, vol. ii, p. 339.

Address, Opening Exercises at the House of Refuge.

1889–91. President's Addresses. *Transactions of the College of Physicians.*

1890. "Injuries to the Peroneus Longus Tendon and its Sheath." *University Medical Magazine*, vol. iii, p. 1.

1891. "Pancreatic Cyst. Removal by Laparotomy; Recovery." *University Medical Magazine*, vol. iii, p. 469.

"Fistula of the Duct of Steno." *University Medical Magazine*, vol. iii, p. 583.

1891. "The Present Status in Brain Surgery Based on the Practice of Philadelphia Surgeons." *University Medical Magazine*, vol. iv, p. 17.

Dr. Agnew could wield a pen exhibiting, to a marked degree, sarcastic retort, combined with humorous comparisons; for example, in talking of religious subjects he said, in regard to certain persons, that "their minds are first made up to a judgment, and then the Bible is subpenaed for its defense, questioned and cross-questioned, threatened and coaxed, put upon the rack of criticism and interpolation, a sentence seized upon here and another there, and these are all marshalled into line, contrary to every rule of grammar and logical interpretation, until an opinion is formed wreaking with the blood of violence. It is not 'Speak, Lord, for thy servant heareth,' with these people, but 'Hear, Lord, for thy servant speaketh.'"

There was a picturesqueness about his style which gives a dash to all of his productions, however dry their character. For example, in speaking on a political subject, he said: "The heart of the old Whig party throbbed its last pulsations with the death of Henry Clay, and the American organization known by the *sobriquet* of 'Know-Nothing,' which came forth with the growth of a fungus in a night, like Jonah's gourd, has passed away as the morning-dew, leaving the shillalah and shamrock as invincible as ever."

In speaking of certain members of the Board of Guardians, he said: "They clung to office like barnacles to a ship's bottom."

In the early part of this biography a valedictory address, delivered by Dr. Agnew at the School of Anatomy, was given, which casts interesting side-lights on Dr. Agnew's thoughts, education, and belief of that day; in Chapter VIII are given two examples of his style of pursuing strictly scientific investigations; later in the work will be given his last didactic lecture. There remain yet two phases of his career as a writer untouched. One is his manner of preparing an ordinary medical essay; the other, his expression of his beliefs on the relations between his profession and ordinary daily life.

They are all easy reading, for Dr. Agnew always used the simplest, most direct words and statements in dealing with any subject. Two of them are given here, as a sample of his work; the first paper shows his clearness of thought and argument in dealing with a difficult medical question which has become a knotty legal problem; while the other paper is on the interesting subject of the "Relation of Social Life to Surgical Disease." Both were read before the American Surgical Association and published in *The Medical News* of Philadelphia.

These papers require no explanation, while they throw incidentally more side-lights on Dr. Agnew's nature, life, and character than would many pages of description :—

MEDICO-LEGAL ASPECTS OF CRANIAL AND HEART WOUNDS.

An Address Delivered before the American Surgical Association.

Is it possible for an individual, with suicidal intent, and in quick succession, to inflict a perforating shot wound of the head and another of the chest implicating the heart? Or, reversing the proposition, is it incredible that a person, bent on self-destruction, can, with his own hand, shoot himself in the heart and in the head?

These questions have a medico-legal bearing of no small import, and have been suggested as the subject of the present paper by a murder committed, during the spring of 1886, in the town of Newport, Rhode Island.

A colored man, long a resident of Newport, well known both to the permanent inhabitants of and to many of the transient visitors to this place of fashionable resort, was found, one morning in his house, dead under the breakfast-table, having in his mouth some food unswallowed, and with a bullet wound in his head and another in his chest. A coroner's jury, after holding an inquest, brought in a verdict of suicide, and the body, under this finding, was interred.

Some weeks later, through the suggestion, I believe, of one of the local physicians, that it was impossible for the deceased to have inflicted these double wounds with his own hands, both involving vital organs, the authorities ordered the body to be disinterred and the inquest to be reviewed. The autopsy revealed a perforating shot wound of the skull, the pistol-ball (22-calibre) having entered the right parietal bone, about two inches above and anterior to the ear, making a clear-cut perforation of the skull and lodging in the posterior part of the left half of the cerebrum, having passed from left to right and from before backward.

Another ball had penetrated the thorax at a point three inches to the right of the left nipple and two inches to the left of the median line. " The ball," as was stated, " was found to have passed through the left ventricle of the heart, entering the base and emerging at the apex." It is probable that the exact point at which the ball entered the chest was not accurately noted, as it would have been an anatomical impossibility for the missile, entering the thorax at the position stated, to have traversed the heart from base to apex, the base of the organ being on a level with the second costal cartilage.

The finding of the coroner's jury, based on the evidence developed by this second examination, was " murder by some person or persons unknown." Suspicion now fell upon the son-in-law of the dead man, who lived at home with his father-in-law.

This colored man, named Dorsey, was a graduate of Lincoln University and had attended two courses of instruction in the Medical Department of the University of Pennsylvania. He was immediately arrested, imprisoned, and held to answer for the murder. He stoutly denied any participation in or knowledge of the crime, and as the young man had, both during his student life at Lincoln University and at the Medical

Department of the University of Pennsylvania, borne a remarkably excellent character, and as no possible or sufficient motive
at the time could be divined for such an act, many of his friends
were disposed to regard him as innocent. These convictions
were strengthened by the rumor that Burton, the murdered
man, was hopelessly embarrassed financially and had, I understand, on the very morning of his death, a note at maturity,
without the means to cancel it.

At the trial of Dorsey, the prisoner, five medical experts
were examined on behalf of the prosecution. One witness testified that either wound must have caused nearly instant death;
or, if the brain received the first ball, such a degree of unconsciousness would have ensued as to incapacitate the victim for
inflicting the second wound.

A second witness declared that the wounds were entirely
inconsistent with the idea of suicide. The three remaining witnesses testified that if not more than one minute elapsed between the shots, the case was one of homicide and not suicide.
Such were the answers as given to me by the prosecuting attorney in the case. Entertaining a different view from that expressed by the medical experts, Dr. William Hunt, one of the
surgeons of the Pennsylvania Hospital, and myself, at the
urgent solicitation of the friends of the prisoner, went to Newport on the last day of the trial. We arrived at the place in
the night, expecting to go on the witness-stand the following
morning; but, in the meantime, the trial was brought to a sudden termination by the confession of the prisoner's wife, in
which both her husband and herself were implicated in the
murder. And now the question recurs,—are such wounds as
those described inconsistent with the idea of suicide?

If the testimony given by the medical experts in the case
just detailed is to pass unchallenged, then it follows that an
innocent person, arrested and tried for murder in a case where a
shot wound of the head and of the heart existed, might be condemned to death, even though the other evidence did not raise

the connection of the prisoner with the deed above a mere possibility. In examining this question, I shall assume that it is possible for a shot wound of the head and of the heart to be suicidal; and as to the precedence of injury,—the head or the heart,—it is not essential to the case.

First, however, let us consider the subject in the order of a shot wound of the head and of the heart. There are two conditions which would disqualify an individual bent on self-destruction from inflicting the second wound in the chest, namely, the suspension or loss of consciousness and paralysis, partial or complete, of one or both upper extremities. The loss of consciousness, in a given shot wound of the brain, is not due to the mere passage of the missile through cerebral matter. You can thrust a finger, a trocar, or a knife into portions of the brain, without affecting either sensibility or consciousness. Loss of consciousness is due generally either to fragments of bone carried before the vulnerating body and buried in the cerebrum, to some large vessel or sinus being open, causing profuse hemorrhage, or to transmitted vibrations resulting from the impact of a ball against the skull, thus causing a molecular disturbance of its contents and momentarily deranging the orderly operation of the intellect.

Indeed, I believe that the sudden suspension of consciousness in many of these shot injuries of the head is due more to this contact of the missile with the cranial wall than to its passage through the brain. It is common to see a person fall to his knées or prone upon the ground when struck upon the head by a pebble or fragment of a stone; in an instant he is again on his feet. The fall does not necessarily imply loss of consciousness, though it does mean an interruption to muscular co-ordination.

Every surgeon can recall instances of the most dreadful injury to the skull and brain without destroying the conscious volitions of the patient. During 1885 Dr. William Hunt and myself were called to see a man who had been run over by a street-railway sweeper during the night. He was seen to arise immediately after the accident and walk to his house, on Spruce Street, two squares from the scene of injury. Opening the door with his dead-latch key, he passed up-stairs to his room, on the second story, and went to bed. The family in the morning found him unconscious. On examination, portions of the parietal and temporal bones were found driven deeply into the brain.

A prominent physician of Philadelphia was run over by an unmanageable horse, and dashed against the corner of an iron pillar, causing a frightful comminuted and depressed fracture of the frontal bone, tearing the membranes of the brain and injuring its substance. I applied the trephine in two places and removed twenty-seven pieces of bone, and yet, although unable to stand, neither mobility nor consciousness was destroyed, for the patient gave intelligent instructions in reference to being carried to his home.

I recall another case of still more extensive damage to the skull; one in which, by the bursting of a fly-wheel, quite one-half of the frontal bone was carried away, and with it a considerable portion of the prefrontal lobes of the cerebrum. Only for a few moments was the man dazed; he ultimately made a good recovery.

The famous case occurring in the practice of Dr. Harlow, and figured in some of the books on surgery, is another one in point. A bar of iron, having entered the face below the zygoma, passed through the skull and the brain, emerging near the vertex, without destroying consciousness. A private ("Surgical History of the War," part i) named Solomon, Company G, New Jersey Volunteers, received a shot wound at the Battle of Bull Run. The ball entered the skull below the tip of the left ear; the man fell, but retained his senses. The surgeon passed a probe two inches into the brain in the track of the ball.

In a letter, received recently from Sir William MacCormac, of London, the writer says that he thinks it entirely within the bounds of possibility for an individual with suicidal intent to shoot himself in the head and in the heart, or in the heart and afterward in the head, and furnishes the following cases, which render such a statement entirely possible: The first was that of a suicidal case, under the care of Mr. Hulke, where the ball traversed the head from temple to temple, but did not emerge. The patient lived fourteen days, but did not lose his consciousness until a short time before his death; he was fully able to inflict any other wound had he been so disposed. In a second case, under the care of Dr. Smith, a bullet traversed the skull from temple to temple; the patient not only preserved his consciousness, but finally recovered.

A soldier at the Battle of Pultuska, in Poland, as related by Hennen, received a remarkable wound of the brain. A ball carried away the bayonet of a musket, which entered the right temple of the man two inches above the orbit, and, passing backward and downward, emerged through the maxillary sinus of the left or opposite side. The soldier, aided by two comrades, tried in vain to withdraw the weapon. The surgeon-major, M. Fordeau, made a similar attempt and failed, when at length the task was accomplished by a strong soldier placing the man's head upon the ground and his foot upon the head and making traction upon the missile. The patient ultimately recovered, and, as it is distinctly stated that he joined his own efforts with those of his fellow-soldiers in their attempts at extraction, it follows that neither consciousness nor motility was lost.

The second disqualifying condition for inflicting another wound after one in the head is paralysis.

The very great advance made in the last few years in regard to the functions of the brain and the topographical relations existing between the exterior of the cranium and definite cerebral convolutions enables us to locate with considerable accuracy intra-cranial lesions from the symptomatic phenomena which may be present. The local areas or centres of muscular power have, for the most part, been clearly established.

It will, I think, be conceded that, so long as the middle portion of the ascending frontal and corresponding portion of the ascending parietal convolutions remain uninjured, the power to use the arms is retained.   The motor centres are all grouped about the fissure of Rolando, and, unless a shot or other missile trenches on these special regions, motility remains; although it may, after a time, be lost by the extension of hemorrhage or from inflammatory products. ˙So common is it to see shot and other wounds occurring without material impairment of muscular motion that I do not think any one can challenge this statement.   Indeed, the cases already cited in support of personal consciousness after wounds of the brain are, most of them, equally pertinent when applied to the maintenance of motility. Nor does the fact that a man falls, or is unable to rise, after a perforating shot wound of the skull, prove that the power to use his arms is lost.   The missile may damage the leg-centres and not affect the arm-centres.

Let us next change the proposition by altering the order of wounds, the heart wounds taking precedence.

The unconsciousness and loss of power which follow wounds of this organ are due to hemorrhage; the vessels ˙of the brain and other nerve centres being suddenly emptied of their blood, fatal syncope ensues; hence wounds of the heart are generally considered to be instantaneously fatal.   Yet there are many—very many—exceptions to this rule.   Fischer, in an analysis of 452 cases of wounds of the heart, gives no less than 35 recoveries; 72 were shot wounds. with 12 recoveries. Dr. Purple, in his collection of heart wounds, states that in 42 cases, 12 of which were shot wounds, death did not take place immediately.

While it is true that these statistics are not altogether free from criticism, yet they possess an intrinsic value in establishing the general statement that these injuries are not necessarily or immediately fatal in all instances.

The following cases, culled from different sources, will go to sustain the object most needful for my present purpose.   In the "Surgical History of the War," part i, pages 530–31, there is recorded the case of Private Lanning, Co. A, Pennsylvania Volunteers, who was shot in the chest, the ball entering the right auricle of the heart. The patient persisted in sitting up and walking about his room. He lived for fourteen days. The same author mentions the case of a private named Wright, Co. C, Fourth Regiment of the Veteran Reserve Corps, shot at Quincy, Ill., who lived forty-six hours. The ball passed through the lung, the left auricle, the auriculo-ventricular septum, and the left ventricle.

In two instances, given by Jamain, the patients lived six months after a shot wound of the left ventricle of the heart. Ferrus mentions a case in which a man lived twenty days with a skewer through his heart.

Sir William MacCormac writes me that Mr. Durham had a case of bayonet wound of the heart, in which the patient survived fifty-six hours. The wound implicated both ventricles, the septum and auricle, and yet the man walked some yards after receiving the injury. Dr. Andrews reports a case under the care of Professor Bergman, of Dorpat, where the injured man traveled fifteen miles to Dorpat and finally recovered.

In the *Lancet*, January, 1879, a case is reported where a man received a perforating shot wound of the left ventricle, which did not prove fatal for fifty-four days, the patient having, in the meantime, returned to his work.

In Rankin's "Abstract of Medical Sciences," vol. xxxi, page 165, Mr. Jackson reports the case of a man who received two shot wounds, one of the balls passing through the right ventricle. He lived for three and a half hours and was able in the meantime to make a deposition and name his assassin. A case of assassination was tried before a British court in India. A native named Kadir was shot through the heart, June 2, 1873, while lying on his cot. It was stated in evidence that the victim, after receiving the fatal wound, recognized and denounced his murderer, a man named Meera Khan. On the

DR. AGNEW IN 1879.

strength of this testimony the assassin was found guilty. An appeal was made and the case carried to another court, and the verdict reversed on the ground that death must have been instantaneous. Mr. W. Curran, Brigade-Surgeon, in comment-ing on this case, stated that the decision of the former court was, in his judgment, correct, as, in his own personal experience, shot wounds of the heart were not necessarily immediately fatal.

On May 11, 1812 (*Lancet*, April 2, 1887), Mr. Percival was shot by Bellingham in the heart. At the trial a witness testified that after the firing he saw the murdered man rush hastily through the crowd toward the place where he was stand-ing, looking first in one direction and then in the other, and, after taking a few steps more, reeled and fell to the ground.

I may also mention the case of a woman brought into the surgical ward of the Pennsylvania Hospital during my term of service. The left ventricle had been pierced by a butcher-knife. She survived for two and three-quarter hours, and for one-third of that time her mental condition was perfectly clear.

Can any one doubt that, in most of the cases cited, these patients, had they been so disposed, could have inflicted a shot-wound of the head?

And now, third and last, are there any instances in which a suicide has actually inflicted the two wounds which I have been considering?

Dr. Macleod, Professor of Surgery in Glasgow University, Scotland, furnishes me the case of a suicide which came directly under his observation, which is to the point. A student shot himself in a closet, the ball entering the head. Finding that he had not accomplished the work of self-destruction, he went to his bed-room, along a passage, and shot himself in the heart. He lived only a few moments after this last injury.

In turning to the records of the coroner's physician in Philadelphia, I am able to furnish the following cases:—

1. A policeman shot himself, first through the head; the ball, entering the right temple, was found lodged in the cranial

vault on the opposite side. A second shot was fired into his chest, the bullet cutting the right side of the heart. Death from internal hemorrhage followed in about five minutes. This was done in the presence of witnesses.

2. A boy, aged 19, inflicted four shot wounds from a revolver on his own person. The first bullet entered the forehead and, after taking a circuitous route, lodged about the middle of the left temporal lobe. A second ball was fired into the chest, and, passing through the sternum, cut through the left ventricle of the heart on a level with the mitral valve. A third shot passed into the abdomen, and a fourth into the neck. Death ensued from pericardial hemorrhage.

3. A grocer was found dead in his room, having locked the door. A pistol was still clutched in each hand; one bullet had passed through the brain and a second through the heart.

4. A man committed suicide in the park; one ball entered the brain, a second the chest.

In all these cases the suicide was not assumed, but proved beyond all reasonable doubt.

From the foregoing facts, which are thus hastily thrown together, I think I am at liberty to draw the following conclusions :—

First. That it is possible for a ball to enter the brain without destroying consciousness, although it may, for a few minutes, cause some mental confusion.

. *Second*. That a ball may traverse the brain without causing muscular paralysis.

Third. That a suicide may, with his own hands, if so disposed, first shoot himself in the head, and, within the lapse of a minute, inflict a similar wound on the heart, and that there is a sufficient number of cases on record to establish the feasibility of the self-infliction of the two shots; and

Fourth. That a suicide may first discharge a ball into the chest, wounding the heart, and immediately after send a second ball into the brain.

In the second article by Dr. Agnew, he studies the tendencies of modern life as related to surgical disease. It has been stated by many authorities that this essay should be found in every household in America:—

THE RELATION OF SOCIAL LIFE TO SURGICAL DISEASE.

President's Address Delivered before the American Surgical Association.

There is no tyranny more exacting or despotic than that exercised by the conventionalities which govern our living. All stages of life, from infancy to old age, are under its domination. It dictates the education, the manners, the walk, the dress, the forms of speech,—in fine, the whole being. Beyond all contradiction, the behests of fashion are vastly more influential in governing public conduct than any argument drawn from the teachings of structure and function. As a rule, when the conflict is between taste and reason, the victory will be on the side of taste. In nothing is this more forcibly displayed than in the apparel used to protect the body.

It is not an agreeable task to peer into the wardrobes or dressing-rooms of our fair country-women. I have no especial taste for exploring museums or *bizarre* collections. Indeed, without a key to interpret the curious and ingenious mechanisms for clothing the form divine, such an exploration would be like an archæologist attempting Egyptology ignorant of cuneiform inscriptions.

I have, however, some knowledge of human anatomy in its broadest sense, and when I look upon the master-pieces of the human form, whether in marble or on canvas, a Belvidere Apollo or a Venus de Medici, and contrast these with the specimens of modern men and women, I am forced to admiration; not so much at the amazing ingenuity displayed in concealing the divinely appointed form as at the plasticity and patient submission of mortal clay under the despotism of a conventional inquisition.

Were these processes of mutilation and abnormality harmless,—did the body consist of a mere mass of protoplasm capable of assuming protean shapes, the subject might be passed over with the feeling of a naturalist; but this is not so. These violations of the laws of structure bring with them serious penal inflictions which, did they terminate with the original offender, might be dismissed with a sentiment of pity; but projecting, as they do, their baneful consequences to successors, they become proper subjects for criticism.

Let me name a few examples as illustrative of my subject. For some time the profession has been speculating on the causation of *nasal and post-nasal catarrh*, with its accompanying auditory defects, the growing frequency of which cannot have escaped general observation. Doubtless no single agency will explain the presence among us of this unpleasant disease; yet there are facts connected with this affection which, to me, are very suggestive. I cannot recall an instance in which I have met with the disease among women belonging to the Society of Friends, Dunkards, or Mennonites. If this, on more extended observation, proves to be true, may not the head-dress peculiar to these people be accepted in explanation of their exemption.

The bonnet which, at one time, overshadowed the entire head, as all know, has been gradually shrinking in its dimensions until it has become a mere shadow of its former self and offers no protection whatever to the head. As a substitute, I would not insist upon the quaint head-gear of the Friend, but I believe that any modification which will protect this part of the body will lessen the tendency to catarrhal inflammation of the naso-pharyngeal mucous membrane.

A legion of physical imperfections arises from *muscular restraint*. Among these may be mentioned weak ankles, narrow or contracted chests, round shoulders, projecting scapulæ, and lateral curvature of the spine.

The foolish concession to appearance and the unwise partiality of parents for enforced systems of education, the demands of which bear no just proportion to the capacity of the juvenile mind, constitute the initial or determining force of these phys-ical imperfections. In many cases the weak ankles of children, characterized by eversion of the feet, thus allowing the super-incumbent weight of the body to be transmitted to the latter, inside of the proper centre of support, is largely chargeable to the miserable practice of placing on the little ones, long before they are able to walk, boots tightly laced up the limb some dis-tance above the ankles. The confinement of the flexor and extensor muscles by this constriction prevents that free play of movement which reacts so favorably on all the elements of an articulation, and that, too, at a time when the growing forces are at full tide; so that, when the time arrives for standing and walking, the muscles are unequal to the firm support of the joint.

The consequence of this feebleness is soon seen in the turn-ing outward of the feet, throwing the strain on the internal lateral ligaments, which, in turn, become elongated through growth, and thus the defect becomes established. But the evil does not stop here. The calcaneo-cuboid and the astragalo-scaphoid ligaments, losing the proper support of the tendon of the posterior tibial muscle under the abnormal tension, begin to yield, and to the deformity of eversion is added that of "flat-foot." That this is not a mere hypothetical expla-nation of the ankle defects I have many times verified by find-ing the threatening symptoms disappear after liberating the imprisoned muscles and subjecting the enfeebled parts to a ju-dicious massage. Under no circumstance, as is too often the case, should instrumental apparatus be applied, unless in cases in which, from neglect, the deformity is thoroughly established and is progressive.

Take another deformity, that of "bow-legs." On the earliest signs of the unsightly curve, the limb is too often tram-melled with irons and the growth of the muscles arrested, when it is well known that if manual force be systematically applied two or three times a day the limbs will gradually assume their typical form.

Again, in further illustration of our general text, take as an example a child who, for one long or two short sessions for five days of the week, sits over the study desk, compelled to assume a position in which, from the inclination of the body, the shoulders fall forward, the head being supported generally on the elbows and the hands. In such a posture the great serratus, pectoralis major and minor muscles are in a state of relaxation, while the erector spinæ and trapezei muscles are in a state of tension. This change in the position of the shoulders gives the shoulder-blades over, without antagonism or resistance, to the action of the rhomboidei and the levatores angulæ muscles, which, acting conjointly, cause that projection of the lower angle of the shoulder-blades which the older anatomists termed "scapulæ alatæ."

To all this must be added the very important factor of four to six hours in the school-room and two hours, at least, of home preparation for the following day's recitations, during which time the respiratory functions, having been reduced to a minimum of activity, the muscles of the chest are comparatively passive and aëration of the blood tardy. Certainly no combination of conditions could be better devised for forming contracted chests and round shoulders.

It is not long before the watchful eye of the mother detects the change in the figure of her child. She will probably discover this condition and take alarm, even when the pale face, the languid air, and the capricious appetite of the child causes no anxiety; and then comes the second act in the drama of physical deterioration,—a resort to shoulder-braces and stays in order to accomplish that which the muscles should be taught to do without restraint or incumbrance.

While it is true that *lateral curvature* of the spine depends upon causes both central and peripheral, yet in no small num-

·ber the deformity is clearly attributable to influences of a social nature. The spinal column, by reason of the non-union of the epiphyses and diaphyses and the supple character of its ligaments, is extremely flexible. Whatever, therefore, destroys the muscular equipoise, however inconsiderable the force, if persistently repeated, changes the centre of gravity and develops primary and compensating curves.

For nine months in the year, any fine morning, groups of young children may be seen plodding along our streets with a miniature library of books suspended from one shoulder. To the already preponderating scale of the balance add the additional factor, a badly-arranged light in the school-room, compelling these little *savants* to assume a lateral inclination of the body in order to obtain the necessary illumination of the subjects of study, and you have all the conditions necessary for perpetuating the lateral deformity. "Just as the twig is bent the tree's inclined." As in the case of round shoulders, in order to prop up the falling column, instrumental contrivances are immediately called into requisition. The body is encased in a formidable coat of mail, to be followed by muscular atrophy and permanent distortion of the most beautiful piece of mechanism in the human frame.

It is true that in most educational institutions for the young provisions are now made for physical culture, and these are, in some measure, antidotal to the evils complained of; but, in my judgment, these factors do not at all compensate for that free unstudied romp in the open air so fascinating to the young child, untrammelled by the hard and fast rules of calisthenics or gymnastics. Nor does the evil end here. While the forcing process, which is to stimulate the mental powers far beyond the real capacity of the immature and growing brain to receive, is in progress, another is inaugurated which is to qualify, especially the female child, to acquit herself with distinction when the time arrives for entering the great world of society, or, as Thomas Brown would style it, "for the frivolous work of polished idleness." The gait and carriage must be reduced to prescribed rules, the voice toned down to a drawl; the muscular apparatus of the face must be taught to express not the spontaneous and natural outcome of feeling which wells up unbidden from the magic chambers of the heart, but rather to produce an effect. And so this work of transformation goes on until it culminates in the full-blown "society girl." Is it any wonder that—under such a scheme of education, conducted throughout by a studied disregard of both the physical and mental constitution, and exercising, as it does, such tremendous drafts on the nervous system—the world is being filled with a class of flat-breasted, spindle-limbed young women, unfitted for the varied and responsible functions of womanhood; qualifications, too, which, under a different regimen and directed into proper channels, would exert a most potential influence on all the great social and moral problems of the age?

While thus plain spoken on the frivolous methods of living, I do not wish to be understood as being unfriendly to the highest cultivation of the mental and physical powers, if conducted on lines in harmony with the organization, nor to any technique which may conduce to personal grace or elegance of manners, so that the manly or womanly personality of the individual be not sacrificed to the Molech of sentiment and sham. Indeed, indifference to these matters is inexcusable in either man or woman, as not only lessening their influence in the world, but, in many respects, disqualifying them for the highest discharge of the duties of modern life. Valuable as may be the unpolished diamond, yet it is only after the wheel of the lapidary has worn away the dull incrustations that its true brilliancy is revealed, and the gem is fitted to adorn the brow or breast of beauty.

In the further discussion of my subject, I may next notice the *evils of visceral displacement* consequent on abdominal constriction. Whatever may be said in regard to Greek and Roman life, the infinite care which these people displayed in developing and maintaining the very best type of the human form is worthy of admiration and emulation. The Ionic "Cheton," spoken of by Attic writers, and so often represented by the bronzes of Herculaneum, while it would not exactly satisfy the modern idea of dress, was, at least, free from the charge of interfering with the contour of the human figure.

The painters and sculptors of those classic days were reverent students of Nature. Their delineations were true to life. Their works furnish us with no hour-glass contractions of the human body. The constriction of the waist operates injuriously on both the supra- and infra- diaphragmatic organs. Any force acting on the base of the thorax and preventing the expansion of its walls concentrates the function of respiration, which should be general, on the apices of the lungs; and hence, under these circumstances, the movements of breathing are for the most part confined to the summit of the chest. As the seat of tuberculosis is generally located in the upper part of the lungs, may not the inordinate work entailed on these parts by constriction have some influence in hastening such deposits in the female when the predisposition exists?

It is this forcing inward of the costal border of the thorax which causes the groove on the anterior surface of the liver so familiar to anatomists. The pressure cannot fail to interfere with the descent of the diaphragm, and with the functions of the gall-bladder and duodenum, and exercises no small degree of influence in favoring the formation of gall-stones, females being peculiarly prone to such concretions. The extent to which the liver may be damaged by extreme constriction of the waist is well illustrated by a case recently reported in the *British Medical Journal*, in which a considerable portion of the left lobe of the liver had been separated from the right, the two being connected only by a band of connective tissue, which enabled the operator to remove the detached mass without difficulty.

The evil effects of this constriction on the viscera of the abdomen and pelvis is most strikingly witnessed in the embarrassed portal circulation, in the different uterine displacements, elongation of ligaments, displaced ovaries, tubal inflammations, hemorrhoids, hernia, and other morbid conditions, which either prevent or disqualify the woman for the exercise of the functions of maternity, and which, in addition to reflex influence, entail a host of functional disorders reaching into every avenue of the body and invading both the mental and moral constitution of the victim.

So prolific have these infirmities become that a new department of surgery has been organized for their special management. To what, if not to social causes, can be these morbid changes of structure in the pelvic organs, especially of the uterus and its appendages, be attributed? Why should laceration of the cervix uteri be so common an accident? Labor is a natural process, and ought not, under ordinary circumstances, to be attended by lesion of uterine tissue. I can conceive of no agency more likely to induce that muscular degeneration which predisposes to this accident than the modes and methods of modern living, especially among the inhabitants of great cities. In the expression "modern living," much is embraced. It includes culinary pharmacy, overfeeding and overdrinking, insufficient or injudicious exercise, improperly heated apartments, and a disproportion between the hours of exercise and rest.

Contrast, if you will, the muscles of the hardy country housewife, who, bearing the cares and responsibilities of a dependent family, bustles about the livelong day, in-doors and out-of-doors, eats with a relish her plain and simple fare, repairs at reasonable hours to bed, sleeps the sleep of the just, undisturbed by dyspeptic night-mares, and, rising with the golden dawn, resumes the round of domestic toil with a clear head and supple limbs; I say—contrast this type of a class with that of another,—the woman born to luxury and ease, whose capricious and exacting taste taxes the arts of the professional caterer, who drags out the morning hours toying with some crazy piece of embroidery or trashy novel, lunches at one, rides out in the afternoon for an airing of two or three hours, returns to a dinner of five or six courses at seven, completes the evening at the opera, the theatre, or the assembly, and, coming home after midnight, crawls into bed, weary and exhausted in mind and body, only to rise, with the best hours of the morning gone, for another day of aimless, routine life.

Can it be doubted that in the first case, with a digestion unimpaired, with the products of textural change consumed by functional activity and eliminated through the proper emunctories, the woman should possess a vital resistance and a tone of tissue altogether superior to that of the other, whose habits of living must necessarily favor their faulty metamorphosis?

To these same agencies must be attributed that brood of nervous and hysterical evils for the relief of which the gynecologist too often, I fear, invades the domain of womanhood around which her whole sexual nature revolves, and which, save in the direst extremity, should be sacred against all operative intrusion.

Late marriages constitute another social evil, the penal inflictions of which involve both sexes alike. Pride and luxury determine long engagements or deferred proposals. Marriage, it is believed, necessarily involves an establishment, a display, a retinue of servitors. The good old notion of two souls being united in wedlock for the purpose of being mutual helpmates, and patiently together working up from modest beginnings to affluence, seems to be entirely at variance with the modern idea of this relation. In the meantime the young man is betrayed into unlawful sources of gratification, alike destructive to moral and physical purity, the pollution of which incontinence is often communicated to and perpetuated in wife and offspring. I would not dare to say how many cases of this nature have been entrusted to my professional confidence, although I doubt not my experience does not differ from that of many of my professional brethren.

It may be thought by some persons that the subject of the *foot* and *shoe* is not of sufficient dignity to appear in a public address. The Romans and the Greeks thought differently. The literature of both people is full of reference to the shoe worn by both sexes. So important, indeed, are the feet to the well-being of the body that whatever impairs their usefulness, either for support or locomotion, becomes a positive calamity. Nothing, scarcely, is less like the human foot than the modern shoe. Let any one leave the impress of his or her foot in the wet sand of the sea-shore and then place alongside of the imprint a fashionable shoe; that the two were intended for each other would scarcely strike a child of the forest. The North American Indian entertains greater notions about clothing this portion of his body than does the civilized denizen of New York or Philadelphia.

Compare the moccasin with the French shoe of the city belle. Compare the σανδαλον or the περσιχαι of Pollux and Aristophanes with the same, and we shall see that the savage and the polished Greek alike understood the value of sound feet in the race of life. It is the imperfect adaptation of the shoe to the foot which constitutes the fruitful source of tired ankles, corns, bunions, overlapping of the toes, and ingrowing nails. Some idea may be formed of the magnitude of the evil from the fact that, of 800 patients under the care of a prominent chiropodist of Philadelphia, the great majority of the defects were entirely attributable to the contracted toes and high heels of the shoes. Especially do these physical incumbrances arising from a blind submission to social laws operate disadvantageously to our fair women at the beginning of the new dispensation, requiring both muscle and brain, and when her friends propose to sweep away all the old traditions and claim for her the earth with all its masculine employments.

Games and amusements, which, in themselves, are proper and praiseworthy, too often become developed into a craze, working both moral and physical mischief. In the national game of base-ball there is the "pitcher's arm," a condition of overtaxed function, and one in which all the anatomical elements of the upper arm are involved. There is also the "tennis arm" and the swollen, supersensitive prostate of the bicyclist, both due to abuse of proper popular amusements.

Defects of refraction, or defects of vision, constitute another class of affections fairly attributable, in many instances, to social influences. The number of children who may be seen on our streets any day wearing glasses has become a matter of common observation. It is far from being probable that the most exquisite piece of mechanism—the human eye—came from the Divine Artificer imperfect.

Because eyes are young, it does not follow that they are thereby better fitted to sustain prolonged use. Just the reverse is true, and it is high time that parents and educators begin to realize this fact. The power of the eye for continued use, like that of other organs of the body, is one of gradation. It moves in the general procession and strengthens with the advance in life until development has attained its zenith. Not only so, but the eye, being a part of the body, must suffer or rejoice through the operation of general causes. A bone may have its normal curves changed, a tendon may slip from its appointed groove, or a blood-vessel be destroyed, and yet very little disability be realized; but the eye is made up of such extremely delicate structures, and acts according to fixed physical laws, that not the slightest alteration of a curve, or the mobility or density of its media, can occur without great vitiation of function.

To exact long hours of study from children of a tender age involves a degree of functional strain altogether disproportionate to the structural resources of the organ, and, by disturbing the orderly processes of nutrition, gives rise to hypermetropia, asthenopia, astigmatism, and its companion, headache. That the picture is not too highly colored or the sensation overstrained, we have only to contrast the children born and reared in those portions of the country not too much dominated by the methods of modern civilization and who rarely demand a resort to artificial aids to provide for abnormal-

ities of vision. The only remedy for the evil, where infantile
scholarship is insisted upon, is the kindergarten, or object
system,—the most natural and effective plan of impressing the
young mind.

Is there any reasonable explanation drawn from sources of
a social nature for the great frequency of those renal diseases
which come more particularly under the care of the surgeon as
crystalline deposits and calculi? For maintaining the general
health at the highest physiological standard, a proper quality
of food and the proper disposal of tissue waste are essential
conditions. Along with wealth and luxury come the abuses
of the table. Americans are fast becoming a nation of dys-
peptics. The country is so rich in the products of every zone
that nowhere else in the world can you find such a variety of
of foods, animal and vegetable. These foods, manipulated in
a thousand ways by the subtle art of the professional cook,
almost necessarily betray one into excess and also create the
desire for wine and other alcoholic beverages to aid the stomach
in disposing of its plethoric supply.

In great cities, which furnish relatively the largest number
of cases of renal disease affecting pre-eminently the mercantile
and sedentary classes, we find just the conditions favorable to
their development. The competitions of trade keep the merchants always at white heat. Time is golden, and the street-car
and other means of conveyance annihilate distance and the ride
is substituted for the needful one. A hasty lunch at the most
convenient restaurant satisfies the inner man until the business
of the day is closed, when, weary and worn, he is driven to his
home to partake of a course dinner, the balance of the evening
to be spent on the lounge with the evening paper or the latest
periodical. To the literary man, the fascinations of the study
and the library charm him away with their syren voices from
the fields and highways until bodily exercise grows distasteful
and repugnant. In the meantime there has been no provision
made for the waste or tissue metamorphosis of the body through

that great agency, exercise. These accumulate in the blood. The internal eliminating organs, of which the kidneys are chief, are overtaxed, and then follow the evils of malassimilation and of excretion, in the form of urates and oxalates, often resulting in the formation of calculi.

In conclusion, may we ever hope for a time when the race will realize that these bodies which we wear, which God has so highly honored by His own incarnation, are sacred temples, to be kept in harmony with recognized physical laws, and not to be made instruments of mere animal gratification.

CHAPTER X.

THE GARFIELD CASE.

On the 2d of July, 1881, James A. Garfield, then President of the United States, was shot in the Baltimore and Potomac Railway Station, at Washington, by Charles J. Guiteau. The motive of the assassin was never fully determined. It was discovered subsequently, however, that he was one of that vast swarm of applicants for position who fill Washington at all times, demanding or begging favors of government officials. He had written to the President asking for the Paris consulship; his application had been referred, with thousands of others, to the proper department. Guiteau undoubtedly was consumed with an overweening desire to become notorious, in which ambition he was not restrained by the possession of a strong moral nature, or any great degree of mental power. With the cunning of his low intellect, he reasoned that if he should remove the President, naturally all eyes would be attracted to him, and his name would be on every tongue. There would be thrown around his name the romance of a Wilkes Booth, while he would be protected from punishment by the opposing branch of the President's party, out of gratitude for placing them in power by the change.

President Garfield was on his way to a reunion of his class at Williams College; accompanied by Mr. Blaine, Secretary of State, and Colonel Rockwell, he was standing in the ladies' waiting-room at twenty minutes past nine on the morning of July 2d. The assassin approached him from the rear, coming within a distance of six feet, firing two shots from a powerful revolver of 42-calibre. One shot went through the President's coat-sleeve, but the other struck him in the back, felling him to the ground. He was carried at once to the second story of the station building and placed upon a mattress, several physicians

(220)

who happened to be in the vicinity administering stimulants to him.[1] At the suggestion of Mr. Robert Lincoln, Secretary of War, Dr. D. Willard Bliss was summoned.

Dr. Bliss found that the point of entrance of the ball, which was oval and sharply marked, was on the right side, in the tenth intercostal space, four inches from the median line of the spine, and on a line with the eleventh rib. A slight discharge of blood was oozing from this orifice, and had stained the clothing. Dr. Bliss passed a Nélaton probe through the tenth intercostal space, downward and forward for a distance of three and one-half inches from the surface of the body, to what appeared to be a cavity, but he was unable to detect any foreign substance, beyond the rib, to indicate the presence of fragments of bone or the missile. In attempting to withdraw the probe it became engaged between the fractured fragments and the end of the rib, and could not be freed until pressure was made upon the sternal end of the rib. Dr. Bliss then passed the little finger of his left hand, to its full length, into the wound, which showed the character and extent of the fracture of the rib; but he was able only to reach a point on a line with the inner surface of the rib, where his finger came in contact with what appeared to be lacerated tissue or comparatively firm coagula of blood—probably the latter.

After withdrawing his finger, Dr. Bliss made an exploration with a long, flexible, silver probe, which he suitably curved before introducing, and gently passed it downward and forward, and downward and backward, with a view of determining the course of the ball, if it had been deflected by contact with the rib; but, meeting with resistance from soft parts in all directions, Dr. Bliss desisted, being inclined to the belief that the ball had entered the liver, which, if true, would not warrant further exploration in that direction.

By this time a large number of physicians had gathered in the room, and Dr. Bliss gave them a hurried account of his

[1] The physicians in attendance immediately after the shooting of the President were Drs. Townshend; Purvis, Reyburn, Norris, Lincoln, Patterson, and J. B. Hamilton.

examinations and expressed the opinion that no further explorations should be made during the stage of collapse, and that stimulants by the stomach should not be given at that time, as the President was suffering from constant nausea, and in his condition absorption would not take place. The President repeatedly requested that he be taken to the White House, and, after a further consultation and a full understanding of the manner and detail of his transfer, his speedy removal was agreed upon.

Temporary dressings were applied to the wound, and the President was placed upon a stretcher, carried down-stairs, and placed in an ambulance in waiting. The vehicle was driven with great care to the White House, the President not experiencing any discomfort. He was taken to his room, which was known as the Southwest or family room of the house. On the arrival of the President at the White House a careful examination was made of his condition. His pulse continued feeble, frequent, and exceedingly compressible; the respiration was slow and sighing; his extremities and the surface of his body were cold; he had been vomiting freely; his entire body was bathed in a profuse perspiration; his voice was husky; he constantly complained of severe pains in the limbs. He was placed on his right side, so as to make the wound dependent, to facilitate drainage, and keep the viscera in contact with the injured walls, looking for the possible adhesion of the injured parts to the peritoneum. It was deemed improper to remove his clothing at this time. Water was given in small quantities, often repeated. This was necessitated by the extreme thirst from which the patient suffered. A hypodermatic injection of $\frac{1}{8}$ grain of morphine and $\frac{1}{80}$ grain of atropine was administered, to control the pain in the extremities and as a more permanent stimulant to assist reaction.

This was at 10 o'clock on the morning of July 2d. There was but little change in the condition of the patient, either in temperature, respiration, or pulse, until 11 o'clock, when it was determined to repeat the morphine in a dose of $\frac{1}{8}$ grain.

This had the effect of modifying the pain and discomfort, and the respiration became more frequent and easy. The pulse responded, however, but feebly to the stimulants. Nausea and vomiting continued at intervals of thirty minutes during the entire day and until 7 in the evening, when it became less frequent, being simply a regurgitation of fluids from the stomach. This condition returned at longer intervals until 6 o'clock the following morning.

At 5.30 P.M., in accordance with a previous understanding with the physicians, the clothing was cut from the body in such a way as to prevent any motion or agitation, and to permit a more successful application of dry heat by warm flannels to the entire body, which had been imperfectly accomplished before. Examination showed a well-defined field of dullness over the region of the wound, thought to be due to hemorrhage from the substance of the liver, along the supposed track of the ball, extending seven and a half inches antero-posteriorly and five and a half inches laterally. At the evening consultation, held July 2d at 7 P.M., the opinion was expressed, as a result of this examination, that internal hemorrhage had taken place, and that, in consequence, the distinguished patient would not survive the night. At 10 P.M. the pulse was 158; temperature, 96.5° F.; respiration, 35; but at 11.20 P.M. the evidences of reaction began at last to manifest themselves. The pulse diminished to 120; the temperature and respiration became normal.

From this time till 2 P.M. on July 3d the variations of the pulse were comparatively slight, ranging from 104 to 120, the respiration and temperature being normal. The patient slept at short intervals, generally arousing with an effort at regurgitation of the contents of the stomach, but otherwise expressing a feeling of comfort and showing evidences of rest. During the night he seemed to be refreshed, and was comparatively free from pain. There was no period up to this time that the patient was not perfectly rational, and he often made brief, pertinent inquiries as to the character of the wound and his condition.

There was some oozing of dark venous blood during the night, sufficient to saturate the carbolized cotton, which was used as a dressing, and stain the bed. On the following morning the hemorrhage had entirely ceased, and the dressings became adherent to the skin. The physicians invited by Dr. Bliss to visit the bedside were Surgeon-General Wales of the Navy, Surgeon-General Barnes of the Army, Surgeon J. J. Woodward, Dr. N. S. Lincoln, and Dr. Robert Reyburn. At the consultation held the morning of July 3d, the patient was found with a pulse of 115, with his temperature and respiration nearly normal. He was cheerful, gave evidence of being rested, and made definite inquiries regarding his condition and prospects. The use of morphine hypodermatically, in doses of sufficient quantities to control the pain in the extremities, was continued.

At this time the resumption of all the normal functions of the kidneys, bladder, and intestines showed that no internal organ had been injured. Slight tympanites was detected, but there was no other evidence of anything, during the whole course of the case, which pointed toward the existence of peritonitis.

Immediately after this consultation, the subject of medical attendance was considered by the President. He placed himself formally in Dr. Bliss's professional care at this time, and requested him to select his own counsel.

Dr. Bliss, realizing the great responsibility of his position and the necessity of selecting such medical authorities as would universally be conceded to be the leaders of the profession in America, decided to summon Dr. D. Hayes Agnew, of Philadelphia, and Dr. Frank H. Hamilton, of New York. At the same time Mr. Wayne MacVeagh, the Attorney-General of the administration, had also urged upon Mrs. Garfield the propriety of taking Dr. Agnew into the case.

Dr. Agnew received the message that he was wanted, at

midnight of July 3d. He was at that time spending the summer at his country place, "Wyndrift," at Haverford, near Philadelphia. Attorney-General Wayne MacVeagh telegraphed to Mr. A. J. Cassatt, at Haverford College Station, requesting him to determine whether Dr. Agnew would come at once to Washington, and, if so, to make arrangements for a special train. It was necessary to repeat the message at Philadelphia, where it was shown to the Night Dispatcher of the Philadelphia Division of the Pennsylvania Railroad, who, anticipating the orders that he knew he would receive, immediately dispatched a special train to Haverford College Station. So quickly was this done that the train reached the station before the message returned to the dispatcher, and by the time Dr. Agnew was dressed and ready he was carried, without a second's delay, to Philadelphia. The train left Gray's Ferry, Philadelphia, at 1.10 A.M., and arrived at Washington at 4.01 A.M., making the run of one hundred and forty miles in one hundred and seventy-one minutes, being the quickest trip on record, between Philadelphia and the Capital, up to that time. Dr. Frank H. Hamilton quickly followed from New York.

The President had passed a comparatively comfortable night, awakening every twenty or thirty minutes, taking water or liquid nourishment in small quantities each time, and dropping quickly to sleep. The nausea had subsided, and the pain and soreness of the lower extremities were controlled by the administration of morphine. A careful review of the case from the time Dr. Bliss first saw the President was given to his new consultants, with the request that they, with the data before them, examine the case thoroughly, as if it were their own, and express freely their views of the character and gravity of the injury and the course of treatment of the case up to that time. Dr. Bliss also gave them a detailed account of the explorations made in the wound, and the unsettled convictions then held as to the course of the missile, and the organs involved in the injury.

15

The new consultants examined the case separately with great care. They studied the data of the progress of the symptoms for the first forty-seven hours, and examined the wound thoroughly. The more prominent data upon which the diagnosis could be based were as follow: The relative position of the assassin to the President at the time of the shooting; the direction of the ball through the tissues, so far as safe exploration could determine; the appearance of severe pains and hyperesthesia in the limbs, especially on the right side, with their gradual subsidence or modification; the repeated unsuccessful efforts to pass a probe or flexible instrument more than half an inch in any direction beyond the fractured rib, except in a direction downward, a little forward and anterior to the twelfth rib, a distance of about two inches. The fact was also considered that explorations had twice been made with the finger, once by Dr. Bliss soon after he reached the injured President, and subsequently by Surgeon-General Wales, of the navy, on the occasion of the consultation on the evening of July 2d, when in each instance it was found impossible to explore successfully beyond the inner border of the fractured rib. The consultants did not underestimate the significance of the profound shock, nor the unusual period of collapse which followed, and which seemed to point to extensive injury of important viscera. The hyperesthesia and continued pains, more marked on the right side, pointed to a moderate degree of laceration of nerve-trunks, but there was no evidence of injury to the spinal cord or its bony column.

The consultants did not attempt to force their probing with too great vigor; the condition revealed at the autopsy showed the wisdom of this policy. Probing sufficient to have gone any distance into the wound would undoubtedly have done fatal harm, as will be shown later, while it could not have revealed by any possibility the location of the ball.

The possible course of the ball was decided to be in one of three directions: (1) either into or through the liver; (2) backward at a right angle so as to involve the spinal column, or (3) downward behind the peritoneum into the pelvic cavity. In regard to the first supposition, the consultants did not believe that the ball had passed through the liver, as had been surmised at first by Dr. Bliss. The suggestion that it had been deflected to the left and had injured the spinal column was considered, but the absence of paralysis showed that the spinal cord was uninjured; the tingling pains and hyperesthesia were probably produced by injury to some nerve-trunks or were reflex in character. The third supposition, that the ball had been deflected into the pelvic cavity behind the peritoneum, seemed the most probable, although this theory was not accepted as positive, being regarded by Dr. Agnew merely as a possibility.

There was absolutely no data to show the course of the ball or its location to these men, whose trained minds would have detected the slightest indications, had they existed.

The propriety of making extensive incisions and dissections so as to explore the fractured ribs and remove as much as might be necessary to reveal the true course of the ball was considered, but the opinion was held by all the physicians that the favorable progress of the President thus far did not warrant such interference, believing that such an operation would seriously complicate the case and diminish the prospects of recovery. The fact, well known in military surgery, that bullets become enveloped in cysts of connective tissue quickly, and remain frequently for years in living tissues without causing damage, also influenced somewhat this decision.

On the evening of July 4th the pain, hyperesthesia, and vomiting had nearly disappeared, but soreness of the feet continued for several days.

The President's condition remained so satisfactory that Dr. Bliss did not deem it necessary to call in the consultants again until July 23d. They were kept informed, however, by long, daily telegrams, of the condition of the distinguished patient.

The case progressed favorably, with fluctuations, until July 23d, when a chill occurred at 7 o'clock in the evening. Two days previous to this a pus-sac had been detected beneath the skin, extending down below the twelfth rib toward the erector spinæ muscle and underneath the latissimus dorsi; it was carefully evacuated by gentle pressure. The consultants did not feel satisfied, however, that this superficial and limited collection of pus, which was so readily evacuated, was the principal cause of the aggravation of the symptoms present; so a free incision was made into the pus-sac, which afforded a more direct and dependent channel to the fractured rib, from which a small fragment of bone was removed. Pressure, made backward and upward upon the abdominal wall, caused a flow of peculiarly white and firm pus.

After this operation the improvement was not as prompt as the consultants had expected; and on July 26th the opening between the ends of the fractured eleventh rib was enlarged, and a small detached portion was removed. This facilitated the discharge of pus, and. as a result, a more uniform condition of the symptoms was maintained until August 6th, when a slight exacerbation in temperature was noticed, which continued. It was discovered at this time that pus had dissected its way down behind the peritoneum into the right iliac fossa; this was corroboratory of the supposition that the ball had followed this course. It was necessary to evacuate this channel; consequently, on August 8th the President was etherized, and an operation making a point of exit in the dependent portion of this pus-sac was done, the incision being carried downward and forward through the skin, the subcutaneous fascia, external and internal oblique muscles, to the sinus or pus-channel. It was discovered at this point that there was a deeper channel, which had not been exposed by the operation thus far, and the incision was carried through the transversalis muscle and the transversalis fascia, affording a free opening for the passage of all the pus.

The President did fairly well again, after this operation, until August 14th, when it was found necessary to resort to feeding by the bowel until August 17th, owing to the nausea, vomiting, and general prostration which appeared. At this date the stomach was quieted gradually and the enemata were discontinued.

On August 18th a slight swelling of that portion of the right parotid gland which lies directly in front of the ear was noticed. With this swelling there was no pain or tenderness on pressure. This parotitis presented many of the characteristics of an ordinary carbuncle, and was unaccompanied by any other abscesses in the adjoining tissue. This swelling went on until suppuration was established, when mental disturbance, vomiting, and restlessness occurred. During the progress of this parotitis, facial paralysis occurred, and continued, with slight improvement, until the time of death. When the climax of suppuration was reached, a free discharge of ichorous pus followed, with a rapid abatement of the more urgent symptoms; and after the separation of the slough, which was limited in extent, a corresponding reparation was rapid and complete throughout the entire suppurating surface, as well as in the several incisions which had been previously made to liberate the pus.

The question of malarial complication was discussed at this time, but eliminated. During this time the pus-channel, which had opened, had been kept free from accumulations by washing it frequently and thoroughly with solutions of carbolic acid or permanganate of potassium.

During the latter part of August, a number of pustules of suppurating acne appeared in the armpits, and, later, four or five on the surface of the body. They were superficial, numbering ten or twelve, being about the size of large peas; they were opened as soon as suppuration took place, healed without recurrence, and were believed to have been due to the septic condition of the system. The small carbuncle mentioned in the report of the autopsy was doubtless referable to the same cause. The above were the only suppurating surfaces, excepting the incisions made into the wound, and four small superficial bedsores formed on the back, which were observed during the President's illness.

The subject of the removal of the President to a more healthful locality had been discussed for some time; in fact, it had been considered all summer. The heat and oppressiveness of a Washington summer are to be dreaded, even by one in perfect health, although an efficient apparatus had been introduced into the President's room, giving an adequate supply of cold, dry air. The subject of his removal was urgently presented at the consultation of August 25th; but, as at this date the discharge of pus from the parotid gland had not taken place, the majority of physicians present considered that his removal at this time would be attended with very grave peril. His diet throughout the summer had been of a thoroughly and scientifically practical kind; it undoubtedly kept the President alive under the most adverse conditions of continued gastric disturbance.

On August 26th there was a discharge of pus from the mouth, and from the ear through the auditory canal. It was believed that the pus which discharged in the mouth dissected its way along the course of Steno's duct, as there was rigidity of the masseter muscle; but the jaw was fixed so as to prevent the possibility of opening the mouth sufficiently for a satisfactory examination. During this period the patient occasionally wandered in his mind, although, when his attention was fixed by an attendant, his mental condition seemed to be comparatively perfect.

An interesting fact connected with the inflammation of the mucous membrane of the mouth was, that it extended by continuity to the pharynx, larynx, trachea, and bronchi. The physical signs developed the fact that acute bronchial catarrh had followed. Hypostatic congestion of the lungs had been observed for some weeks before, more extensive on the right side than the left, because of the President's position in bed. An improved condition appeared when the pus began to discharge from the parotid gland.

DR. AGNEW IN 1882.

Consequently, it was decided, early in September, that the patient was in a condition to be removed to the sea-shore. The details of his journey from Washington to Elberon, and the precautions taken to secure a safe and speedy transit, were perfect in every particular. Every provision was made to meet any emergency that might arise in the course of the journey, even suitable places along the line of the road being selected to which he could have been removed in case evidences of exhaustion had appeared. His transfer from the Executive Mansion to the cars was made with the least possible disturbance, without accident, and with perfect satisfaction and comfort to the patient. During the journey his pulse and temperature were taken from time to time, and frequent examinations made to determine the effects of the motion at different rates of speed. It was found that the President rested better when riding at the rate of sixty miles an hour. During the last hour of his journey he showed symptoms of fatigue, which would have prevented a longer journey, had such been required to reach his destination.

This journey of the wounded President was unique in the literature of railroad management. At every station along the line of the road crowds of men and women appeared,—the former uncovered and with bowed heads, the latter often weeping. No sound of bells or whistles was heard; train-men vied with each other in aiding the physicians. On arriving at the temporary track laid to the Francklyn Cottage, it was found that the engine had not the weight and power sufficient to pull the train up the steep grade; instantly hundreds of strong hands laid hold and pushed the coaches up to the level.

The President bore the journey well. It was the 6th of September, 1881, and the bracing air of the early fall at the sea-shore and the sound of the waves afforded him the greatest delight and satisfaction. The heat of the two succeeding days made but little impression on the distinguished patient. For eight or ten days his general condition visibly and continuously improved. The President was so much pleased with his improvement that he expressed a desire that the number of his professional attendants should be reduced. Accordingly, only Drs. Agnew, Hamilton, and Bliss remained in charge of the case.

During the evening of September 15th, however, the inevitable change took place, his pulse slightly increasing, occasionally reaching 120 during the night. On September 17th, at 11 A.M., a severe chill of half an hour's duration occurred, followed by a sharp rise in temperature. The mental disturbances were more noticeable during the febrile rise, but the stomach was still able to retain the nourishment and stimulants.

This chill was accompanied by agonizing pain over the chest, which the President compared to the pains in angina pectoris. These pains were subsequently believed to have been caused by the rupture of the aneurismal sac of one of the splenic arteries, the coat of which had been injured by the bullet in its course. This attack of pain was followed by others at intervals of six to twelve hours, which were undoubtedly due to the progressive dissection, at irregular intervals, of the blood into the surrounding tissue, until finally it burst into the abdominal cavity. On September 18th another chill occurred, followed by a febrile rise. At 8 A.M. on September 19th the President's pulse was fast and feeble; his temperature was 108° F., and all the conditions unfavorable. In half an hour afterward there was still another chill, followed by febrile rise. At 8 P.M. on September 19th the President's pulse was still fast and feeble, temperature being 108.8° F. During the periods of chill and fever he was more or less unconscious. At 10.10 P.M. the President sank into an unconscious and dying condition, and expired twenty-five minutes later. The brave and heroic sufferer, the Nation's patient, for whom all had labored so cheerfully and unceasingly, had passed away.

The post-mortem examination was made the following afternoon at 4 o'clock. It was necessary to determine the exact track of the ball and the parts involved; also, to ascertain the immediate cause of death. The autopsy was performed by Dr. D. S. Lamb, assisted by Dr. J. J. Woodward.

Record of the post-mortem examination of the body of President James A. Garfield, made September 20, 1881, commencing at 4.30 p.m., eighteen hours after death, at Francklyn Cottage, Elberon, New Jersey.[1]

Behind the right kidney, after the removal of that organ from the body, the dilated track of the bullet was dissected into. It was found that from the point at which it had fractured the right eleventh rib (three and one-half inches to the right of the vertebral spine), the missile had gone to the left, obliquely forward, passing through the body of the first lumbar vertebra and lodging in the adipose connective tissue immediately below the lower border of the pancreas, about two and one-half inches to the left of the spinal column, and behind the peritoneum. It had become completely encysted.

The track of the bullet between the point at which it had fractured the eleventh rib and that at which it had entered the first lumbar vertebra was considerably dilated, and the pus had burrowed downward through the adipose tissue behind the right kidney, and thence found its way between the peritoneum and the right iliac fascia, making a descending channel which extended almost to the groin. The adipose tissue behind the kidney, in the vicinity of this descending channel, was much thickened and condensed by inflammation. In the channel, which was found almost free from pus, lay the flexible catheter introduced into the wound at the commencement of the autopsy; its extremity was found doubled upon itself, immediately beneath the peritoneum, reposing upon the iliac fascia, where the channel was dilated into a pouch of considerable size. This long, descending channel, now clearly seen to have been caused by the burrowing of pus from the wound, was supposed, during life, to have been the course of the bullet.

The last dorsal, together with the first and second lumbar vertebræ, and the twelfth rib were then removed from the body for more thorough examination.

When this examination was made, it was found that the bullet had penetrated the first lumbar vertebra in the upper part of the right side of its body. The aperture, by which it entered, involved the intervertebral cartilage next above, and was situated just below and anterior to the intervertebral foramen, from which its upper margin was about one-fourth of an inch distant. Passing obliquely to the left, and forward

---

[1] The general condition found at the autopsy is omitted, only the portion referable to the wound being copied.

through the upper part of the body of the first lumbar vertebra, the bullet emerged by an aperture, the centre of which was about one-half inch to the left of the median line, and which also involved the intervertebral cartilage next above. The cancellated tissue of the body of the first lumbar vertebra was very much comminuted, and the fragments somewhat displaced. Several deep fissures extended from the track of the bullet into the lower part of the body of the twelfth dorsal vertebra. Others extended through the first lumbar vertebra into the intervertebral cartilage between it and the second lumbar vertebra. Both this cartilage and that next above were partly destroyed by ulceration. A number of minute fragments from the fractured lumbar vertebra had been driven into the adjacent soft parts.

It was further found that the right twelfth rib also was fractured at a point one and one-fourth inches to the right of the transverse process of the twelfth dorsal vertebra; this injury had not been recognized during life.

On sawing through the vertebra, a little to the right of the median line, it was found that the spinal canal was not involved by the track of the ball. The spinal cord, and other contents of this portion of the spinal canal, presented no abnormal appearances. The rest of the spinal cord was not examined.

Beyond the first lumbar vertebra the bullet continued to go to the left, passing behind the pancreas to the point where it was found. Here it was enveloped in a firm cyst of connective tissue, which contained, besides the ball, a minute quantity of inspissated, somewhat cheesy pus, which formed a thin layer over a portion of the surface of the lead. There was also a black shred adherent to a part of the cyst-wall, which proved, on microscopical examination, to be the remains of a blood-clot. For about an inch from this cyst, the track of the ball behind the pancreas was completely obliterated by the healing process. Thence, as far backward as the body of the first lumbar vertebra, the track was filled with coagulated blood, which extended on the left into an irregular space rent in the adjoining adipose tissue behind the peritoneum and above the pancreas. The blood had worked its way to the left, bursting finally through the peritoneum behind the spleen into the abdominal cavity. The rending of the tissues by the extravasation of this blood was undoubtedly the cause of the paroxysms of pain which occurred a short time before death.

This mass of coagulated blood was of irregular form, and nearly as large as a man's fist. It could be distinctly seen from in front through the peritoneum, after its site behind the greater curvature of the stomach had been exposed by the dissection of the greater omentum from the stomach, and especially after some delicate adhesions between the stomach and the part of the peritoneum covering the blood-mass had been broken down by the fingers. From the relations of the mass, as thus seen, it was believed that the hæmorrhage had proceeded from one of the mesenteric arteries, but, as it was clear that a minute dissection would be required to determine the particular branch involved, it was agreed that the infiltrated tissues and the adjoining soft parts should be preserved for subsequent study.

On the examination and dissection, made in accordance with this agreement, it was found that the fatal hemorrhage proceeded from a rent, nearly four-tenths of an inch long, in the main trunk of the splenic artery, two and one-half inches to the left of the cœliac axis. This rent must have occurred at least several days before death, since the everted edges in the slit in the vessel were united by firm adhesions to the sur-rounding connective tissue, thus forming an almost continuous wall bounding the adjoining portion of the blood-clot. Moreover, the periph-eral portion of the clot in this vicinity was disposed in pretty firm con-centric layers. It was further found that the cyst below the lower mar-gin of the pancreas, in which the bullet was found, was situated three and one-half inches to the left of the cœliac axis.

Besides the mass of coagulated blood just described, another, about the size of a walnut, was found in the greater omentum, near the splenic extremity of the stomach. The communication, if any, between this and the larger hemorrhagic mass could not be made out.

The surgeons assisting at the autopsy were unanimously of the opinion that, on reviewing the history of the case in connection with the autopsy, it is quite evident that the different suppurating surfaces, and especially the fractured, spongy tissue of the vertebra, furnish a suffi-cient explanation of the septic conditions which existed during life.

(Signed)   D. W. Bliss,
J. K. Barnes,
J. J. Woodward,
Robert Reyburn,
D. S. Lamb.

There never was a case in the history of medical literature whose entire course was followed so anxiously, so closely, and so intelligently, by so many millions of people. The surgical aspects of the case became so familiar to the millions who scanned the daily bulletins and read the daily papers that many surgical methods and many technical terms which hitherto had been the exclusive property of the profession, became perfectly familiar to all. Undoubtedly, before the summer was over, the public were able to discuss the case from its purely medical aspect with the greatest thoroughness and intelligence.

Of course, with so many minds studying the same subject, enhanced by the natural obscurity of the case, considerable discussion arose as to the proper treatment. Sensational newspaper-writers, anxious to boom the circulation of their journals, attacked the judgment of the physicians; medical men, eager for notoriety, worked out hypothetical cases in the privacy of their offices, and, fitting the President's condition to their theories, rushed into print. To the credit of the public and physicians in charge of the case, it must be said, however, that the great mass of the public and the majority of newspapers accepted the treatment as correct, as it was outlined in the daily bulletins.

Through all this storm of excitement, criticism, doubt, and responsibility, the little *coterie* of physicians in charge of the President's case maintained a dignified silence. It was encouraging to see that they were not driven from the decision which they had reached, by this great storm which raged throughout the American world. In the sober light of after-judgment it was universally conceded, not only by the nation as a whole, but by the better class of the press[1] and the entire medical profession, that the case had been perfectly treated, and that nothing had been left undone, either in the way of meeting existing conditions or anticipating possible contingencies.

The questions to be discussed in deciding upon the correctness of the treatment are as follow:—

1. *Was the wound necessarily a mortal one?* This question was, of course, of the most vital importance, in which all-

---

[1] It is curious to note that in the thousands of newspaper clippings on Dr. Agnew's life, published at the time of his death, there were but two unfavorable notices found. One of these appeared in a Brooklyn paper, written by some journalistic genius who stated that he knew all about the condition of the vertebra of President Garfield, as revealed at the autopsy, long before he died. The other appeared in a journal published in Salt Lake City under Mormon management. It stated that Dr. Agnew put President Garfield under a course of treatment that would have killed a well man.

considerations as to diagnosis, treatment, and the precise mode of death would be, in comparison, of secondary moment, although, in the consideration of the attending physicians, these points were just as material. In the event of the plea of malpractice being offered in the Guiteau trial, this would have been the principal question to have been determined, from a legal stand-point. In this connection, the discussion in the *North American Review* for December, 1881, by four leading medical authorities of this country,—Dr. John Ashhurst, Jr., Dr. J. Marion Sims, Dr. John T. Hodgen, and Dr. William A. Hammond,—is to the point.

Undoubtedly, the strongest arguments on both sides of the case are presented in this symposium. The only one of the four to take the ground that the wound in the vertebra, in the case of President Garfield, was not necessarily mortal was Dr. William A. Hammond. Dr. Hammond rested this proposition entirely on a few quotations from surgical literature, from which he endeavored to show that patients may recover from gunshot wounds of the vertebræ. The quotations made by him are garbled in the extreme; portions of the statements being quoted, qualifying or explanatory portions being left out, and conclusions being reached wholly unwarranted by the quotations selected. Further, in such cases as are cited no attempt was made to prove their similarity in any essential particular to the case of President Garfield. It was a matter of surprise to many who did not know Dr. Hammond that he should have dared to risk the positive assertion that death was not inevitable from such a wound, based on such insufficient and deceptive data.

On the other hand, the other three authorities, Drs. John Ashhurst, Jr., J. Marion Sims, and John T. Hodgen, agreed that the President's wound was necessarily a mortal one. The real status of the literature of surgery on the subject was fully expressed by Dr. J. Marion Sims, when he wrote that "*our whole medical literature does not contain a single well-authenticated case of recovery from such a wound.*"

2. *Did the position of the President and the assassin at the time of the shooting offer any clue as to the track of the bullet?* It was overlooked by many critics of the treatment that this point was carefully considered at the time of the shooting and subsequently. The fact that the ball, on entering the body, struck the eleventh rib and was deflected at almost a right angle from its original course, immediately on entering the body, together with its zigzag course later,—revealed at the autopsy,—showed that there was no satisfactory data to be obtained from this source.

3. *Could the ball have been detected and located by the use of probes?* The track of the bullet as seen at the autopsy showed the wisdom of the physicians in their refusal to persist in probing. The ball, after fracturing the eleventh rib, was deflected downward, comminuting the twelfth rib; it then passed through the fibres of the psoas magnus muscle, which run longitudinally; these fibres undoubtedly closed soon after the passage of the ball, eliminating all possibility of following its course, so that the track of the ball disappeared within a short distance from the skin. If the probing had been persisted in, undoubtedly the aorta, the thoracic duct, or the vena cava, would have been in danger of being ruptured, for the vessels lay, with their delicate walls, in the direct course of the probe; such an accident meant instant death. If this greater danger had been avoided, the foramen opening into the uninjured spinal canal might have been entered, with unfortunate results. It would have been impossible to have reached the opening through the body of the vertebra; even if it had been reached, the ball would have lain undiscovered on the other side of the spine. Persistent attempts at probing would have killed the President at once, without possessing the slightest chance of revealing the position of the ball. If the ball had been found it would have made no difference in the result, for it had become encysted, as was expected, and was doing no harm.

4. *Were there any symptoms which pointed to the injury in the spinal column?* Many readers, confused by the similarity of the words "spinal cord" and "spinal column," imagined that the spinal cord had been injured. On the contrary, the autopsy revealed the fact that it was uninjured, the spinal column, or its bony support, being the portion fractured by the ball in its passage. If the spinal cord had been injured, it would have been discovered, but no positive symptoms existed of the injury to the vertebra; in fact, beyond a few tingling sensations and the hyperesthesia felt on the right side of the body below the waist, there were no nervous symptoms at all. To have based a diagnosis of fracture of the vertebra on such data as this would have been poor surgery, for these slight symptoms are not at all characteristic of such an accident. The possibility of this injury had been considered, however, by the consultants at their first meeting, but there was a total absence of data on which to base such a belief. The probe, as has been shown, could not have revealed its existence. The vomiting and collapse, which were extreme, are symptoms of shock, and are common to that condition. Their existence, to an extreme degree, suggested the possibility of injury of some important viscera, but all other traces of such a calamity were absent during the entire course of the case. All those persons who revealed the fact—the majority of them after the autopsy—that they had diagnosed this fracture of the vertebra based their opinions on data too weak to be anything more than mere guesswork.

5. *Should an exploratory operation have been performed to search for the bullet and to reveal the condition of the wounded parts?* From a study of the answers to the previous questions, it can be seen that there was no clue as to the direction in which such an exploration should have been made. As was believed at the outset, it would have added greater peril to the case, without improving in any way the prospects of the wounded President.

Undoubtedly, the fatal issue of the case was due to this

injury of the vertebra. The septicemia, or blood-poisoning, which appeared can be traced to this source. The injury of the cancellated structure of bone is peculiarly prone to be followed by the production of blood-poisoning. It was a matter of surprise to the public to learn that such is the case; it is due to the fact that the open venous sinuses in the cancellated tissue of bone, bathed in ichorous pus, are most favorable conditions for absorption of this poison and the production of this state.

There was no criticism made at any time by any one as to the nursing and feeding and the general hygienic treatment of the patient. This was acknowledged by all to have been superb, undoubtedly prolonging the President's life for many weeks. It is certain that no improvement could have been made in the treatment, had the injury to the vertebra been known. The treatment throughout was in accord with the rules of the strictest antiseptic surgery. Dr. Hammond wrote in the article quoted: " I desire to express my profound admiration for the fidelity, devotion, and assiduity displayed by the attending and consulting surgeons. Rarely has any man, whether of high or low degree, had a more laborious and dutiful body of medical and surgical attendants than had President Garfield, and I believe that in no other country in the world could such entire abnegation of self as they exhibited have been obtained from physicians and surgeons in attendance on prince or potentate." Dr. Hammond attacked only the surgical treatment of the first forty-eight hours as not being in accordance with surgical precepts. This was before the consultants were called in; but as they concurred in the correctness of this treatment, its responsibility fell on them also.

It was thought probable that the bullet had been deflected into the right iliac fossa; but this belief was not held unreservedly by the attending physicians, and by Dr. Agnew it was regarded as a mere possibility. As to the course of the ball, it was not an error of diagnosis, but simply an absence of diagnosis. Such conditions are every-day occurrences in surgery.

As to the immediate cause of death, it was believed by Dr. Hammond, in the article just quoted, that it was due to heart-thrombus, and that the pus-sac was the sole cause of the blood-poisoning. It was acknowledged by all, however, excepting this author, that the principal source of septic infection was the wound in the lumbar vertebra, and that death was due to the rupture of the aneurismal sac of the splenic artery, either from its injury by the bullet in its course or from the extension of the process of inflammation to the artery from the track of the ball. Dr. Hammond claimed the possibility of the rupture of the aneurismal sac by the injection of the embalmer, overlooking the fact, pointed out to him by Dr. William Hunt, in the *New York Medical Record* (November 26, 1881), that the blood in the abdominal cavity could not have been pushed out of the splenic artery by the embalming-fluid, for the reason that there is nothing in arteries which can be pushed out after death, these channels being empty at this time. Moreover, the arrangement of the clot in concentric layers showed that the hemorrhage must have occurred during life.

These statements and opinions of Dr. Hammond are supposed to represent the strong side of criticism as to the management of the President's case. They are based on data pitifully weak, and they fall entirely short of proving that any essential difference in the mode of treatment would have resulted any more favorably. Dr. Hammond did not claim that the ball could have been found, much less abstracted, or that any system of drainage of the wound in the vertebra could have been established, thus removing the principal if not the sole cause of the blood-poisoning, and possibly preventing that depraved general condition of the system which superinduced the rupture of the aneurism. On the other hand, the other three physicians quoted above frankly acknowledged as follows: Dr. John Ashhurst, Jr.—" Looking at the whole case from beginning to end, I do not see that the treatment could have been altered in any way to the advantage of the illustrious patient; nothing was done that should have been omitted, and nothing was left undone that could possibly have been of benefit." Dr. J. Marion Sims— " The President's surgeons did all that men could do, all that the present state of science would permit, and all that could have been done even if they had at first ascertained the course and direction of the ball. Our whole medical literature does not contain a single well-authenticated case of recovery from such a wound. He had not the least chance of recovery under any circumstances or any treatment." Dr. John T. Hodgen— " In reviewing the history of the case of President Garfield, I can find no reason for adverse criticism of any part of the management."

So universally was the correctness of the treatment of President Garfield conceded, that the legal counsel defending the assassin Guiteau did not attempt to use this point in his defense, resting instead on a claim of insanity. Guiteau himself, however, alternated between an expressed belief that the doctors had killed the President and that that official had been removed by divine command; he was unable, however, to explain the discrepancy existing between these two beliefs. The first belief was brought out at the commencement of his trial in the following incident. Colonel Rockwell had been placed on the witness-stand, by the prosecution, to prove the shooting of the President. After a number of questions had been asked him, the counsel for Guiteau arose, and, claiming that the questions asked were irrelevant, said, " We do not deny, your honor, the killing of the President." Guiteau immediately sprang to his feet and exclaimed, " Yes, we do, your honor; we admit the shooting of the President,—not the killing."

The remarkable trial, subsequent conviction, and execution of Guiteau have become a portion of American history.

Through the terrible ordeal and frightful monotony of eighty days of prolonged suffering and of incessant watching, the wounded President bore all with incredible patience and the most Christian-like fortitude. He constantly maintained a cheerful aspect; his words and actions were always courageous, although undoubtedly he was deeply impressed with the probable issue of his case. When he asked Dr. Bliss at the outset, if there was any chance for recovery, Dr. Bliss replied: "Mr. President, your injury is formidable. In my judgment, however, you have a chance for recovery." The President replied, with a cheerful smile: "Well, Doctor, we will take that chance." This was his attitude through his entire illness. In everything he aided the physicians and nurses in their difficult work without murmuring or faltering.

The history of this famous case and the course of treatment are given and explained with a moderate degree of detail, because to a large portion of the American public, outside of Philadelphia and its vicinity, it was the chief means of acquaintanceship with Dr. Agnew's name. It has been stated that Dr. Agnew's connection with the Garfield case was the circumstance which made him famous. In regard to a portion of the laity, this is undoubtedly true, for the environments of a physician's life are such that there is no way for him to become known nationally except by connection with some such incident. The degree of celebrity attained by Dr. Agnew from his connection with this case cannot be under-estimated. This was the beginning of that acquaintanceship with his character and career which have, therefore, become known until now there is probably not a hamlet in the United States in which a fair knowledge of his career and a good estimate of his character and services are not possessed by the intelligent citizen. His connection with this case was so indissoluble that it was seen even in the streets of his own city, where his fame and achievements were no new thing; it was a common experience for patients sitting in his office to hear passers-by say something of this purport: "Here is Dr. Agnew's office,—don't you remember; he was Garfield's surgeon?"

At the same time, it is not fair to Dr. Agnew to say that it was this connection which made him a famous man. The

medical profession of the world had regarded him as the leading surgical authority in America and probably the most expert
operator in the world, long before he was consulted by Dr. Bliss.
Dr. Bliss, in his selection of the President's chief consultant,
simply voiced the general opinion of the medical profession.
Certainly there was no educated physician who had not been,
previously, familiar with Dr. Agnew's career and teaching.

While the Garfield case made Dr. Agnew better known to
the general public, at the same time he would have been as
much beloved and as well known to the larger portion of the
intelligent American world without it. That this is true is
shown by the tremendous variety of locations from which his
patients came. It was a common experience to find clustered
in his waiting-room patients from far-distant points. For example, one of his friends remembers to have seen, waiting to see
Dr. Agnew at one time, a patient from San Francisco, another
from New Orleans, and a third from Boston. They came from
everywhere, even as far as from India and different portions
of Europe.

The strain and annoyance caused by this case on the attending physicians can never be known. Looking simply at
one phase of it, it is hard for any one to realize the espionage
under which each physician rested, and the constant pressure
brought to bear by persons seeking information as to the President's condition. Not only was Dr. Agnew constantly besieged
by visitors, but even his servants were not exempt from interviews. It was the custom for Dr. Agnew and Dr. Hamilton to
go alternately to Washington or to Elberon certain days in the
week. Of course, this had a bad effect upon Dr. Agnew's
practice, as it made him unable to attend to much of his work,
and also made him uncertain in his town visits; and, on
the other hand, many patients from this cause came to him
simply out of curiosity. His limited time in town caused his
waiting-room to be crowded always. Not only was the room
full, but the windows, the hall-way, steps, and frequently the

street in front. Often some waiting patient, whose time hung heavily on his hands, would count from seventy to one hundred people waiting to see Dr. Agnew. On such occasions Dr. Agnew never hurried over the patients; he examined each case that presented itself as carefully as if it were the only one. This was always his custom,—he never hurried a patient out of his office. When his time was exhausted, he would step into his waiting-room and say: "I have seen all that I can to-day; those who still care to see me will please come at my next office hours."

No one can ever know the terrible, protracted strain on all the physicians in this case. The letters received by Dr. Agnew formed a part of this ordeal. Frequently a stack of letters a foot high would be received in one day, telling him what to do, what not to do, suggesting remedies, threatening, inquisitive, and impudent.

One unpleasant phase of the illness of the President was the eagerness with which certain unscrupulous persons used the condition of the President as a means to better their financial condition. So alarming was the condition of the President from the outset, and so anxious was the public to ascertain his condition, that newspapers issued editions at night. Two or three stout-lunged fellows with great rolls of papers under their arms would start round some quiet street in the small hours of the night, and by their shoutings would awaken nearly the entire block. The half-awake citizen, hearing a jumble in the street, and catching a fragmentary word here and there, naturally imagined that some fresh calamity had befallen the nation. He would purchase the paper, and by the time he had examined it, only to find that it contained nothing of special importance, the energetic newsboy would be out of reach.

When the Committee sent by Congress to obtain from Dr. Agnew his bill for attending the President came to Philadelphia to his office, Dr. Agnew said: "Gentlemen, I present no bill for my attendance to President Garfield. I gave my services freely and gratuitously." He persevered in his determination to present no bill, despite the advice and solicitation of the Committee who had charge of the arrangements.

Undoubtedly the attendance on this case, and the subsequent treatment which he received, killed Dr. Bliss. During the eighty days which the President lived, after receiving his injury, Dr. Bliss' attention was unceasing. The strain, both mental and physical, which he endured, so broke down his health that he was unable to resume practice for a long time afterward. The terrible ordeal through which he had passed, the attacks made upon him, and the accusations both as to his professional and moral abilities, shattered him completely. He found, in consequence, that his practice had been largely scattered, and he realized that he was not equal, physically, to the effort of regaining it. In consequence, his income, which had averaged $20,000 a year before his assumption of the President's case, fell to almost nothing. The last blow which he received was the niggardly manner in which he was treated by the government. His claim for $25,000 for his attendance on the President, which was a very modest sum, under the circumstances, was cut down, and he received $6500. He never recovered from this last action, which he regarded in the light of an insult, and his death occurred not long after. Although Dr. Agnew would present no bill, his claim was made equal to that of Dr. Hamilton's, $15,000, while each of the other attending physicians put in a claim for $10,000. Congress appropriated the sum of $35,000, with which to pay the expenses of the case. As has been said, Dr. Bliss received $6500; Drs. Agnew and Hamilton, each, $5000; Dr. Reyburn, $4000; the nurses, Drs. Boynton and Edson, received $4000 and $3000, respectively.

After paying these sums to the physicians in attendance, the remainder of the money which Congress had voted to the physicians was returned to the Treasury by the Board of Audit, although they had been instructed to distribute the whole amount. Of the *coterie* of physicians who attended President Garfield, Dr. Robert Reyburn is the only survivor. This experience of Dr. Bliss with the Garfield case is not an unusual one in medicine. It is a good commentary on the value of publicity to a physician.

The position which Dr. Agnew held in the Garfield case was that of chief consulting surgeon. He was recognized by the patient, by the attending physicians, and by the public as the man to whose judgment the greatest importance was attached. His selection for this position was spontaneous and undisputed, and he performed all the operations which were done, exhibiting his usual dexterity and skill. It has been said that when Dr. Bliss handed the keen-bladed knife to Dr. Agnew the eyes of the Nation were upon that blade; and yet, in no way did the distinguished surgeon show that there was any unusual stress on his nerves, or that he was affected by the unusual importance of the situation.

In a recent letter of condolence from Mrs. Garfield, she places the following estimate upon Dr. Agnew's services at the bedside of her distinguished husband: "Dr. Agnew's faithful attendance at the President's bedside through his days of suffering won our deepest gratitude and our entire confidence in his distinguished ability as physician and surgeon. His presence was a constant source of encouragement and comfort to General Garfield, and his ever-entertaining discourse tided my husband over many dark hours."

Dr. Agnew never took a hopeful view of the President's case. He was most eager, of course, to hope that a favorable issue would follow, but he never allowed himself to be deceived by delusive beliefs. He knew that deep-seated, undiscoverable mischief was at work. One day at Elberon Dr. Bliss, in speaking of the President's case, said that the world would soon see the most wonderful cure in medical history. The same evening, in conversation with Dr. Agnew, some one gave expression to the enthusiasm of Dr. Bliss and the joy the country would feel at the rescue of the stricken President. Dr. Agnew listened attentively, and said, in his quiet way: "I pray every hour for this consummation; but when I first saw the President I felt that death had claimed him. I would be the happiest man in Elberon to believe as Dr. Bliss does. The President may live the day out, and possibly to-morrow; but he cannot live a week." Garfield died the next day.

This case of President Garfield made a difficult and unpleasant task for his attending surgeons. There was apparently to the public but small chance to exercise great diagnostic judgment or operative skill. The course laid out by the consultants required but a few operations, which were only moderately difficult in their performance, and not especially dangerous. This lack of opportunity for the performance of some brilliant surgical operation by which, after taking great risks, the President could have been restored to health, was deplored by many. On the contrary, no better illustration exists, in his whole career, of the character of Dr. Agnew than that, under the stress of outside influence, he did not swerve a fraction of an inch from his better judgment and attempt a brilliant exploratory operation instead of adopting the course he did. He did what he felt to be his duty,—what his judgment dictated,— without regard to its effect on the outside world. He had no desire to kindle admiration or create excitement.

The great importance of the service rendered by Dr. Agnew in the case of President Garfield can scarcely be appreciated, after it was accomplished. The credit of this is due largely to Dr. Agnew, because, while all the surgeons were unanimous in their conceptions of the treatment of the case, yet, undoubtedly, had Dr. Agnew advocated another plan of treatment, it would have been followed out. The President's assassination threw the whole country into a state of the greatest excitement, alarm, and apprehension. If the President had died at once, there is no telling what might have happened. Especial apprehension was felt in regard to the line of succession to the Presidency, in case anything should happen to the Vice-President.

This contingency had never been provided for by the founders of the government. It was a peculiarly dangerous period, especially on account of the numerous insane persons throughout the country who are on the outlook for such occasions, and who always come forward at such times, producing the most calamitous consequences. If the President had died at once, or soon after the shooting, probably the excitement, publicity, and apprehension would have brought forward a Guiteau for President Arthur. The President being kept alive, all feelings of uneasiness and resentment passed away. The government had an opportunity to arrange its workings, and the whole country subsided into a calmer mood. This work of keeping a mortally wounded man alive for nearly three months was most stupendous in its accomplishment and in its results for the country at large.

Moreover, its value to President and Mrs. Garfield should not be overlooked. It gave opportunity for the settling of the business of the President and the arrangement of his spiritual affairs, which was most comforting to the living and the dying.

CHAPTER XI.

DR. AGNEW'S HOME-LIFE.[1]

So many know of Agnew the surgeon, and so few know of Agnew the man! This was unfortunate, for it was under his own roof-tree, and in the midst of his own little family that the most beautiful side of his character was shown. It was my privilege to have lived with this good man for a period of fifteen years. We were not a large family; there were only four of us,—Dr. and Mrs. Agnew, and their two nieces, Miss Ella P. Irwin and myself. This number formed, in Dr. Agnew's estimation, a perfect family; four at home, and in travel being a complete number.

In their earlier life in Philadelphia Dr. and Mrs. Agnew had been in the habit of spending their summers in travel, or in resting at some quiet sea-side resort, near enough to the city to allow him to go there daily. For several years they had a cottage at Atlantic City, being among the first to realize the benefits and disadvantages of that city by the sea.

In 1872 Dr. and Mrs. Agnew decided to go abroad; they sailed in June and returned in September. This was the only time Dr. Agnew ever crossed the ocean. He was always hoping for a time to come when he might throw off every care and take a more satisfactory European trip; for, unfortunately, this trip was saddened by the sudden and serious illness of Mrs. Agnew. She was taken sick in Geneva, Switzerland, where she lay in a critical condition for some time. When she had improved sufficiently to be moved, she was taken to Paris, where Mr. John Russell Young, then correspondent for the *New York Herald*, kindly placed his home at her disposal.

While at Geneva, Dr. Agnew performed several operations; for he could not, even on a pleasure-trip, leave his work

---

[1] This chapter was written by Margaret Agnew Adams.

wholly behind him. In consequence of Mrs. Agnew's illness, Dr. Agnew was unable to visit many of the European hospitals or to form the acquaintance of the medical men whom it would have been a mutual pleasure to have met.

Yet, when Dr. Agnew returned from Europe, he came home with a much higher respect for American medicine and surgery. He said: "Here we feel that the welfare of the patient is our first and highest duty. Abroad, especially upon the Continent, this seems to be a secondary matter. There they are more anxious to find out what is the matter with the patient, and look more eagerly for an autopsy than for a recovery."

In 1875 they spent the summer at Atlantic City, where Mrs. Agnew contracted a severe attack of typhoid fever, following which for eight months she hovered between life and death. By the summer of 1876 she had sufficiently recovered to be taken to the country, and she was moved to Bryn Mawr. They had learned so to dread the bad drainage of hotels and sea-side resorts and the exposure incident to travel, that they determined to purchase a permanent country home, in which they could spend the summer.

Feeling well satisfied with the purity of the air in the vicinity of Bryn Mawr, and its nearness to the city, Dr. Agnew, in the fall of 1876, purchased a number of acres at Haverford College Station, on the line of the Pennsylvania Railroad, one mile east of Bryn Mawr.

He was one of the pioneer settlers in this region, which has since become so popular and fashionable among rich Philadelphians. Here he built his country home, "Wyndrift," in which he spent, subsequently, so many happy hours. A portion of his property he disposed of, the following summer, to his intimate friend, Mr. Crawford Arnold.

This Haverford home was to him the resting ground for the few leisure hours which he took from his work. Always an extremely early riser, here he arose at 6 o'clock in the morning, bathed, shaved, and breakfasted by 7 o'clock, and walked to the station, a distance of about three squares, and took the 7.11 A.M. train for the city; this enabled him to be in his office by 10 minutes of 8 o'clock each morning. In the summer-time he had no afternoon office-hour, remaining in his office until half-past 11 or 12 o'clock; then he ate a light lunch, consisting invariably of cream-toast, milk, and a soft-boiled egg. These articles of food constituted his principal diet, for he was always most abstemious with food and drink. Then he saw the patients who required visiting for the day, always planning, if possible, to return home about 5 o'clock in the afternoon.

He usually sat, on his way to town, with his friend Dr. Walter F. Atlee, whose station was several miles west of Haverford, thus giving him greater advantage in the selection of a seat. The seat which they generally occupied would not have been considered desirable by most people; it was the one at the extreme front of the car, just back of the door, but it suited them, and, being conservative men, they did not change after once having made their selection. Often they would spend the short half-hour in conversation—sometimes earnest, serious talks; again, merry tales and anecdotes. Indeed, Dr. Atlee proved to be such a sparkling *raconteur* that it became quite the thing for us to look forward to an evening dinner-hour, when our dear doctor would sooner or later begin, with a smile of pleased recollection, "Atlee was telling me to-day,"—and then would follow "Atlee's latest."

Often, however, the thirty minutes were spent in reading. Dr. Agnew was never without a book, generally a volume similar in size and style to the series of the "Little Classics."

When Dr. Agnew could come out to his country place he left behind him all the worries and anxieties of his busy professional life. Probably it required a visit to Haverford to see him in his pleasantest, easiest moods. Here he dropped all thought of hurry or business, and lost that reticence which was somewhat a characteristic of his work, with those with whom he was not fully acquainted.

He made a most charming host; he was affability and hospitality itself, and he possessed that rare faculty of making his guest quickly and thoroughly at home. Many people, awed by his presence and reputation, have often said that they were afraid to unbend before him; but here he placed himself in the mood of all those with whom he came in contact. He was a brilliant conversationalist, and possessed that rare faculty of bringing out in those around him their own ideas and thoughts. He was able to talk with every one who came to his house on their own daily work in a surprisingly familiar way, and he was that rarest of rare beings,—a sympathetic listener. Quietly adding a word here and there, even the most diffident school-girl was at ease with him.

He loved to entertain his friends. Many persons imagined him to be stiff, dignified, and devoid of humor. On the contrary, while thoroughly dignified, he never impressed any one, with whom he was fully acquainted, with any severity of manner, and his sense of humor and of the ridiculous was very marked. He would see instantly any ridiculous situation or incident, and could tell a story with the greatest clearness and force.

No one approved of pure fun or humor more thoroughly than Dr. Agnew; but he was sensitively averse to gossip,—even so-called innocent gossip he abhorred; and I have seen him look pained and embarrassed while within ear-shot of idle chatterers whom he could not rebuke. In his own family, he simply would not brook anything which even savored of gossip, saying always, "If you cannot speak well of a person, it is best to say nothing."

When Dr. and Mrs. Agnew built their country home, it was with the intention of spending six months of the year there, continuously, Dr. Agnew intending to take a week or two off in the summer; but he soon found that Haverford was not the haven of rest he had desired, for his patients sought him out even there. So it naturally came about that every summer Dr. Agnew found it necessary, in order to obtain any rest at all, to take a short outing, lasting regularly from ten days to two weeks, and, although no one enjoyed traveling more than he, he allowed himself only one of these during the year. Short as these trips were, much pleasure was crowded into them. We usually started on our little jaunt about the second or third week of August.

These outings were always most pleasant to us and most eagerly looked forward to; for at these times we had our dear doctor all to ourselves, while at home his whole time belonged almost exclusively to the ailing public. A doctor's life is trying not to himself alone; his whole family is called upon to make many sacrifices. Indeed, a doctor's household is perhaps more thoroughly identified with his work than that of any other professional man. Of social life a successful doctor has almost nothing. How many, many times, when we have been all ready for a dinner or reception, messages have come calling our doctor away! We were never sure of a quiet half-hour with him, even at meal-time.

When away on one of these trips, he enjoyed nothing better than a good novel. The class of stories which he read were such books as "Lorna Doone," the tales of Scott, "Rab and His Friends," "Uncle Remus," etc.; he was particularly fond of dialect tales, especially such Scotch and negro stories as illustrated the traits, customs, or thoughts of their heroes.

Many persons at such times noted with surprise how difficult it was to get him to his meals when he was immersed in the excitements of a well-told story. One of the last novels he read was "Kidnapped," by Robert Louis Stevenson. He entered into its exciting vicissitudes with all the enthusiasm and delight of a boy.

It was always a great pleasure to travel with him; he had friends everywhere, and every one was anxious, even eager, to serve him. Hotel proprietors instinctively gave him the best rooms; even the porters on the trains in some mysterious way knew him.

There was some subtle influence about him, which made even strangers vie with each other to increase his comfort and do him homage. Perhaps it was the uncommon make-up of the man; his splendid physique and general ruggedness, softened by the crown of soft, white hair, and the mildness of very clear blue eyes. Dr. Agnew, like his father and uncles before him, was like unto the sons of Anak for goodly height and manly proportions. He stood six feet one inch in his stockings.

As he grew older, he grew more imposing in appearance. His hair, which was always light, whitened in his early manhood; in his early years he wore a full beard, but later in life discarded everything except a moustache, which he allowed to grow rather long. There was a great deal of character in his hands; they were strong, white, and wonderfully supple, and beautifully cared for. In his dress, Dr. Agnew was plain to a marked degree, generally wearing a black frock-coat, black vest, and black, or sometimes gray trousers. The only latitude he allowed himself in dress was in the selection of neck-ties. Although usually wearing a black four-in-hand tie, the supply of which was always kept full by a patient, yet he sometimes would appear in a garnet satin bow-tie.

In the fall of 1886 Dr. R. J. Levis determined to sell his residence at 1601 Walnut Street. Dr. Agnew, who had lived at 1611 Chestnut Street for almost twenty-one years, and who had been for some time on the lookout for a house adapted to the purposes of a physician, heard that the Levis house was for sale and lost no time in securing it. This house was rebuilt by Dr. Levis, and was especially planned for a surgeon, having its offices on Sixteenth Street, entirely separate from the rest of the house and not interfering in any way with the domestic arrangements. The house has frequently been called the "Surgeons' House," for it was occupied originally by Dr. Edward Hartshorne, surgeon to the Pennsylvania Hospital.

I think sufficient emphasis has not been placed upon Dr. Agnew's magnificent constitution, which enabled him to perform the tremendous amount of work that he did. Until within the last five years of his life, he was never known to have an ache nor pain excepting an occasional attack of rheumatism. How often, when some member of his family complained of headache, he would say, quizzically, "Headache, what is it? I have never had it in my life!"

He was one of the most pains-taking, tireless workers that ever lived, toiling steadily and patiently from early morning until far into the night. He really seemed to find recreation in work, and after doing the work of three ordinary men during the day—work of the most difficult, delicate, and nerve-trying character—he would come home in the evening and go to his office to write with all the freshness and zest of a boy.

His freshness and enthusiasm made him seem always young. He never gave the effect of being old, and, compared with many who were no older than himself, he seemed very youthful in his ways and thoughts. This was due partly to the fact that he adapted himself quickly and thoroughly to any improvements in modern life as easily as he did to those in medicine. While he loved and revered the good old customs of by-gone days, he did not cling blindly to old traditions. As he said himself: "I am not one of those who believe that the old is always better than the new; that we should always hold to the traditions and methods of the past. The past has gone into history, and can only be useful to us in so far as it will serve to illuminate the present and the future."

A propos of this youthful effect upon his intimate friends and relatives, I well remember my intense indignation when, as a young girl, I was asked the name of the "old white-haired gentleman who sat so far front in the Second Church." White-haired, to be sure; but old—never!

Dr. Agnew's belief in his ability as a worker in any field was always of the humblest character. He never trusted in his own powers, but always before an operation asked for divine guidance during its performance. He carried the same humble opinion into his church-life. He was chosen four times to the eldership in his church, but each time he declined the call because he deemed himself unworthy for this sacred office.

Trained from childhood to the strictest observance of the Lord's day, Dr. Agnew rigidly upheld all the old customs in his own home. Sunday-morning breakfast was, if anything, earlier than that of the other mornings of the week. After a chapter in the Bible and a prayer for divine guidance through the day, the family separated, to meet again in a few hours at church. Service over, we walked quietly home and sat down to a plain dinner, for Dr. Agnew was strongly opposed to "first-day feasts." After dinner followed a happy home-hour, in which the sermon of the morning was discussed, questions in the catechism were asked and explained, and favorite hymns were sung. At 2.30 we separated again, the doctor going to visit his patients and the younger ones going to Sunday-school. At 6 o'clock came supper, after which another chapter from the Bible and a prayer for divine protection during the hours of the night, and the doctor would spend the intervening time before evening service in reading the Bible or his favorite "Life of Guthrie"; 9.30 o'clock found the house closed for the night.

As a child, how I dreaded those Sundays! No Sunday-school books, no walks, no gazing out of the front window at the altogether too attractive dresses of other little girls! How hard, how tiresomely hard it all seemed! As I grew older, however, those dear Sundays at home became to me the sweetest days of all the days of my young womanhood; and I shall always hold them in blessed memory.

Dr. Agnew never had a Sunday office-hour,[1] and never,

---

[1] He observed the custom, however, of seeing patients in his office at 5 o'clock Sunday afternoon, whose condition demanded attention, but who were not sick enough to be confined to the house.

unless kept away by some ailing one, missed the morning and evening service at the church he so dearly loved.

He was particularly attracted to clergymen, esteeming it the greatest honor and privilege to entertain them. I can see him now—the dear old man—with face all aglow, sitting on the porch of his country home, in close converse with his dear friends MacIntosh and Hoge. These men were to his later years what Beadle had been to his younger manhood. What delight he took in them ! What joy it was to him to entertain them ! In the days he spent with them, it seemed as though his heart were kindled afresh with the fires of youth. And with what glee would he listen to their anecdotes, and, in his quiet way, add boyish reminiscences of his own !

He was extraordinarily well acquainted with theology, and could argue on a doctrine or discuss a theological movement with the greatest vigor and comprehensiveness. He undoubtedly would have made a good minister. He could talk beautifully and simply on religious subjects, on which he felt a great courtesy toward the feelings and opinions of all. He would frequently allow points to pass in which he did not believe, simply from a desire not to wound the feelings of his guest.

There was always a great source of affinity between members of other religious beliefs and Dr. Agnew. Although he was of the strictest Calvin Presbyterian belief, yet he was very tolerant of other beliefs, and formed many of his friends among people who were most diverse to him in religious opinions. Roman Catholics seemed particularly attracted to him, especially members of the priesthood and sisterhood. It was no uncommon sight to see four or six nuns sitting in his waiting-room. He expressed great sympathy and admiration for the works of these orders, and under no circumstances would he charge them for his services any more than he did the Protestant clergy. In return, they appreciated his kindness and skill and made him the recipient of many beautiful presents.

The number of presents which Dr. Agnew received was

simply tremendous. They consisted of everything imaginable: handsome carriages, thorough-bred horses, registered cattle, watches, canes, barrels of oysters, terrapin,—in fact, everything fancy could suggest. He smoked the very best brands of cigars and cigarettes, which were always kept in stock by his admirers. Even his ice-house each winter was filled with particularly pure ice sent by a patient from northern Pennsylvania. Without going more into detail, this will give an idea of the infinite variety of presents received by him.

It always annoyed and displeased Dr. Agnew to be complimented for his work or praised for his skill; he had no craving for such return, and he always tried to avoid it. At the time of the semi-centennial celebrations of his entrance into the medical profession, there were so many laudatory expressions poured forth on him by the medical profession, his patients, by the newspapers, and from the pulpit that he said it made him uneasy. He feared that the good people of Philadelphia would want to banish him, impelled by the same reason that the Athenians ostracized Aristides—because they had grown weary of hearing him called "the Just."

Doctors are only human, and they have instinctively their likes and dislikes among their patients; they live in a little world of their own, of which they are the centre, and in which they come into the most confidential relations with those who have intrusted to them their health. This relation is often even more confidential than that which exists between pastor and people.

The responsibility which a true physician feels toward his patients is something which bears heavily upon him, and yet, at the same time, brings him the keenest pleasure. Dr. Agnew always regarded his duty to his patients as a most sacred trust, allowing nothing to interrupt its performance.

While Dr. Agnew did not allow himself to be biased by his personal feelings, still, like other physicians, he had his attractions and repulsions among his patients. No one among them, however, ever knew when he experienced the latter feeling;

on the contrary, they rather regarded themselves as the favored ones. Fortunately they were few in number, for Dr. Agnew was as fond of the majority of his patients as they were of him. Once in a while, however, he would meet with a patient who tried his forbearance to the utmost. Every practising physician has some such patients, the very sight of whom tires him as soon as they enter his office-door.

These patients have usually been seriously afflicted with some ailment at one time, from which they have recovered, but they have been unable to rid their minds of the delusion that they are still suffering from disease. Dr. Agnew, by his prominent position and well-known forbearance, attracted to him from time to time a number of these hypochondriac cases. He knew too well beforehand the repetition of the long, unnecessary recital of their peculiar woes.

During his illness of a year ago, there was one patient who called on him regularly every day to see if he were well enough to attend to her wants. Her all-consuming concentration on her own sorrows had dimmed her anxiety for his condition, excepting the desire that she wanted him to get well enough to attend to her. She impressed upon those whom she met the great devotion which Dr. Agnew felt for her, and said: "If he knew I were down-stairs, sick as he is, he would get up and come down and see me." So persistent was she in her daily calls that when the doctor finally recovered sufficiently to see a few selected cases occasionally, her name, without his knowledge, was put among the first on the list. As soon as his eye caught this fact he exclaimed, "I would give a hundred dollars not to see that chatter-box. Write and tell her that I cannot see her." When he was expostulated with that she would know that he was seeing other patients, he said, "Well, tell her I have gone to Europe to be gone indefinitely; or make any other excuse, I don't care what." The sequel proved, however, that, in his kindness of heart and forbearance, she had the privilege of seeing him among the first, after all.

Dr. Agnew, like most public men, was a target for all sorts of cranks seeking advancement or self-advertisement. Just as his connection with the Garfield case brought him hundreds of letters, giving him all sorts of presumptuous advice, so in his own case in his final illness. His mail at this time was filled with all sorts of communications telling him how he should be treated.

How tender and beautiful was his love for his semi-invalid wife! Always extremely delicate, her life was saved many times by his matchless skill and unsleeping care. During one of the serious illnesses of Mrs. Agnew's life, such was his devotion to her that for over three months he never went to bed nor caught more than a few momentary snatches of sleep. It was his terrible expenditure of medical skill and nursing which brought her back to life many times, after she had laid at death's door for many months. The devotion of these married lovers for a period of fifty-one years was such as to call forth the admiration of all who saw them together; and yet, with the curious irony of fate, she, who had depended upon him almost for existence itself, outlived all his splendid vitality.

In the bigness of his heart, Dr. Agnew found room also for the rest of his little family. How gently and kindly we were treated! How many pleasures he gave us!

A more uncomplaining, easily satisfied man than Dr. Agnew never lived; never depressed, but always cheerful, with a pleasant word and smile for every one, and a kindly courtesy which extended to the youngest member of his household and the humblest servant, small wonder it was that we should vie with each other in our attentions to him. Nothing but the best was good enough for him, and in return how we treasured his words and looks of thanks!

In all the years which I spent with him, although he was grieved and hurt many times, never once did an angry word escape his lips. How marvelously he forebore to visit us with his righteous indignation when we so richly deserved it!

I will give two little instances of his forbearance: In the fall of 1880 I was intrusted with a large roll of manuscript of his work on surgery. This represented the work of years. I was to bring it from his office, 1611 Chestnut Street, to Haverford. On the way out I made several stops, and by the time I reached Haverford I became painfully aware that the manuscript was not with me. I went in fear and trembling and made known my loss. Not a hasty word did he utter. He simply *looked* at me, and said "That was the work of years." My feelings can be better imagined than described. A thousand scoldings would have been as nothing compared to that gentle reproof. He proved that he could bear the loss of the work of years, like Sir Isaac Newton, with equanimity. Telegrams were sent in all directions; the *dépôt* and the car in which I rode to Haverford were thoroughly searched, but the manuscript could not be found. The next day, half dead with grief and anxiety, I went to the city determined to get that manuscript. At the first place to which I went I found the roll, just where I had, with childish heedlessness, put it the day before.

In the summer of 1881, during President Garfield's illness, Dr. Agnew was waylaid by reporters from papers all over the country. Our house and grounds were in a state of siege, while a group of reporters always clustered about the station at the hours at which Dr. Agnew was expected to come from the city. At the end of a month we were mildly indignant; at the end of six weeks we were desperate. One night a dapper little reporter came to get a correct account of the President's condition. He left his hat and stick in a dark corner of the porch. Knowing Dr. Agnew's thorough dislike of interviews, as a childish revenge we collected a few pins and placed them in the hat of the "knight of the pencil," where they would be most effective. We then retired behind a bow-window and awaited results. We had not long to wait, for Dr. Agnew was brief in his interviews. The reporter bowed himself out and then placed his hat firmly on his head; but he quickly took it off and said something energetically under his breath. The next day we had forgotten all about it, but the unfortunate reporter evidently had not, for half a column of the first page of his paper, commencing in great head-lines, expressed in a humorous style his appreciation of the trick. On account of the tremendous publicity given to it, I felt, in my childish mind, that I had disgraced not only myself, but my dear uncle, and I trembled to meet him; but when I finally mustered up courage to see him he laughed, and referred to it subsequently as a good joke.

Dr. Agnew was often urged to write an autobiography; he was frequently told by relatives and friends that the story of his life, as told by himself, with his own description of his struggles, ambitions and successes, would be wonderfully interesting and absorbing, as well as the greatest encouragement to younger men in the profession. Dr. Agnew, however, could never be induced to undertake this task, undervaluing the probable interest of the world in the details of his life.

He grew fonder of poetry as he grew older, and nothing pleased him more than to listen to the reading or recitation of some poetical selection. He was also very fond of hymns, especially those of Charles Wesley. After his death, the following verse was found between the leaves of his favorite Bible, and was, probably, one of the last things he had copied and kept. This hymn must have seemed to him, in his weakened state, most applicable to himself; it certainly voiced his feelings, —the first natural fear of death overcome by the thought of an eternity made beautiful and blessed by the Master he had so long and faithfully served. This hymn had been written by the good and pious Wesley as he was dying:—

> " In age and feebleness extreme
> Who shall a helpless worm redeem ?
> Jesus, my only hope thou art,
> Strength to my failing flesh and heart ;
> Oh ! could I catch a smile from thee,
> Then drop into eternity."

Dr. Agnew was the humblest, the most consistent Christian I have ever known. Of all his kindness, generosity, goodness, and purity the world will never fully know. His earnest life, unswerving piety, and truly Christ-like efforts to help the needy and afflicted brought their reward ; for when the summons came, " Good and faithful servant, enter thou into the joy of thy Lord," the white head and gentle face of this grand old saint upon earth was suddenly beatified with a light of such clear shining that heaven and earth seemed very near. Can we doubt, with this manifestation to our earthly eyes, that the heavenly welcome and crown were wanting ?

CHAPTER XII.

Dr. Agnew's Later Life.

Dr. Agnew's later life did not differ in its details and methods from the work of the years that preceded it. He had not changed as he grew older; he remained the same mild, unaggressive, hard-working surgeon He rarely showed his strength. There are many workers in different fields who use at all times all the power and influence which they possess, but Dr. Agnew was not one of these. His only exhibition of his influence was in his efforts to forward the position and standing of his friends and students.

He never refused to aid a former student, and many a physician to-day can recall some deed or letter of Dr. Agnew which has opened new fields or made paths easier for himself. This interest in his brother-workers was one reason why Dr. Agnew became the idol of his professional brethren. A single instance of it is shown in the following incident, which repeated itself innumerably in his career. The circumstance is told by the physician to whom it occurred :—

"Twenty years ago, when a young man just pushing my way into practice in my native place, a very sad case came into my hands from some very much older men. Worried very much indeed about it, and sorely in the dark how to avoid a renewal of the failures that had met my predecessors in the case, I called one evening at Dr. Agnew's old home on Chestnut Street, and, although it was long after office hours, he received me, and listened attentively to my list of troubles.

"Then, beginning at the bottom of my case, he unraveled the whole thread, showing me where the failures were long before they seemed failures, and sent me away not only master of my case, but kindly assured of his interest in my success, and with an appointment to see him again in a few weeks, that I might report to him the history of my success.

"With the remembrance of that circumstance in my mind, I have always felt that a large portion of the success which has come to me here was owing to the advice given me by Dr. Agnew, which made me successful where others had failed, and brought a young M.D. into the prominence which gave him the opportunity of earning his position."

During these later years of his life Dr. Agnew became more active in society life, being elected president of a number of societies of which he had been a member; so that he became more prominent than he had been in his earlier years in this branch of work.

Dr. Agnew never was an office-seeker, and never wished to be one; the minutiæ, the intrigues, the wire-pulling, and tact which are necessary for successful society work are just as well marked in medical politics as in other forms, but they never fascinated him. He was too busily engaged in the practice of his profession to turn aside for the honors and emoluments of such work. When any position was offered to him of trust or honor he accepted it gratefully, as a manifestation of the wishes of his friends, but he was not a man who cared to organize societies or carry out their routine.

At the same time he was honored by being elected to the presidency of every medical organization of which he remained a member. The first medical society which he joined was one in which he had been instrumental in organizing,—The Lancaster County Medical Society; while in the country he had joined with a number of fellow-practitioners in the formation of this influential body of medical workers. The following letter in this connection explains itself:—

LANCASTER, February 21, 1889.

MY DEAR DOCTOR: On the morning of the 14th day of February (St. Valentine), of the year 1844, twenty-three physicians, then residents of the city and county, assembled in an upper room, third floor, of Krampf's building, corner of North Queen and Orange Streets, in the city of Lancaster, for the purpose of organizing the Lancaster City and County Medical Society.

If memory carries you back to the time stated, do you remember being present on that occasion and taking part in the proceedings? The record marks your presence.

The Society has just passed its forty-fifth anniversary, and I am selected to write briefly and congratulate *you* with myself that of these twenty-three physicians there are but two survivors (Drs. Agnew and Ehler.) If your general health is good and physical activity alike good, you are up to my standard. I perform the active duties of my profession as of yore. I am free of pains and aches, sleep well, have a good appetite, eat all the good things that come my way, and do not refuse a glass of " champy, " to wash the cobwebs from the fauces. If you have a fondness for *old things*, I send list of *original twenty-three* as they appear on the minutes of Society.

With kind regards, very truly yours,

J. Aug. Ehler.

To D. Hayes Agnew, M.D., Phila

On his advent in Philadelphia, the first society to which Dr. Agnew was elected was the Philadelphia County Medical Society, in 1858. It will be seen that he lived in Philadelphia ten years before he became a member of this great society. This action on his part is a sufficient commentary of his position toward societies at the time. He was rewarded for his long service in the society by his election as president of this influential body in 1872.

In 1859, one year after his election to the County Medical Society, he was made a member of the College of Physicians,— the oldest and one of the most distinguished medical associations in this country. After a membership in this society for a period of thirty years, he was made the thirteenth president, February 6, 1889. He was the third surgeon to receive this honor in the history of its existence, the first surgeon being William Shippen, who was made president in 1805, succeeding John Redman, who had been the first president for sixteen years, while the second had been Thomas Hewson, in 1835.

Dr. Agnew, while at the head of this august body, according to the traditions of the society, delivered three annual addresses,—December 4, 1889; December 3, 1890; and December 2, 1891, at which latter date he retired from the presidency. This last address was remarkable, as being the last one which he delivered in any official capacity. He was elected a member of the Medical Society of the State of Pennsylvania in 1870, and he was invited at the twenty-seventh annual session of the society, held in Philadelphia in May and June, 1876, to deliver "The Address on Surgery." He made this report of the progress in surgery for the year one of his clear, characteristic papers. At the twenty-ninth session of the society, held in Pittsburgh, in May, 1878, Dr. Agnew delivered the President's address, taking as his subject, "Errors of Diagnosis." He had been elected President of the Society the year before, at the meeting held in Harrisburg, June 14, 1877.

He was elected a Fellow of the American Surgical Association in 1882; this society had been recently founded, in 1880, by the late Professor Samuel D. Gross. Dr. Agnew was elected President of this association May 14, 1887. His impromptu remarks on being elected President were considered so excellent by the members of the society, at the time, that they were inserted in the preface to the volume of that year's Transactions. He spoke extemporaneously as follows:—

"I confess that this announcement is to me one of regret as well as of surprise and pleasure; regret because when I look over this distinguished body of men—of representative men—I see many who would discharge the duties of this office with more dignity and more efficiency than I shall be able to do. I have never been an office-seeker, and never wish to be one. I experience also a feeling of pleasure, because it is no small honor to preside over a body of distinguished men like yourselves. I accept the office not so much for the honor it confers, but because it comes to me unsolicited, and conveys to me the good wishes and good feeling of a body of men whom I love."

On September 20, 1888, he delivered his address as President of this association, taking as his subject "The Relation

of Social Life to Surgical Disease."[1]   At the meeting of the
society, held September 20, 1891, at Washington, D. C., he
delivered the opening address, taking as his subject "The
Present Status of Brain Surgery." Although this was the last
paper that he prepared, he displayed in it even more than his
usual care and brilliancy in deducing conclusions from the data
of which he treated. One of the most distinguished surgeons
present at the meeting said, on hearing this paper read: "These
are revolutionary times, and it is to me a great satisfaction to
hear the present Nestor of American surgery take such an advanced position in favor of operation in every case of depressed
fracture, with symptoms or without symptoms."

At the Congress of American Physicians and Surgeons,
held at Washington, D. C., in September, 1888, Dr. Agnew, as
President of the American Surgical Association, was First Vice-
President, *ex-officio*, of the Congress. On the fourth day of its
meeting, Thursday, September 20th, at the convention of the
delegates in the hall of the National Museum, to listen to the
address of the President on "Medical Museums," Dr. Agnew
presided.

To render social intercourse among medical men more
frequent and at the same time to diffuse among them professional knowledge of the day, certain well-known physicians
formed clubs, which met one evening every week at the residence of each member in rotation. The entertaining member
invited other physicians not belonging to the club, to the number of twenty or more. The refection given was limited to tea,
coffee, bread and butter, and cakes, and the conversation was
usually on professional subjects.

The Monday-Evening Club was probably the oldest among
these. It included such men as Drs. Franklin Bache, Henry
Bond, Isaac Hays, Hugh L. Hodge, Samuel Jackson, Charles
D. Meigs, George B. Wood, and Francis D. Condie. Next in
seniority was the Friday-Evening Club, among whose members

[1] See page 207.

were Drs. Robert Bridges, Joseph Carson, George Fox, W. W. Gerhard, Caspar Morris, and Geo. W. Norris. The "Social Medical," or Thursday-Evening Club, was a still later organization. Its members were Drs. D. Hayes Agnew, John B. Brinton, Edward Hartshorne, Samuel Lewis, J. H. B. McClellan, J. Forsyth Meigs, John Neill, Edward A. Page, William Burd Page, William Pepper, R. A. F. Penrose, B. Howard Rand, Lewis Rodman, Robert E. Rogers, W. S. W. Ruschenberger, Francis G. Smith, Alfred Stillé, and Ellersley Wallace,—in all nineteen, of whom five are living. This list constituted the club for 1873–74.

The Social Surgical Club was started in 1877, as a medium for different surgeons of the city to meet occasionally for mutual improvement scientifically and acquaintanceship socially. The first meeting of the club was held in the office of Dr. John H. Packard, to whose exertions the existence of the club was chiefly due. It was the original intention of the incorporators of the club to invite one or two surgeons from each hospital in the city to join, each member bringing cases for mutual study, reading papers, and carrying on discussions on medical subjects. The refreshments were to be limited to something very mild, such as beer and pretzels. Under these conditions the society continued to meet for some time. Its original members were Drs. Agnew, Brinton, S. W. Gross, Hunt, Levis, Morton, Maury, Reed, Packard, and Mears,—the membership being limited to ten. In 1879, on the death of Dr. Maury, Dr. S. D. Gross was elected to the vacant place. After the admission of this last distinguished surgeon, no new members have been admitted to the "Surgical Club," as it is familiarly called.

By this time the social side of the society had become so pronounced that the medical features sank into insignificance. The cost of the dinner gradually increased, and the *ménu* became correspondingly more elaborate; still, in the matter of beverages, only beer and sherry were allowed. Tradition reports that only once was this rule broken and champagne indulged in.

At the suggestion of the elder Gross, soon after his admission to membership, the scientific and social features, which had long been estranged, were totally divorced in 1879. The society continued to meet and retain the social features, inviting distinguished visitors who chanced to be in the city to its dinners. There are now but three living members of the club, Drs. Brinton and Packard having resigned, Drs. Agnew, Levis, Maury, Reed, and the two Grosses being dead.

The Academy of Surgery was started to revive the lagging medical features of this surgical club. The Academy was founded April 21, 1879, and incorporated December 27, 1879. Dr. Agnew was one of the founders, and in January, 1880, was elected the first Vice-President. Its first President was the gentleman who was responsible for its existence, Dr. S. D. Gross. In October, 1884, Dr. Agnew was elected to the presidency; this post he retained until January, 1891, when he resigned, being succeeded by Dr. William Hunt.

Dr. Agnew delivered the annual oration before the Academy in 1882, his subject being "The Life and Writings of Baron Larrey." He was always active in its work, and the minute-book contains many references to his contributions to the proceedings of the Academy.

Among the societies of which Dr. Agnew was a member, none gave him more sincere pleasure than the little undergraduate society named in his honor. It was not merely the fact that it was named in his honor that made it dear to him, but more because he was peculiarly fond of medical students and solicitous for their welfare. His relations with his students were always like that of a father to his sons. He had the happy faculty of impressing upon his scholars the fact that he took a personal interest in each one. This interest was genuine and unaffected. He always did everything in his power to further the advancement of those who had studied under him.

This Agnew Surgical Society was founded in the winter

of 1887–88, by a *coterie* of students who intended to devote as
much time as possible to the study of surgical matters. In
order to accomplish this, it was the intention of the society to
invite authorities in different branches of medical work to
lecture before them, in addition to the preparation of papers by
individual members. This kind of work had been done before
by other medical societies, to a certain extent; but it was carried out more fully and more comprehensively by the Agnew
Society. Of course, the founding of such a society, with three
well-grown, active societies in opposition, was at first somewhat
of a difficult matter; but the name of Agnew is one to conjure
with, and in less than three months the new society took a
foremost position in undergraduate life.

It started with a course of brilliant lectures by leading
authorities; it did much original work, but particularly in its
banquets was it happy. It accomplished in its first year what
had never been done before by medical undergraduate societies,
—that is, gathering together nearly the entire Faculty at its first
annual banquet. These banquets undoubtedly were a great
feature in the life of the undergraduate who was fortunate
enough to be a member. The opportunity to come in close
contact with the Faculty,—especially with Dr. Agnew,—the
stimulus, the inspiration, and the pathos of the occasion, made
it such an event that it was not very quickly forgotten by its
participants. Dr. Agnew was president *ex-officio* of this society.

On February 21, 1891, at the annual banquet for that
year, Dr. Agnew presented to this society a "loving cup," from
which each year each member was to pledge his renewal of
good fellowship. On one side is the Agnew coat of arms, on
the other the motto "Sapientia cum latitia."

Hawthorne has said, somewhere, that there are chasms
between men which can never be thoroughly bridged over; that
there can never be that thorough interplay of feelings, thoughts,
and emotions as exists between man and woman or among
women. The nearest approach to the removal of this isolation

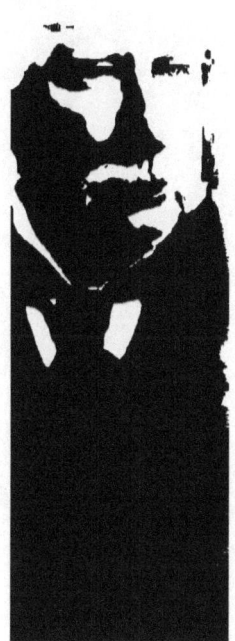

DR. AGNEW IN 1881.

existed, undoubtedly, in this little Agnew Surgical Society, between Dr. Agnew and his students.

Another society of which Dr. Agnew was a member, but
which was not medical in its nature, was the Wistar Association, which gave the famous "Wistar Parties." This Association, which had ceased to exist in 1863-64 on account of the
political excitement which was developed at its meetings, was
re-established in 1886 by Dr. Casper Wister, one of Dr. Agnew's
most intimate friends. This organization was called, later, "The
Saturday-Night Club." These meetings were held on Saturday
evening, beginning at 9 o'clock, and each member was entitled
to invite a certain number of outside guests to them. They
formed gatherings remarkable for their social and intellectual
attractions.

Dr. Casper Wistar, the former Professor of Anatomy at the
University of Pennsylvania, was the originator of the "Wistar
Parties." He was in the habit of receiving his friends and
scientific strangers at his house on Sunday evenings, and upon
his death, in 1818, a social circle was formed among the members of the Philosophical Society, to which was given the name
of "Wistar Parties." The meetings were held subsequently on
Saturday evenings, continuing until 1863-64.

Dr. Agnew was also a member of the medical fraternity
A M Π Ω, being elected in 1891.

Dr. Agnew rightfully believed that, to succeed in medicine,
every energy and every thought must be concentrated by a
physician on his life-work, hence he did not seek outside work
or positions; yet he held a few positions of honor and trust, not
of a medical character, which came to him at different times.
He was appointed a Manager of the House of Refuge by the
Judges of the Courts of Common Pleas of Philadelphia in 1859.
He was at the time of his death by far the oldest member of
the Board, so much so that none of the present members have
personal knowledge of the condition of affairs when he was
appointed. They all have a tradition, however, that he worked

great changes in the sanitary department, which subject was very little understood by the public at that time. As an example of this reformation, at the time he became manager it was customary to have the towels used in common by the inmates, and, in consequence, a large part of the time, many of the children suffered with sore eyes. At Dr. Agnew's suggestion this was altered, so that each inmate was given his or her own personal towel. So much information is given in the resolution adopted by the Board of Managers, of his relation to this institution, in reference to Dr. Agnew, after his death, that it is quoted in full :—

"Dr. Agnew has been a member of this Board of Managers for the past thirty-three years, always manifesting a deep interest in the administration of the institution and the welfare of the children. Ready at all times to advise upon the sanitary and hygienic problems frequently arising in the administration of so large an undertaking, his counsel has been invariably sought and cheerfully given.

"His interest in the work and appreciation of its usefulness grew with his years, and it was not until after a personal inspection of the site selected for the new Institution at Glen Mills that the contract for the purchase was entered into. His approval of the system to be employed there was unqualified.

"In recording his generous and philanthropic spirit and the deep sympathy evinced by him with the unfortunate children committed to our care, we are but uniting in the universal testimony to those qualities which he exhibited throughout a long and distinguished professional career, devoted to good deeds and generous acts."

Mr. Collins, who died November 27, 1892, the venerable President of the Board of Managers of the House of Refuge, had been in the board twenty years; this made him quite a youth compared with Dr. Agnew's service of thirty-three years.

Dr. Agnew was a member of the Board of Directors of the Union Trust Company, one of the largest financial concerns of Philadelphia. This company was a conception of Colonel William C. Patterson, of Philadelphia, its charter being obtained on the 16th of October, 1882. Dr. Agnew was made a mem-

ber of the Board at the first meeting of the Company, and continued in active service up to the time of his death. He was
always in attendance at the meetings of the Board, unless prevented by his professional duties, and his advice and counsel
were always sought and esteemed to be of great value. He
did not waste much of the time of the Board in long discussions, but he did not hesitate to express his views very freely,
when the occasion required it.

At a meeting of the Trustees of the Philadelphia Dental
College, held November 29, 1881, Dr. Agnew was unanimously
elected a member of the Board. On April 19, 1872, he was
made a member of the American Philosophical Society for Promoting Useful Knowledge. He was also a member of the
Franklin Institute.

On February 19, 1872, Dr. Agnew had been elected one of
the Consulting Surgeons to the Presbyterian Hospital; in 1890,
he was made Honorary Surgeon to the same institution, the first
time such a position had been created.

At the meeting of the Alumni Society of the Medical Department of the University of Pennsylvania, held May 6, 1891,
he was elected Vice-President of the society. This was an
unusual honor, as the officers in this society, as a rule, are not
chosen from among the members of the Faculty.

Dr. Charles T. Hunter, who had been Dr. Agnew's Demonstrator of Surgery for many years, resigned from this position in
1882; he was advanced to the position of Demonstrator of
Anatomy. His place was taken by Dr. J. W. White, who assisted
Dr. Agnew in much of his work until the latter's retirement
permanently from professional duties.

Dr. Agnew delivered the introductory address to the course
of the winter 1881–82, and the valedictory address to the
graduating class in 1885.

At the time of the consideration of the necessity for the
establishment of a compulsory fourth year, in 1887, Dr. Agnew
was one of its most eager advocates. The successful establish-

ment of this medical advance at the University met with his warmest approval.

Dr. Agnew continued his lectures at the University until the spring of 1889. During the winter he intimated his desire to retire from active service, which was accomplished by his election to the post of Emeritus Professor of Surgery and Honorary Professor of Clinical Surgery, January 11, 1889. By the former position he was still a member of the Faculty with all its privileges; by the latter title—one never given before in the history of the University—he was enabled to deliver cliniques to the students whenever he so desired. This intention he carried out from time to time until within a short period before his death.

The incidents and anecdotes which throw side-lights on a man's character and career are often fortunate in revealing the colors and details of a human life which would otherwise be lost forever. There are many such anecdotes that remain of Dr. Agnew's career which tell, far more forcibly than mere description, of many of his characteristics; some of them demand a place in the story of his life, for their value in thus disclosing glimpses of himself or of the environments of his life-work.

His regular attendance at church was so marked, especially in such a busy physician, that the following little incident, which shows his arrangement of his work in order that he could get to church, will not only serve as a lesson for practising physicians, but also emphasize the sacrifices to which he put himself, in order to be present at divine worship :—

In the early seventies he asked a young surgeon of the city to accompany him to Gloucester, New Jersey, to see an interesting case of abdominal tumor in a woman. It was necessary to see the case the next day, which happened to be Sunday. The young surgeon suggested 10 o'clock as a good hour for starting; his surprise can be imagined when Dr. Agnew told him he would stop for him with his carriage at half-past four in the morning. Dr. Agnew arrived on time, and they reached the ferry by 5 o'clock, took the first boat over, and Dr. Agnew was back in his office by 9 o'clock.

Dr. Agnew's quickness of retort and his ability to see the humorous side of things are shown in the following incident: A gentleman in the country was unfortunate enough to swallow a set of false teeth while eating oysters; they stuck in his throat, from which position they could not be dislodged by the efforts of the country physicians who were called to attend him. In consequence, the gentleman came in great distress to town to see Dr. Agnew. After a little manipulation the doctor removed the teeth from the throat of the unfortunate gentleman, and left him in a condition practically as good as before the accident.

The news of this incident spread through the city, and consequently a reporter called on Dr. Agnew about midnight of the day of the extraction. As was Mrs. Agnew's custom, in order to save her husband as much exertion and exposure as possible, she answered the call to the night-bell. She told her husband that there was a person down stairs who wanted to know about the man who had swallowed his teeth, and had been operated upon that day. Dr. Agnew laughed and said: "Tell him that if he doesn't go away from my door there will be another man in Philadelphia to-night with his teeth down his throat."

In the *Medical News* of July 28, 1883, under the head of "Correspondence," are a couple of letters on a publication, entitled "An Epitome of Medicine, Surgery, and Obstetrics, by Alfred Stillé, D. Hayes Agnew, and R. A. F. Penrose. Published by Samuel M. Miller, M.D." The following explains itself:—

To the Editor of the Medical News.

Sir: I am receiving letters from various sections of the country asking for information in regard to my connection with a little volume published by a Dr. Samuel Miller, and entitled "An Epitome of Medicine, Surgery, and Obstetrics, by Drs. Alfred Stillé, D. Hayes Agnew, and R. A. F. Penrose." I have no desire to increase my correspondence, already too onerous, and, therefore. deem it best to avail myself of the columns of your widely-circulated journal to inform my professional brethren that I disown any relation whatever with this miserable piece of literary larceny, published entirely without my knowledge, and only remarkable for inaccuracy, stupidity, and audacity on the part of its author.   Yours, truly,

                                        D. HAYES AGNEW.

July 21, 1883.

An injunction was granted subsequently against Dr. Miller, · restraining him from publishing and selling this medical work. On behalf of the defendant, it was argued by his attorney, E. Spencer Miller, that an oral delivery of matter to persons, who attended such lectures on invitation or otherwise, became common property to those who were present and remembered the subject discussed. He said that the students had never been notified that the lecturers reserved the right of property in their lectures, but, on the contrary, directed their students to take copious notes of the lectures. Judges Hare, Mitchell, and Fell refused to dissolve the injunction, saying there was not sufficient evidence shown to induce the court to dissolve it. Still later, in the case of appeal of Dr. Samuel M. Miller from the decree of Court of Common Pleas, No. 2, the Supreme Court confirmed the decree of the lower court; so that the book was permanently suppressed.

The following incident occurred many times in Dr. Agnew's career when he was called into consultation. He would meet the attending physician at the house of the patient, examine the case, and retire to an adjacent room in which to talk over the case. As Dr. Agnew was discussing the problems presented, he would be at the same time glancing around the room. On every side he could see evidences of a long, unsuccessful struggle against poverty. The threadbare carpet; the dingy furniture; the pinched, wan face of the wife or mother,— all told their story of a bitter struggle. When the time came for him to go, as was customary in these cases, the attending physician would ask Dr. Agnew his charge. Dr. Agnew would mention the amount of his bill, the physician would confer with the mother of the family, and Dr. Agnew would be paid at once. On the way to the door, Dr. Agnew would find some pretext to see the woman unobserved and slip back into her hand the money which he had just received. In a second he was gone and no one was the wiser of the act, not even his family or the attending physician.

It has been wisely said that a fool cannot lose his temper, and a wise man does not. Dr. Agnew's control of temper was not due to any inability to see harm done him, or provocation aroused. He could, on occasion, be most stern and decisive in his words and actions. They seemed all the sharper and sterner because they were so far apart. He had a considerable amount of the old Scottish blood in him. An incident will illustrate this: In his earlier years Dr. Agnew attended a woman suffering from an incurable affection,—chronic tubercular peritonitis. Eventually, despite all that was done for her, she died. In the course of time Dr. Agnew presented his bill to her husband. He knew that the man had been put to considerable expense and was not in the best of positions financially. His bill, even at the moderate charge which he was accustomed to make, came to $180, but he divided it by ten and sent a bill for $18. A year rolled by, and as the bill was still unpaid Dr. Agnew sent his collector, who was subjected to a considerable abuse. Somewhat later this man sent the bill, with a check, to Dr. Agnew, with the following letter:—

DR. AGNEW.

DEAR SIR: I enclose your bill with check therefor. Kindly receipt it and return to me. I will say that I never paid a bill under greater protest. You promised to cure my wife and you failed to do it. I feel that you are an inefficient physician and incapable of giving proper medical attention to your patients.   Yours, etc.,

——— ———.

Dr. Agnew sat down, receipted the bill and folded up the check, and put them together in an envelope, with the following note:—

DEAR SIR: I enclose you the receipted bill, also the check which you sent. Permit me to say that I never promised to cure your wife. That is a power which belongs only to God, and if He does not bless our efforts our medicines are of no avail. I will only ask one favor of you. It is that you will never darken my office-door again.

Yours sincerely,
D. HAYES AGNEW.

Such discourtesy was most unusual in Dr. Agnew's experience. The receipt of such letters as the following was, on the other hand, a common experience:—

MY DEAR DOCTOR: Twenty-three years ago, on the 14th of March, I went out to O——— in the morning full of health and vigor, and returned in the afternoon a sad cripple, my right ankle-bones broken in pieces, having received a compound comminuted fracture—the most terrible accident of my life. Then it was that, by your skillful and careful treatment and watchful attention, assisted by Dr. Smith, that you placed me upon my *two* feet again, and, instead of ever thereafter limping along, I have traveled life's journey for twenty-three years longer, *sound in both limbs*. And as to-day is the anniversary of the accident, I wished to write you a few lines and tell you I bear in my heart the grateful remembrance of all your kindness to me. The poet says: "A thing of beauty is a joy forever." To me, a *kind act* is a most precious memory, and throws a brightness over all my after life. And can I forget your friendship, with all the kindness I have received from you? *Never.* Years may and do bring many changes, but the heart that is true remains the same.

So, believe me as ever, affectionately yours,

Dr. Agnew's study of human nature was often most marked, so that frequently he would let drop a remark which would linger for years in the minds of his auditors. For example: a gentleman, in explaining to him the condition of a patient, said, "Doctor, my father is in the habit of taking a couple of ounces of raw whisky before dinner. Do you think he ought to give it up? Do you think it has a bad effect upon his disease?" Dr. Agnew replied: "No; a man of seventy should never break up even a bad habit."

A gentleman calling on the elder Gross one morning noticed lying on his desk a copy of "Agnew's Surgery," which was then just published. He asked Dr. Gross what he thought of the work. In the impressive style for which Dr. Gross was noted, he said, "I want you to listen to what I am going to say. I sat up nearly the whole of night before last reading this work, and I will venture to assert that 'Agnew's Surgery' will be read and consulted by the medical world long after the dust has settled forever on the covers of similar works." The visitor asked, "How do you think it compares with your own work?" Dr. Gross modestly replied, "Why, sir, mine is, in comparison, a pigmy."

The following interesting letter, written to Dr. Agnew by Dr. Gross in regard to his "Surgery," shows the friendly relations existing between these two great surgeons:—

PHILADELPHIA.

MY DEAR DOCTOR AGNEW: I thanked you in advance last week for your kindness in sending the second volume of your "Surgery." Now that an opportunity has been afforded me of scanning its ample pages, let me thank you again,—not in a cold and formal manner according to the world's fashion,—but with all my heart and soul. You have produced a great and noble work,—one creditable alike to yourself, your profession, and your country.

I hope and pray that the great and good God—the Father of us all—may give you health and strength and a long life to enjoy the well-merited fruits of your labors.   Ever faithfully your friend,

S. D. GROSS.

Dr. Agnew did not keep many of his letters or other data in reference to his work. He was in the habit of destroying everything as soon as he had digested its contents; and although he left considerable material, it was not one-hundredth of the amount which he destroyed. This is unfortunate for posterity, for it limits considerably the outlines of his life.

A Southerner who had come to Dr. Agnew for advice, after leaving his office, went into a neighboring drug-store to have a prescription filled, asking if "this Agnew over the way was the

celebrated Agnew." Being assured that it was, he seemed to
hesitate, and then said, "I came from far south and brought a
thousand dollars in my pocket to have Agnew give an opinion
upon a malady of mine, but I got that opinion and he only
charged me three dollars, and I don't understand it." The
druggist asked if he was slighted in any way; he replied,
"Slighted! No; on the contrary, he could not have treated me
better; but why he did not charge me more I don't know.
He merely said that that was his regular charge for office advice."
This disregard of Dr. Agnew for possible advantages that he
might take of those who came to him and his exceeding fairness
toward all people were strongly marked through his whole career.

Dr. Agnew said one morning to a friend, "I saw in my
office this morning forty patients. How much money do you
suppose I charged and received for my morning's work?" The
friend being unable to estimate, Dr. Agnew said, "Twenty dollars."
In other words, he charged only one out of four or six patients.
If he had only collected what even his moderate charges were,
his estate would have been at least three times larger than it
was at his death. This had an unexpected effect on the other
physicians in the town. If Agnew charged so little it was difficult for other less well known practitioners to charge more.
Undoubtedly, Dr. Agnew's scale of fees had a bearish tendency
in the great medical market. This circumstance did not always,
however, deter other physicians from charging their usual
prices, even when called into consultation at the same time that
Dr. Agnew would also be called. For example, for seeing a
patient outside the city, Dr. Agnew presented a bill for $50,
while another professional gentleman, who accompanied him
also to see the case, younger and less well known, sent a bill
for $250.

There were a number of incidents which occurred in Dr.
Agnew's work at this period which are of sufficient importance
to demand attention. One of these was the occurrence of a
death; the only one which happened to Dr. Agnew in the whole

course of his professional career, in which the patient died while under the influence of ether. As the case is of great value as a lesson in etherization, its outlines are briefly presented. Although the death was proved to be unavoidable, it is most fortunate for the medical profession, not only from the rareness of the incident, that it occurred at all, but that it fell to the lot of Dr. Agnew, and not to some less well known operator.

After forty years of surgical work, often of the gravest character, and sometimes requiring prolonged anesthesia, without a single accident, Dr. Agnew had come to believe that the exhibition of ether, unless recklessly administered, was entirely free from danger. He was aware that several deaths had been reported from time to time from its use, even in the hands of the most careful operators, but he could never divest his mind of the idea that in these cases there was some undetected element involved more influential in the issue.

Dr. Agnew was engaged in preparing to operate on a gentleman, 45 years of age, for the removal of two ulcerating hemorrhoids. The patient was in good health, the heart and kidneys not being diseased. One year before Dr. Agnew had operated for fissure of the sphincter ani on this same patient, at which time he had done well under the ether. At the time of the second operation, nothing occurred during the early stage of the inhalation other than what is witnessed every day when ether is exhibited. In the course of fifteen minutes, the patient was placed across the bed, one of the tumors was drawn down, transfixed, and ligated with a double ligature. When about to seize the second, the breathing, which had been strong and free, suddenly ceased. The operation was immediately suspended, and the usual methods for resuscitation instituted. Notwithstanding these measures were persisted in for at least three quarters of an hour, during twenty-five minutes of which time the pulsations of the heart could be recognized, not a single effort of natural respiration occurred. The post-mortem, made by Dr. Formad, the coroner's physician, revealed complete collapse of the lungs; marked traces of an old meningitis, attributed to a former sun-stroke; and what satisfactorily explained the sudden termination of life, the rupture of a calcified vessel in the floor of the fourth ventricle, the recognized physiological centre of respiration. All the vessels comprising the circle of Willis were in a similar state of atheromatous degeneration.

It was evident, therefore, that the increased vascular tension of these cerebral vessels, caused by the ether, determined the lesion,—a result which might have followed any unusual mental or physical excitement. Under the circumstances this sad disaster could not have been avoided by any human foresight. The ether was pure, not more than five ounces had been inhaled, and there had been a sufficient admixture of atmospheric air. During life it was impossible to ascertain the state of the blood-vessels of the brain as disclosed at the autopsy,—a very improbable condition in a man of 45 years.

Dr. Agnew had, curiously, about the same time, a case in which he was called to see a woman more than 70 years of age, who was suffering from strangulated hernia. They were just preparing to give her the ether, when the patient gave a sudden convulsive movement and expired in a moment. Had the etherization been commenced or the operation begun before the death of the woman, the fatal result would have been attributed either to the anesthetic or the knife.

The following tribute of respect to Dr. Agnew's memory was written by a former patient. It expresses two such good points that it is quoted:—

"His manner in the sick-room is worthy of study; he would first shake hands with his patient in the most kindly and courtly manner and sit down as quietly and composedly as if he had not another patient in the world, and evidently intended to remain until everything had been discussed and considered. He would listen patiently to the explanations of his patient, give his decisions and advice quickly and incisively, and then refer to some topic of pleasant conversation which he knew would be of interest to the patient. When he went, he had made all feel that nothing had been left unsaid or undone. Frequently, after he was gone, my wife would say, 'Oh, dear, the doctor never sees me when I am bad'; the fact being that she forgot her suffering, and, after the questions as to her treatment had been decided, she had been endeavoring to entertain him by showing him whatever new shell, butterfly, or beetle she had received.

"Of Mrs. Agnew but little has been written. The world should know what a loving and kind-hearted woman she is, and what a help-meet she was to her husband. As a matter of fact, he owes a large part of his success in life to her,—not, of course, his professional success, but it was by her great and unceasing watchfulness over him in sickness and in health, and relieving him from all business matters, from all petty annoyances, that enabled him to devote his undivided attentions and energies to his professional work. Never was there a couple better suited to each other."

Dr. Agnew's influence as an expert in medico-legal cases was a natural outgrowth of his work in other directions. His appearance on the witness-stand was always a source of impregnable strength for the side on which he testified, for his vast erudition and experience, combined with his well-known honesty and conscientiousness, made it possible for him to rebut any testimony contrary to his own which might be offered by an opposing attorney.

Dr. Agnew's testimony as an expert led him frequently to testify in cases in which he felt that he should place on record his experience, especially when such expert testimony was given that he believed was doing an injustice in any way to an innocent person. For example, he went to New England in the spring of 1886 to testify in a case of a poor colored man who had been charged with murder, in which the case turned upon the point, whether it is possible for an individual with suicidal intent to inflict a shot wound in the brain and another in the heart.[1]

---

[1] See page 197.

Dr. Agnew was so honest that he frequently failed to see the intrigues of others; in consequence, he allowed himself occasionally to be the source of advertisement to those who were seeking to advance their own interests. This tendency on his part increased as he grew older; in his later years he permitted many things to pass which, occurring earlier in his life, he would have quickly stopped. This tendency was recognized by his friends, and it did not create the surprise which might have otherwise naturally arisen.

All through this decade Dr. Agnew was endeavoring to decrease his work; he resigned, in 1884, from the Pennsylvania Hospital, and in his practice he limited his work as far as possible. Still, he did far more work than he had outlined for himself.

When Dr. and Mrs. Agnew came to Philadelphia, they joined the church of the Rev. T. H. Beveridge, at Twenty-second and Race Streets. This was an Associate Presbyterian Church, of the same division of Presbyterianism of which Dr. Agnew's parents had long been members. Subsequently, they transferred their membership to the Tenth Presbyterian Church, at Twelfth and Walnut Streets, at that time under the charge of the Rev. Henry Boardman, D.D. They remained regular attendants at this church until 1865, when they joined the Second Presbyterian Church, where, until his death, Dr. Agnew was a regular attendant.

In 1863 Dr. Agnew began his romantic attachment with the late Rev. Elias R. Beadle, D.D., when he had the pleasure, first, of hearing this gifted minister preach. It was in the Tenth Presbyterian Church where this occurred. Dr. Beadle took charge, temporarily, of the congregation of Dr. Boardman and of Dr. Crowell during the absence of these pastors in the summer-time. He entered the church and took a back-seat on a side-aisle, until the hour for service arrived; then he arose, walked with a rapid, nervous step down the aisle, and ascended the pulpit. There was something about the man which im-

mediately awakened Dr. Agnew's interest. The sharply cut
features, the deep lines which furrowed a thoughtful face, and
the quick, nervous movements, all revealed the fire which flamed
beneath the surface. The voice and manner, the form and force
of expression, the elegance of diction, all conspired to make
one magnificent harmony. Dr. Agnew, as well as others, at
once recognized that in the delicate, wiry body of the speaker
God had enshrined a soul full of beatitudes.

Notwithstanding the heat of midsummer and the depopu-
lated state of the city, Dr. Beadle soon attracted large congre-
gations of highly educated and appreciative hearers. The
following year Dr. Beadle spent in Rochester, N. Y., supplying a
vacant pulpit in that city; but the rigor of the climate compelled
him to seek a more congenial spot, and, in 1865, he was called to
the Second Presbyterian Church of Philadelphia, then situated
on Seventh Street, between Market and Arch.

In consequence of the drift of population westward and
the encroachment of trade, a process of disintegration had been
going on for years in this historic old church which rendered a
change imperative. When a few remaining worshipers turned
their backs on the church hallowed by so many sacred memories,
it was with sad hearts; after leading a nomadic life for some
time, this body at length selected the site at Twenty-first and
Walnut Streets, and there erected, in 1876, the present imposing
edifice, where the last, and not the least, prosperous years of Dr.
Beadle's singularly successful ministry were spent.

Dr. Beadle, after his license to preach in 1835, had been,
for several years, a missionary to India and Syria; but his health
did not permit of his continuance in this work, and he had
returned to America in 1843. From this time he worked in home
fields. His intimacy with Dr. Agnew was marked from the outset
of their acquaintance. It was partly through Dr. Agnew that he
was called to Philadelphia; scarcely a day passed during the
following years that they did not see each other. Dr. Beadle
was fond of calling on his friend at supper-time; he would run

in unannounced at this time, and these two workers would spend an hour or so in congenial talk.

On Sabbath morning, January 5, 1879, Dr. Beadle preached with his usual earnestness and power, and at the close of the service touchingly announced the consummation of a long-cherished hope,—that he had lived to see cancelled the onerous debt which had hung over the beautiful temple in which he and his people had worshiped, at the same time saying, "My work is now done." The words were prophetic; it was his last Gospel message; his work was done.

One hour later Dr. Agnew was hastily summoned to his aid. On entering the room in which he was placed, Dr. Agnew found the poor sufferer seated on a sofa, but, alas! how changed. He had been seized with the agony of cardiac angina, and the face that an hour before had been beaming with exultant joy was now shrunken, the wrist pulseless, and, with the desperate clutch of the fingers, was heard the half-suppressed moan of one in mortal trouble. Shortly after midnight the gentle spirit of Beadle was released from its mortal environment and passed from the Church Militant to the Church Triumphant.

In 1880 the Rev. John S. MacIntosh, D.D., of Belfast, Ireland, was called to the empty pastorate. He had charmed and delighted Philadelphia by his brilliant and feeling sermons the year before, during the Council of the Presbyterian Alliance. Dr. MacIntosh accepted the call, and was installed in 1881. Dr. MacIntosh's own words in the estimate of Dr. Agnew's career, and his funeral sermon, express the relations that existed between Dr. Agnew and himself.

These suggestive notes and reminiscences are furnished by Dr. Agnew's pastor, who, despite the fact that he preached two sermons on Dr. Agnew's life in quick succession, still had left these beautiful thoughts touching his dead friend:—

"It was my happy fortune to be thrown very closely with Dr. Hayes Agnew from the very first moment of my return to Philadelphia, and it is a matter of highest satisfaction to my-

self that the succeeding years only tightened the bonds of intimacy, until we became the very closest and most confiding
of friends. During the later years of Dr. Agnew's life, it is, I
think, the simple truth for me to say that no man was honored
with his closest confidences as I myself was, and no man saw
or heard so much of his inner life.

"But a great deal of that which was thus in the freedom of
frankest friendship unveiled to my eye must, through the sacred-
ness of affection and a solemn sense of duty to the dead, remain
forever sealed up in my own memory and guarded in my own
heart. To rest a welcome guest at a man's fireside; to sit at
his table; to share his home-life; to enter into his sick-chamber;
to talk with him when laid upon his bed; to read his uncovered
spirit-life and enjoy his trustful confidences, and then go out
and talk about him and tell what was never expected to be
told, and set in cold print what was only opened by a loving
heart to a loving eye,—what true man, with tender heart and
high sense of honor, can ever bring himself to play such a part!
Therefore, it is not for me to say much of this inner life, and
open up to the public eye many of these holy confidences.

"But times come and calls are heard when speech about
your absent friend is the purest loyalty of the loving heart, and
there are seasons when busy men and women, struggling to do
the right and to grow better, have a just claim upon those that
knew the purer and truer souls; knew them not simply for themselves, but for the help of their fellows, and for the glory of that
God who, by his grace and presence, made these bright spirits
very much what they were. There are a few choice souls whom
their fellows need to know, and it brightens the world to see
them in their home-life and know a little of the play of their
great, honest hearts. There are strong and sympathetic brothers
whose inner life is the secret of their outer strength. The man
in his home and the man before God explain the man among
men and the man at his work.

"The wish to know the hidden man is right. Ever and

19

anon there walks among the crowd one whose face shines, though he himself wists it not, and his wondering fellows, looking with awe and admiration on him, want to know whence comes that sweet but awful light; and when they learn the secrets of the brightness it betters and sweetens their own spirits.

"Since Agnew went away from us there are many feeling poorer by his very loss, and they are asking those of us who knew him best, whence came and what formed that singular wealth of personality which made richer those who touched our departed friend, by their very contact with him? Hard, indeed, it is to pack such a man and the secret of his life into a few sentences. Yet were it serious wrong to him if speech were unduly long or praise grow fulsome. The calm, severe dignity of this modest and self-hiding man demands that words be few and well ordered.

"What manner of man was this, as he lived among his more intimate friends and moved in the sweet circle of his home? He was a man of moral symmetry. He was a man of purest kindliness; of most devout piety; of settled faith and strong convictions; of broad catholicity and spiritual generosity.

"*His Moral Symmetry.*—In the human form what is more winsome than symmetry; fine balance of parts; harmony; true proportions and perfect articulation? To see a youth of symmetric form is indeed a joy forever, but there is a symmetry of soul, there is a moral balance, an equipoise which is finer and sweeter by far than the bodily; a symmetry of soul where great qualities meet and are harmonized. Hayes Agnew carried with him this great and singular beauty of spirit.

"Looked at from the moral point of view, there were few things lacking in his spiritual make-up, and there was nothing out of proportion. He was marked by clearest truth, by child-like simplicity, by sweet modesty, heroic firmness, steady earnestness, winsome gentleness, unchanging cheerfulness, peculiar conscientiousness, and holiest reverence. Every one who knew

Dr. Agnew in 1887.

him well would admit that each one of these high qualities of mind
and heart and spirit was found in him, and that they all made
themselves felt by those who came in contact with him, and that
they shone forth brightly upon those who lived in the close rela-
tionships of near friendships and the home. And yet a singular
fact was that you scarcely knew which of these was the master
feature, for in him truth and gentleness, modesty and firmness,
simplicity and earnestness, conscientiousness and forbearance,
cheerfulness and reverence went together. One quality was
checked by another; one feature balanced another, and they
were combined into a sweet unity of a great, strong, good man.
In the number, in the variety of his moral characteristics, lay
much of the strength of his character, but the chief power of it
was found in the happy balance of his features of soul. It was
the strength of his character that tells largely the secret of his
remarkable hold upon the community. Confidence in the man
himself was, perhaps, as marked as confidence in the surgeon of
unrivaled skill.

"*His Purest Kindliness.*—Agnew's eye was remarkable.
Those who knew him well know and recall that fact. There
was a steady penetration in it that seemed to go right down to
the bottom of the person or the thing he looked at. But there
was also in it a serene pity that made you feel you had found
not a patron in him, but a friend. It was a joy to him to do an
act of kindness, and that was almost an hourly deed. During
the later years of his life, when it became tolerably well known
that he and I were very close, intimate friends, I was constantly
approached by those who were in need of help of various kinds
and desired an introduction to Dr. Agnew. Wherever and
whenever such an introduction was given, the applicant, whether
in suffering or in want, was sure of a kindly hearing, and, with
scarce an exception, received help and attention. There were
three classes whom he recognized as having what he called
'first claim on my care.' These were: doctors in suffering,
sick and struggling ministers, and those of God's poor who

were in special pain or burdened with incurable troubles. The most of his own profession have testified in public to his open hand and open heart in meeting the calls of his suffering brethren, and the generosity with which he ofttimes administered to the wants of those who, through physical infirmity or some inexplicable break-down in their professional life, were no longer able to provide for themselves.

"It may be permitted me to say that if he was the doctors' doctor he was also the pastors' physician. Since his death there have multiplied to me singular testimonies of the pure kindliness and thoughtfulness of my departed friend to the members of my own profession. Just last week it so chanced that public duty called me to a neighboring town, where, in a goodly company of Christian ministers, the conversation drifted to Dr. D. Hayes Agnew. In the course of that talk this fact was pressed home upon my attention: that every clergyman there present knew several instances where Dr. Agnew had, for a longer or shorter time, ministered to some suffering preacher or given advice and lent his skill for the recovery of some member of a ministerial household.

"One witness gave the following illustration: 'A brother minister of mine went to Philadelphia to consult Dr. Agnew about a severe trouble of his own. He saw the doctor, who examined him carefully, prescribed for him, and told him when to return. This care and ministration went on in the case of the suffering pastor for well nigh two years, until, through the blessing of God and the skillful treatment of Dr. Agnew, the minister was restored to perfect health and strength. Some little time after his recovery the clergyman wrote to Dr. Agnew, asking for his bill, and received the following remarkable and touching answer:—

"'REVEREND AND DEAR SIR: That I have been permitted to minister to your relief and, through the blessing of God on my efforts, have been enabled to be of help to you, is a source of greatest gratification to myself. You owe me nothing. To your Master and my own I owe all things, and to serve one of His poor, suffering messengers is but a little service rendered to Him who gave Himself for me. All I ask is that you pray for me; that is the richest return that you can make.

"'I am yours in Christian friendship,

"'D. HAYES AGNEW.'

"Another minister present at the table said: 'Well, I know a preacher who was tended by Dr. Agnew for nearly a year, and when he was quite better asked the doctor what he was in his debt. With one of those kindly smiles that marked Agnew and a gentle tone Dr. Agnew asked him: "How much do those people down in the country give you?" The preacher named a very modest salary. "Oh, well," said Dr. Agnew, "when they quadruple your salary come back and tell me and we'll talk about the fee."'

"I can myself testify that on very many occasions I have spoken to him about some poor man or woman whose peculiar case demanded special advice, and I have never so spoken to him that he has not either gone to see the sufferer or had the patient come and see him, and it was all done with a sweet courtesy and a tender sympathy that showed that Dr. Agnew felt himself blest and honored in being permitted to help any of the deserving poor.

"*His Devout Piety.*—If there ever were a simple-minded, humble, devout Christian man, it was D. Hayes Agnew. He was a man of prayer. For himself he felt and owned the need of daily and close communion with God. An early riser, the first part of the day was consecrated to this fellowship of the Spirit with his Father in Heaven; and it was a rare thing, indeed, when he allowed the most sudden and urgent call, even at an unusually early hour, to take him from his home without first bending at the family altar, and leading with earnest tone and reverent spirit and loving heart the thoughts of his family up to God, and seeking for them the Divine blessing and for himself the Divine guidance in his work and the help of the Great Physician in the discharge of his own professional duties. More than a score of times have we talked together upon the power and necessity of prayer to men living public, noisy, professional lives. It is the close hold of a man's soul upon the unseen God that makes him strong for duty and kindly among his fellows. That was a realization of Dr. Agnew's experience.

"He was a diligent student of the Bible. His habit for years had been regularly and systematically to read through the entire Word of God. This work was not done as a mere piece of routine. It was not done for the mere sake of doing it. He read thoughtfully; compared scripture with scripture; *searched* the scriptures, and had the Word of Christ dwelling in him richly, in all wisdom and spiritual understanding. If you made Dr. Agnew a present of a book, there was no gift that he welcomed so gladly and with so profuse thanks as some work casting fresh light upon the Word of God. Travels in the Holy Land, descriptions of Biblical life and customs, accounts of explorations making more intelligible hints and references contained in the Old Testament, were all eagerly hailed by him and carefully studied. He was one of those who *meditated* on God's word. It was a very common thing for him to have for his more intimate clerical friends a number of very difficult questions in connection with the meaning of scripture, and as he would put these to you you felt immediately that you were dealing with a man who had thought very deeply upon the subject presented to you for explanation. One of the last topics on which he and I conversed together was the nature and meaning of the demoniacal possessions referred to in the New Testament.

"He was a lover of the Sabbath. He did, indeed, count it an honor and a delight, and resolutely and reverently set it apart for spiritual rest and refreshment. As he himself said, he had an abhorrence of 'Sunday physic.' He regretted exceedingly whenever necessity and the supreme call of mercy required him to give up to professional work and duty any part of the sacred hours of the Lord's Day. And with that quiet dignity that so strongly marked him when he chose to show it, he resented anything like an impertinent interference with his quiet enjoyment of his time of rest and worship. The inner circle that knew him best knows full well the pained look that came across his face when some one with abundance of leisure intruded himself upon the quiet, thoughtful, Christian man, enjoying the calm of the Sabbatic afternoon, to obtain advice that could just as easily have been had upon the morrow.

"He was a constant attendant upon church ordinances, and morning and evening his tall, erect form was seen in the House of God, and from the beginning to the end of the service his reverent attention never faltered, and his manifest enjoyment was clearly written upon his countenance.

"*His Settled Faith and Convictions.*—He was a man of settled faith and of strong convictions. He knew what he believed and why he held his faith so fast. He had searched and tried himself in the realized presence of God. He had carefully compared scripture with scripture. He had earnestly and steadily faced and fought his doubts and difficulties. He had groped through many an hour of thick-set darkness. He had plumbed the deep, sullen waters of perplexities and seeming contradictions. He had pushed his way through stormy seas of controversies, and the end of it all was: 'I know whom I have believed, and I am persuaded that He is able to keep what I have committed to Him against the day.'

"In the closing years of his life, his mind was at perfect rest in the clear, serene light of established trust and convictions, yet was he ever ready to face and fairly consider every new question reverently put and backed up with arguments of seeming strength. During these past ten years not a single subject of debate has come up upon the confessional field, or within any of the great ecclesiastical lines, on which he and I have not talked frequently and fully. He had thought each one of them out for himself, and arrived at clean-cut and definite conclusions. He rested implicitly in the Word of God. He was satisfied that when the last full word was spoken by science, it would be in accord with the Word of God, or, at least, in no antagonism to it.　He held firmly by the unity of truth, full truth, simple truth.

.　"As to his creed and church, he was a positive Presbyterian. Privately and publicly, with great gladness of heart, and yet with no offensiveness, he avowed himself a lover of the old blue banner.　He honored her history; he loved her simple ways. He delighted in the direct and unimpeded intercourse which she gave the soul in her address to God and her manner of communion with Him and the seeking of His face.　In the later questions, stirred within the pale of his own communion, he took a very lively interest, and held strong, clear opinions.

"*His Broad Catholicity of Spirit.*—He was settled in his own convictions, but he was tolerant of the opinions of others, and catholic in the true sense of the word.　He loved his own church best, but was generous in thought and kindly in feeling toward all.　He had many friends in all the churches, and in all the communions of Christ he recognized admirable features. He was intelligently acquainted with their doctrines, with their history, and their forms of worship, and he recognized the good that was in each of them.　Standing firmly upon his own Presbyterian foundation, he said, from the depth of his heart: 'I believe in the communion of the saints.'　He preferred the characteristic worship of the church of his fathers, but felt by no means a stranger in any of the sanctuaries of his Christian brethren.　Wherever the message of his Master came to him, he received it reverently and lovingly, no matter what mouth spake it or in what peculiar form of worship it found its place. Thus I recall him, the man who gathered unto himself and sweetly combined and harmonized so many moral excellences; the man of gentle speech and kindly spirit; the man of deep, humble piety, of settled faith and broad catholicity; and, as I think of him, I see him in the happy quiet of his summer home, in the early hours of the Sabbath morn, with his open Bible by his side, wherein for a good, long hour ere I came upon him he had been reading; the still, serene light of a happy, restful soul lying softly on his countenance, and the deep, calm joy of a Christ-kept spirit shining through his eyes, and the suggestive, quiet speech of a God-taught believer coming to me helpfully when I entered on the duties of the day.

"Once again I see him, a sick and suffering man, leaning back, weak, in his arm-chair; lifting his wasted hand to take mine, and raising his kindly eyes to me and thanking me for a simple prayer which, he said, 'has done me the most good, and has made my heart to rest.'

"Thus I bid him farewell, until the shadows flee away and the morning breaks for both."

CHAPTER XIII.

THE JUBILEE OF DR. AGNEW.

ON the 10th of April, 1879, the *confrères* of Dr. Gross, in commemoration of the fifty-first year of his entrance into the profession, gave him a complimentary banquet at the St. George Hotel, at which Dr. Agnew presided. The number of subscribers was limited to one hundred. Among the invited guests were many of the most prominent surgeons and physicians in the United States. The Committee on Arrangements originally consisted of Drs. D. Hayes Agnew, Thomas G. Morton, and Richard J. Levis, to whom was afterward added Dr. J. Ewing Mears, as Secretary. The undertaking had its origin in the Surgical Club of Philadelphia, a private association which met once a week during the autumn and winter for mutual improvement and the cultivation of kindly feeling. It had been the intention to extend this compliment to Dr. Gross the year before, on the occasion of his semi-centennial professional birthday, but the celebration had to be postponed on account of the death of his wife.

"Professor Agnew[1] announced the first toast of the evening, 'Our Guest,' and, addressing Dr. Gross, indulged in the following eloquent strain, which was repeatedly applauded during its delivery :—

"The honor of speaking to this toast devolves upon myself, and I may say that it gives me great pleasure to be the medium of extending to you, on this occasion, the friendly congratulations of your professional brethren here present.

"Fifty-one years is a long time, my dear sir, for a man to labor in any department of knowledge. Will you recall for a moment just a few of the events which have transpired during this period? Two generations have played their part in the great drama of life, and have left the stage.

---

[1] The remainder of the report of this banquet is taken from Dr. Gross' autobiography.

Dynasties which bid fair to rival in perpetuity that of Rome itself have risen, flourished, and passed into decay. Engineers have struck their levels, and laid down great iron roadways from one end of this continent to the other, uniting together the waters of the Atlantic and the Pacific. The most distant parts of the earth have been reached by threads of iron, over which pass the thoughts of men in chariots of electric fire. The telephone has made the world a great whispering gallery; the powder-cart and the subtle arts of diplomacy have reconstructed the entire map of Europe; and an American medical and surgical literature has grown up to which you have been one of the largest contributors,—a literature which is not only read on this side of the Atlantic, but in every civilized country on the face of the globe. And yet here you still remain, my good friend, sturdy and strong as a great oak of the forest; or, like Moses, with eye undimmed and strength unabated.

"It is, I fear, too commonly thought, in these days of mad haste for preferment, place, or power, that men, when they have passed three-score and ten years, should gracefully retire to the shades of private and inactive life, leaving the field to younger athletes.

"This is a great mistake. Look at old Plato, at eighty-one, delving away at his studies with all the enthusiasm of youth; at Isocrates, delivering his great Panathenaic oration at ninety-six. No, no! There is something in the grace and dignity of age. Its serene complacency of mind, when coupled with an affluent wealth of knowledge and rich stores of observation and experience, renders the presence of old men in our midst pillars of strength, not only in a profession like our own, but to the community at large; indeed, to the world. The wisdom of old Fabius was more than a match for the trained legions of the youthful and wily Hannibal. It was not for men like Milo, or Ajax, for which the Captain of all the Greeks prayed, in order that he might humble the proud battlements of Troy, but for men like Nestor. Long may you yet live, my dear sir, actively to engage in the duties of the profession which you have dignified and honored! And when the inevitable hour comes, as come it must to each and all of us,—that supreme hour, on which all the hours of human life concentrate,—may your eyes close on the scenes of earth calm and quiet as a summer evening!

"It only remains for me to place on the lapel of your coat this little decoration. It is the gift of the gentlemen who sit around this board. And also this book, which contains the names of those who participate in this interesting ceremonial. These souvenirs may serve, when you shall have laid aside the harness of conflict, to recall some pleasant memories of the past; and they may also tend to fire the ambition of your sons to emulate the ambition of their noble sire.

"When Professor Agnew had finished his address, he attached to the lapel of Dr. Gross' coat a gold medal, having on one side the monogram, 'S. D. G.,' in diamonds and brilliants, and on the other this inscription: 'Presented to Dr. S. D. Gross by his medical friends in commemoration of his fifty-first year in the profession, April 10, 1879.' The memorial book, containing leaves of tinted paper on which were written the names of the invited guests and subscribers, was presented at the same time."

Nine years later Dr. Agnew celebrated his own jubilee; he had graduated ten years later than Dr. Gross, although he was thirteen years younger. In those nine years much had happened,—Dr. Gross had died; Dr. Agnew had given up the larger part of his hospital work; he had cut down his practice, and was concluding arrangements by which to retire from the University. It was the nine years filled with the most momentous changes in his life.

As the spring of 1888 approached, it was felt by the members of the medical profession that some public recognition should be given Dr. Agnew for the completion of so long and so remarkable a professional career, for on a spring day fifty years before he had graduated from the University of Pennsylvania. For the purpose of carrying out this intention, a preliminary meeting was held in the Council-room of the College of Physicians, Tuesday, January 31st. This preliminary call was signed by Drs. S. Weir Mitchell, Ellwood Wilson, John H. Brinton, J. Solis Cohen, J. M. Da Costa, William Pepper, James H. Hutchinson, and Thomas J. Yarrow. At this meeting, held January 31, 1888, on motion of Dr. S. W. Gross, Dr. S. Weir Mitchell was chosen chairman of the meeting, and Dr. Horace Y. Evans secretary. Dr. H. C. Wood moved that the form of the testimonial be a public reception; Dr. John Ashhurst, Jr., amended the motion, with the suggestion that it be made a banquet by the members of the medical profession, which was adopted by vote. It was decided, therefore, that a dinner be given to Dr. Agnew, the subscription being fixed at twelve dollars, two dollars of which and the balance that might remain after the dinner to be used in procuring an oil portrait of Dr. Agnew, to hang in the hall of the College of Physicians.

A Committee of Arrangements of twelve was appointed, which consisted of Drs. J. M. Da Costa, Ellwood Wilson, Owen J. Wister, Richard A. Cleeman, J. Solis Cohen, Alfred Stillé, John Ashhurst (Jr.), William F. Norris, Samuel W. Gross, Lewis Rodman, William Pepper, James H. Hutchinson, and S. Weir Mitchell. Dr. J. M. Da Costa was appointed Chairman of this Committee.

Dr. Agnew accepted the invitation of the committee, leaving the date of the dinner to be fixed by them. The committee accordingly selected the 6th of April as the most appropriate date for the banquet. At its meeting on March 3d the committee approved a list of physicians to be invited to subscribe to the celebration in Philadelphia. It was decided that the physicians outside of Philadelphia to be invited to subscribe be limited to those living in towns in neighboring States, within a radius of forty miles of Philadelphia. It was resolved that certain physicians from other cities be invited as guests, as reported by the same committee. This list was afterward revised by Dr. Agnew.

The banquet was confined entirely to medical men, with two exceptions, these being the pastor of Dr. Agnew's church, Rev. Dr. John S. MacIntosh, and his cousin, Rev. Dr. Benjamin L. Agnew. More than two hundred physicians promptly accepted the invitation of the committee, and the banquet took place, on the evening of the appointed day, in the foyer of the Academy of Music. One table was placed parallel with the northern wall, at which sat the chairman of the committee, Dr. J. M. Da Costa, with the honored guest of the evening, Dr. Agnew, on his right, and the Rev. Dr. MacIntosh on his left. Three long tables at right angles to this reached nearly to the southern end of the room.

At no period in his life was there a greater display of the magnetism which surrounded Dr. Agnew's personal presence. His modest manner only seemed to heighten the enthusiasm and love lavished upon him by his colleagues and former students. These characteristics brought out one of the most curious features of the success of Dr. Agnew,—the remarkable lack of ill feeling and jealousy which surrounded his advance. Although the attendance at the banquet was made up largely of his life-long associates in the medical profession, there was no one to begrudge his honors or belittle his fame. It was demonstrated to the public again that Dr. Agnew was truly, as was said of him later, "the doctors' doctor."

The opening speech of the evening was made by Dr. J. M. Da Costa, who proposed the toast, "The Honored Guest of the Evening." He spoke as follows:—

Fifty years ago, on this very day, there stood, with the honors of a University just received, a young man on the threshold of his life. His thoughts were the pleasant ones of the occasion; his aspirations had hardly taken shape; he was the popular comrade of the one hundred and fifty-five whose real life, like his own, was to begin. Fifty years have passed, and their Agnew has become our Agnew, of the many thousands of the medical profession.

Honored Guest: In addressing you to-night I feel that I speak not simply for those who are gathered around you, nor for those in this Commonwealth whose interests will centre here, but for the whole profession, who hold you in such esteem, and whose sympathetic thoughts, could they reach you, would come to you in messages of such good will and affection as to overwhelm you with their warmth.

Your career has been indeed a remarkable one, and you must pardon me and let the occasion be my excuse if in your presence I allude to its success and the main causes of that success. Nor is it wholly unfitting in one to do so who has known you and watched your progress with friendly interest almost since you came to this city to try your powers in a wider field. The training you brought with you as a rural practitioner of note was indeed valuable. Self-reliance and cool judgment under difficult circumstances are not the least reward of a country physician's hard life.

You enrolled yourself as a teacher of medicine in its most laborious branch, and fittingly took charge of a school which has been the nursery of famous anatomists and surgeons,—where Godman's practical skill was displayed, and Joseph Pancoast laid the foundation of that intimate knowledge of the human frame which made him afterward so great a surgeon.

The Philadelphia School of Anatomy, in College Avenue, has, indeed, left its mark in the history of medicine. It has been to us what the Windmill Street School was to London, of William and John Hunter, of Hewson, of Cruikshank, of Baillie, of Benjamin Brodie, of Charles Bell. Its rickety structure harbored not only anatomists,—some of them your own pupils, who are to succeed you as celebrated teachers,—but its dingy walls heard eloquent discourses on diverse branches from more than one of your future colleagues. In its garret, independent and fruitful researches on the textures of the body were pursued; in its cramped lower room, physiological experiments were carried on, which have made their deep impress on the science of our day.

For ten years, working in this school of anatomy, you lived laborious days and nights, and in its stern training your classes grew until the narrow quarters would hold them no more, and you became the popular, admirable teacher you have proved yourself on a larger scale and on a different branch, as professor of the principles and practice of surgery in the famed University with which your reputation is forever identified.

You learned to present facts plainly and impressively, to teach nature's truths with nature's simplicity, and without a deadly paralysis of words. But in these ten years of unremitting work you did something more than teaching,—you laid, by exact knowledge, by steadiness of purpose and affability, the foundations of that large practice which you have since enjoyed, developing more every day into the trusted surgeon, whose deft hand and cool judgment caused his advice to be generally sought.

You have been tried in many a hard case; in none harder than when your reputation caused you to be selected among the counselors at the couch of that wounded one for whose relief millions were anxiously watching. That in these trying times you bore yourself with the same calmness and dignity we know in you, every one in these millions recognized.

Your success as a surgeon of great repute must indeed have been gratifying to you; not only for the opportunities it afforded you of doing so much active work in your profession, not only because it gave a personal value to your writings, especially to your opinions expressed in your elaborate work on surgery, but because it enabled you to carry out a plan of action of which I may not speak,—one which showed you

to be possessed of the same high sense of honor for which Sir Walter
Scott has received the unbounded admiration of mankind.

May you, dear sir, who have these many claims to distinction and
esteem; may you on this the fiftieth anniversary of entrance into a profession which you have graced by your industry, your sagacity, your
skill, your character; may you accept the homage of those who are
engaged with you in the same pursuit, as a sign of widely-felt regard and
appreciation. May your vigorous frame preserve your power of doing
good, of teaching truths, for many a long year. May there always remain with you the assurance that, as age gently lays its hand upon you,
the chilling finger of time will not lessen the respect nor benumb the
tenderness of feeling with which young and old alike regard you.

At the close of the speech by Dr. Da Costa there was great
cheering for some time, and, quiet finally being restored, Dr.
Agnew arose. This movement was greeted with enthusiastic
cheers. He said:—

Mr. Chairman: When I glance over this table and see so many
distinguished and representative men, of my own profession, who have
come to do honor to one of the humblest of their guild, I confess it is
with a deep sense of embarrassment that I wish to respond to the complimentary sentiment embodied in your toast and in your address. I can
say, without affectation, that, had it been the pleasure of my friends, a
less conspicuous demonstration of their good-will than the present
would have been more in consonance with my feelings and taste.

It is a great distinction for any man, in whatsoever sphere of life
he may move, to win the confidence and esteem of his fellows. And it is
scarcely necessary for me to say how profoundly I realize this mark of
your respect.

Any man who has lived long in this world, and has taken a
thoughtful retrospect of his past life, must be forced to confess that
the influences and forces which have conspired to mould his character and
to shape his destiny, are most mysterious indeed. Plans constructed
with infinite care have miscarried; fondly-cherished hopes have been
suddenly crushed with a shock; glowing anticipations, just about to become realizations, are dissipated in a moment into thin, viewless air, like
earth-mists before the morning sun. One of Scotland's gifted, but
unfortunate sons, has condensed these thoughts into the expressive
couplet:—

> " The best laid schemes o' mice and men
>   Gang aft aglee."

And the great bard of England—rather, the bard of all people and all times—has crystallized the same sentiment in those expressive lines :—

"There is a divinity that shapes our ends,
Rough hew them as we may."

And a greater than either has said : "It is not in man to direct his steps."

About thirty-five years ago, I came to this city a stranger. Although previously enjoying a large practice in a wealthy and populous district, yet the field was never a satisfactory one. The horizon seemed too contracted, the prospect uninviting. Possessing naturally strong anatomical taste, I was able to ratify these only to a moderate degree, by dissections of the human body and the bodies of animals ; the prejudice against studies of this nature was calculated to render their prosecution unpopular, not to say very embarrassing. The desire, therefore, to obtain a larger field for the gratification of the idol of my thoughts induced me to make Philadelphia my home.

The scene of my early labors, as most of you know, was in College Avenue. in the Philadelphia School of Anatomy. This institution —not a chartered, but a private one—had both an ancient and an honorable history. It was here that Godman and Webster and the elder Pancoast and Allen laid the foundation of their reputation. It was, indeed, a school of the prophets ; a gymnasium in which were trained the great majority of the men who, as teachers and writers, have filled so large a place in the medical world. Among these names may be mentioned that of Gerhard; the pioneer of physical diagnosis in America ; of Wallace, who became Professor of Obstetrics in the Jefferson Medical College ; of Bridges, Professor of Chemistry in the Philadelphia School of Pharmacy ; of Keating, elected Professor of Obstetrics in Jefferson College, but compelled to resign on account of ill health ; of Henry H. Smith, Professor of Surgery in the University of Pennsylvania ; of Francis Gurney Smith, Professor of Physiology in the same institution ; of your honored chairman, Professor of the Principles and Practice of Medicine in the Jefferson Medical College ; of Penrose, Professor of Obstetrics in the University of Pennsylvania ; of Brinton, one of the Professors of Surgery in the Jefferson Medical College ; Garretson, the author of a popular work on "Oral Surgery "; and of Keen, Professor of Surgery in the Women's College of Philadelphia. It was here that Brown-Séquard delivered his lectures on operative physiology, and it was here that Mitchell conducted his classic experiments on snake-poison, and on many physiological problems, which have placed his name alongside that of Ferrier and given him a high place among the scientists of the present day. It was in this institution that for many years, summer and winter, night and day, rarely taking a vacation, I studied the mysteries of this wonderful organism of ours, with a love and a zeal which never flagged, and drew around me, notwithstanding the hostility of the two great medical schools, from a small beginning of nine 'medical students, the largest private classes—only limited by the capacity of the building—that had ever followed a private teacher in this country.

Those were happy days: yes, I think the happiest days of my life. I was master, then, of my own kingdom. Those old, dingy rooms had more attractions for me than the frescoed and fretted walls of a palace, and those anatomical odors were sweeter far than those of Araby the blest.

When I was induced to accept the Demonstratorship of Anatomy in the University of Pennsylvania, it was with reluctance and regret that I left the old Philadelphia School of Anatomy. It was entirely natural that my thoughts should linger about College Avenue, for it was here that I formed those friendships which, like hooks of steel, have bound me to the medical men of every part of this country, and to not a few across the sea.

In 1854 a united effort was made to reopen the Philadelphia Hospital for medical teaching. The doors of this institution had been closed for several years. History furnishes innumerable instances in which the most momentous events have been determined by the most trivial accidents. All these fade into insignificance when contrasted with that which closed the doors of this great clinic against the profession. The cackle of a few geese saved Rome, but a presumptuous cockroach closed the gates of the Blockley Hospital to clinical teachings. Let me say here in parenthesis, that to Dr. Henry H. Smith and Dr. J. L. Ludlow, more than to all others combined, the profession and the country at large are indebted for the restoration of this important hospital to clinical instruction. By their unwearied and indefatigable perseverance, by their unceasing importunity, like the widow with the unjust judge, these men succeeded in revolutionizing the antagonistic and settled ideas of the Board of Guardians, and gained this great contest. On the same day that the Hospital Committee made their favorable report, Dr. Smith and I were elected surgeons in the institution, and for twelve years, save for a short interregnum, when self-respect demanded the resignation of the Medical Board, I continued to discharge the duties of a clinical teacher of surgery in the hospital. In 1864 I was elected one of the surgeons to the Wills Hospital for Diseases of the Eye,—fulfilling the duties of the physician for a period of six years. In 1865 I was honored by an appointment on the surgical staff of the Pennsylvania Hospital, and for about eleven years continued my service in that venerable institution until the inauguration of a policy which compelled me to resign.

Let me say here that I have tried to make it a rule of my life never knowingly to violate my sense of duty. And, with the help of God's grace, it has never cost me one moment's hesitation to turn my back on any proposition or place, however tempting, the acceptance of which would compel me to surrender my conscientious conviction of right.

In 1877 the Board of Managers, of its own motion and unsolicited, with a cordiality and unanimity which I can never forget, re-elected me to my former place on the surgical staff. In 1867 I was elected one of the surgeons to the Orthopedic Hospital, then situated on Ninth Street, which has now grown to be one of the important institutions of the country for the treatment of deformities. In 1870 the Trustees of the University of Pennsylvania elected me to the Chair of Clinical Surgery in that institution, and a year later to the Chair of the Principles and Practice of Surgery, and on the completion of the University Hospital Building I was appointed one of the clinical professors of surgery.

Why I should have all these honors thrust upon me I do not know. (A voice: "We know.") Other and abler men could have filled them. But this much I can say,—I never schemed or planned for one of them. Any place in the republic of medicine was honorable enough for me. I knew there were golden apples in the garden of the Hesperidës, but I was too much in love with my own particular study to attempt to play Hercules and the Dragon.

My love for the profession was inborn, wrought into the very fibre of my mental organization, and inspired not by the honors at her command, but from the unspeakable satisfaction and pleasure of being able to use her resources for the benefit of our common humanity. How long I may be able to continue in this service I know not. This I leave to the wisdom of Him who numbers the hairs of the head and notes the flight or the fall of the sparrow; but, come when that supreme moment must, I shall be satisfied. I have had all that I could wish,—more than I deserve.

And now, gentlemen, this is a great honor which you have done me; to be the guest of such a company should satisfy the most exacting ambition. And let me say, to each and all of my professional brethren here to-night, that I have no words which can fittingly express the profound obligation under which I am placed by your generosity and kindness.

Dr. Lewis A. Sayre, of New York, being called upon by Dr. Da Costa, spoke as follows, in response to the toast, "Our Invited Guests":—

MR. CHAIRMAN AND GENTLEMEN: I very fully appreciate the distinguished honor conferred upon me by being requested to respond to the toast of "Our Invited Guests" on this momentous occasion, when we have assembled to commemorate the fiftieth anniversary of the professional life of one of America's greatest living surgeons, Dr. D. Hayes Agnew. I most sincerely regret that some one more worthy, or at least more competent, had not been selected to perform this pleasant duty.

There is no physician—and particularly no surgeon—in the broad expanse of this whole country who would not most thankfully embrace the opportunity of adding his leaf to the "laurel crown" so richly earned by our distinguished friend, and which, to-night, we so cheerfully accord to him.

Why is it that, without a single dissenting voice, the entire profession of this vast country unite in harmony with us in doing honor to Dr. Agnew? Many others have lived and practiced the profession for more than fifty years, and yet have not been singled out for this distinction. Why is it, then, that this large gathering of the most distinguished members of our profession, and from the most distant sections of our vast territory, has assembled here to-night to do him honor?

It is because of his pure and unsullied life, his strict integrity, his close and constant devotion to the improvement of surgical science, his careful and conscientious investigation of all new suggestions, and his ready approval and adoption of all such as he could prove to be true, after such investigation.

Another great charm of his character—and which has endeared him to so many—is his earnest desire to impart to others all the information that he had obtained himself by diligent and careful application. And he thus became the disseminator of important knowledge to the thousands of students who listened with rapture to his eloquent and instructive teachings.

This is not the fitting time nor place to review in detail the immense improvements — in fact, I might almost say the marvelous improvements—that have been made in the science and practice of surgery within the past half-century. Yet, I cannot refrain from briefly referring to a few.

Take, for instance, the cases of compound comminuted and complicated fractures that were formerly condemned to amputation, and that are now successfully treated, resulting, in many instances, in useful limbs and also in movable joints. Wounds and injuries of the intestines, bladder, kidney, liver, and even of the stomach, which were formerly considered necessarily fatal, are now, by proper antiseptic precautions, successfully treated, and, in many instances, with rapid recovery, without any constitutional disturbance, or even the formation of a drop of pus. The *exact* localization and successful removal of tumors and abscesses of the brain; the union of *all* wounds by first intention, under proper antiseptic precautions,—these are some of the marvelous advances in surgery which, had they been described fifty years ago, would not have been believed.

But our distinguished friend, in whose honor we are assembled here to-night, has kept himself well abreast with all these recent improvements, and taught his recent classes the *exact* science of surgery, as understood and practiced at the present time.

His has been a great gift,—the gift of the mastery of the mystery of healing; the wielding of the necromancer's wand over bodily deformity and suffering; and the still greater gift, the ability to impart to others, through his instructive teachings, the knowledge he himself possessed.

Our Divine Master, who commanded, "Visit the sick in their afflictions," He who made the blind to see, the lame to walk, the deaf to hear, the dumb to speak, appears in this capacity in His very sublimest character, that of the "Great Physician,"—the ideal Christ,—Christ, the healer.

And surely, no other comes quite so near the great exemplar of Christianity as he who most successfully relieves human afflictions.

This, so far as I understand the character of Dr. Agnew, has been the principal or leading object of his life for the past fifty years.

Let us all imitate his noble example.

Dr. S. Weir Mitchell then read a poem in honor of the occasion. It was as follows:—

Poem by Dr. Mitchell. Read at the Dinner Commemorative of the Fiftieth Year of the Doctorate of D. Hayes Agnew, M.D., April 6, 1888.

GOOD CHAIRMAN, BROTHERS, FRIENDS, AND GUESTS,
   all ye who come with praise
To honor for our ancient guild a life of blameless days,
If from the well-worn road of toil I step aside to find
A poet's roses for the wreath your kindly wishes bind,
Be certain that their fragrance types, amid your laurel-leaves,
The gentle love a tender heart in duty's chaplet weaves.

I can't exactly set the date,—the Chairman, he will know,—
But it was on a chilly night, some month or two ago.
Within, the back-log warmed my toes; without, the frozen rain,
Storm-driven by the angry wind, clashed on my window-pane.
I lit a pipe, stirred up the fire, and, dry with thirst for knowledge,
Plunged headlong in an essay by a Fellow of the College.
But, sir, I've often seen of late that this especial thirst
Is not of all the varied forms the keenest nor the worst.
At all events, that gentleman,—that pleasant College Fellow,—
He must have been of all of us the juiciest and most mellow.
You ask his name, degree, and fame; you want to know that rare
    man?
It wasn't you,—nor you,—nor you ;—no, sir, 'twas not the Chairman !

For minutes ten I drank of him, quenched was my ardent thirst,
Another minute, and my veins with knowledge, sir, had burst ;
A moment more, my head fell back, my lazy eyelids closed,
And on my lap that Fellow's book at equal peace reposed.
Then I remember me the night that essay first was read,
And how we thought it couldn't all have come from one man's head.
At nine the College heard a snore and saw the Chairman start,—
A snore as of an actor shy rehearsing for his part.
At ten, a shameless chorus around the hall had run,
The Chairman dreamed a feeble joke, and said the noes had won.
At twelve the Treasurer fell asleep, the wakeful Censors slumbered,
The Secretary's minutes grew to hours quite unnumbered.
At six A.M. that Fellow paused, perchance a page to turn,
And up I got, and cried, " I move the College do adjourn."
They didn't, sir ; they sat all day.   It made my flesh to creep.
All night they sat ; that couldn't be.   Goodness ! was I asleep?
Was I asleep?   With less effect that Fellow might have tried
Codeia, Morphia, Urethan, Chloral, Paraldehyde.

In vain my servant called aloud, " Sir, here's a solemn letter
To say they want a song from you, for lack of some one better.
The Chairman says his man will wait while you sit down and write ;
He says he's not in any haste,—and make it something light ;
He says you needn't vex yourself to try to be effulgent,
Because, he says, champagne enough will keep them all indulgent."

I slept—at least I think I slept—an hour by estimation,
But, if I slept, I must have had unconscious cerebration ;
For on my desk, the morrow morn, I found this ordered verse :
Pray take it as you take your wife,—" for better or for worse."

MINERVA MEDICA.

A golden wedding; fifty earnest years
　This spring-tide day from that do sadly part,
When, 'mid a learned throng, one shy, grave lad,
　Half conscious, won the Mistress of our Art.

Still at his side the tranquil goddess stood,
　Unseen of men, and claimed the student boy,
Touched with her cool, sweet lips his ruddy cheek,
　And bade him follow her through grief and joy.

" Be mine," she whispered in his startled ear,
　" Be mine to-day, as Paré once was mine;
Like Hunter mine, and all who nobly won
　The fadeless honors of that shining line.

" Be mine," she said, " the calm of honest eyes,
　The steadfast forehead, and the constant soul,
Mine, the firm heart on simple duty bent,
　And mine the manly gift of self-control.

" Not in my service is the harvest won
　That gilds the child of barter and of trade ;
That steady hand, that ever-pitying touch,
　Not in my helping shall be thus repaid.

" But I will take you where the great have gone,
　And I will set your feet in honor's ways ;
Friends I will give, and length of crowded years,
　And crown your manhood with a nation's praise.

" These will I give, and more ; the poor man's home,
　The anguished sufferer in the clutch of pain,
The camp, the field, the long, sad, waiting ward,
　Watch for your kindly face, nor watch in vain

" For, as the sculptor years shall chisel deep
　The lines of pity 'neath the brow of thought,
Below your whitening hair the hurt shall read
　How well you learned what I my best have taught!"

The busy footsteps of your toiling stand
　Upon the noisy century's sharp divide,
And at your side, to-night, I see her still,
　The gracious woman, strong and tender-eyed.

O, stately Mistress of our sacred Art,
　　Changeless and beautiful, and wise and brave,
Full fifty years have gone since first your lips
　　To noblest uses pledged that forehead grave.

As round the board our merry glasses rang,
　　His golden-wedding chimes I heard to-night;
We know its offspring; in a hundred towns
　　His pupil children bless his living light.

What be the marriage-gifts that we can give?
　　What lacks he that on well-used years attends?
All that we have to give are his to-day,—
　　Love, honor, and obedience, troops of friends.

The reading of this poem was followed by an address by
Dr. R. A. Cleeman, to whose energies much of the success of
the banquet was due. Dr. Cleeman made a brief but eloquent
speech preceding his formal motion to adjourn, which was afterward withdrawn, at the request of the Chairman, Dr. Da Costa,
to give Dr. Thomas Wistar an opportunity to read his verses
written in honor of the guest of the evening:—

Ode to Professor D. Hayes Agnew, M.D., LL.D., on the Fiftieth Anni-
versary of his Graduation in Medicine, April 6, 1888.
By Thomas Wistar, M.D.

The winter whiteness glorifies thy brow,
　　The summer sunshine lingers on thy face;
　　Upon thy heart the years have left no trace,
Warm as it kindled first, we feel it now.
Here age and youth alike before thee bow,
　　Each rivals each with every kindly art
　　To do such honor to thy head and heart,
　　As friendly words and one brief hour allow.
Thy constant home is in the loving heart,
　　Still loved the most by those who know thee best.
　　As if the Truth had claimed thee for her own,
Thy honest soul disdains each doubtful art.
　　By such as thou the world is richly blest,
　　For good men rise from high example shown.

There are who stand aloft before men's eyes,
    Like crumbling castles better seen afar,
    Whose grandeur oft a nearer view would mar,—
    Such dire defect in seeming greatness lies.
The truly great beget no sad surprise :
    Humble art thou and gracious to thy kind ;
    No loud pretense betrays the little mind,
    No affectation weakness underlies.
Hippocrates and Galen—could they rise
    From honored tombs and be with us to-day,
    With kindred souls who speak the ages through—
The master-minds, the great, the good, the wise—
    Glad would they crown thee with immortal bay,
    Beloved by all, because to all so true !

Transcendent master in thy noble art !
    In mortal throes and danger imminent
    Thy skilled hand needs no other precedent.
    Who, like to thee, can bid the pulses start,
Tears cease to flow and wasting fear depart ?
    When Garfield fell and horror filled the land,
    A nation breathed when thou didst show thy hand,
    If not to heal, at least to soothe the smart.
Thou, too, art honored as a teacher great !
    Benign, as on a lofty mission bent,
    No secret does thy candid bosom hold ;
But free to all who on thy wisdom wait,
    Athirst for knowledge and with high intent,
    Thou dost the riches of thy lore unfold.

Though grudging Fate prescribe a narrow bound,—
    Though Genius does not kindle with its flame,
    Or grant to scale the starry height of fame
    To all ; yet from thy higher ground,
How ready was thy big heart ever found,
    At every lesser brother's call in need,
    To give, on the equal terms, the kindest heed,
    Though to thyself no vantage should redound !
No empty praises do we sing to thee :
    Could weary hospitals thy goodness tell,
    Could countless homes thy benefits unfold,
Glad from the skies would Love and Sympathy
    With Earth's too sordid children straightway dwell,
    Drawn by the story, if the half were told.

In vain do these too hurried numbers tell
    The peaceful triumphs of thy fifty years
    Vain our applause, vain Friendship's holy tears
    That all unbidden from our eyes upwell—
While lovingly we on thy virtues dwell—
    Unless to us thy grand achievements give
    Some quick'ning energy like thee to live,
    And like to thee in living worth excel.
The evening shadows lengthen o'er thy way,
    Around thee falls a mild and mellow light,
    Surely from care thou needest some release :
Well mayest thou rest while yet the lingering ray
    Of sunset splendor waits upon the night,
    And earth and heaven and thy own soul say "Peace!"

The photograph of each gentleman who participated in the Jubilee Dinner of Dr. Agnew, was taken by the photographer, W. Curtis Taylor, and mounted in a specially prepared album, and presented to Dr. Agnew as a souvenir of the occasion.

This brought the formal proceedings of the banquet to a close, although the medical men lingered long afterward to listen to the informal speeches, and to shake hands with Dr. Agnew before he left the Academy. At a meeting of the committee, held April 23, 1888, Drs. S. Weir Mitchell, J. H. Hutchinson, and S. W. Gross were appointed the committee on the portrait. Bernhard Uhle was selected as the artist, and the splendid picture which he produced, and which hangs in the College of Physicians, is regarded by many as the first of his masterpieces.[1] Dr. S. Weir Mitchell made the presentation speech, and the picture was received by Dr. W. W. Keen, on behalf of the College, at a dinner held April 22, 1890. Thus was consummated a most heart-felt tribute to a great man, beloved by his colleagues, and without an enemy in the profession which he had made his life-work.

On April 19, 1890, when the committee met to settle its

---

[1] See Frontispiece.

affairs, it appeared that a large surplus remained. It was then resolved that the balance of the fund be expended for a portrait of Dr. Alfred Stillé, provided that disposition of the money seemed appropriate to Dr. Agnew. Such disposition was sanctioned by Dr. Agnew, and the fine picture of Dr. Stillé was painted by the same artist, Uhle, and hangs near the portrait of Dr. Agnew in the hall of the College of Physicians.

On April 24, 1888, the Faculty of Medicine and the students of the Medical Department of the University of Pennsylvania, held their celebration of the fiftieth anniversary of the graduation of Dr. Agnew. On this occasion the exercises were held in the Chapel of the University. A reception consumed the early part of the evening, and at 9 o'clock Provost Pepper, of the University, made an introductory speech. Dr. Pepper then introduced Professor Samuel W. Gross, of the Jefferson Medical College, who made an address, taking the career of Dr. Agnew as an object lesson. He concluded by saying: "In England they call Gladstone the Grand Old Man; to me, Agnew is the Dear Old Man. Long may he live to adorn our profession; long may he live to shed additional lustre upon the institution with which he is connected." William R. Lincoln, of the Class of 1888, followed with a speech appropriate to the occasion, and in behalf of the undergraduates presented Dr. Agnew with a gold medal as a souvenir of the occasion.

Dr. Agnew then replied to the remarks which had been made. He pointed out the fact that Dr. Leidy and himself were then the only links that connected the old University with the new. He then spoke earnestly to the students, and in turn addressed himself to the Faculty and Alumni, and urged them all, in his characteristic style, to use their best endeavors to further the interests of the University. The proceedings included a banquet and songs by the University Glee Club. The committee in charge of the banquet, selected J. H. Adams, of the Class of 1889, to write a song suitable for the occasion, the music to which was the work of Hugh A. Clarke, Professor of Music at the University.   It was as follows:—

SONG.

Fifty years of strong progression!
  Half a century of rise!
Noblest in a great profession.
Highest far, by all confession,
  But gentle, as thy name implies.

In the midst of Time's swift eddy,
  Fraught with wrecks of human life;
Thy figure stands out strong and steady,
For thy duty, calm and ready,
  Never blinded by the strife.

The lone cripple in the alley,
  For thy skill, holds life more dear;
And thy students, as they rally,
Bless thee now from hill and valley,
  Indian jungle and wild frontier.

When the Leader of the nation,
  Low was laid by insane will;
From the wide-spread consternation
Grew the patient resignation,
  Trusting to thy matchless skill.

With swelling hearts, we meet thee,
  Thou, the guider of our way.
With loving awe we treat thee,
With humblest pride we greet thee,
  On this, thy natal day.

Before the banquet each gentleman present was invited to register in a large memorial album, which was presented subsequently to Dr. Agnew.

It was regretted by many non-professional friends of Dr. Agnew that there was no demonstration paid him in which they could take part.   The demonstration paid Dr. Agnew by his fellow-physicians was a most remarkable display of admiration, appreciation, and love which was deeply and fully appreciated by him, and which had a marked effect upon the public, but many persons in other branches of life expressed a great desire to join in some celebration to his honor. The possibilities of the magnitude and note of such a gathering can be estimated when the interest of the public, as manifested in his death and funeral, are considered. This complaint was rendered partly unjust by the action of the Penn Club, which gave a reception for Dr. Agnew in April, 1888. By this means a large number of distinguished Philadelphians were enabled to meet and do him honor.

CHAPTER XIV.

DR. AGNEW'S RETIREMENT FROM THE UNIVERSITY OF PENNSYLVANIA.

IN contrast with this jubilee banquet was the last didactic lecture delivered by Dr. Agnew at the University of Pennsylvania, April 5, 1889. This lecture was probably one of the pleasantest and yet saddest experiences in his long career. To understand his emotions we must know the circumstances surrounding the occasion.

The jubilee dinner of the year before lost much of its saddening influences through the warmth of the enthusiasm and love displayed, through the flood of pleasant memories that poured their mellowing influence over all, like the beauties of a glorious sunset; but, like the sunset, the banquet was simply a glorification of the present; it showed nothing of the future.

This last lecture, on the other hand, was the quiet, practical separation of Dr. Agnew from the most loved portion of his life-work. His chiefest energies had been expended in teaching. He had been an active teacher for 38 years.

As has been shown in the chapter on Dr. Agnew's connection with the School of Anatomy, he delivered, while connected with this institution, over 1800 lectures. As Demonstrator of Anatomy at the University of Pennsylvania, a rough calculation shows that he must have delivered at least 600 lectures while holding this position. In his position as Professor of Surgery he must have delivered at least 2000 lectures, including his cliniques, making a total, at the University, of about 2600 lectures.

During his ten years' service at the Philadelphia Hospital, and twelve years at the Pennsylvania, he delivered, probably, 600 more, making a grand total of 5000 lectures. In the thirty-eight years that he lectured, there were, on an average, 310

(318)

working days, making a total of 11,780 days. Dr. Agnew's vigorous application to his work is shown when it is seen that he lectured on 5000 days, or nearly every other day, including winter and summer vacations, holidays, etc., for 38 years. No better commentary on his application to work than this exists, and, yet, this was only a small portion of his daily work.

In the lecture, which is included in this biography, there are, approximately, 3000 words. As each lecture was about fifty-five minutes long, while this last one was only thirty-five, it is but fair to say that he used about 5000 words in a lecture; so that, in his lectures, he gave enough medical instruction to fill a series of volumes containing 25,000,000 words, which would make a fair-sized library, filling over two hundred volumes the size of this biography. The magnitude of this service can be seen when it is shown that these lectures were delivered to about 12,000 students, who subsequently became physicians. As there are about 90,000 practising physicians in the United States, the extent of Dr. Agnew's force as a factor in medical education can be estimated approximately.

It made no difference as to the subject of his lecture; his audience at once perceived that he was not merely rehearsing to them a lesson which he had himself just learned for the occasion, but that he was laying before them the results of practical acquaintance with his theme in all its bearings. Possessing the happy faculty of being able to tell what he knew, impressing it on the minds of his students indelibly, he had spent the happiest portion of his life in this work.

He was now resigning from his professorial chair not because he felt unequal to the work before him, but because he feared that such a time might come upon him unawares. As he said in his little speech at the close of this lecture, "God has given me the sense—the good sense—to enable me to resign while I feel that I am yet in full enjoyment and possession of all my faculties." He knew well that surgery is a cruel mistress; he knew that when her servants grow old, their minds less active, and their fingers less nimble, she holds these failings up to the pitiless gaze of all. She does not permit that greatest gift of old age,—the power to rest on the laurels of a life's work, to maintain the present by the memories of the past. On the contrary, she is as relentless to the old, tried follower of fifty years as to the newest tyro of to-day. This is one of nature's cruel but necessary provisions. Nothing earthly is as precious as human life; and when the operator grows unfit for his work, an All-wise Providence proclaims it widely. Dr. Agnew realized this hard side of his profession, and he stood more than ready to accept its conditions.

His students, as usual, singularly in full sympathy with his feelings, had decorated the lecture-room with flowers and plants. A wreath of laurel had been placed on the central chandelier so as to crown, unconsciously, the head of their beloved lecturer.

What visions of the past and future must have swept before the old teacher's eyes! There were memories of the dim long ago, when he had been a student in the old Ninth Street School. Then there were the happy days of teaching at the School of Anatomy, followed by the long train of years at the University. These were all now ended. He saw the future too clearly to delude himself with false hopes. He saw that he had reached the last great mile-stone in his career; and yet, except for an occasional hesitancy in manner and speech, and a certain subdued softness, nothing marked his outward demeanor different from his wont. His long schooling in the repression of his feelings stood him in good stead. This modern gladiator, who had fought the better fight for health and happiness, who had wrung many victories from disease and death, as hard fought as that of Hercules for the life of Alcestis, must have felt, as he gazed on those tiers of benches,—so singularly suggestive of the old Roman arena and amphitheatre,—like the gladiators of old, as they gazed on Cæsar with the cry on their lips, "Those who are about to die, salute you!"

So much has been written of Dr. Agnew's lectures that this last lecture is here incorporated. It was a short lecture,— twenty minutes shorter than the usual length. He always spoke extemporaneously, without notes excepting occasional memoranda of the heads of the subjects to be discussed for the day. This lecture was reported stenographically, and is printed exactly as he delivered it, without additions. As he lectured, he pointed out the various anatomical points on appropriate charts and performed the various operations of tracheotomy on the body of a dead child on the desk before him. This ability to work and talk successfully at the same time is a most difficult task, but, as has been said, it was another of Dr. Agnew's accomplishments.

TRACHEOTOMY.

*Last Didactic Lecture Delivered by Dr. D. Hayes Agnew, at the
University of Pennsylvania, April 5, 1889.*

" Tracheotomy is one of those operations that I think every medical man should be able to perform. There are two operations which, I have frequently said, every practitioner should qualify himself to do, in consequence of the danger which results from the loss of time. One of these operations is for strangulated hernia, and the other is tracheotomy; minutes count, and count dearly, when any delay about operations of this nature ensues.

" The subject of tracheotomy is one that requires, in the first place, a certain amount of knowledge of anatomy; a knowledge of the relation of the trachea to the two sets of great blood-vessels of the neck, and also to the arteries and veins which are placed immediately in front of it. A few moments will enable me to call your attention to the leading anatomical facts in connection with this subject. You will see upon the blackboard a diagram which represents the trachea and the great vessels which cross it, or are related to it at the root of the neck, and also those which are placed upon its side. Here you have the arch of the aorta giving off, as the first blood-vessel, the innominate and then the innominate dividing into its two principal trunks, the subclavian and the carotid, and, on the opposite side, the carotid coming off as a primary vessel from the aorta.

"Then, here is the trachea disappearing, crossed by this important vein, which is the transverse vein, a vein which, when there is any difficulty in the respiration, often becomes distended to more than three times its normal size, and therefore is within reach of the knife when you are making an incision into the trachea, provided that the knife is carried down too low. Not only so, but you notice that a portion of the trachea is covered up by the part of the innominate artery which is a little to the right of the median line, and, consequently, if your knife should run a little too far in this direction this vessel would be wounded. By keeping clearly in your minds the relations of these structures to the trachea itself such errors are not likely to occur.

"The trachea is covered by skin, superficial fascia, and the platysma, and, joining in the median line, the sterno-hyoid and the sterno-thyroid muscles, with the deep fascia, and, next in order, the tracheal fascia. Crossing the trachea, we have the thyroid body, which, in consequence of the great size of the middle portion or isthmus, may sometimes interfere somewhat with the operation.

"There are various operations done in the median line of the neck, all of which can be explained to you in a few moments if you will look at the skeleton of the trachea and larynx.

"Always pass your hand over the neck before beginning your operation, so as to make yourself entirely familiar by touch with all the topographical features. This you should do before dissecting any region, so as to notice clearly and distinctly all the swells and depressions. Every part ought to be so clearly recognized that you could produce a mental image of it at any time if you desired. Pass your hand down the median line of the neck and you feel first the hard body of the hyoid bone and then you feel the most salient portion of the neck, the angle of the thyroid cartilage; then, if you pass a little further down, you come to another prominence which is not so large, but which gives you the idea of a dense ring; this is the cricoid cartilage. Now, if you let your finger slip down in the median line just below the thyroid, you will find that it drops into a little soft space which separates the thyroid from the cricoid,—the crico-thyroid space. Below the cricoid cartilage you come to the receding portion of the trachea, the part which leaves the surface and sinks deeper in the neck, and which causes, as it drops beneath the sternum into the chest, this fossa which we speak of as the supra-sternal fossa.

"We come now to consider the operations which may be performed to open the respiratory apparatus. First, there is the operation which consists in opening the crico-thyroid membrane. This allows the free admission of air to the trachea, but it is not a space which gives any great room for removing a foreign body, or in which it is desirable to keep a tube for any length of time. It is only an extemporaneous operation to save a patient from perishing from a foreign body which may have lodged in his larynx, or when you have not the instruments at hand to do a formal tracheotomy. The next operation is one in which you open below the cricoid; this is tracheotomy, whereas, the one higher up is laryngotomy, because it is within the limits of the larynx. These operations become necessary from a great variety of causes, which I shall not stop to-day to detail, but I will pass at once to the *technique* of the operation itself.

"What vessels are there which must be kept clearly in mind during this operation?

"First, if you perform the operation of laryngotomy,—that is, opening through the crico-thyroid space,—there are four vessels, all coming from the crico-thyroid arteries. These divide each into two branches and send one small trunk along the lower border of the thyroid and one along the upper border of the cricoid; sometimes these arteries are very large. Here, on this specimen, is one as large as the radial artery. If your knife were to divide that, you would have a furious hemorrhage, and if you carried your incision far enough to open the larynx the blood would probably enter and destroy the life of the patient. But rarely is the artery so large as it is here. Still, when you are opening this space, remember the existence of these two branches and make your incision exactly in the middle, neither too near the cricoid nor too near the thyroid.

"Then you have the other small branches which you meet with in passing down the neck, but which are practically of little import unless you have present that vessel which is called the middle thyroid, or the artery of Neubauer, for the anatomist who first discovered it. It arises from the innominate, rarely from the arch of the aorta, and comes directly up on the middle of the trachea. Before any operation is performed, always examine by the touch to see if you can find any pulsation there. This artery is sufficiently common to make it possible that you may encounter it in an operation of this character.

"At the root of the neck is a plexus of veins called the thyroid plexus. This preparation enables me to exhibit to you all the vascular parts that are of interest in the operation. Here you have the crico-thyroid arising from the superior thyroid and supplying the crico-thyroid space. Then you come to this, which is the thyroid body, whose isthmus lies directly across the trachea covering in one, two, or three rings, and sometimes more of the trachea itself. Then from the bottom you see this intricate plexus of veins, with very distensible walls, which become very much distended during the difficult respiration which accompanies croup; so that often, when you have opened the neck and have exposed the tracheal fascia, you will be almost deterred from inserting the knife among the large blue veins which cover it,—if you are not familiar with the operation. These veins run down and empty into the transverse vein. Next you see the trachea covered in by the innominate artery, showing that it is quite possible to open it if the knife is carried too far. I saw such an accident once. The knife was carelessly handled by an operator while opening the trachea, and he cut but did not sever entirely the innominate. The patient died, and I had that specimen for many years while I was teaching anatomy; but it has disappeared, like many other anatomical specimens, which, you know, are difficult to keep.

"Next you notice the transverse vein, which might be opened, especially if it was greatly distended on account of difficult respiration.

"The great point in all operations here is to keep accurately in the median line, for then it is not necessary to divide any muscular tissue whatever. You have this linea alba, you may say, or raphe of the neck, separating all the muscular tissues. If you go to one side or the other and cut into muscular tissue, you become confounded and greatly embarrassed in this simple operation. I say simple, although it is not always a simple operation, especially in that class of cases on which you will usually operate,—children with short, fat necks, with a movable trachea rising and falling with each difficult respiration.

"The administration of an anesthetic is preparatory to the operation. Many cases do not require it; the patient is in a semi-unconscious state and will make very little resistance, especially when operation has been postponed, as it too often is, to so late a period that changes have probably taken place in the lungs, making the operation futile. It is well in ordinary cases to give the child a whiff of chloroform or ether,—chloroform often better than ether, because less likely to excite spasm and more kindly received by the patient,—enough, at least, to deaden the sensibility until you can complete that which is the sensitive part of the operation, namely, dividing the skin and subcutaneous tissue.

"The instruments required for that purpose are, first, a scalpel, a pair of forceps,—the ordinary instruments that you have in your operating cases,—and a director, ligatures, and

tenaculum; and then you are to be provided with such instruments as will enable you to keep the wound in the trachea
patulous. We have various instruments for that purpose.

"This is the old tracheal tube, as it is termed. It is sometimes of metal, sometimes of hard rubber,—the latter is not reliable, as it is apt to be broken. This should be largely, if not
entirely, a silver instrument, so as to keep it from tarnishing. It
is simply a double canula with two shoulders, so arranged that
you can introduce tapes or a little sticking-plaster,—preferably
the former,—in order to hold it in the opening. One tube
comes out of the other. You can disarticulate the inner tube
by turning it half-way around; the object of this is that the tube
may be kept perfectly clean. With a little screw at the top it
is fixed in place. These tubes are curved, and the length of
them must depend largely on the age of the patient on whom
you operate.

"Then you want something to enable you to guide the
canula in after you have opened the trachea, and, very frequently, this is a difficult maneuvre, and is sometimes the most
difficult and embarrassing part of the whole operation. Your
tube is apt to get to one side or the other, and it slips in between the tracheal fascia and the trachea itself, but, by introducing something that will act as an obturator and round off the
extremity of the canula, you can usually get it in without much
difficulty; and so, in well-appointed operative cases, you have
this instrument which acts as a pilot, and, by its conical form,
serves to conduct the canula into the opening. You can get
along very well,—and economy is a great matter, especially with
medical students and young practitioners,—as a rule, without
any instruments of this kind, by taking a soft catheter and passing
it through the canula till a small portion of it projects at the
end.

"Then you require other instruments. For example: you
may need a little dilator to expand the orifice you are making,
in case you are operating for a foreign body in the trachea or

bronchi. That you could do with a pair of forceps; but, still, this is a useful instrument.

"Then you require an instrument to take out foreign bodies that are in the trachea. You may introduce this delicate, curved pair of forceps down till you reach the bronchial tube, if necessary, and take out a coin, for instance, which may be there.

"Then here is another instrument for which you could very well substitute a feather or a camel's-hair brush. It is nothing more than some bristles twisted into a wire, which is meant to keep the trachea clear from the secretions which accumulate and tend to close up the tube.

"Here are two instruments which will save you from what is always a dangerous thing to do, but which has been done as an evidence of the boldness and self-sacrifice of surgeons, namely, applying the mouth to the tube and sucking it clear when the trachea would otherwise have been closed from the accumulations in it. Here is a syringe by which you can draw out the accumulations that are there, or by which you can keep up artificial respiration, which is sometimes necessary from the operation having been delayed so long that the patient is practically moribund when it is undertaken. By forcing in air through this tube, and then compressing the chest again, patients have been revived, by keeping up artificial respiration for some time.

"The retractors are these two instruments which you see here; and now you have the whole armamentarium which goes to make up a complete case.

"The operation is done as follows: Have an assistant to take charge of the ether and give his whole attention to that. You may stand in one of two positions, either where an etherizer usually stands, at the head of the patient, or you may take your position at the side and cut either from below upward or from above downward. That is a matter of taste altogether. Then, if you are going to open simply the larynx for temporary relief, you palpate and touch the hyoid bone, the thyroid and cricoid cartilage, and then you return and sink your finger into the crico-thyroid space and immediately drive your knife vertically into the larynx; or you may pass it in transversely, which is better; or you may, if you please, make a crucial cut. In this way you may save your patient's life, though it is an operation of only temporary value.

"It is very easy to expose the whole laryngeal box by an addition to this operation which we have spoken of as laryngotomy. If the knife is turned on its back and you cut directly upward in the median line, you separate the two halves of the larynx and expose it and make it easy to remove a growth from the vocal cords or any other part of the larynx. Sometimes this portion, which we speak of as the angle, is so thoroughly ossified as to require either bone-forceps for clipping it, or the cartilage-knife.

"But suppose you are going below and are going to open the trachea, for example, for croup. Then your incision should commence at the bottom of the thyroid cartilage. It is a great convenience to give yourself ample space, so far as the soft parts are concerned, and so begin the incision that you will have a clear view of the median line and carry it down almost to the top of the sternum. The first incision should go down to the superficial fascia; then pick up the superficial fascia, little by little, and divide, and then the deep fascia next. When you have divided the deep fascia, you have exposed at once the edges of the sterno-hyoid muscles, and then your knife is laid aside and you take your director and pass it into the median line, working up and down so as to separate these muscles.

"You have divided no muscular tissue if you have been careful to maintain the median line.

"Then you come to the connective tissue between the sterno-thyroid muscles. Divide that and go down till you come to a loose fascia, and in that perhaps you will see the veins bulging up directly into the wound, and you must get rid of them.

"Sometimes you can press them off with your finger or director sufficiently to enable you to get them out of the way; but if you cannot there is no use tying them individually, but you are to take them up in a bunch and put a ligature of cat-gut around the entire mass.   Next, breaking up the tracheal fascia, I put my finger in and feel to see if the middle thyroid artery is present.   If it is not, I go on clearing away the loose connective tissue from the front of the trachea, which is another very important part of the operation, in order that the last steps of it may be successful.

"Many unsuccessful attempts to get a tube into the trachea have been due to the fact that the trachea has not been cleaned. If you have time, clean it till you feel your director running freely over the cartilaginous rings.

"Sometimes you are embarrassed by the middle lobe of the thyroid gland.   Sometimes you can put the director under the whole isthmus and push it up toward the thyroid cartilage.·   If you fail to get rid of the isthmus in that way, and it is often very vascular, you are to take a curved needle and pass it under the isthmus, bring the thread out above, and allow a double liga-ture to remain, tying the isthmus on either side.   This is valuable for another purpose, for you can steady the trachea very much by these two threads; though we have another method of doing that.   Pass the director under the isthmus and divide it between the two ligatures.   After having exposed the trachea, the next point is to open it.   It is well enough to have all hemorrhage arrested, though there is a certain amount of oozing that will not be stopped by ligatures, but stops the moment you put the tube in.

"You must fix the trachea when you open it.   An ordinary tenaculum is to be put in quickly, because the trachea is mov-ing up and down.   It may be necessary to have retractors to keep the wound open.   Catch the tenaculum in the cellular tissue about the cricoid.   Keep it steady for a moment and lift it out of its deep sulcus.   Then take a sharp-pointed bistoury and make your incision in the trachea by cutting from below upward, for by so doing you are cutting away from danger. The knife is dipped into the trachea, and the division of two or three rings exactly in the middle line is made.

"When the incision is made, the next thing is the introduction of the tracheal tube, which goes through the wound in the neck into the trachea, and it may be secured by tapes or adhesive plaster, the tapes being better. Some put a suture directly through the sides of the wound and through the shoulders of the tube. This, however, is painful to the patient, and is a practice which ought not to be followed.

"Now comes a very important part of this subject, and it is the after-treatment. That treatment consists in having a skilled nurse who shall be at the side of the bed—never leaving it for a moment; or, if so, she shall be replaced by another of equal intelligence. Her duty is, with a feather or brush, to keep the tube clear of mucus that constantly wells up into it and has to be wiped away. Not only so, but the temperature of the room is a matter of some importance. It ought not to be below seventy degrees, and sometimes it is better to have it a little more. Then there is need of something to prevent the intrusion of foreign matter from the air, and even the air itself is harmful until it has been modified a little by passing through some medium. We usually take a little gauze and place it over the tube, and we may moisten it with a little boracic-acid solution, so that the air is strained of its impurities and the lungs saved from irritation. Two or three stitches are put in to close up part of the external wound and keep the tube in position.

"The length of time the tube is to be retained depends very much on the morbid conditions that have existed before the operation. Ordinarily it is kept in several days, but sometimes several weeks. A very good way to tell whether it should be taken out is to place your finger over the end of it and compel the patient to breathe through the natural passages;

and if he breathes with ease for a considerable period, it is time to remove it.

"These constitute the leading points in connection with the operation of tracheotomy."

After this lecture he addressed the class as follows :—

"And now, gentlemen, I have delivered the last of the lectures that it has been my privilege and my pleasure to deliver to you. In taking my leave from the associations of nearly my whole life-time, I cannot do so without dwelling for a moment on the reflections that this occasion gives rise to. I have been connected with this Institution since its earliest days, through its rapid growth to where it stands to-day, in the front rank of the medical institutions of the country. With a feeling of satisfaction that I can thus behold this Institution which we love so dearly, I turn to contemplate the retirement which I have sought.

"There comes a time in the life of every man when he wants to be free, when he feels that even the pleasant duties and congenial tasks which have been his lot grow heavy,—I have reached that time. I feel like the galley-slave, who, with manacles thrown off, breathes the air of freedom. For over forty years I have been, as they say in theatrical parlance, on the boards before the public, and, as I glance backward over that long period of almost a life-time, three most delightful thoughts come to me. The first of these is, that at no time have I ever been received by any act of discourtesy or unkindness by any of the gentlemen whom I have had the honor to address here (prolonged applause). The second is, that the post of responsibility which it has been my cherished privilege to hold here was one that I had never sought. It came to me unbidden. And the third thought is, that God has given me the sense—the good sense—to enable me to resign it while I feel that I am yet in the full enjoyment and possession of all my faculties. These I have endeavored to strengthen, to broaden, and to render useful in the sphere of my professional life, for I feel that I have lived to very little account if I have not lived to learn.

"In a few days we part, some of us, perhaps, to meet no more. How eagerly and deeply would I impress on you your duties as physicians. You have chosen a profession which is one of the highest and noblest that a man can make his calling. See that, by your faithful zeal and application, you endeavor to maintain it in all the dignity that belongs to it.

"As we take this leave, I wish that all of you may prosper; that it may be your aim to elevate your lives and to round them off in the fullness of an undeviating regard for duty and high purpose; that, in short, you may be good men and true, good physicians, and pure, good, and honorable citizens. I trust, in the effort to attain these high marks in the life that stretches out before you, that you may continue in a reverent regard for the faith that has sustained you, guarded you from the paths of evil. I can say no more. God be with you."

No one realizes, until he attempts it, how difficult it is to talk to medical students in the strain as that shown by Dr. Agnew in this little speech. He knew, of course, that the class represented the most diverse religious beliefs. There were all kinds and divisions of Christians, as well as Agnostics, Israelites, Persians, Mohammedans, Japanese, etc. To be personal and appealing without wounding their religious feelings is a very tactful and difficult task.

A few days later, at the One Hundred and Fifteenth Annual Commencement of the Department of Medicine of the University of Pennsylvania, held May 1, 1889, at the Academy of Music, a painting of Dr. Agnew was presented to the University by the three undergraduate classes of the Medical Department. It has been the custom from time immemorial to present the portrait of a professor retiring from his department, to hang in the hall of the Wistar and Horner Museum. This collection has grown to be the most valued possession of the Medical School, as was shown at the fire in May 1888, when the students, at the risk of their own lives, saved these paintings, although warned by the firemen not to attempt such foolhardy risks.

The invitation-cards engraved for this commencement had in the corner a representation of the head of Dr. Agnew, in honor of the occasion. Dr. Joseph Allison Scott, of the graduating class, in a few appropriate words made the presentation. "This is our Agnew Day," he said, "and well may we be impressed by its solemnity, for it is the last time that we shall see our beloved professor before us in his official capacity."

Then the veil, which had concealed the portrait, was

DR. AGNEW IN CLINIQUE.

slipped off, showing a life-size likeness of Dr. Agnew standing in the clinical amphitheatre, having just completed an operation,—removal of a cancer of the breast. All the figures in the group were taken from life. His assistants are dressing the wound, while Dr. Agnew has stepped to the rail of the clinique-seats and is explaining what he has done, and its *rationale*.[1]

The painting is seven by eleven feet without the frame, and is regarded as one of the masterpieces of that famous artist, who has made a specialty of medical subjects, Thomas Eakens.

The treatment of the subject is an amplification of the portrait of Dr. Gross done by the same artist. The picture incidentally shows an interesting change in surgery, the white garments of Dr. Agnew and his assistants being an innovation due to antiseptic surgery, unknown in Dr. Gross' time.

This picture has been criticised, not for the ability of the artist, or for the artistic merit of his work, for the portrait of Dr. Agnew is as life-like as is possible and the delineation of the clinique-room is perfect, but for the idea embodied,—that of presenting Dr. Agnew in the act of operating. While a surgical operation is rarely pleasant to a layman, and, consequently, such a subject must be more or less repulsive to the general public, yet at the same time it was this work which made Dr. Agnew famous. This picture, intended to be hung in the Medical School, is certainly not unworthy, as it represents the most important side of Dr. Agnew's life-work; for its resting place it is perfectly proper.

While engaged in painting this picture, the artist discovered forcibly one of Dr. Agnew's peculiarities. Dr. Agnew had been represented with blood attached here and there to his hands; noticing this point, at once he objected most strenuously, and, despite the artist's protests for fidelity to nature, he ordered all the blood to be removed.

---

[1] The following is the inscription on the frame of the painting : " D. Hayes Agnew, M.D. Chirurgus expertissimus ; scriptor et doctor clarissimus ; vir veneratus et carissimus," which, being translated, reads : " The most experienced surgeon, the clearest writer and teacher, the man most beloved and venerated."

The criticism is made that surgeons grow brutal, but here was a surgeon, who had been accustomed to working in blood for fifty years, who had not had his sense of propriety blunted in the least.

The portrait was received on behalf of the trustees by Dr. S. Weir Mitchell, Chairman of the Medical Committee of the Trustees. In a brief speech he accepted it in his usually happy style, concluding: "Whenever you become involved in doubt and uncertainty, think what Dr. Agnew would have done, and you will be sure to have done the right thing."

When Dr. Mitchell sat down, there was a loud cry of "Agnew" from all parts of the house. In response to the call, Dr. Agnew rose slowly and stepped to the foot-lights. This was the signal for a universal burst of applause and a deafening clapping of hands. When the noise had subsided, Dr. Agnew turned smilingly to his counterpart in oil and said that though he had often heard of "speaking likenesses," this did not hold in the present instance, however excellent the representation, for he would be compelled to do the speaking himself. Continuing, he said: "Perhaps you have not all heard the story of the old woman who had spent her life toiling in a kitchen in London. Finally, being placed in a position to follow out her inclinations, she determined to free herself from all the trouble and turmoil of this life, and accordingly she built for herself a mansion outside of the city, fitted out with every modern luxury. But every once in a while she became tired of her comforts and an ungovernable longing came over her, and she would come back occasionally to London to her old kitchen, to 'smell its grease.' So, now that I have retired into comparative ease, if life should become unbearable to me, I shall still retain the consolation of going across the river occasionally to hear the boys' yell."

At this, Dr. Agnew "heard the boys' yell" where he stood, and such was the din that he was unable to proceed for several minutes. When the house had quieted down finally, he addressed a few words of earnest advice and exhortation to them, and he was just turning to his seat when he staggered. A thrill of horror ran through the house, but he caught himself almost immediately, and before Provost Pepper, with his usual tact, could go on with the program, to conceal the occurrence, he recovered his equilibrium and, turning again to the students, said, in a firm, distinct voice, "I wish you all success in your profession." He did this to assure them that nothing serious had happened.

He had been suffering all the morning from a very acute attack of indigestion, which brought on a considerable amount of dizziness. This, with the glare and heat of the foot-lights over which he was standing, the moving sea of upturned faces, and, possibly, with some natural emotion under the circumstances, caused this momentary indisposition. It gave the students a chance to study that imperturbability of manner under the most startling circumstances which Professor William Osler, in the valedictory address a few minutes before, had declared so necessary in the young physician.

Dr. Agnew, by his resignation from the teaching force of the University, sought more time for leisure. It was his intention to devote less time to work and more to recreation. As he said in his speech, he had reached the time when he wished to be free from the exacting duties of his life, and, moreover, his experience as a physician had taught him that he had reached that time of life when he must naturally expect to lessen his output. His life became more social, he began to spend more time with his family, and his home-life, which had been seriously interfered with throughout his whole life, was now fuller and more satisfactory. Dr. and Mrs. Agnew were able, at length, to devote considerable time to each other.

Thus quietly and unostentatiously Dr. Agnew's life sped on, broken only by such occasional incidents as those just related. He sought rest more and more from his labors, although his nature and obliging disposition led him to work far more than he intended, and far more than he should have done. He found it impossible to shake off a large part of his work. He was still wanted at operations, and even if he would not operate many physicians wanted him present, simply to give his opinion and sanction as to the course pursued.

Dr. Agnew's reputation, at this period, had grown so great that it was no longer an honor for him to be associated with an institution, but, on the contrary, an honor to the institution. By this time he had been made consulting or honorary surgeon to nearly all the hospitals and dispensaries in town, such as the Gyneceau Hospital, the Kensington Hospital for Women, the Philadelphia Dispensary, etc.

In these later years Dr. Agnew took more interest in politics. He had been a life-long Democrat, although never active in political work. The rejuvenation of the Democratic Party by President Cleveland aroused his flagging interests, and he eagerly watched and commended the beliefs and actions of this Democratic Moses.

A representative from the University of Pennsylvania, who visited, in the course of his duties, a large proportion of the universities of Europe, had the curiosity to inquire of the different officials, professors, and students what men at the University of Pennsylvania they were familiar with. He found, of course, that in their own lines of work the different European scientists were acquainted with the men doing that line of work at the University, but he found that there were but two men who were universally known, and their career and deeds recognized and appreciated. These were Leidy and Agnew. Knowing that so much of Dr. Leidy's work was of such a kind that it would be distributed throughout the educated world, it was not a surprise to find his name so familiarly quoted, but, as Dr. Agnew worked in a field and in a way which was naturally far more local, his constant recognition was rather surprising.

Undoubtedly, if Dr. Agnew had gone abroad in the last few years of his life he would have received many honorary degrees from European universities, as did Dr. Gross.

The degrees which he received were few in number: as has been said, in 1861 he received from Princeton College the honorary degree of A.M., which was followed, in 1874, by the conferring of the degree of Doctor of Laws by the same institution. On June 6, 1888, the University of Pennsylvania conferred on him the degree of LL.D.

Dr. Agnew's last appearance at a public meeting of any sort was at the Musical Fund Hall, February 27, 1892, on which occasion he responded to a toast on the professors of his youth, at the first triennial banquet of the combined Alumni of the University of Pennsylvania. He found, when he began to speak, that his voice, which was usually so distinct, would not respond to the demand made upon it, and, although the hall has excellent acoustic properties, it was only by the strictest silence that his remarks could be heard. He spoke on a favorite topic,— the outlining of the characters and careers of his early teachers. In such delineation as this he was peculiarly happy. Like the artist who, with a few quick, bold strokes of his pencil, gives the outline of a figure, in which what is left out is suggested, so Dr. Agnew, in a half-dozen terse phrases, could etch the personality of one of these former giants. He felt very much dissatisfied, after his speech, with what he had said, although to his auditors it was an unusually interesting and absorbing narration. He was compelled, on account of feeling ill, to hurry home that night, directly after the delivery of his speech.

Judge M. Russell Thayer, who also replied to a toast at this same banquet, brought out a curious and beautiful coincidence in his own career, which applied unconsciously, but equally well, to Dr. Agnew. The substance of what he said is as follows: "Fifty years ago I graduated from the University of Pennsylvania. The Commencement exercises were held in this hall. During this long period of time the course of events has carried the University far to our westward, and for many years this old historic building stood alone and deserted in this rather disreputable portion of the city. Now that the western portion of the city has been built up, attention has been turned back again to this old site, and it has been rejuvenated, and our alumni banquet is held within its walls, and here I am speaking again in the hall which I left as a graduate fifty years ago. It seems as if the cycle of my life has been made complete and I have returned to the spot from whence I started, after a life's journey."

CHAPTER XV.

Dr. Agnew's Final Sickness, Death, and Funeral.

Dr. Agnew's death came as he desired it,—a quick transition from a busy life to an eternal reward. He found in later years that, after undue exertion on his part, he was subject to slight attacks of angina pectoris, due, as was afterward proven, to the ossification of the coronary arteries. He had, in the winter of 1889–90, a severe attack of epidemic influenza, from which he never fully recovered. Following this, he had an attack of broncho-vesicular catarrh, of moderate severity. On several occasions he had passed renal calculi, and there had been slight manifestations both of diabetic and albuminuric conditions. On Wednesday, the 9th of March, 1892, after operating, he returned home at 3 o'clock, when, remembering that he had forgotten to see a case, he went out.

During this last operation, which he performed on this day, it was necessary to give him brandy a number of times, although the operation lasted but half an hour. Immediately after the operation, before he left the house of the patient, the attack became so severe that he became firmly possessed of the belief that he was going to die then and there.

On his return home the second time, he was seized again with anginose symptoms, and was compelled to remain in his office for a number of hours before he could be removed to his bedroom. For the next two or three days he improved to such a degree that he saw several of his friends. In the evening of Saturday, March 12th, he became much worse. His condition from this time until the day of his death was simply a fluctuation from slight hope to positive hopelessness. During this time he was thoroughly conscious of his physical condition, and controlled largely the treatment of his case. On Sunday, March 20th, he fell into a comatose condition, in which he remained

(339)

until the moment of his death, which was at twenty minutes of three on the afternoon of March 22, 1892. The immediate cause of his death was uremia, due to the failure of the kidneys to perform their usual functions.

An autopsy was held on March 23, 1892, at which time there were revealed the conditions which had been diagnosed before death. He had met with a severe fall a couple of years before his death, and the members of his family were anxious to determine whether the injury at the base of his skull could be in any way connected with the diabetes which subsequently appeared. There was the trace of nothing abnormal in his brain; it was rather small in size, but the convolutions were most tremendously marked and totally dissimilar in each hemisphere.

The American Anthropometric Society desired to secure his brain, that it might be placed in their collection alongside of that of Dr. Leidy. The object of this society is to place the study of the human brain upon a satisfactory scientific basis. Cerebral topography is in many respects incomplete; brains of low, if not degenerate, type have furnished, for the most part, the results which have thus far been obtained. It is evident that this is not desirable. Knowledge should be drawn from sources which indicate, so far as it is possible so to do, the peculiarities of brain-structure of all classes of society. While it is comparatively easy to secure the brains of criminals and those who have been inmates of city hospitals, it is quite difficult to obtain brains of a higher expression of cerebral structure, and to study such with the aid of complete histories. To meet and overcome these difficulties, the society has appealed to the educated classes for assistance. They request the members of the higher classes of America to bequeath their brains to the use of the society.

As Dr. Agnew had not joined the society, although he was cognizant of its existence, Mrs. Agnew did not feel that it was his wish to have his brain added to this collection; and as she felt, personally, a great repugnance to such an idea, she did not consent to their request.

On March 24th a plaster-cast was taken of Dr. Agnew's head, face, and hands by Mr. Thomas Eakens, the artist, and Mr. Samuel M. Murray, the sculptor. On the evening of March 23d the Philadelphia County Medical Society held a large meeting, at which appropriate resolutions in regard to his death were passed. The following evening the College of Physicians called a meeting for a similar purpose.

On Friday, March 25th, Dr. Agnew was buried. At half-past 1 P.M. private services were held at his residence, 1601 Walnut Street, by the Rev. W. Hamilton Miller, D.D., pastor of the Bryn Mawr Presbyterian Church, which Dr. Agnew attended in the summer months. The funeral *cortege* then moved out Walnut Street to Twenty-first Street, where the funeral services were to be conducted in the Second Presbyterian Church. Eight members of the Agnew Surgical Society bore the body to the hearse. Probably never has there been a more impressive and solemn procession on Walnut Street than this one. As the long, stately line moved along in the bright sunshine of a glorious spring day, it seemed as though Nature were rejoicing to receive into her embrace all that was mortal of him.

"Not since the burial of Lincoln has there been in this city such a demonstration of distinguished homage as was manifest at the funeral of Dr. David Hayes Agnew. The great church was crowded to its outer doors with a patient congregation, glad even to be near a service in which they could not all participate by reason of their multitude. Hundreds tried in vain to join those who filled all the available space within, and many lingered near at hand on the sidewalk to the close of the services. Of those who filled the body of the church, representing all classes of society, the majority were men of all the learned professions beside those of medicine and surgery. In weight of character, in wealth of learning, in dignity of exalted position, a nobler or more notable array of the living never joined in such a tribute to the honored dead."

No mere professional and scientific eminence would have drawn out such a tribute. Behind the physician, behind the man of talent, learning, and skill there was a personal character which gave all these a value higher than their own. His professional fidelity and success were such as to command the respect and admiration of his associates and the love and confidence of the subjects of his skill. He had the incommunicable graciousness of one who humbly recognized and leaned on a higher than human power in all he learned and achieved. He wielded to the full an influence which mere ability and skill will never possess. By professional brethren and pupils, no less than by unlearned and trustful patients innumerable, he was consulted, cherished, revered in a way possible only toward one who is at once a Christian and a physician.

Such a man deserves to be set before the community, and especially before the rising generation of medical students and practitioners, as an ideal and an inspiration. Unhappily, there is often a divorce between the dual ministrations of soul and body, although God has wedded them in a union sacred and lasting as life. Jesus Christ was himself a physician alike to the physical and psychical diseases of men. He was the divine healer alike of the sick and the sinful. And while, in the economy of grace, there is properly a difference of function between the medical doctor and the Gospel minister, they represent the two sides of one and the same work. The physician who is wise enough not to ignore the pharmacy of grace, and the minister who is wise enough not to ignore the potency of medicine, in so far fulfills the ideal of his vocation. Occasionally the two are combined in one, as in the case of St. Luke, " the beloved physician." They are divinely fulfilled in one glorious ideal in the person of " the Son of Man."

The large congregation mourning the death of Dr. Agnew were but the inner group of a vast multitude scattered everywhere throughout the land, who, in their indebtedness to the great physician for themselves or their loved ones, mourn that they shall see his face no more.   And whether they consciously recognize the secret of it or not, there can be no question that they largely owe their debt of gratitude to the personal virtue going out of him as a Christian physician.   Others of the great throng, sincerely mourning his loss, will cherish him as an illustrious instance of one who combined the most eminent scientific ability and culture with unfaltering faith in revealed religion and in Jesus Christ as the Divine Healer of all the ills of man.

Clustering in chairs on the centre of the platform were the Rev. Moses D. Hoge, of Richmond, Virginia, a life-long friend of the dead master; the Rev. J. Addison Henry, D.D., Moderator of the Presbytery of Philadelphia ; the Rev. C. A. Dickey, D.D., representing the Presbyterian Hospital; the Rev. George Dana Boardman, D.D., as Chaplain of the University of Pennsylvania ; and Dr. John S. MacIntosh, Dr. Agnew's pastor.

When Dr. MacIntosh entered the pulpit, he uttered a brief prayer, and then announced the hymn beginning,

> " Come unto me when shadows darkly gather ;
>   When the sad heart is weary and distressed,"

and added that all the hymns to be sung during the service were very dear to Dr. Agnew.

Prayer was then offered by the Rev. J. Addison Henry, in which he feelingly spoke of the death of the eminent surgeon, saying: "We thank Thee for this beautiful life taken from us,— so faithful, so true, so loving, so wise.   He cared for us in our sickness ; watched most tenderly over our loved ones who have passed away.   So true to the interests confided to him, we rejoice that he was so faithful to Thee.   He loved the Master and served Him most faithfully all the days of his life, and he loved the Church of the living God.   Thou hast taken him to Thyself; to the society of those who loved and feared Thee when on earth."

The Old Testament Scripture lesson was read by the Rev.
George Dana Boardman, and, by request, he selected the 39th
and 23d Psalms, the former beginning: " I said I will take heed
unto my ways."

Then in sweet, low tones was sung the familiar hymn,
" Nearer my God, to Thee." This was followed by the reading
of the Epistle of the Resurrection by the Rev. C. A. Dickey,
who, by special request, selected the Scripture commencing:
" If the dead rise not, then is not Christ risen."

Following the Scripture lesson, Dr. MacIntosh delivered an
address, founded on the 31st verse of the 16th chapter of
Proverbs: " The hoary head is a crown of glory when found in
the way of righteousness." He said:—

" Crowned with glory is his hoary head! Yes, that hoary
head we all knew so well and loved so deeply through these
many years is crowned to-day; crowned with the mournful
respect of this sore-stricken community and this saddened land;
crowned with the tearful love of countless bereaved friends,
many of them the best and foremost of our time; crowned by
the sincere affection, love, and high-heaped honors of the noble
and ennobling profession wherein he stood foremost and was
greeted as a father; crowned by his church and the broad
Christian brotherhood that knew his earnest, simple piety, his
sincere convictions, and his life-long manifestation of Christ-like
virtues; crowned by us all, and right worthily, for this man of
science and of skill was a man of goodness and of God; and
he, if ever another, was always found in the way of righteousness. So, 'tis fitting that we should think of him who was to
us so helpful and inspiring.

" Another friend has gone! Ah! how true he was to all
he loved! Another helper passed away from struggling humanity! Ah! how ready he was with words of cheer and
works of mercy! Another master foremost in wisdom silent
forever! Ah! how fondly loved for his own unique worth and
his stored wisdom that we may use no more! And another

member gone out of this flock of. Christ that needed him so
much; but gone from us to the light and peace of the eternal
fold, the welcome reward of his Father and his God.

"He was one over whom we may well lift our praises, both
for his own sake and still more in honor of Him who, as our
friend himself was ever first to say, had made him all he was.
For this beloved physician ever stood forth the conscious steward
of the good gifts of God, humbly owning the Hand that had
guided him, lovingly tracing the wisdom so manifest throughout his life, and daily recognizing his supreme obligation to his
Eternal Judge.

"*He was a gift, a glory, and a benediction.*

"*He was a gift!*   Yes; a right royal gift he was from the
Giver of every good and perfect gift.   There is the gift of healing.
Let us recognize it, and let us own Him out of whose hands we
get it for our health and our comfort!   If with clear eye we behold
in the Aholiabs and the Bezaleels of the plastic fingers and the
witty inventiveness; if we find in the statesmanship and leader-
ship of a Moses and a Joshua; if we greet in the righteousness
of a Samuel and the poesy of a David; if we own in the far-
sighted philosophy of a Paul, or the high-soaring genius of an
Isaiah or a John, a gift from God to man, shall we not as truly,
as wisely, and as reverently find a heavenly gift in a Luke, who, as
'beloved physician,' comes with healing powers to stricken, suffering humanity, to troubled households, to great, useful lives that
need to be kept alive and made whole for the communities in
which they are strengths and lights and joys, and so reveals
himself to us as a very gift from on high?   Right worthily does
the Great Apostle class with the 'Word of wisdom' and the
'Word of knowledge' the 'Gift of healing,' and recognizes in it
the hand of the administrative and enriching Spirit of God.
And such a gift we had in this student of tireless patience, who
started with no special advantages of position; in this strong
soul of thoughtful resolution, who honestly willed that nothing
to be learned in his profession or in the gathering lights of

advancing science which might minister unto human help should
be for him unknown; in this keen-eyed investigator, who was
as busy, as eager and hungry for the last facts of real knowledge
in his riper years as he was in the days of adventurous youth;
in this ever-growing man of power, so quietly won and honestly deserved and sweetly used; in this modest spirit, so firm,
so gentle, who by his rare capacity for tireless application, by
his life-long, yet intensifying devotion to a beloved and entranc-
ing calling, by his pure and unselfish surrender to the exacting
demands of an enormous practice, and by his embracing all the
large possibilities of his lofty professional chair, has risen, without
stirring jealousy or envy amid the plaudits of his brethren, and
the glad heart of the community in which he was a member, to
be a master in medicine and our chief in surgery; in him shall
we not own a gift—yes, here, and in this hour recognize a gift
loaned for a while and now recalled? And in doing so we only
take what I can here, as his pastor and his closest friend, all
solemnly affirm to have been his own view of himself and his
work. For, he owned himself a steward of the good gifts of
God; acknowledged himself the servant of all, bound to go
about continually doing what good he might, and openly con-
fessed and worshipped and lifted up before him as his model
that one Divine Master, the Great Physician, who Himself went
about continually doing good.

"Well do I remember how, on one occasion, as I was
speaking of the relation of Jesus Christ to the medical profession,
and calling Him the ideal for all to whom the work of healing
was committed as a life-task, the strong face of my friend flushed
and his eyes brightened and the lofty form grew more erect!
And the next morning brought me, as was not unusual, the
loving note of thankfulness that told me how the man's heart
had answered to the preacher's words. No wonder the community to-day feels poor and we stand bereaved.

"*He was a glory! Agnew, of Philadelphia!* That was his
name. The name and the man were an honor and an ornament
to our city and to our University.

"Well do I recall the days abroad, when in Edinburgh and Glasgow, and in Belfast and Dublin, in Paris, in Berlin and Vienna, my Philadelphia heart has bounded within me and swelled with generous pride as the great surgeons of those great schools would name him with praise, and tell of his achieve-ments and repeat some of his words of wisdom.   To-day, how-ever, is not the season, for long time must not be taken, to speak at length of what a glory, and dignity, and attraction, and inspiration he was to those ardent youths, to those thronged and eager classes that, year after year, crowded the old room, ever so dear to himself, back of St. Stephen's, and to those who, in later days, from packed University benches, watched the marvel-ously swift sweep of those unique hands right and left,—each firm, both sure and quick,—and listened almost breathlessly to the unrivaled clearness and briefness, but comprehensiveness, of his own luminous discourse, and gave him not infrequently the outbursting cheer that made even the old man once more a boy, and bound 'the boys,' as he loved to call them, closer to him-self and made them love him as a father; and not a few of them weep over him, as I myself have seen, with a grief that unfitted some of them—not the weakest of men—for immediate duty, and made them seek their offices for thought, if not for prayer.

Himself and his University are indissolubly wedded.   She, the great and growing University, gave to him the splendid arena where, before the New World and some representatives of the Old, he proved his acknowledged greatness as an oper-ative surgeon; she placed him, year after year, in those fresh circles of young, eager life, which, in his clinics, freshened and inspired him; she joyously yielded to him homage, generous praise, and largest encouragement; she opened to him a clear path to his own primacy, and welcomed ever his counsels for her wise changes and continuous enlargement.   And he, on his side, lent to her much of his own calm and elevated dignity, graced her with a large measure of his own honor, summoned hundreds to her halls year by year, made her light more brilliant, and threw about her much of his own rich and pure renown. The city and college were proud to call him ' ours,' and each was better, stronger, nobler, and more widely known because he was one of ourselves and in our midst,—' a glory and a safeguard!' Yes; he was a glory.

"*And he was a benediction.* There are men who, by their very presence, confer a benefit upon all who know them. He was of such a very foremost chief. There are men who can see moral greatness; there are men who can picture greatness; but there are men themselves so great they think not of it, yet ever stamp on all they meet some of their own overflowing greatness, and make moral strength beautiful to all who touch them. Of such, he was one. There are men who are bettered by a noble profession; there are a few men who better even the two noblest callings on this side of the grave, and among the latter he whom we have lost stood very high-raised indeed.

" Now, such a surgeon and physician as was Dr. Agnew,— joining a whole-souled self-surrender to his profession with a wholly unselfish fulfillment of its exacting and lofty duties; joining a majestic calmness of judgment with piercing and instantaneous insight; joining the sympathetic tenderness of a fatherly heart to the singular coolness of the most perfect self-control; joining the daring courage of a fearless operator to the soberest caution of supremely-felt responsibility; joining the broad, comprehensive wisdom and knowledge of a great physician to the skill and power of the master-surgeon, and lifting all this splendid and singular combination up into the unity of his own dignified, modest, gentle, and responsive personality,—such a man is a rare benediction. Benediction,—yes; one of the rarest, if he stand in his ever-widening circle of influence, ready to pour out the treasures of his skill, to devote the forces of his soul to all who may be helped, to use the powers of his hand and the wealth of his genius and character upon his younger brethren of his own profession and upon any sick and wounded ones who, on the Jericho road of our common distress, appeal to him for succor

DR. AGNEW IN 1890.

and sympathy. All this, yea, more, do we all know that he was, and for long years proved himself to be.

"Ah, what a gap he leaves! As great as he was good, and better, even, than great! But we yet stand too close to take aright his measure, and so learn our loss. Yes; he was a gift, a glory, and a benediction.

"Brethren of this glorious profession, still so dear to me because of many a precious memory; young men, candidates for fellowship in this goodly guild; Christian men and women gathered in this silent sorrow, what calls to holy living are sounding in our ears! What thrilling inspirations come in this sad hour of parting! What a cloud of witnesses from the spirit-world group themselves in cheering circles round us! Rise to these stirring summonses; answer nobly to these voices; throw your heroic manhood into the good fight; make your woman-hood lovelier by sweeter services and more Christly charities. Let us not forget that out of this pew passed the pure-souled Lenox Hodge, and out of that has just gone the princely Agnew; and moved by their bright examples, and moulded into saintly symmetry by the same Spirit's hand, and mastered by the same Lord and His love, let us as heavenly children work the will of our Heavenly Father while it is called to-day."

The Rev. Moses D. Hoge, D.D., of Richmond, Va., an old-time friend of the lamented surgeon, who had been very dear to him all his long life, closed the services with an address and with a benediction.

"As the years wear on," he said, "all true ministers of Christ are conscious of an ever-increasing desire to comfort those who need consolation. The Pastor has to bear the sorrows of a great multitude. Every time a member of his flock is afflicted his heart is smitten, and there are times when he feels how inefficient all his efforts are to console those who need con-solation. But sympathy will not accomplish everything. What could we do, my dear ministerial brethren, were it not our priv-ilege, when we go to homes made dark and desolate, to say :—

> " ' Come, ye disconsolate, where'er ye languish,
>   Come to the mercy seat, fervently kneel ;
>   Here bring your wounded hearts ; here tell your anguish ;
>   Earth has no sorrow that Heaven cannot heal.'

" When I look over this vast assemblage, hushed and still, and see the tears not only of bereaved relatives, but of a bereaved community, I cannot but feel that we all constitute one sorrowing brotherhood and need consolation. Not only in this city, but in how many homes in this great land, from the North to the South and from the East to the West, are there those who to-day stand before God smitten and afflicted! I know it is true in the home I have left to come and pay this loving tribute to one who was dearer to my heart than any man north of the Potomac.

" But I come here not to speak of the good citizen, nor of the successful teacher, or the eminent author; not even of the man, endeared as he was to us by his many attractive virtues.

" I come to speak of the humble Christian, the servant of God, and for His sake the servant of the church he loved so well; and to the Pastor, who to-day mourns a loss which even his words cannot give us an adequate conception of. I come to speak of one who was an honest servant of the Church and of the community whose throes he felt so keenly, and to which he ministered with a tenderness of his own.

" I come to magnify not the man, but the grace of God that most ennobled his life, and that made so tranquil and peaceful his death.

" Physical strength may be entwined with the most charming grace of character, but the time will when even that strength will fail. The only staff is the one the preacher alluded to in the Twenty-third Psalm, that of the Good Shepherd. Honor and power give no joy to the heart that lies still in the coffin, and all the music of the world's applause fails to penetrate the dull, cold ear of death.

" As I look over this audience and see in it such a large

proportion of young men who have in view one of the noblest callings of life, I am reminded of the propriety of saying a word in regard to the bearing of science and Christianity. I know very well that the heart of our friend was often troubled at the skepticism which prevailed among scientific men, and I stand here on this occasion to bear testimony to the fact that, the more he investigated the ideas and teachings of the scientific studies to which he gave his life, the firmer became his confidence in religion. In one of the last letters he wrote to me he said: ' Christ to me is all, and my aspiration is for the immortality to come.' His testimony is something worth treasuring in your memories.

"His was a complete life. Do you know of anything in which it was incomplete? There are very few complete, symmetrical, well-rounded lives.

"How often it happens that the historian does not live to complete his final volume, or the sculptor his final work of art! Not so with this complete life—an honored life, a peaceful end, and heaven to crown it all.

"And now we are to follow him to the tomb and lay him there, in the sure and blessed hope of a certain resurrection; and in the midst of our grief let us be grateful that the ties of friendship, when sealed by the blood of Jesus, are ties which nothing can finally sever. For these associations shall have a resurrection beyond the grave. It is but a little time, and we look forward to the season of union and recognition in the everlasting glory. In the midst of our grief we can say: ' Glory to the Father, and to the Son, and to the Holy Ghost, as it was in the beginning, is now, and ever shall be, world without end. Amen.'"

Under Dr. MacIntosh's instructions the great throng which crowded the aisles and the seats slowly passed the casket, and many were there who sobbed as they looked their last upon him they knew well and loved.

Memorial sermons were preached on Dr. Agnew by several

ministers. Dr. MacIntosh, on Sunday, April 3, 1892, delivered a memorial address, taking as his subject, "The Beloved Physician," his text being Colossians, iv, 14. The Rev. Thomas A. Hoyt, D.D., pastor of the Chambers Presbyterian Church, preached, on the same day, from the same text. On Sunday, March 27th, Rev. W. C. Rommel, at the Gaston Presbyterian Church, preached a sermon on Dr. Agnew, taking as his subject, "The Blessed Physician." On this same date, Rev. T. De Witt Talmage, of Brooklyn, also delivered a sermon, taking Dr. Agnew and his life as his subject.

There were innumerable other sermons preached which contained more or less reference to Dr. Agnew and his career. On April 13, 1892, Dr. De Forest Willard read before the Philadelphia County Medical Society, by invitation, a paper on Dr. Agnew's life and surgical work.

The newspaper notices on Dr. Agnew's death were tremendous. Out of the eighty thousand periodicals in this country, over nine-tenths contained considerable accounts of his life and work. It was surprising to note the familiarity of each journal with his name and life-work.

After Dr. Agnew's death there were a number of suggestions made that a suitable permanent memorial should be made in his name. Certain of his admirers went so far as to offer, through the columns of the *Public Ledger*, large sums of money if some one would take hold of this movement. A number of letters received from different portions of the country also gave voice to the same sentiment. As yet this movement has not taken shape, but undoubtedly, if it were pushed properly, a suitable memorial could be made for him.

A mausoleum has been erected in the beautiful cemetery of West Laurel Hill, sacred to Dr. Agnew's memory, and here, near the country home he had loved so well, his ashes will rest in peace.

CHAPTER XVI.

ESTIMATE OF DR. AGNEW'S POSITION IN SURGERY.

DR. AGNEW was undoubtedly fortunate in the time of his birth. It occurred just as modern medicine was beginning to grow; during his life-time medicine developed into a great science, and his death did not come until surgery—his principal life-work—stood on a well-nigh perfect foundation.

This century, which has seen so many other professions and industries spring, Minerva-like, into full-grown existence, has been as fully acquainted with wonderful strides in medicine. It is no exaggeration to say that medical study has made a greater advance in the past ninety years than it did in the entire previous history of the world.

There was a culmination of conditions which brought about this wonderful change. The phenomena of disease are so varied and require such a tremendous range of observation over such long periods of time, that no one man, or even set of men, could arrange them on a scientific basis. It required the simultaneous and continued action, for a long series of years, of a large body of scientific observers, working under the most favorable circumstances, to bring medicine anywhere near the condition of a science. Taking up the application of remedies for the cure of disease, the discovery of the proper drugs was a slow, uncertain, and discouraging work; for, even when apparently powerful remedies were discovered, the proper means to determine the efficiency of these agencies were unknown.

The crude manner in which this investigation was carried on, as a brilliant therapeutist has said, was somewhat as follows: When Adam was sick, Eve—for undoubtedly the first physician was a woman—administered to him some preparation made from an herb, plant, or shrub. If Adam recovered from his illness, the data were jotted down in the old lady's memory,

—for she must have been old by this time,—and when Adam was sick again and presented the same symptoms she gave the same remedy. The fact that Adam recovered was sufficient proof to her of the efficacy of her treatment. The suggestion that he might have recovered from his illness despite her medicine, or that her drugs had had no effect upon him either way, never entered into her decision of the case. Seeing the disease, giving the remedy, and getting the relief was the natural method of primitive therapeutists. Thus there grew up in every community a system of empiricism or treatment based upon experience, which, as seen to-day, could easily be wholly and radically wrong.

Not only was the work, even when done in a natural and practical manner, misleading, but there were also a number of factors which retarded medical progress terribly. One of these was the attitude held by the olden masters of medicine, who constantly looked for curious solutions to medical truths. For the human mind, ever eager to find great governing laws of nature to control the phenomena of disease, was not content with these slow, uncertain processes of discovery. Hence began that fruitless search for some hidden law which should govern the application of drugs in disease. For example, there sprang up in the Middle Ages the doctrine of the "Law of Signatures," which taught that a drug should be given which resembled in appearance the organ which was supposed to be diseased. For example: in liver diseases there should be given aloes, from its fancied resemblance to this organ. Through coincidence aloes did do good occasionally, by its purgative action; hence, on such deceptive data as this, the therapeutists of the Middle Ages felt that they had established a great law in medicine. In a similar manner there arose other absurdities, such as Perkin's Tractors, the law of "Similia Similibus Curantur," etc.

The result of these curious delusions was that clear-headed observers became disgusted with the efforts which they were making for the cure of disease, and so the natural reaction to this misleading tendency came at last; it was seen to its fullest extent in the Viennese school. The masters of this great centre of medical education swung to the other extreme of the pendulum, and became therapeutic nihilists, believing that medicines were of no avail whatever in disease.

This unconsciously gave the great opportunity which was to advance medicine, for under the sway of these teachers the natural history of disease, uninfluenced by the effects of medicine, was studied for the first time. The pure phenomena of diseased conditions were seen and described at last, as a basis for all future medical study and comparison.

The real condition of affairs in medical circles two centuries ago was seen by many clear-headed observers. For example: when Boerhaave, the great Leyden physician, died, he left a handsomely embellished volume, in which he said would be found all of the real medical literature of the world and all of the valuable precepts of medical teaching. When the book was opened it was discovered that it consisted almost entirely of blank pages. Only one page contained any statement; on this it was written, "Keep your feet warm, your head cool, and your bowels open." Thus did the great Dutch physician aptly express the real extent of medical teaching at that period. It is true that a great many facts and a great many disconnected points relating to medicine were already known, but they projected here and there, like disconnected mountain-peaks, and there had been thrown between them no connecting links of joining knowledge. They were useless to the profession.

Here and there a far-sighted practitioner, living in advance of his age, such as Benjamin Rush, or John Hunter, saw far enough into Nature's truth to prescribe courses of treatment which, even to-day, must be regarded as quite scientific and proper; but at the beginning of the century the great cloud of superstitious knowledge still hung over the mass of the medical profession of the world.

Thus it was that at the beginning of the nineteenth century light was beginning to break on medical fields. Medical men were slowly emerging out of the mists and uncertainties of this strange search for specifics in disease. They were just beginning to learn that the way to acquire Nature's truths is to study Nature's phenomena. It seems a curious thing that it required so many hundreds of years to reach this apparently obvious and natural method of studying disease. Pathology was beginning to be comprehended; obstetrics was being elevated into the dignity of a distinct branch of medical study; gynecology was discovered; while surgery was making a few bold, incisive intrusions into a largely unknown region, and therapeutics, the basis of all medical work, was beginning to grow into an accurate science through the medium of experimental study upon animals. In all this advancing work the American physicians were eagerly pushing to the front, although they were terribly handicapped by the fact that the majority of their number were dependent for their livelihood upon their practice, and hence could not spare the time for original work or laboratory investigations.

It was at this time that Dr. Agnew was born. There was growth in every direction at this period throughout the civilized world. America was rapidly spreading out her domains farther and farther in every direction. The growth of railroads, the introduction of the use of steam, the use of electricity, the extension of the use of the printing-press, and all the varied factors which make up modern life were just budding into active existence.

The same conditions which caused Dr. Agnew to fail as a business man were to extend a thousand-fold his opportunities as a physician.

The medical journals of the day were becoming important; their pages were filled with the new successful work which was being poured forth by many encouraged workers. Dr. Agnew grew up with this inspiring condition of affairs surrounding him.

Following his graduation came the most wonderful discovery, as far as he was concerned, that ever occurred in medicine. It shaped his future career after he felt that he had decided it for himself. This was the practical application of the use of chloroform and ether in surgery. The power of these drugs to produce a condition of unconsciousness had long been known,[1] but whether they could be safely used had not been determined. This does not detract from the fame of the bold men whose names are associated with their introduction. These operators, unenlightened by any precedent, who pushed the application of these drugs on their patients until they sank into that profound stage of unconsciousness which is necessary for surgical work, were as bold as Columbus when he dared to push his vessel's prow persistently to the westward in search of the Indies.

To us of the present day, who are so familiar with anesthesia and anesthetics, it is scarcely possible to estimate the importance of these discoveries in the field of surgical activity. On them is dependent the present condition of surgery. The existence of the pains of consciousness prevented the great majority of the major operations in surgery, while those that were done were performed only through the greatest courage on the part of the operator and patient. Time was so valuable, on account of the intense agony of the patient, that only a few hurried cuts could be made in the course of an operation; in consequence, no careful work could be done, no dissecting out of tissues, or removal of any considerable amount of flesh; for example, in the removal of the breast for cancer, it had to be cut out in two or three quick strokes. All that was done had to be done almost instantaneously. No careful dissection of diseased tissues, or of glands in the neighborhood, which might be infected, was possible. Dr. Agnew was so vividly impressed with the horror of these operations that, quite frequently, in

---

[1] For example: Dr. J. Marion Sims relates that in Georgia, long before the introduction of surgical anesthesia, the young people engaged in "ether frolics," in which the use of ether was pushed to a great extent, even occasionally to unconsciousness.

describing an operation performed before the introduction of anesthesia, his manner and words showed that even the lapse of fifty years, and familiarity with thousands of operations in the meantime, had not lessened the horror of these memories.

The surgeons of that day were obliged to reduce the patients to as near a state of unconsciousness as could be safely done; in order to accomplish this they were frequently narcotized with large doses of laudanum, or they were even bled until consciousness was nearly lost. Then, limp and weak, the patient was placed on the operating-table, his limbs being strapped down so that in his struggles he could not move sufficiently to interfere with the accuracy of the surgeon's knife, while the operator hurriedly made the few cuts which were essential.

In consequence of this state of affairs, the reputation of the surgeon of that day was dependent largely on his ability to work with great rapidity; while his operations were comparatively few in number. The surgeon of that day, of necessity, must have been far more dextrous than one of the present. His work was far harder than at present, and the results he obtained were far less satisfactory. It has been said that Physick's reputation as a surgeon depended largely on his quick and accurate cut through the perineum in operating for stone in the bladder.

The introduction of the use of ether and chloroform into surgery changed all this condition of affairs. The possibility of the production of a state of unconsciousness, in which a surgeon could operate on his patient as painlessly as if it were on an inanimate object, made it possible for the rapid and thorough advance of surgical training and ability by giving him complete control of the patient for a comparatively long period of time. This terrific impetus given to surgery occurred just as Dr. Agnew was merging into the great stream of the medical profession.

Dr. Agnew saw the great future opening in surgery, and the fact that he determined to take advantage of this opportunity is shown in his attempts to commence dissecting in the country under such unfavorable circumstances as have been

described.   He knew that such work must make him unpopular and his immediate future most uncertain.' The opposition
aroused among his country friends and patients and the consequent loss of practice only urged him to seek such a field
where he could continue it at a still greater advantage and to a
fuller extent.   This ability to grasp and keep up with the current progress of medicine in every department was ever a most
marked characteristic of Dr. Agnew's disposition.   He used, to
the last, the latest instruments and the newest drugs.

It has often been remarked, as a matter of surprise, that in
a prescription of Dr. Agnew would often be seen a drug or preparation which had been before the profession for a comparatively short time, and which many men half his age had not
yet learned to use.   In no point was there a greater sign exhibited of this tendency on his part than in his relation to the
introduction of antiseptic surgery.   Dr. Agnew, at the time of
its introduction to the profession, was, undoubtedly, in a position
as a medical authority either to aid or to retard it considerably.
The weight of his great experience and training would have
had great force not only with his students, but with the medical
men of the country.   The fact is well known that Dr. Agnew
was one of the first to adopt thoroughly and fully all the precepts and practices of antiseptic surgery.   He saw at once the
great advantages to be derived from its application, and he was
its most enthusiastic advocate.

The advantages of the training of such a school as the
School of Anatomy to a surgeon have been stated elsewhere.

The conflict of the great Civil War, with its thousands of
wounds and injuries, with its innumerable diseases caused by
the life necessarily led by soldiers, was another great opportunity to Dr. Agnew.   It came also, fortunately, at a time of
life when he was fully prepared to meet its tremendous exactions,
and when his reputation was sufficient to enable him to grasp
readily the positions necessary to exercise his skill.   At the
beginning of the War he stood as a clear-headed and careful

anatomist and a skillful surgeon. His appointment at the
Mower Hospital, Chestnut Hill, where he saw constantly thousands of gunshot wounds daily, and where their course and
treatment were brought thoroughly to his mind, was but a
natural selection of the most eminent man for the position. He
was, at that time, only about forty years of age, but already one
of the leading surgeons of the country.

Again, in other connections, Dr. Agnew was fortunate in
the time of his birth. In his early days there was no such strict
division between medicine and surgery as exists to-day. In
consequence, Dr. Agnew's medical training was fully as thorough and complete as his surgical, and he was valued until his
death as a most skillful and competent consultant, in many conditions purely medical in their nature. At the same time, somewhat later in his career, there was yet no division of the specialties ·
among surgeons, and Dr. Agnew was at one time a distinguished
gynecologist, ophthalmologist, a genito-urinary specialist, and a
syphilographer, as well as a leading authority on gunshot wounds,
on orthopedics,—in fact, on everything in surgery. Undoubtedly, the field of general medicine and general surgery has
grown too broad for such specialists on everything to exist again.
Those who are pursuing specialties are going so deeply into
their subjects, and are becoming so unusually expert at their
work, that, doubtless, no one man can hope to compete with
them in their special lines of work. This was one of the corollary results that followed the admission of Dr. Agnew into
medicine.

His pre-eminent position in surgery was shown to the
American world when he was selected as President Garfield's
chief consultant. The chance for such a demonstration, fortunately, never occurred before in the history of American surgery.

Of course, his fortunate time of birth and his fortunate
career cannot be ascribed in any way to luck. He reached his
goal through the most distressing and discouraging of circumstances. The first fifteen years of his professional life seemed

to him to have been spent in a fruitless and unsatisfactory search for a proper field. The fact that such great opportunities existed should not blind our eyes to the equally important fact that Dr. Agnew was great enough to seize his opportunities. To show how rare a combination this was, it is only necessary to note how few of his colleagues accomplished similar results.

As a man and as a physician he was thoroughly honored. His calm, grave face, so ready to light into a smile, and never wanting its kindly aspect, will ever remain in the hearts of his admirers. He was never morose, never discouraged; always calm exteriorly, yet, after forty years of continuous teaching, he was agitated by an approaching lecture. He was very reticent and undemonstrative, yet always cheerful—a cheerfulness born of his love of God, his profession, and his fellow-men. It was pain for him to be unable to do a friendly act.

Dr. Agnew was thoroughly honest in thought, in speech, and in action. He was honest as a surgeon; he always did the thing which he believed to be the best for his patient. He had no jealousies. His hand was ever ready to assist the weak and struggling practitioner, and the profession of Philadelphia was, through him, raised to a higher plane. His success in life was achieved not by any sudden turn of fortune, but by patient industry, by tireless application, by wise judgment, by thorough knowledge, by consummate skill, and by honest purpose of word and act. He was never ostentatious in anything.

One point in Dr. Agnew's character which strikes most forcibly is the fact that he had but few qualities considered in this day to be necessary to success. Young men are admonished that the way to be successful is to be grasping, selfish, and pushing, and insensibly they grow up with the idea of each man for himself; but here was a man who achieved success in life by a diametrically opposite course. He was modest, retiring, kind, gentle, and devoid of all ambition. Truth was the object of his search; he endeavored to ascertain the facts and draw the right inferences; justice was the bedrock of his character.

There was a singular purity about his very presence; God gave him natural gifts of a high order, and he had a perfect body. He owed his success largely to a singular balance of mental and moral qualifications. Novelties never too much tempted nor too much repelled him. He was intellectually very honest. The surgeon is sometimes apt to become dramatic, to love display of his own skill. Dr. Agnew had none of this. He once said that "the immense amount of unpaid service to physicians and their families was hard on busy people; but then," he added, "it is, after all, a great help to one's self. We ought to be thankful that we are not always making mere money."

Many men change radically as life goes on; but Agnew was, from first to last, young or old, the same man. A certain simplicity was in all his ways; the outcome of action from belief was fearless and unquestioning.

In our American world, given to haste, to pressure, and to longing for speedy results and quick returns, he stood a crowning example of those patient and persevering powers which moved steadily to an appointed end without haste and without rest. In a self-seeking, grasping age he never swerved from the high standard of a self-sacrificing profession. In days given to self-advertisement he patiently waited, without self-assertion, until fame came as the fit fruit of the union of genius and character. Years were needed to make his worth known and to round out the full measure of public and professional recognition, but it came, in later years, in an overflowing flood.

Dr. Agnew always intimated the idea that his profession was "a calling," that the healing of his fellow-men was not only the practice of medicine, but a sacred duty. He felt himself, in a sense, a trustee of his vast knowledge and wonderful skill. He did not regard them as commodities commanding, by reason of their rarity, the highest market-price. He did not, in short, make his fees parallel with the inflection of his reputation.

Undoubtedly, if he could have afforded it, he would have done his work without remuneration.

He was possessed of great natural ability and strong common sense; these traits would have given him eminence in whatever vocation he might have followed; had he continued in business he would ultimately have become a great and far-seeing financier; had he turned to legal pursuits he would have been a judge on the bench, learned in the law; or, drifting in a political life, a senator; had he been a theologian he would have been a moderator of assembly, or, in other church relations, would have graced an Episcopal Chair.

In no profession or vocation in life are there more varied, or different, or stronger attributes required than go to make up the elements necessary for the production of a successful practising physician. Many professions or vocations overlap, in their requisites, the essentials in medicine; but none require more. In the first place, a physician requires a great natural endowment of intelligence. Without it, under the veneer of pleasant or polished manners, a certain degree of success can be attained, but no commanding height can be reached.

Again, a great degree of manual dexterity is needed, especially in the surgeon. A great surgeon must be a great mechanic. He must be as adept in the use of his hands and in the various laws of mechanics as a carpenter, a sculptor, or a mechanical engineer. Again, he must possess the most imperturbable manner,—must not be upset or disturbed by anything. He is expected to be cool, collected, and active in the most startling or sudden emergencies. He must possess more or less of an agreeable manner and pleasant appearance. Of course, as a physician grows older and his real worth is better known, this is not so essential; but in the young physician this is absolutely demanded. He must possess concentration. He must be able to reach conclusions definitely and quickly, from the various data which are presented to his mind. He must proceed to formulate his diagnosis like an arithmetician working out a problem. He must be willing to work at all times, day and night; to expose himself to all sorts of dangers and hardships,—in short, to live a life in which the precepts which he teaches are almost entirely disregarded. He must expect to do a large proportion of his work without hope of remuneration,—in fact, he can never look forward to any extraordinary degree of income.

As he becomes more in demand he will be able, only to a slight extent, to use assistants or substitutes. It is himself and his own opinion that are wanted; and he is unable, as in other vocations, to employ a corps of workers to aid him in his daily work. Of course, to a certain extent, this can be done, but not at all as it is done in many other professions.

On the other hand, the advantages of such a position as that held by Dr. Agnew were equally great. He was beloved by every one; his words, deeds, and thoughts were quoted and copied everywhere as almost infallible. To the American world, who dearly loves a hero, he stood the ideal of the prowess of the American surgeon. The name of Agnew has always been associated with the description of the great Larrey, the French surgeon, by Napoleon: "He was the best man I ever knew."

The extraordinary reputation, honor, and romantic position of Dr. Agnew in the world of medicine was not without its effect upon his profession. He placed the ideals of the profession upon the highest levels, where they will permanently remain. For his life-work, the accomplishment of this object was enough in itself alone. The American public have been taught by his example what a physician can be.

His fame, attracting the eye of young America, has created a great *furore* for surgery. The aspiring collegian looking for a profession is frequently influenced to take up medicine, and particularly surgery, as a life-work, simply from his impressions of Dr. Agnew. Undoubtedly Dr. Agnew's reputation has caused the surgical world to be filled to overflowing by aspiring applicants. It has given an impetus to American surgery which will redound forever to the credit of the New World.

APPENDIX.

CREDITS FOR MATERIAL USED IN THE AGNEW BIOGRAPHY.

IN preparing this biography it was the object of the writer in all cases to go to the original sources for obtaining data. In all cases where it has been possible this has been done. In obtaining this material it has been verified or disproved by parallel comparison as fully as possible. This was possible to do, as nearly every bit of information has been received from two or more wholly different sources.

Of course, the greater part of the material comes directly from Dr. Agnew himself, or from material furnished by Mrs. Agnew. In all cases of dispute Mrs. Agnew has been the judge, and to her judgment has been submitted every point of dispute. Thanks are due to Mrs. Agnew for this service which she has rendered, especially as, being in poor health, she has fulfilled the painful duty of examining and verifying the story of her husband's life, in order to get it into proper shape for this biography. Without her assistance much of the record would be totally wanting.

Dr. Agnew's lectures, private notes, books, and letters have been carefully gone over in order that nothing might be missed which could be with propriety included.

Credit is due to the following books from which information was obtained :—

The Homes of Family Names, by H. B. Guppy.

The Origin and Signification of Scottish Surnames, by Clifford Stanley Sims.

The Genealogical and Heraldic Genealogy of the Peerage and Baronetage, by Sir Bernard Burke.

Debrett's Peerage, Baronetage, Knightage, and Companionage, 1892, 179th year of publication.

Men of Mark of Cumberland Valley, Pennsylvania, 1776–1876, by Alfred Nevin, D.D., LL.D.

Strong Bow's Conquest of Ireland, edited by Francis P. Barnard, M.A., London, 1888.

English History from Contemporary Writers.

Colgrave's History of the Norman Conquest.

Chambers' Lives of Eminent Scotchmen.

Dictionary of National Biography, MacMillan & Co.

Biographical Encyclopædia of Pennsylvania of the Nineteenth Century.

Hereditary Sheriffs of Galloway, by Sir Andrew Agnew. For a copy of this extremely rare and interesting book, thanks are due to the son of the author, the present Sir Andrew Noel Agnew. The book has been given to the Historical Society of Pennsylvania, where it may be consulted by those desiring to study the history of the Agnew family more in detail.

The Biographical Outline of the American Agnew Family, compiled by Smith Agnew (unpublished). For the opportunity to study these sets of remarkably complete genealogical tables, thanks are due to his grandson, Mr. Smith Agnew, of Pittsburgh.

Carson's History of the Medical Department of the University of Pennsylvania.

Catalogues of the University of Pennsylvania, 1830–1892.

Philadelphia Hospital Report, vol. i.

Reports of Philadelphia Hospital to Board of Guardians, 1856–1870.

History of Chester County, by J. Smith Futhey.

History of Lancaster County, by Franklin Ellis and Samuel Evans.

History of Philadelphia, by Scharf and Westcott.

History of Delaware, by Scharf.

History of Jefferson College.

Gross' Autobiography.

Sims' Story of My Life.

In addition to these works, thanks are due to Mrs. Mary A. Wallace, of East Earl, Pa., and her daughter, Mrs. Mary A. Falls, of New Castle, Pa., Dr. Agnew's half-sister, and her daughter, and to Mrs. Mary Irwin Agnew, niece of Dr. Agnew, and Miss Martha A. Agnew Stuart.

In the description of the student life at the University from 1835 to 1840, thanks are due to Dr. Alfred Stillé, of Philadelphia, and Dr. Traill Green, of Easton, Pa., each of whom prepared a special original article on this subject for this biography.

Thanks are also due to Dr. James L. Tyson, of Penllyn, Pa., who prepared the description of Dr. Agnew as a student at this period. Dr. W. S. W. Ruschenberger also supplied some interesting reminiscences which have been used.

Credit is due to Iron Making and Coal Mining in Pennsylvania, by James M. Swank, for verification of much of the material collected from family stories and from a survey of the business world of this period.

The History of the Philadelphia School of Anatomy, a lecture delivered by Dr. W. W. Keen, March 1, 1875, at the closing of the school, forms the basis from which has been prepared the history of the connection of the different teachers of this school, with the exception of Dr. Agnew, down to 1875. The story of Dr. Agnew's connection with this school has been prepared from many different sources; among them, from a paper prepared on this subject by Dr. James E. Garretson, and from information furnished by two of Dr. Agnew's former demonstrators of anatomy, Dr. Robert Bolling, and Dr. John W. Lodge. The history of the school since 1875 is compiled from the owners of the school at the periods mentioned.

The account of Dr. Agnew's connection with the Philadelphia Hospital was prepared from his own data, and from the original records of the hospital, through courtesy of Dr. Charles K. Mills.

The official report of Dr. Agnew's services during the Civil War was furnished from the records in the Surgeon-General's office in Washington, through the courtesy of Dr. John S. Billings, U. S. A., and Deputy Surgeon-General Charles R. Greenleaf. Drs. Lodge and Morton also furnished data in this connection.

Dr. Agnew's connection with the University of Pennsylvania was prepared from the minutes of the meetings of the Trustees of the University of Pennsylvania, through the courtesy of the Rev. Jesse Y. Burke, and from the minutes of the meetings of the Faculty of the Medical Department, furnished through the courtesy of the gentlemen composing this distinguished body. To Mr. William H. Salvador thanks are also due for the use of his inexhaustible supply of information on this subject.

The account of Dr. Agnew's connection with the Wills Eye Hospital was prepared from data furnished by Dr. Charles A. Oliver.

Dr. Agnew's connection with the Pennsylvania Hospital was written from material furnished by Mr. Benjamin H. Shoemaker, President of the Board of Managers of that institution.

The account of Dr. Agnew's connection with the Orthopedic Hospital was prepared from data furnished by Dr. Frank S. Pearce.

The estimate of Dr. Agnew's services in the Faculty of Medicine was written by Dr. William Pepper.

The article by Dr. De Forest Willard on the life of Dr. Agnew has been freely quoted, as has also a similar one by Dr. John Ashhurst, Jr., published in the *International Clinics* for July, 1892.

The material used in the Garfield case was prepared from the original notes of the case as written by the attending physicians. To Dr. Robert Reyburn thanks are due for the privilege of examining these documents. Dr. Bliss' article in the *New York Medical Record* and the editorial comments in the same journal have also been used when essential.

The account of the jubilee of Dr. Agnew was taken from the original manuscript in the hands of the speakers and writers.

For various facts and data, thanks are due to Drs. Wharton Sinkler, Frederick P. Henry, Wm. M. Capp, James Tyson, J. M. Da Costa, Francis E. White, Lewis A. Sayre, Wm. Goodell, H. C. Wood, John Marshall, R. A. Cleeman, S. Weir Mitchell, Thomas S. Neilson, J. Ewing Mears; also to Messrs. Coleman Sellers, Crawford Arnold, J. Simpson Africa, Hon. Andrew G. Curtin, Gregory B. Keen, Col. A. J. Rockwell, Henry Chapman, A. J. Cassatt, Mrs. James A. Garfield, Jos. H. Swain, Rev. E. R. Craven; Frederick D. Stone, Librarian of the Historical Society; Manzo Kushida.

INDEX.

Abolishment of hereditable jurisdictions, 16
Abolition of slavery, speech on, 129
Abolitionists, 128
Abraham Lincoln, 128
Academy of Surgery, 271
    annual oration before, 271
Accident, run-away, 73
    while fox-hunting, 57
Adams, J. H., 315
    Margaret Agnew, 250
Address, at banquet to Dr. Gross, 298
    at funeral of Dr. Agnew, 344–351
    by Dr. Agnew on retirement from University, 331
    valedictory, 116–126
Addresses, at jubilee, 304–307, 315
    by Dr. J. M. Da Costa, 302
    by Dr. Lewis A. Sayre, 308
    by Dr. R. A. Cleeman, 312
    by Prof. Samuel W. Gross, 315
    by Provost Pepper, 315
    by William R. Lincoln, 315
    before American Surgical Association, 197–219, 263
Agneaux, a village in Northern France, 1, 2
    derived from the Latin term agnus, 1
    family name derived from, 1
    Norman-French for "lamb," 1
Agneaux, d', Jean Jacques René de Ste. Marie, 4
    Marquis de Ste. Marie, 2
    Sir Fulke, 4
    Sir John, 4
    Sir Philip, 4
    Sir William, 4
    Ste. Marie, 4
Agneaux, heraldic achievements of the, 3
    Robert and Antoine, 4
Agneaux de l'Isle, 3, 6
    descendants of, 4
Agnew, a town in Nebraska, 1
    Andrew, 10
    Benjamin S., 34
    Cornelius R., 34
    Daniel, 34, 135
    David, 24, 63
        descendants of, 24
    David Hayes, 21, 25, 36
    Dr. D. Hayes, year of birth, 19
        year of death, 19
    Erwin, 33
    family, American branch of, 23
        baronetage of, 17

Agnew family, coat of arms of, 19
    earliest record of, 1
    great height and splendid physique of, 22
    knighthood of, 17
    lineage of, 1
    prolific offspring, 23
    prominence in religious matters, 23
    prominent in early history of America, 21
    royal descent of, 11
    Scotch branch of, 5
    General James, 14, 29, 30
    James, 21, 23
        descendants of, 24
    John Holmes, 33, 41, 126, 135
    John P., 63
    Patrick, 11
    Prof. John Holmes, 135
    Rev. David C. A., 3
    Rev. Dr. Benjamin L., 301
    Rev. John Holmes, 41, 126
    Robert, Dr. Agnew's father, 25, 26
        description of, 26, 27
    Samuel, 21
    Sir Andrew, 10, 11, 18, 126
    Sir Andrew Noel, 19
    Sir Patrick and descendants, 18
    Smith, 23
    Surgical Society, 271, 341
        its banquets, 272
    various ways of spelling, 1
Agnew, a brilliant conversationalist, 253
    a "born doctor," 36, 39
    a charming host, 253
    a consistent Christian, 264
    a Christian from childhood up, 38
    a Consulting Surgeon to the Presbyterian Hospital, 275
    a famous sportsman, 55
    a Fellow of the American Surgical Association, 268
    a good judge of a horse, 58
    a life-long Democrat, 336
    a member of Board of Directors of the Union Trust Company, 274
    a member of the American Philosophical Society for Promoting Useful Knowledge, 275
    a member of the Franklin Institute, 275
    a member in the Board of Managers of the House of Refuge, 126, 273

24

Agnew, a member of the Philadelphia County Medical Society, 126
a member of the American Colonization Society, 128
a member of the Medical Examining Board for Volunteer Surgeons, 131
a member of the Medical Society of the State of Pennsylvania, 268
a member of the A M H Ω, 273
a member of the Faculty of Medicine in the University of Pennsylvania, 139, 152, 156
a society named after, 271
a strict Calvin Presbyterian, 258
a student at Jefferson College, Cannonsburgh, Pa., 40
a student at Newark College, Del., 41
record of his experience there, 41
a student at the University of Pennsylvania, 42
a tireless worker, 256
a Trustee of the Philadelphia Dental College, 275
abstemious with food and drink, 252
again locates in Philadelphia, 73
ambidextrous, 169
an ideal teacher of surgery, 157
an example of punctuality, 169
an early riser, 251
appointed Surgeon of Volunteers, 131
approved of pure humor, 253
as a lecturer, 49, 138, 155, 166, 318
as a publisher, 193–196
as a surgeon, 164
as a syphilographer, 160
as a writer, 113–116, 193–219
as Acting Assistant Surgeon in the United States Army, 131
as an expert in medico-legal cases, 285
as an operator, 166
as consulting surgeon, 131, 152, 165
at Mower General Hospital, 131
as Curator, 113
as Demonstrator of Anatomy in the University, 138
as Professor of Surgery, 154–172
assisting his father in his practice, 54
at the battle-field of Gettysburg, 133
attracted to clergymen, 258
averse to gossip, 253
banquet to, 300
before the State Legislature, 158
changes his residence, 153
comes to Philadelphia, 72
death of, 340
decides to become a surgeon, 70
description of, in 1838, 51, 52
disliked by country people because of his method of studying anatomy, 71
duck-shooting, 57, 58

Agnew, elected Attending Surgeon at Pennsylvania Hospital, 144, 145
Attending Surgeon at Wills' Eye Hospital, 142
Professor of Clinical and Demonstrative Surgery, 139, 141
Emeritus Professor of Surgery at University, 276
establishes the Pathological Museum, 113
fond of hymns, 263
of medical students, 271
of reading, 252, 254
fox-hunting, 56
funeral of, 341
gives up practice, 55
reasons for, 60
gold medal presented to, 315
had friends everywhere, 254
Honorary Professor of Clinical Surgery at University, 276
Honorary Surgeon to the Presbyterian Hospital, 275
in the Garfield case, 224, 249
Orthopedic Hospital, 108, 149
Pennsylvania Hospital, 107
Philadelphia Hospital, 107
School of Anatomy, 76
University Hospital, 108
Wills Eye Hospital, 108
joins the College of Physicians, 126, 267
locates in Soudersburg, 73
loved to entertain his friends, 253
made Emeritus Surgeon to Wills' Eye Hospital, 142
meets with a run-away accident and is seriously injured, 73
not opposed to the higher education of women, 148
one of the founders of the Atheneum Literary Society, 41
operating at Geneva, 250
plain in his dress, 255
practising at Cochranville, 70
at Nobleville, 55
at Pleasant Garden, 55
President of the American Surgical Association, 268
of the Medical Society of the State of Pennsylvania, 268
progressive, 359
receives honorary degrees of A.M. and LL.D. from Princeton College, 159
returns again to medicine, 70
seemed always young, 256
sickness of, 339
speaks on the abolition of slavery, 129
studying anatomy, 52, 71
Surgeon-in-Charge at Hestonville General Hospital, 131
" the doctors' doctor," 302

Agnew, tolerant in religious beliefs, 258
 town of Agnew, Nebraska, named in
  honor of, 1
 tribute of respect to, 284
 Vice-President of Alumni Society of
  Medical Department of University
  of Pennsylvania, 275
 well acquainted with theology, 258
 well known to the profession in Europe, 336
 well received in Philadelphia, 106
Agnew's address, at banquet to Dr. Gross,
  293
 before the American Surgical Association, 268
 on cranial and heart wounds, 197–206
 on relation of social life to surgical
  disease, 207–219
 on retirement from the University,
  331
 addresses at jubilee, 304–307, 315
 annual visit to parents, 69, 70
 appointment as Professor of Surgery at
  the University, 154
 at the Orthopedic Hospital, 149
 attendance on General Winfield S. Hancock, 133
 on President James A. Garfield, 224–
  249
  Mrs. Garfield's estimate of, 247
 belief in divine guidance, 257
 birth, 25
 birthplace, 26
 boyish life in the country, 39
 business venture, 60, 75
 calm exterior, 361
 cheerfulness and forbearance, 261, 262
 classical education, 39
 class-mates and fellow-graduates, 50, 51
 connection with hospital duties, 107
  with the Philadelphia School of
  Anatomy, 76, 105
  with the Pleasant Garden Iron-Works,
  60–69
 courtship and marriage, 54, 55
 degrees, 337
 dislike for compliments, 259
  toward the mixed clinique, 148
 duty to his patients a sacred trust, 259
 early life, 36
  in Philadelphia, 106–127
 education at Jefferson College, Cannonsburgh, Pa., 40
 European trip, 250
 experience as a country physician, 55
 first appointment at the University of
  Pennsylvania, 136
 first meeting with his future wife, 38
 freshness and enthusiasm, 256
 graduating thesis, 53, 54
  destroyed during fire at University, 53

Agnew's graduation, 50
 Haverford home, 251
 home-life, 250–264
 ingenuity, 174
 jubilee, 298
 kindness of heart, 132, 265
 last appearance at a public meeting, 337
 last didactic lecture, 321–331
 later life, 267–297
 life from 1860 to 1870, 128–153
 love for his wife and family, 35, 261, 265
 love for the study of anatomy, 52
 magnificent constitution, 256
 most important position in operative
  work, 143
 objection to female students, 145
 observance of the Lord's Day, 257
 original investigations, 177–192
  work in surgery, 173–192
 parents, 25, 39
  description of, 26–29
 personal appearance, 165
 portrait (frontispiece), 314
 position in surgery, estimate of, 353–364
 presents from his admirers, 259
 progress, 107
 relatives prominent in history of Pennsylvania, 29–34
 respect for American medicine, 251
 retirement from the University of Pennsylvania, 318–338
 return to Nobleville, 54
 school days, 37
 separation from the School of Anatomy,
  105
 services as a surgeon, estimate of, 171
 sickness, death, and funeral, 339–352
 splendid physique, 255
 summer trips, 254
 "Surgery," 160, 281
 valedictory addresses, 116–126
 writings, 193
"Agnew's Hill," 6
Agnews, American, genealogy of, 23
 of Lochnaw, 16, 22
 of Pennsylvania, 21, 22
 of the South, 21
Alaric, 123
Alencourts, line of the, 4
Almshouse Hospital, 47
Alumni Society of Medical Department of
  University of Pennsylvania, 275
Ambidexterity, 170
American Colonization Society, 128
 Philosophical Society for Promoting
  Useful Knowledge, 275
 physicians, 356
 surgery, Nestor of, 269
 Surgical Association, addresses before,
  197–268
Amusing story of "Blockley," 109

Anatomical dissections, 53
" Anatomy Acts," 90
Andrew Agnew, 10
Anecdotes, 276
    of Dr. Agnew's boyhood days, 36–39
Anesthesia, 357
Appendix, 365–368
Armorial bearings, 3, 4
" Armorial de France," 4
Articles and books published by Dr. Agnew, 193–196
Athenæum Literary Society, 41
Atlee, Dr. Walter F., 252
Autopsy on President James A. Garfield, 233–235

Banquet to Dr. Gross, address at, 298, 299
Banquets at Agnew Surgical Society, 272
    to Dr. Agnew, addresses at, 300–317
        ode read at, 312
        poem read at, 309
        song, written by J. H. Adams, 315, 316
        music to, by Hugh A. Clarke, 316
Barnes, Surgeon-General, 224–235
Baron Larrey, 130, 271
Baronets of Nova Scotia, 17
    of Ulster, 17
Barton, John Rhea, Professorship, 141
Battle of Chippewa, 29
    of Germantown, 14, 29, 30
    of Gettysburg, 133
Bay of Larne, 9
Beadle, Rev. Elias R., 286
" Birchen age " of American education, 37
Birth of Dr. D. Hayes Agnew, 19
Black Douglas, 9, 10
Blair Castle, 12
    defense of, 13
Bleeding in surgery, 358
Bliss, Dr., in the Garfield case, 221–249
" Blockley," 108
    amusing story of, 109
Boerhaave, 355
Books and articles published by Dr. Agnew, 193–196
Brig O'Doon, 9
" Broad hints " of Sir Andrew Agnew, 15
    humorous story of, 15
Bruce, Edward, 7
    Lady, 15
    Robert, 7
Burying-ground at Gettysburg, 22
Business venture, Dr. Agnew's, 60

Camp-meeting, 37
Camp-story, 14
Castle of Lochnaw, 6, 7
    captured by one M'Clellan, 8
    retaken by one of the Agnews, 8, 9
Charles I, 17

Charles II, 18, 20, 21
Charles V, 120
Chloroform in surgery, 357
Church of Ireland, 20
Civil War, 48, 91, 108, 113, 131, 359
Cleeman, Dr. R. A., address by, 312
Clinical instruction at the University, 139–142
    Surgery, Chair of, 139
Club, Friday-Evening, 269
    Monday-Evening, 269
    Penn, reception to Dr. Agnew, 317
    Saturday-Night, 273
    Social Surgical, 270
    Thursday-Evening, 270
College of Physicians, 126, 267, 341
Colonization of the North of Ireland, 20
    Society, American, 128
Colony, Liberian, 128
Commencement eve at Musical Fund Hall, 50
Comment vous portez vous, 15
Conquest of Ulster, 6
Constable of Lochnaw, 7, 9
Consulting surgeon, Dr. Agnew as, 131
Cornelius R. Agnew, 130
County Wigtown, 5, 21
    Hereditary Sheriff of, 5
Cranial and heart wounds, medico-legal aspects of, 197–206
Cromwell, 18
Curator, Dr. Agnew as, 113

D'Agneaux, see Agneaux.
Da Costa, Dr. J. M., address by, 302
Daniel Agnew, 34, 135
David Agnew, 24, 63
    descendants of, 24
David Hayes Agnew, 21, 25, 36
Death of Dr. D. Hayes Agnew, 340
    of President James A. Garfield, 232
Delaware College, 41
Department of Manche, 2
Derivation of family name of Agnew, 1
Douglas, Black, 9, 10
    Earl, 8, 9
    Sir William, 9
Dr. D. Hayes Agnew, year of birth, 19
    year of death, 19
Duck-shooting, 57, 58
Dukes of Argyle, 16

Earl Douglas, 8
Earl of Moray, 7
    of Strigul, 3
Earliest record of the Agnew family, 1
Earls of Rothes, 16
    of Tyrone and Tyrconnel, 19
Early life of Dr. Agnew, 36–59
    in Philadelphia, 106
Edward Bruce, 7

Eels as assistants in studying anatomy, 71
Emigration to Pennsylvania, 20
Erwin Agnew, 33
Ether in surgery, 283, 357
  frolics, 357
Exiles from France, 3

Faculty of the University of Pennsylvania, 43, 47, 137
Family name of Agnew, derivation of, 1
  tradition, 3
Favorite Galloway story, 11
" Fax mentis honestœ gloriœ," 18
Female students, Dr. Agnew's objection to, 145
Ferdinand de Soto, 123
Feudalism, essence of, 6
Fire at the University of Pennsylvania, 53
Firth of Clyde, 7
Fox-hunting, 56
Francklyn Cottage, 231
Franklin Institute, 275
  Medical College, 96
French chivalry, knights of, 3
Friday-Evening Club, 269
Frolics, ether, 357
Funeral of Dr. D. Hayes Agnew, 341
  address at, by Dr. MacIntosh, 344
  services at, 343–352

Galloway, 5, 7, 8
  lordship of, 10
  Scots of, 8
  sheriff of, 5, 18
  story, favorite, 11
Garfield case, 220–249
  discussion on treatment in, 236–242
  incident in the, 168
  physicians in attendance, 221, 224
Genealogy of the American Agnews, 23
General James Agnew, 14, 29, 30
  Winfield S. Hancock, 133
" Gentlemen's law," 6
Gettysburg, Battle of, 133
" 'Ginny students," 48
Gold medal presented to Dr. Agnew, 315
Goldsmith, 118
Graduating thesis, Dr. Agnew's, 53, 54
" Green Box," or " Green Room," 50
Gross, Prof. Samuel W., address by, 315
Guiteau, 220, 242
Gunshot wounds, 132

Hamilton, Dr. Frank H., 224–249
Henderson, James N., 29, 37
  Rev. Ebenezer, 25
Heraldic achievements of the Agneaux, 3
  bearing of Agneaux de l'Isle, 3, 4
" Here me is," 38
Hereditable jurisdictions, abolishment of, 16
Hereditary Sheriff of Wigtown, 5, 8

Hereditary Sheriffs of Galloway, 18
Hestonville General Hospital, 131
Hoge, Rev. Moses D., 258, 343, 349
Hospital, Almshouse, 47
  Blockley, 108
  Hestonville General, 131
  Mower General, 131, 133, 360
  Orthopedic, 108, 149
  Pennsylvania, 46, 47, 107, 143
  Philadelphia, 47, 90, 107, 108
  Presbyterian, 275
  Satterlee General, 131, 133
  University, 154
  Wills' Eye, 107, 142
House of Refuge, 126, 273
Huguenots at time of Reformation, 3
Hunter, Dr. Charles T., 159
  John, 355
Hymn, Wesley's last, 263

Infidels, services against, 4
Instruments devised by Dr. Agnew, 174–177
Iron industry of Pennsylvania, 63
Irwin & Agnew, firm name, 67
  failure of, 67, 68
Irwin family, 54
  Margaret Creighton, 38, 54

James Agnew, 21, 23
  descendants of, 24
James I, 19, 20
James II, 20, 21
Jean Jacques Renò de Ste. Marie d'Agneaux, 4
Jefferson College, Cannonsburgh, Pa., 40
John Brown's invasion of Virginia, 91
John Holmes Agnew, 33, 41, 126, 135
John P. Agnew, 63
" John Rhea Barton Professorship of Surgery," 141
Journals, medical, 356
Jubilee of Dr. Agnew, 288–317
Judge M. Russell Thayer, 337

Kane, 124
Kepler, 125
King David II, 7, 9
King James I, 10, 17
King of Ireland, 7
King Robert Bruce, 7
Kirkcudbright, 5
Knights of French chivalry, 3

La Manche, 2
" Lacon," 124
Lady Bruce, 15
Laird of Lochnaw, 9
Lamb, Dr. D. S., 233, 235
Lammermuir lion, 14
Lancaster County Medical Society, 266
Larne, bay of, 9

Larne, Lord of, 6, 7
  lough of, 7
Latta, Rev. Francis, 39, 40
Laudanum in surgery, 358
Law of Signatures, 354
Lectures, Dr. Agnew's, 49, 138, 155, 166, 318
  last didactic lecture at the University
    of Pennsylvania, 321–331
Leidy, Dr., at the University, 78
Liberian colony, 128
Life, Dr. Agnew's early, 36
  in Philadelphia, 106
  of Dr. Agnew from 1860 to 1870, 128
Lincoln, Abraham, 128
  Dr. N. S., 224
  William R., address by, 315
Line of the Alencourts, 4
Lineage of the Agnew family, 1–35
Lochnaw, 6, 7
  castle of, 6, 7, 9, 10
  Constable of, 7, 9
  Laird of, 9
  loch of, 9
Lord of Alencourt, 4
  of Larne, 6, 7
  of l'Isle and Auval, 3
    his heraldic bearing, 3
Lords of Ulster, 7
Lordship of Larne, 6
Loving cup, 272

MacIntosh, Rev. John S., 288, 301, 344
  his reminiscences of Dr. Agnew, 288–297
MacVeagh, Wayne, 224
Marquis de Ste. Marie d'Agneaux, 2
Mason's and Dixon's Line, 64, 70
Mausoleum at West Laurel Hill Cemetery, 252
Medical instruction of fifty years ago, 45–50
  Institute, 49, 96, 140
  journals, 356
  Society of the State of Pennsylvania, 268
Memorial sermons, 351, 352
Memorial to Dr. Agnew, 352
"Merchant of Venice," 119
Mitchell, Dr. S Weir, poem by, 309
"Mixed cliniques," 148
Monday-Evening Club, 269
Moscow Academy, 39
Mower General Hospital, 131, 133, 360
Murrays of Philiphaugh, 16
Museum, Pathological, 113
  Wistar and Horner, 332
Museums, medical, 269

Name, Agnew, numerous ways of spelling, 1
  derivation of, 1
Napoleon, 40. 123
Nestor of American surgery, 269

Newark College, Delaware, 41
Noble family, 28
Norman conquest of England, 3
Normans, or Norsemen, 2
Nova Scotia, baronets of, 17
  special honors granted to, 17

Ode by Dr. Thomas Wistar, 312
Olderfleet Castle, 7
Origin of name of Agnew, 1
  of town of Agnew, Nebraska, 1
Original investigations, 177–192
  work in surgery, 173
Orthopedic Hospital, 108, 149

Painting of Dr. Agnew, 332
  presentation remarks by Dr. J. A. Scott, 332
  reception speech by Dr. S. Weir Mitchell, 334
  reply of Dr. Agnew, 334
Pathological Museum, 113
Patrick Agnew, 11
Penn Club reception to Dr. Agnew, 317
Pennsylvania, emigration to, 20
Pennsylvania Academy of Medicine, 101
  Hospital, 46, 47, 107, 143
  Medical College, 110
Pepper, Provost, address by, 315
Perkin's tractors, 354
Philadelphia Anatomical Rooms, 78, 82, 83
  Association for Medical Instruction, 96, 97
  County Medical Society, 110, 126, 149, 267, 341
  Dental College, 275
  Hospital, 47, 90, 107, 108
  Polyclinic and College for Graduates in Medicine, 95
  School of Anatomy, 74–116
    its history, 76–105
    receipts from, 92
  School of Operative Surgery, 84
    fees from, 92
  University of Medicine and Surgery, 154
Physicians, American, 356
Pleasant Garden Iron-Works, 54, 60, 63, 66
  ruins of, 68
Portrait of Dr. Agnew (frontispiece), 314
  of Dr. Alfred Stillé, 315
Post-mortem of body of President Garfield, 233–235
Presbyterian Hospital, 275
Princess Margaret, 10
  Mary, 10
Princeton College, 159
"Principles and Practice of Surgery," 160
  translated into Japanese, 163
Private classes, 48, 49
Protestant exiles from France, 3
Providence, 116, 127

Quiz classes, 49, 76
  clubs, 49
  work, 95

Rebellion, War of the, 128
Record of the Agnew family, earliest, 1
Reminiscences of Dr. Agnew, 288–297
Resurrectionists, 89
Retirement from the University of Pennsylvania, Dr. Agnew's, 318–338
Rev. David C. A. Agnew, 3
  Elias R. Beadle, 286
  Francis Latta, 39, 40
  John Holmes Agnew, 41, 126
  John S. MacIntosh, 288
  Matthew Brown, 40
Reyburn, Dr. Robert, 224, 235
Richard de Clare, 3
Robert Agnew, Dr. Agnew's father, 25, 26
  description of, 26, 27
Robert and Antoine Agneaux, 4
Robert Bruce, 7
Robert III, 9
Royal descent of the Agnews, 11
Rush, Benjamin, 355

Sabbath, Dr. Agnew's observance of the, 126, 257
Saint-Lo, city of, 2
Samuel Agnew, 21
"Sapientia cum latitia," 272
Satterlee General Hospital, 131, 133
Saturday-Night Club, 273
Sayre, Dr. Lewis A., address by, 308
School, Viennese, 355
School of Anatomy, 52, 74, 116
  of Medicine, 96
  of Operative Surgery, 84, 92
Scotch branch of Agnew family, 5, 8
Scots of Galloway, 8
Sermons, memorial, 351, 352
Services against the infidels, 4
Sheriff of Galloway, 5, 18
  of Wigtown, 5, 8, 9, 16
Sickness of Dr. D. Hayes Agnew, 339
Signatures, Law of, 354
"Similia Similibus Curantur," 354
"Sinister hand of Ulster," 6
Sir Andrew Agnew, 126
Sir Andrew Agnew, a famous soldier, 11, 18
  "broad hints" of, 15
  camp-story in reference to, 14
  favorite Galloway story of, 11
  his prejudice against the French, 15
  incidents of, described by Sir Walter Scott, 12
Sir Andrew Agnew, Bart., M.P., 10, 18
Sir Andrew Noel Agnew, 19
Sir Fulke d'Agneaux, 4
Sir John d'Agneaux, 4
Sir Philip d'Agneaux, 4

Sir William d'Agneaux, 4
Sir Patrick Agnew, 18
  descendants of, 18
Sir William Douglas, 9
Slavery, the subject of, 52
  address on, by Dr. Agnew, 129
Smith Agnew, 23
Social life, relation of, to surgical disease, 207–219
Song, written by J. H. Adams, 315, 316
  music to, by Hugh A. Clarke, 316
"Southern Agnews," 21
Southern students, 91, 129
Specialties, 360
Speech on abolition of slavery, 129
Ste. Marie d'Agneaux, 4
Stillé, Dr. Alfred, portrait of, 315
  Library, damaged during fire at University, 53
Story, favorite Galloway, 11
"Strong Bow," 3
"Summer Association," 97
  brilliant teachers and writers, 100
Surgeon of Volunteers, Dr. Agnew, 131
Surgeons, distinguished, fifty years ago, 47–49
"Surgeons' House," 256
Surgery, bleeding in, 358
  chloroform in, 357
  ether in, 283, 357
  laudanum in, 358
Surgery, Clinical Chair of, 139
  Dr. Agnew's original work in, 173
  position in, 353–364
  John Rhea Barton Professorship of, 141
  "Principles and Practice of," 160, 281
  translated into Japanese, 163
Surgical Club, Social, 270
Surgical disease, relation of social life to, 207–219
  operations before introduction of anæsthesia, 47

Thayer, Judge M. Russell, 337
Thursday-Evening Club, 270
Tractors, Perkin's, 354
Tradition, family, 3, 8
Translation of "Virgil" into French in 1582, 4

Ulster, baronets of, 17
  conquest of, 6
  lords of, 7
  sinister hand of, 6
Union Trust Company, Dr. Agnew a Director of, 274
University of Pennsylvania, 42, 47, 52, 108, 137, 154
  Alumni Society of, 275
  clinical instruction at the, 139–142